LENNOX BERKELEY : A SOURCE BOOK

The Berkeley Family, photographed by Jan Traylen

LENNOX BERKELEY

A SOURCE BOOK

compiled by

STEWART R. CRAGGS

Ashgate

Aldershot • Burlington USA • Singapore • Sydney

© Stewart R. Craggs, 2000

All rights reserved. No part of this publication may be reproduced, stored in a retrieval system, or transmitted in any form or by any means, electronic, mechanical, photocopying, recording, or otherwise without the prior permission of the publisher.

The author has asserted his right under the Copyright, Designs and Patents Act, 1988, to be identified as the author of this work.

Published by
Ashgate Publishing Limited
Gower House
Croft Road
Aldershot
Hants GU11 3HR
England

Ashgate Publishing Company
131 Main Street
Burlington
Vermont 05401–5600
USA

Ashgate website: http://www.ashgate.com

British Library Cataloguing-in-Publication data

Craggs, Stewart R.
  Lennox Berkeley : a source book
  1. Berkeley, Lennox, 1903–1989 — Criticism and interpretation
  I. Title
  780.9'2

Library of Congress Cataloging-in-Publication data

Craggs, Stewart R.
  Lennox Berkeley : a source book / Stewart R. Craggs.
  Includes index.
  1. Berkeley, Lennox, Sir, 1903–1989   Bibliography.   2. Berkeley, Lennox, Sir, 1903–1989   Discography.   I. Title.
  ML134.B48C73   2000
  780'.92—dc21   99-36002
                      CIP

ISBN 0 85967 933 0

Typeset in Goudy by JL & GA Wheatley Design, Aldershot and printed on acid-free paper and bound in Great Britain by MPG Books Ltd, Bodmin, Cornwall

For

FREDA

without whose help much of

this would not have been possible,

and to the memory of

SHEILA MacCRINDLE
(1931–1993)

who also gave her full blessing

to all my endeavours

Contents

Foreword by Michael Berkeley	ix
Acknowledgements	xi
Alphabetical list of compositions	1
Chronology	11
Catalogue raisonné	49
Manuscripts and first editions, prepared by Joan Redding	123
Discography	296
Select bibliography	311
Appendix 1: Classified index of main works	356
Appendix 2: Lost or missing manuscripts	362
Appendix 3: Personalia	365
General index	371

Foreword

Given the invaluable work that Stewart Craggs has already produced on behalf of composers like Walton and Bliss, I am absolutely delighted that he should now have turned his meticulous attention to my father. Notoriously vague and ultimately stricken by Alzheimers, Lennox left many papers in a somewhat less than resolved state when he died in December 1989. Any work, therefore, that helps to clarify and sort out his manuscripts is not only very welcome but also timely since friends and assistants like Peter Dickinson and Joan Redding still have details and information relatively fresh in their minds.

The Source Book has already afforded me the wicked pleasure of being able to inform several musical acquaintances that Lennox had close links with Darmstadt – only on reading Stewart's book will they be able to resolve their puzzlement and discover that far from an early affiliation with the young Stockhausen, Darmstadt was in fact the birthplace of Lennox's maternal grandmother!

Lennox was not a composer of the grandiose statement; he was, on the whole, happiest while working on small scale canvasses where his love of economy afforded him real mastery. Like Fauré, his tendency to understate means that climaxes, when they do come, are all the more striking for the restraint that surrounds them.

Looking through the catalogue I am now struck by the similarities not only with Fauré but also with Lennox's close friend, Francis Poulenc. Think of the deeply felt sacred music and the love of piano and song. Recently I had the pleasure of revisiting in performance a series of chamber works like the *String Trio*, *Horn Trio* and *Oboe Quartet* as well as some of the songs and piano works and was delighted to discover a veritable Pandora's box of exquisitely turned gems. Then there are the better-known works for small orchestra like the joyous *Serenade for Strings*, the *Divertimento* and *Sinfonietta*, and the profoundly moving *Four Poems of St Teresa of Avila*. All of these pieces and doubtless many more will, I know, stand the test of time and it is because of their quality that this Source Book by Stewart Craggs will gradually assume an ever-growing importance to both musician and music-lover alike.

Michael Berkeley
London, 1998

Acknowledgements

This Source Book (the result of 15 years of research) seeks to document and place in the public domain factual details concerning Lennox Berkeley's life, career and compositions which until now have only been available in scattered form, and known only to those with access to the composer's private papers and composition manuscripts.

I owe a special debt of gratitude to Freda Berkeley for providing me with information over the years, and for giving me permission to reproduce certain items, to Michael Berkeley for writing the Foreword, and to Julian Berkeley for his help in many other ways.

I should also record my thanks to Amanda Arnold of the PRS; Marion Arnold, Northampton County Library; Miss Jill Balcon; Dr A.S. Bendall, Fellow, Librarian and Archivist, Merton College, Oxford; Lady Bliss; Christopher Bornet of the RCM Library; Mrs Clare Brown, formerly of the BBC Written Archives Centre, Caversham; Mr Richard Buckle; Lady Clarke; David Cliffe, County Reference Librarian, Berkshire County Library; Clare Colvin, Archivist, English National Opera; David Cousins, Heritage Services Officer, Kent County Library; Judith Curthoys, Assistant Archivist, Christ Church, Oxford; Pat Curtis, Windsor Public Library; Timothy Day, National Sound Archive; Prof. Peter Dickinson; Prof. John Dressler; Roger Evans, Department of Manuscripts, British Library; Lewis Foreman; the late Mr Frederick Grinke; Mrs Jane Henderson; Mr Colin Horsley; Mr Michael Linsey; Keith Lodwick of the Theatre Museum; the late Sheila MacCrindle of Chester Music; Mr Roger Nichols for allowing me access to his Berkeley chronology, and for many other kindnesses; Andrew Potter, Head of Music at Oxford University Press; Marion Pringle, Senior Librarian, Shakespeare Birthplace Trust; Joan Redding for her contribution to this volume and for all her kind help over the years; Dr Philip Reed, formerly of the Britten-Pears Music Library; Su Roberts of the Performing Right Society; James Rushton, Managing Director of Chester Music; Tony Scotland for allowing me access to the results of his genealogical research about the Berkeley family; Miss Rosamund Strode, former archivist at the Britten-Pears Music Library for all her many kindnesses; Mrs V.M. Thomas of the Merchant Taylors' Company, Dr Tony

Trowles, Librarian, Westminster Abbey, and Mr D. Withey, Reference Librarian, Finsbury Library.

Stewart R Craggs
August 1999

Alphabetical list of compositions

Adeste fideles, 102, 123–4
Adieu, cruelle, adieu, *see* Four Ronsard Sonnets (Set 1)
Afraid, *see* Another Spring
All night a wind of music, *see* Autumn's Legacy
All that's past, *see* Songs of the Half-Light
Allegro for two treble recorders, 90, 124–5
Andantino for cello and piano, *see* A Festival Anthem
Andantino for organ, *see* A Festival Anthem
Andantino for cello and piano (Music for a Prince), 35, 108, 126, 327
Another Spring (Op.93, no.1), 41, 118, 126–8, 296, 327
Antiphon (Op.85), 37, 38, 114, 128–9, 296, 327–8
Aria, *see* Three Pieces for Organ
Ask me no more (Op.37, no.1), 83–4, 129, 328
Aubade, *see* Three Pieces for Organ
Automne (Op.60, no.3), 31, 34, 100, 129–30, 296, 328
(The) Autumn Wind, *see* Five Chinese Songs
Autumn's Legacy (Op.58), 30, 31, 98–9, 130–31, 296, 328

Bagatelle for two pianos (Op.101, no.1), 46, 120–21, 131–2
Ballet (no title), 16, 57, 132–3
Bank Holiday, *see* Two (Auden) Songs
(The) Banquet, *see* Suite from A Winter's Tale (Op.54)
Batter my heart, three person'd God (Op.60, no.1), 99, 133–4, 328
(The) Beacon Barn (Op.14, no.2), 20, 64, 134–5
Because I liked you better, *see* Five Housman Songs
(La) belle dame sans merci, 13, 49–50
Bells of Cordoba (Op.14, no.2), 20, 64, 135
Berceuse, *see* Three Pieces for Piano
Boar's Hill: hymn tune (Hears't thou, my soul), 104

Canon for string trio, 36, 111, 135

Capriccio, *see* Three Pieces for Piano
Carry her over the water, *see* Five Poems of W.H. Auden
Castaway (Op.68), 32, 33, 46, 47, 103–4, 136–8, 328–9
Ce caillou chaud de soleil, *see* Trois Poèmes de Vildrac
Ce premiere jour de Mai, *see* Four Ronsard Sonnets (Set 2)
Cet enfant de jadis, *see* Trois Poèmes de Vildrac
Christ is the World's Redeemer, *see* Gartan: hymn tune
(The) Cockpit, *see* Suite from Nelson (Op.42)
Colonus' Praise (Op.31), 25, 80, 138–40, 329
Comme un void sur la branche, *see* Four Ronsard Sonnets (Set 1)
Common Ground (ballet), *see* Serenade for String Orchestra
Concert study in Eb (Op.48, no.2), 90, 140, 296
Concertino for Chamber Orchestra, 15, 53, 329–30
Concertino for recorder, violin, cello and harpsichord (Op.49), 28, 91, 140, 296
Concerto for cello and orchestra, 20, 47, 65, 141, 330
Concerto for flute and chamber orchestra (Op.36), 25, 26, 84, 141–2, 297, 330
Concerto for guitar and orchestra (Op.88), 38, 39, 115–16, 142–3, 297, 330
Concerto for piano and double string orchestra (Op.46), 29, 93, 143–4, 330–31
Concerto for piano and orchestra (Op.29), 24, 25, 79, 144–5, 297, 331
Concerto for two pianos and orchestra (Op.30), 24, 79–80, 145–7, 297, 331
Concerto for violin and chamber orchestra (Op.59), 30, 98, 147–8, 297, 331–2
Counting the beats (Op.60, no.4), 31, 100, 148–50, 332
Crux fidelis (Op.43, no.1), 27, 89, 150, 332

Day of these Days, *see* Signs in the Dark
De Don Juan, *see* Tombeaux
De Narcisse, *see* Tombeaux
Dearest of thousands, *see* Five Herrick Poems (Op.89)
Deux Poèmes de Pindare, 18, 61–2, 150, 333–4
Dialogue for cello and chamber orchestra (Op.79), 36, 37, 110, 150–51, 332
Diana and Actaeon Waltz, 111, 217–20, 302, 344
(Les) Dimanches, 14, 50
(A) Dinner Engagement (Op.45), 26, 27, 45, 46, 47, 86–7, 151–4, 332–3
Dithyramb, *see* Deux Poèmes de Pindare
Diversions for eight instruments (Op.63), 32, 101–2, 154–5, 297, 334
Divertimento in Bb (Op.18), 22, 24, 70, 155, 297, 334
Domini est Terra (Op.10), 19, 62–3, 155–6, 334–5
Dreaming of a Dead Lady, *see* Five Chinese Songs
D'un Fleuve, *see* Tombeaux
D'un vanneur de blé aux vents, *see* Three Early Songs
Duo for cello and piano (Op.81, no.1), 136, 112, 156–7, 298, 335

Duo for oboe and cello, 111, 157, 298

(The) Ecstatic, 70, 157
Edith Sitwell Memorial Concert (Aubade for organ), *see* Three Pieces for Organ
Elegy for String Orchestra (Op.33, no.2b), 42, 82, 158
Elegy for violin and piano (Op.33, no.2a), 25, 82, 157–8, 298, 335
Eleven-fifty (Op.14, no.2), 64, 158–9
Epitaph of Timas, *see* Three Greek Songs
Eripe me, Domine, *see* Three Latin Motets
Esterel: suite for orchestra, 72
Etude, *see* Three Pieces for Piano
Eyes look into the well, *see* Five Poems of W.H. Auden

Fair Daffodils, *see* Three Songs
Faldon Park (Op.100), 36, 41, 43–4, 45, 122, 159–61
Fanfare for the Royal Academy of Music Banquet, 112, 161–2
Fantasia for organ (Op.92), 41, 117, 162, 298, 335
Fauré, Gabriel –
   Barcarolle No.5 (Op.66)
   Impromptu No.2 (Op.31)
   "Mandoline" (words by Verlaine)
   Nocturne No.6 (Op.63)
   Nocturne No.7 (Op.74)
   Prelude No.5 (Op.103)
   Prelude No.8 (Op.103)
   "Soir" (words by Albert Samain),
    see La Fête Etrange
(A) Festival Anthem, *see* Sion's Daughters, Sons of Jerusalem
La Fête Etrange: ballet, 76, 335
The First Gentleman: music for the film, 24, 78–9
Five Chinese Songs (Op.78), 36, 109–10, 163–4, 298, 335–6
Five Herrick Poems (Op.89), 115, 164–6, 336
Five Housman Songs (Op.14, no.3), 20, 67, 166–8, 299
Five Pieces for Violin and Orchestra (Op.56), 30, 31, 98, 168–9, 336
Five Poems by W.H. Auden (Op.53), 29, 30, 94, 169, 298, 337
Five short pieces for piano (Op.4), 61, 170, 298
Five Songs (Walter de la Mare) (Op.26), 23, 75, 170, 298, 336
(The) Fleeting, *see* Songs of the Half-Light
Florizel and Perdita, *see* Suite from A Winter's Tale (Op.54)
Four concert studies for piano (Op.14, no.1), 20, 22, 66, 171, 299
Four concert studies for piano (Op.82), 37, 112, 171–2

Four pieces for flute, oboe and piano, 51
Four pieces for organ, 51
Four pieces for small orchestra, 52, 172
Four Poems of St Teresa of Avila (Op.27), 24, 77, 172–4, 299, 337
Four Ronsard Sonnets (Set 1) (Op.40), 26, 33, 42, 43, 84, 174–6, 303, 337
Four Ronsard Sonnets (Set 2) (Op.62), 101, 176–9, 303, 337
Four score years and ten, 118, 179
Full Moon, *see* Songs of the Half-Light

(A) Garland for the Queen, *see* Spring at this hour
Gartan: hymn tune (Christ is the World's Redeemer), 99–100, 329
A Glutton for Life: incidental music, 23, 74, 180–81
A Grace, 36, 111, 181

Hail Gladdening Light, *see* Melfort: hymn tune
Hail Holy Queen, 108, 181
(The) half moon westers low, *see* Five Housman Songs
He would not stay for me, *see* Five Housman Songs
Hears't thou, my soul, *see* Boar's Hill: hymn tune
The Hill of the Graces (Op.91, no.2), 39, 40, 117, 182–3, 299, 337–8
(The) Horseman, *see* Five Songs (de la Mare)
Hotel Reservé: music for the film, 23, 71
How love came in, 58, 183, 299, 338
Hurrahing in Harvest, *see* Autumn's Legacy
Hymn, *see* Deux Poèmes de Pindare
Hymn for Shakespeare's Birthday (Op.83, no.2), 113, 183

i carry your heart, 109, 184
I sing of a Maiden, 104, 184, 299, 338
If fortuned out of the thicket wood, *see* Una and the Lion
If Lord, Thy love for me is strong, *see* Four Poems of St Teresa of Avila
If nine times you your bridegroom kisse, *see* Five Herrick Poems (Op.89)
Impromptu for organ, 21, 68, 184–5
Improvisation on a theme by Manuel de Falla (Op.55, no.2), 97, 185, 299, 338
In Memoriam Igor Stravinsky: canon for string quartet, 36, 110, 338
In Wintertime (Op.103), 47, 121–2, 185–6, 299, 338
Incidental music for puppet play and farce (1938), 64, 346–7
Interlude, *see* Suite from Nelson (Op.42)
Introduction and Allegro for double bass and piano (Op.80), 36, 110–11, 186, 300, 338
Introduction and Allegro for two pianos and orchestra (Op.11), 19, 21, 64, 186–7
Introduction and Allegro for violin (Op.24), 75, 187, 300, 338–9

Introduction and Dance, 15, 52, 339
Iphigenia in Taurus: incidental music, 87

Je sens une douceur, *see* Four Ronsard Sonnets (Set 2)
Jigsaw: music for Oranges and Lemons (a review), 79, 216
Jonah (Op.3), 17, 18, 58–60, 188–91, 339–40
The Judgement of Paris (Op.10, no.2), 18, 19, 63, 192, 340
Judica Me (Op.96, no.1), 42, 43, 48, 119, 192–3, 300, 340
Justorum animae (Op.60, no.2), 100, 193, 300, 340

Kissing Usurie, *see* Three Songs

Late Spring, *see* Five Chinese Songs
Lauds, *see* Five Poems of W.H. Auden
Lay your Sleeping Head, My Love (Op.14, no.2), 63, 193–4, 300
Legacie, 70, 194
Lesbos, *see* Autumn's Legacy
Let mine eyes see Thee, *see* Four Poems of St Teresa of Avila
(The) Lion Lord of every beast, *see* Una and the Lion
Look back to Lyttletoun: incidental music, 92–3, 194–7
Look not in my eyes, *see* Five Housman Songs
Look up, sweet babe (Op.43, no.2), 27, 89–90, 197–8, 300, 340
Lord, by whose breath, *see* Wiveton: hymn tune
The Lord is my Shepherd (Op.91, no.1), 39, 116–17, 198–9, 300, 340
Lord, when the sense of thy sweet grace (Op.21, no.1), 22, 71–2, 199–200, 300, 340
The Low Lands of Holland, 77, 200
Lullaby, 70, 200–201

Ma fièvre croist tour jour, *see* Four Ronsard Sonnets (Set 2)
Magnificat (Op.71), 33, 34, 106, 201–2, 301, 341
Magnificat and Nunc Dimittis (Op.99), 44, 45, 120, 202–3, 301
March for piano, 13, 50, 203–4
Marie levez-vous, *see* Four Ronsard Sonnets (Set 1)
Mamillius, *see* Suite from A Winter's Tale (Op.54)
Mass for five voices (Op.64), 32, 37, 48, 102, 204–5, 301, 341
Maupassant, *see* A Glutton for Life
Mazurka for piano (1939), 20, 65, 205
Mazurka for piano (Op.101, no.2), 46, 121, 205–6, 301, 341
Melfort: hymn tune (Hail Gladdening Light), 95, 181
The Midnight Murk, 22, 69, 206

(The) mighty thoughts of an old world, *see* Autumn's Legacy
Minuet for two recorders, 50, 206–7
Missa Brevis (Op.57), 30, 97, 207–8, 301, 341
Mistletoe, *see* Five Songs (de la Mare)
Mont Juic (Op.9), 18, 19, 20, 62, 208–9, 301, 341
(The) Moth, *see* Songs of the Half-Light
Mr Pilkington's Toye, 51, 209
Music for a Prince, *see* Andantino for cello and piano
My God! Look on me, *see* Five Herrick Poems (Op.89)

Nelson (Op.41), 25, 26, 27, 28, 47, 48, 87–9, 209–12, 342–3
Night covers up the rigid land (Op.14, no.2), 63, 212–13, 302, 344
Nocturne, *see* Suite from A Winter's Tale (Op.54)
Nocturne for harp (Op.67, no.2), 105, 213–14, 302, 344
Nocturne for orchestra (Op.25), 23, 75, 214
Now is your turne, *see* Five Herrick Poems (Op.89)

O lurcher-loving collier, *see* Five Poems of W.H. Auden
Oboe Quartet, *see* Quartet for oboe and string trio
Ode (Partition), 57, 215
Ode du premier Jour de Mai (Op.14, no.2), 67, 215, 302
Oranges and Lemons, *see* Jigsaw, and Venus Anadyomene
Otez votre beauté, *see* Four Ronsard Sonnets (Set 1)
Out of chaos: music for the film, 71, 217
Overture for chamber orchestra (Op.8), 17, 58, 217, 344
Overture for chamber orchestra (1947), 24, 76–7
Overture for Light Orchestra (1959), 29, 95

Palm Court Waltz, *see* Diana and Actaeon Waltz
Partita for chamber orchestra (Op.66), 32, 103, 220–21, 302, 344
Pastourelle, *see* Three Early Songs
Paysage [de France] (for piano), 72, 221–2, 302
People hide their love, *see* Five Chinese Songs
Petite Suite, 15, 53–4, 222–3, 302
Piece for clavichord, 56, 223
Piece for Vere (piano or harpsichord), 15, 53, 224
Piece pour flute, clarinette et basson, 54, 224–5
Poem for Easter, *see* Signs in the Dark
Poetry, *see* Another Spring
Polka, Nocturne and Capriccio for two pianos (Op.5), 17, 19, 20, 60, 225–8, 302
Poor Henry, *see* Five Songs (de la Mare)

Portsmouth, *see* Suite from Nelson (Op.42)
Poulenc, Francis – Sonata for flute and piano, *see* Sonata for flute and piano (Francis Poulenc): orchestrated by Berkeley
(La) Poulette Grise, 56, 228–9
Prelude and Capriccio for piano (Op.95), 42, 118, 229, 302, 344–5
Prelude and Fugue for clavichord (Op.55, no.3), 97, 230, 302
Prelude-Intermezzo-Finale for flute, violin, viola and piano, 15, 53, 230–31
Prologue, *see* Suite from A Winter's Tale (Op.54)

Quartet for oboe and string trio (Op.70), 32, 33, 34, 105, 231–2, 302, 345
Quartet for strings no.1 (Op.6), 17, 18, 60–61, 232
Quartet for strings no.2 (Op.15), 21, 22, 67, 232
Quartet for strings no.3 (Op.76), 35, 36, 108–9, 232–3, 345
Quintet for oboe, clarinet, horn, bassoon and piano (Op.90), 39, 40, 116, 233–4, 303, 345

Rachel, *see* Songs of the Half-Light
Redowning tears did choke, *see* Una and the Lion
Regina coeli laetare, *see* Three Latin Motets
Releasing a Migrant Yen, *see* Five Chinese Songs
Rich Days, *see* Autumn's Legacy
(The) Riverside Village, *see* Five Chinese Songs
Rondeau, *see* Three Early Songs
Ruth (Op.50), 28, 29, 91–2, 234–7, 345–6

(The) Sailing of the Victory, *see* Suite from Nelson (Op.42)
Salve Regina (Op.48, no.1), 27, 91, 238, 303, 346
Sarawak National Anthem: arrangement, 68
Scherzo for piano (Op.32, no.2), 25, 81, 238, 303, 346
(The) Seraphina: incidental music, 92, 238–9
Serenade for flute, oboe, violin, viola and cello, 55, 239–40
Serenade for String Orchestra (Op.12), 20, 47, 65–6, 240–41, 303, 346
(The) Seven Ages of Man, *see* Incidental music for puppet play and farce
Seven Songs (Op.14, no.2), *see*
  (The) Beacon Barn
  Bells of Cordoba
  Eleven-fifty
  Lay your Sleeping Head
  Night covers up the rigid land
  Ode du premier Jour de Mai
  Tant que mes yeux

Sextet for clarinet, horn and string quartet (Op.47), 27, 28, 90, 241–2, 303, 347
Shepherd, Shepherd hark that calling! *see* Four Poems of St Teresa of Avila
Shepherd's Dance, *see* Suite from A Winter's Tale (Op.54)
Signs in the Dark (Op.69), 33, 34, 105, 242–3, 347
Silver, *see* Five Songs (de la Mare)
Sinfonia Concertante for oboe and orchestra (Op.84), 37, 38, 113–14, 243–6, 303, 347–8
Sinfonietta (1929), 16, 55
Sinfonietta (Op.34), 25, 82–3, 246, 304, 348
Sion's Daughters, Sons of Jerusalem (Op.21, no.2), 23, 73, 125–6, 162–3, 296, 298, 327, 335
Six preludes for piano (Op.23), 23, 24, 74, 247–8, 304, 348
So sweet love seemed, 95, 248
Sonata for flute and piano (Op.97), 42, 43, 119, 248–9, 304, 348
Sonata for flute and piano (Francis Poulenc): orchestrated by Berkeley (Op.93, no.2), 41, 117, 249, 304, 348–9
Sonata for piano in A (Op.20), 21, 23, 72–3, 249–50, 304, 349
Sonata for viola and piano (Op.22), 73, 349
Sonata for violin and piano, No.1, 16, 56–7, 250–51, 304
Sonata for violin and piano, No.2 (Op.1), 17, 57–8, 251
Sonatina for guitar (Op.52, no.1), 28, 29, 92, 304–5, 349
Sonatina for oboe and piano (Op.61), 31, 100–101, 251–2, 305, 349
Sonatina for piano, 55
Sonatina for piano duet in Eb (Op.39), 27, 87, 252–3, 305, 349–50
Sonatina for treble recorder (or flute) and piano (Op.13), 20, 66, 253–4, 305, 350
Sonatina for two pianos (Op.52, no.2), 29, 95, 254
Sonatina for violin, 53
Sonatina for violin and piano (Op.17), 22, 23, 69, 254–5, 305, 350
Sonatine pour clarinette et piano, 15, 54, 255
Sonette de Ronsard, 14, 50
(The) Song of the Soldier, *see* Five Songs (de la Mare)
Songs of the Half-Light (Op.65), 31, 32, 102, 255–7, 305, 350
Sonnet for high voice and piano (Op.102), 121, 257
Spring at this hour (Op.37, no.2), 26, 84–5, 257–8, 305, 350
Spring goeth all in white, *see* Three Songs
Spring Song, *see* Three Greek Songs
Stabat Mater (Op.28), 24, 26, 42, 77–8, 258–60, 350–51
(The) Station Master, *see* Incidental music for puppet play and farce
(The) Statue, *see* Suite from A Winter's Tale (Op.54)
Still when she slept, *see* Una and the Lion
(The) Storm, *see* Suite from A Winter's tale (Op.54)

(The) street sounds to the soldiers' tread, *see* Five Housman Songs
Suite for flute, oboe, violin, viola and cello, 55, 260–61
Suite for harpsichord, 16, 56, 261–2
Suite for oboe and cello, 16, 55–6
Suite for orchestra (1927), 15, 54, 351
Suite for orchestra (1953), 26, 85
Suite for strings (Op.87), 38, 115, 262–3
Suite: A Winter's Tale (Op.54), 263, 297, 355
Suite: Nelson (Op.42), 89, 264, 343–4
Sur quel arbre du ciel, *see* Trois Poèmes de Vildrac
Sweet was the song (Op.43, no.3), 92, 264, 306
(The) Sword of the Spirit: music for the film, 68
Symphony for string orchestra, 16, 56
Symphony no.1 (Op.16), 17, 20, 21, 22, 40, 69, 264–5, 306, 351
Symphony no.2 (Op.51), 28, 29, 30, 40, 41, 94, 265–7, 306, 351
Symphony no.3 (Op.74), 34, 39, 107, 267–8, 306, 351–2
Symphony no.4 (Op.94), 41, 42, 43, 118–19, 268–9, 352

Tant que mes yeux (Op.14, no.2), 21, 66–7, 269–70, 306
The Tempest: incidental music, 23, 74–5, 270
Theme and Variations for guitar (Op.77), 35, 109, 270–71, 306, 352
Theme and Variations for piano duet (Op.73), 34, 107, 271–2, 306
Theme and Variations for violin (Op.33, no.1), 81–2, 272–3, 306
There was neither grass nor corn, 23, 72, 273
These springs were maidens, *see* Five Herrick Poems (Op.89)
Thou hast made me (Op.55, no.1), 96–7, 273, 306–7, 352
Three Early Songs, 13, 14, 15, 50, 273–4, 298, 353
Three Greek Songs (Op.38), 25, 83, 274–5, 307, 352
Three Impromptus for piano (Op.7), 61, 275, 307
Three Latin Motets (Op.83, no.1), 37, 42, 112–13, 276–8, 307, 353
Three Mazurkas (Homage à Frederic Chopin) (Op.32, no.1), 25, 80–81, 278, 307, 353
Three Pieces for Clarinet, 65, 278–9
Three Pieces for Organ (Op.72, no.1), 32, 106, 279–80, 307, 353
Three Pieces for Piano (Op.2), 58, 280–81, 307
Three poems by Mary Webb, 64
Three short pieces for piano, 15, 53
Three songs for four male voices (Op.67, no.1), 103, 281–2, 307
(The) Three Winds, *see* Signs in the Dark
(The) Thresher, *see* Three Early Songs
To Aster, *see* Three Greek Songs

Toccata, *see* Three Pieces for Organ
Toccata for piano, 14, 15, 51, 282–3
Toccata for violin and piano in E minor (Op.33, no.3), 82, 283, 307, 335
Today a shepherd and our kin, *see* Four Poems of St Teresa of Avila
Tolhurst, George – "I went out full", Air from *Ruth*, orchestrated by Berkeley, 113, 124
(Le) Tombeau de Sapho, *see* Tombeaux
(Le) Tombeau de Socrate, *see* Tombeaux
Tombeaux, 15, 16, 52, 283–4
Tonight the winds begin to rise, *see* Autumn's Legacy
Trio for flute, oboe and piano, 60, 284
Trio for horn, violin and piano (Op.44), 26, 27, 86, 284–5, 307–8, 353
Trio for violin, viola and cello (Op.19), 22, 70–71, 285–6, 305–6, 353
Trois Poèmes de Vildrac, 16, 55, 286–7
Twelfth Night, *see* Signs in the Dark
Two (Auden) Songs, 51–2, 354
Two dances for piano duet, 14, 51
Two pieces for string quartet, 16, 55

Ubi caritas et amor (1969), 34, 107, 287
Ubi caritas et amor (Op.96, no.2), 44, 45, 48, 120, 287–8
Una and the Lion (Op.98), 43, 119–20, 288, 354

Variation on an Elizabethan theme (Sellinger's Round), 26, 85, 289, 308, 354
Variations on a hymn-tune by Orlando Gibbons (Op.35), 25, 83, 289–90, 354
Veni sponsa Christi, *see* Three Latin Motets
Venus Anadyomene: music for Oranges and Lemons (a review), 79, 216
Voices of the Night (Op.86), 38, 40, 114–15, 290–91, 354

(The) Wall of Troy: incidental music, 75–6, 291–2
Westminster Abbey: incidental music, 21, 68, 292
What's in your mind, *see* Five Poems of W.H. Auden
When we were idlers with loitering rills, *see* Autumn's Legacy
The Windhover (Op.72, no.2), 34, 106, 292–3
Windsor Variations (Op.75), 34, 35, 107–8, 293, 354
A Winter's Tale: incidental music, 30, 96, 293–4
Wiveton: hymn tune (Lord, by whose breath), 104–5, 198

Yesterday and Today: incidental music, 69–70, 294–5
Yeux, qui versez en l'âme, *see* Four Ronsard Sonnets (Set 2)
Youth in Britain: music for the film, 93, 295

Chronology

This chronology draws on many available resources, from available correspondence to Lennox Berkeley's autograph manuscripts, diaries and publication assignments with his publishers. I am most grateful to Tony Scotland for showing me his Berkeley family tree, and to Roger Nichols for allowing me to incorporate his Berkeley chronology into my own.

Information about the Berkeley family can be found in H. Costley-White *Mary Cole, Countess of Berkeley: a Biography* (London, Harrap, 1961) and B. Falk *The Berkeleys of Berkeley Square and some of their kinsfolk* (London, Hutchinson, 1944).

1827	Lennox's paternal grandfather, George Lennox Rawdon Berkeley, *de jure* 7th Earl of Berkeley, born (Died 1888)
1831	Lennox's maternal grandfather, James Charles Harris, born in Genoa (Vice Consul in Nice 1881, Consul 1884, Consul for Monaco 1888) (Died November 1904)
1838	
21 September	Lennox's maternal grandmother, Geraldine von Gau, born in Darmstadt (Died 10 February 1912)
1855	
12 November	Lennox's father, Hastings George FitzHardinge

	Berkeley, 8th Earl of Berkeley manqué, Captain R.N. born in Paris (Baptised 1 December 1855)
1860	George Lennox Rawdon Berkeley marries Cecile Drummond, daughter of Edward Drummond, Comte de Melfort.
1863	
11 December	Lennox's mother, Aline Carla Harris, born (Nice?)
1891	
27 January	Captain Hastings and Aline Harris marry at the British Consulate in Nice. "The voice that breathed o'er Eden" (A and M 350) "composed expressly for and dedicated to Miss Aline Harris on the occasion of her marriage with Captain Berkeley."
1898	Geraldine Berkeley (sister) born (Died 1989)
1903	
12 May	Lennox Randal Francis Berkeley, 9th Earl of Berkeley manqué, born at Melford Cottage, Boar's Hill, near Oxford
1909	Family moves into Oxford Lennox is educated at Dragon School
1913	Lennox's mother " … [goes] to hear *Mignon* (Thomas) in Nice."
1914	
September	Lennox goes to Gresham School, Holt
1915	
12 November	Lennox's father celebrates his 60th birthday

1918	Lennox leaves Gresham School
1919	Lennox goes to St George's School, Harpenden
1920	
Easter	Certificate in the Diocesan Scripture Exam
Summer	Takes part in a concert of music for 'cello and piano
November	Speaks in a debate about "that all is Vanity."
1922	
October	Goes up to Merton College, Oxford where he reads French, Old French and Philology. Studies organ with W.H. Harris
1923	
25 May	Elizabeth Freda Bernstein born
11 December	Lennox's mother celebrates her 60th birthday
1924	
April	Composes his *March for harpsichord/piano* at Beaulieu
16 June	*Pastourelle* and *La belle dame sans merci* performed at OUMCU
Late (?) June	Travels to Florence and Assisi with Father Thorne. Goes via Turin and Genoa
16 July	Arrives in Anneçy and stays with his parents
16–26 July	Practises at a local music shop
4 August	Leaves via Paris for Chaumont
20 September	Arrives in London (Royal Palace Hotel with parents) from Chaumont
21 September	To "Gerry's flat" in Meadway Court

4 December	*Sonette de Ronsard* and *Les dimanches* performed at OUMCU
Late December	Travels to Sicily with H.W. Garrod

1925

2 January	Arrives in Palermo, and plans to travel to Rome
12 March	*Two Dances for piano duet* and *The Thresher* performed at OUMCU. Cox of Merton VIII. Arrives *chez* parents in the South of France by train
23 March–26 April	Vere Pilkington and family staying nearby
28 March	All and Vere go to hear *Pelléas and Mélisande* (Debussy) at the Monte Carlo Opera
30 March	Lennox and his mother attend a String Quartet concert in Monte Carlo
11 April	"Lennox's Indian friend, Mr. Gurtu, comes to dinner."
16 April	Lennox and John ? to ballet in Monte Carlo
22 April	Leaves by train
21 July	Lennox joins his parents near Alton
22 August	"Lennox and Colin put in a good bit of tennis."
23 August	"To early church with Lennox."
28 August	"Lennox and Colin left for Town this morning. Lennox went to Oxford."
31 August	"Lennox left early this morning for Amboise." Staying with the de Minvielles
September–October	Composes his *Toccata for piano* at Negron
12 November	Lennox's father celebrates his 70th birthday

1926

	Meets Ravel
6 March	*Toccata for Piano* performed at OUMCU

26 March	*Introduction and Dance* for small orchestra played at a BBC concert at the New Chenil Galleries
June	Takes a fourth in Modern Languages
Autumn	Goes to Paris

1927

	The Thresher published by OUP after revision: his first published work. Finishes his *Three short pieces* for piano
March–April	Composes his *Petite Suite for oboe and cello* in Paris
6 April	*Concertino for Chamber Orchestra* first performed at a British Music Society concert
June–August	Composes his *Prelude-Intermezzo-Finale* in Paris and Veneux les Sablons
22 September	*Concertino* performed at the Harrogate Festival
October	*Prelude-Intermezzo-Finale* performed in London
1 November	*Prelude-Intermezzo-Finale* performed in Oxford
29 December	Composes his *Piece for Vere*

1928

	Received into the Roman Catholic Church
16 February	*Suite* performed at the Salle Pleyel in Paris
Spring	*Tombeaux* performed at a concert in Paris. Works on his *Sonatine pour clarinette et piano*
August	Living at 4 Rue du Ruisseau XVIII in Paris
Christmas	Spends the holiday with the Pilkington family

1929

11 March	*Tombeaux* (with chamber orchestra) broadcast by the BBC

June	Finishes his *Sinfonietta*. Composes his *Trois Poémes de Vildrac* in Paris. Writes his first report from Paris in the *Monthly Musical Record*
September	Living at 19 Rue du Mont Cenis XVIII in Paris

1930

	Composes his *Symphony for String Orchestra*
2 May	*Two Pieces* for String Quartet performed in Paris. Composes his *Suite for Harpsichord* in Paris which is completed in June
31 May	*Suite* for oboe and cello performed in Paris

1931

	Composes his *Sonata No.1 for Violin and Piano*
10 February	*Tombeaux* performed in London at the Aeolian Hall
14 December	*Symphony for String Orchestra* performed at Queen's Hall in London

1932

4 May	*Sonata No.1 for violin and piano* performed in Paris
May–June	Composes an untitled ballet for the Monte Carlo Ballet. Leaves Paris for the South of France
17 June	Attends the unveiling of the Debussy memorial in the Boulevard Lannes, near the Bois de Boulogne, in Paris

1933

	Commences work on his oratorio *Jonah*. The first full score score is dated 1933
11 December	Lennox's mother celebrates her 70th birthday

1934

April	J.& W. Chester begin to publish his works: introduced by Lord Berners. Agree to publish *Sonata No.2 for violin and piano* and the *Polka for two pianos*. Death of Lennox's father
June	Last Paris report in the *Monthly Musical Record*. Composes the *Overture for Chamber Orchestra* (Op.8) at Cap Farrat

1935

	Returns to London and completes *Jonah*
June	OUP refuse to publish *Jonah*
1 October	*Overture* performed at a Promenade Concert
November	*String Quartet No.1* first performed in London
December	Starts to rescore *Jonah*. Death of Lennox's mother

1936

	Living at 1 Cité Chaptal with José Rafaelli Begins composition of *Symphony No.1*
21 April	Meets Benjamin Britten
22 April	Nightclub in Chinatown
23 April	*Overture* performed at the ISCM Festival in Barcelona
25 April	Attend a performance of folk-dancing in Barcelona
June	Living in London at 28 Great Ormond Street
19 June	*Jonah* broadcast by the BBC
25 July	Arrives *chez* Ursula Nettleship. Britten already there. Decide to collaborate on *Mont Juic*, and orchestral suite based on themes that both heard in April

30 July	Lennox returns to London
31 July	Ralph Hawkes accepts the *String Quartet No.1* for publication
August	Flys (for the first time) to Jersey
8 October	Elected provisional member of the Performing Right Society
22 October	Returns to Cité Chaptal
24 November	*Deux Poèmes* conducted by Nadia Boulanger at Queen's Hall, London

1937

5–12 April	Lennox and Benjamin Britten at Painswick; start work on *Mont Juic*
27 April	Peter Burra killed in plane crash
29 April	Attends Burra's funeral
8 May	Lennox visits Brussels, feeling "sterile"
August	Benjamin Britten buys the Old Mill at Snape
7 October	Lennox conducts *Jonah* at the Leeds Music Festival
19 October	Lennox and Britten attend a performance of *Jeu de cartes* conducted by Stravinsky
12 December	*Mont Juic* is completed, and starts work on *The Judgement of Paris*
Christmas	Spends the holiday in a Benedictine monastery at Solesmes. On his way back to Paris, Lennox sees Jean Françaix in Le Mans who was writing "... some rather voluptuous ballet music."
28 December	Death of Ravel
30 December	Attends Ravel's funeral at Levallois-Perret

1938

8 January	*Mont Juic* given its first performance in a BBC broadcast

11 January	*The Judgement of Paris* finished in piano score. Nadia Boulanger and Clifford Curzon play the *Polka* and *Nocturne* (Op.5) in Paris
23 January	Orchestrating *The Judgement of Paris*. Drinks in a Paris hotel with Ralph Hawkes who offers to publish *The Judgement of Paris*
6 February	Returns to England, with Jean Françaix (his first visit)
26 March	Benjamin Britten makes suggestions about the orchestration of *The Judgement of Paris*
5 April	Finishes the revisions to *Domini est Terra*
9 April	Moves into the Old Mill at Snape which he shares with Benjamin Britten. Works on his *Introduction and Allegro* which is dedicated to Britten
19 April	In Paris, at Cité Chaptal
22–30 April	Visits Geneva with his cousin, Claude Berkeley
c. 1 May	Returns to London
10 May	First performance of *The Judgement of Paris* at Sadler's Wells, conducted by Constant Lambert
17 June	*Domini est Terra* performed at the opening concert of the 16th ISCM Festival in Queen's Hall, London
5 July	Orders the score of Aaron Copland's "Piano Variations" from J. & W. Chester's
14 July	Returns to Cité Chaptal, Paris to work on *Three Pieces* (Op.5)
21 July	Leaves Paris for the South of France
8 September	*Domini est Terra* performed at the Three Choirs Festival in Worcester *Three Pieces* for two pianos finished and *Serenade for String Orchestra* begun
23 October	Proofs of *Capriccio* and *Nocturne* sent off. Composes *The Beacon Barn*

December	Composes *The Bells of Cordoba*

1939

March	Buys a 16 hp AC coupé, and travels to Belgium. Mention that the cello concerto is apparently "... going ahead."
April–May	Writes his *Sonatina for recorder and piano*
25 August	Tells his Aunt Annie: "My Cello Concerto is at last finished, but I have still a great deal of work to do on it . . . ."
3 September	World War II begins
5 September	First concert performance of *Mont Juic* at a prom concert is cancelled owing to the declaration of war
Mid-October–Mid-November	Lennox in Paris
21 November	In Chippenham with the Davenports. Finishes the *Serenade for String Orchestra*
24 December	Spends Christmas at Painswick. Composes a *Mazurka* for piano

1940

January	Composes four of the *Five Housman Songs* and works on *Four Concert Studies* at Marshfield. Informs Benjamin Britten that he has finished his *Mazurka*
6 January	Visits Oxford: Sybil Jackson at Boar's Hill, and Merton College
30 January	*Serenade for Strings* first performed in London with Britten's *Les Illuminations*
February	Lennox still at Marshfield. Plans *Symphony No.1*
April	Lennox in Paris
21 April	Writing *String Quartet no.2* at Marshfield
8–10 May	Writes *Tant Que mes Yeux* (Op.14 no.2)

June	Berkeley tells Benjamin Britten that he has written a new *String Quartet* which he had finished in June
17 July	Still at Marshfield
6 September	*Introduction and Allegro* first performed at a Promenade Concert
9 November	Returns to Oxford and Boar's Hill
12 November	Travels to Painswick. Discusses Bartók with Benjamin Britten

1941

31 March	Works on *Symphony No.1* at Berkeley Castle and starts to write his *Piano Sonata*
11 June	The first movement of *String Quartet No.2* sent off to the BBC at Bedford
7 September	His incidental music for the radio feature on *Westminster Abbey* broadcast by the BBC
11 September	Elected full member of the Performing Right Society
October	Composes *Impromptu for Organ* for Colin Gill
6 November	Tells Douglas Gibson at Chester's that he has nearly finished the full score of his first *Symphony*, a work he started to write in 1936
December	Transferred to the BBC European Service (French Department)

1942

3 March	Joins the BBC Music Department in Bedford and works with Herbert Murrill on orchestral programmes
18 March	*String Quartet* turned down by a BBC Music Panel under the chairmanship of Edmund Rubbra

May	Arthur Bliss, Director of Music, commissions a work for Section C of the BBC Symphony Orchestra (*Divertimento*)
Mid-May	*Symphony No.1* played to Adrian Boult at Berkeley's request
June	Bliss contests the refusal of *String Quartet No.2*
12 June	*Symphony No.1* and the *Sonatina for violin and piano* finished
20 June	*The Midnight Murk* broadcast by the BBC

1943

	"Transformed" to Home Service Music Section in Marylebone High Street. Composes the *Trio for violin, viola and piano*
9 February	Clifford Curzon writes to Berkeley about the *Four Concert Studies*
27 May	Article about Britten's String Quartet is published in *The Listener*
8 July	*Symphony No.1* first performed at a Promenade Concert in London
1 October	*Divertimento in Bb* first performed by Section C of the BBC Symphony Orchestra
14 October	Memo from Berkeley about orchestra allocations
23 November	Berkeley in line for a religious music commission from the BBC (*Lord, when the sense*)

1944

20 March	*Symphony No.1* first broadcast by the BBC
August	*String Trio* first performed at the Wigmore Hall
25 September	*Sonatina for violin and piano* first performed in Hampstead by Max Rostal and Berkeley

28 October	Music for the film *Hotel Reservé* recorded by the BBC Northern Orchestra
24 December	*There was neither grass nor corn* first broadcast on the BBC Home Service

1945

	Six Preludes commissioned by the BBC as interludes between radio programmes. Completes the *Piano Sonata* and works on his *Nocturne for orchestra* which is completed in 1946. Leaves the BBC
February (end)	Takes two weeks sick leave and stays in Painswick
May–June	Composes *Sion's Daughters, Sons of Jerusalem* (A Festival Anthem)
30 June	Sends congratulations to Benjamin Britten on the success of his opera *Peter Grimes*
21 September	Conducts the first performance of the *Festival Anthem* at St Matthew's Church in Northampton. Starts to compose the *Six Preludes* for piano which are finished in October

1946

	Appointed professor of composition at the Royal Academy of Music, a post he holds until 1968. Awarded the Collard Fellowship for Music (Worshipful Company of Musicians)
14 January–2 February	Composes his incidental music for *A Glutton for Life*
20 April	His incidental music for Shakespeare's play *The Tempest* is first performed at Stratford
June	Writes his *Five Songs* (Walter de la Mare)
20 August	Agrees to join the score-reading panel at the BBC

14 December	Marries Freda Bernstein at the Church of the Holy Apostles, Claverton Street (Pimlico)

1947

February–April	Composes his *Four Poems of St Teresa of Avila*
May–June	Composes his *Stabat Mater*
27 June	*Overture for chamber orchestra* first performed in Canterbury Cathedral
7 July	The *Six Preludes for Piano* first performed at the Concert Hall in Broadcasting House
14 July	Lennox and Freda visit France and Holland
19 August	Conducts the first performance of *Stabat Mater* in Zurich

1948

	Finishes his score for the *The First Gentleman*
15 March	Trade showing of *The First Gentleman*
4 April	*Four Poems of St. Teresa of Avila* first performed at Broadcasting House, London by Kathleen Ferrier. Works on both the *Piano Concerto* and the *Concerto for Two Pianos and Orchestra*
29 May	Michael FitzHardinge Berkeley (son) born
31 May	*The First Gentleman* goes on general release
31 August	The *Piano Concerto* first performed at a Promenade Concert by Colin Horsley
13 December	The *Concerto for two pianos and orchestra* first performed at the Royal Albert Hall by Cyril Smith and Phyllis Sellick

1949

January	Boult conducts the *Divertimento* in Milan which is a success
January–February	Composes *Colonus' Praise* and starts work on *Nelson*

20–30 April	Visits Jersey
26 April	The *Piano Concerto* is played in Palermo by Colin Horsley at an ISCM concert
30 June	Elected Honorary Member of the Royal Academy of Music
August	Retires from the BBC score-reading panel
13 September	*Colonus' Praise* first performed by the BBC Choral Society and Orchestra at a Promenade Concert
3 October	No. 3 of *Three Mazurkas* for piano first performed in Paris
November	Completes his *Scherzo* for piano

1950

April	Completes his *Elegy for violin and piano*
9 May	BBC talk on composition
6 July	Julian Lennox Berkeley (son) born. Act III of *Nelson* begun
September	Completes his *Sinfonietta* which he started the previous month. Composes the *Three Greek Songs* which are completed in 1951
1 December	*Sinfonietta* first performed at the Wigmore Hall

1951

	Starts to compose the *Flute Concerto* which is completed in 1952
November–December	Composes his *Variations on a hymn-tune by Orlando Gibbons*

1952

21 June	*Variations on a hymn-tune by Orlando Gibbons* first performed at the Aldeburgh Festival
29 October	Asked to write a contribution to *A Garland for the Queen* by John Denison of the Arts Council

December	Completes his *Four Ronsard Sonnets* (set 1)

1953

14 February	Concert reading of *Nelson* at the Wigmore Hall in London by the English Opera Group Association
8 March	*Ronsard Sonnets (set 1)* first performed at the Victoria and Albert Museum
12 April	Attends a Poulenc concert in Monte Carlo
12 May	Celebrates his 50th birthday
1 June	*Spring at this hour* (A Garland for the Queen) first performed in the Royal Festival Hall on the eve of the Coronation
6 June	The *Suite* for orchestra (a BBC commission for Coronation week) first performed by the BBC Symphony Orchestra
20 June	His *Variation (No.3) on an Elizabethan Theme* (Sellinger's Round) first performed at the Aldeburgh Festival conducted by Benjamin Britten The *Stabat Mater* is also performed
7 July	Tells Benjamin Britten that he is seeing Paul Dehn about the libretto [*A Dinner Engagement*] for an opera
29 July	The *Flute Concerto* is first performed at a Promenade Concert
16 October	Completes his *Trio for Horn, Violin and Piano*
November	Starts to compose *A Dinner Engagement*

1954

	Elected Composer of the Year by the Teachers' Association
March	Completes *A Dinner Engagement*
28 March	The *Trio* is first performed at the Victoria and Albert Museum

29 March	The *Trio* is recorded by EMI
17 June	*A Dinner Engagement* is first performed at the Aldeburgh Festival
1 July	First broadcast of *A Dinner Engagement*
31 July	Completes his opera *Nelson*
August	Visits France with Freda
September	Rehearsals for *Nelson* before its first performance on 22 September
7 October	The first London performance of *A Dinner Engagement*, the first of three performances
8 October	*Nelson* performed in Manchester
14 October	*Nelson* performed in Birmingham
3 December	Attends the premiere of Walton's opera *Troilus and Cressida* at Covent Garden
5 December	Finishes *Look up, sweet Babe*

1955

	Appointed Director of the Performing Right Society (until 1983)
18 January	*Sonatina for piano duet* first performed in London
6 March	*Crux Fidelis* first performed at the Victoria and Albert Museum
April–May	Composes his *Sextet*
July	Composes his *Salve Regina*
11 July	First performance of the *Sextet* at the Cheltenham Festival
20 July	First performance of the concert suite from *Nelson* at the Cheltenham Festival
August–7 September	Works on the *Concertino* at Nuttage House, Bucklebury, Berkshire

9–21 September	Lennox and Freda in France. Writes to Benjamin Britten from Blois (10 September) about *Ruth*, and visits Poulenc ("completely recovered"), Poitiers and the Dordogne
October	Starts work on *Ruth* which is completed in July 1956
11 December	First London performance of the *Sextet* at the Victoria and Albert Museum

1956

9 January	Nicholas Eadnoth Berkeley (son) born
24 January	First performance of the *Concertino* from Broadcasting House, London
3 June	Visits the British Embassy in Rome at the end of a holiday
8 August	All the family fly to Jersey
30 August	First London performance of the concert suite from *Nelson*
September	Meets William Mathias and Nicholas Maw for the first time as students at the Royal Academy of Music
28 September	Attends rehearsals for *Ruth*
2 October	First performance of *Ruth* at the Scala Theatre
31 December	Starts to compose *Symphony No.2*

1957

1 January	Appointed Commander of the British Empire (CBE)
26 February	Attends an Investiture at Buckingham Palace
14 March	Guest in "Call the Tune" on the BBC Home Service
April–June	Composes his *Sonatina for Guitar*
7 June	Writes to Benjamin Britten to say that there will be no new end for *Ruth*, and that he is in

	the process of buying Coldblow Cottage, six miles from Gresham's
25 June	Finishes the *Sonatina for Guitar*

1958

	Commissioned for his *Symphony No.2* by the Feeney Trust, for the City of Birmingham Symphony Orchestra. Works on it throughout the year
9 January	Member of the General Council of the Performing Right Society
April–June	Composes the *Five Poems by W.H. Auden*
August–September	Sketches the *Concerto for piano and double string orchestra* at Morston
November	Sir Ashley Clarke commissions the *Sonatina for two pianos*

1959

11 February	Berkeley conducts the first performance of the *Concerto for piano and double string orchestra*
14 February	First broadcast of the *Concerto*
21 February	Talks about his *Symphony No.2* on BBC radio
24 February	The *Symphony No.2* receives its first performance
April	Works on the *Overture for Light Orchestra* at Morston
15 May	BBC interview on his life and music ("The Composer Speaks")
26 May	The *Sonatina for two pianos* receives its first performance
1 June	Finishes the *Overture* and travels to Rome and then on to Assisi
4 July	First performance of the *Overture* at the Royal Festival Hall

August	Spends the summer at Morston
9 September	Conducts the first London performance of the *Symphony No.2*
23 October	First London performance of the *Five Poems of W.H. Auden*

1960

12 March	First performance of the *Missa Brevis* in Westminster Cathedral
16 August	Unable to attend rehearsals for *A Winter's Tale* at Stratford because of an appendix operation
17 September	Visits Venice
October	Commences work on the Suite from *A Winter's Tale* which is completed in December

1961

17 January	Writes to Benjamin Britten about *Billy Budd* and George Malcolm's departure from Westminster Cathedral
February	Tells Douglas Gibson at Chester's that he is "well into" the *Violin Concerto*
April	On holiday at Morston
27 May	The suite from *A Winter's Tale* first performed in Norwich
1 June	*Concerto for Violin and Orchestra* first performed at the Bath Festival. Presents first prize to Jacqueline du Pré (Royal Over-Seas League Music Competition)
25 August	Lunches with Benjamin Britten at Aldeburgh
28 December	Completes *Five Pieces for Violin and Orchestra*

1962

	Awarded the Cobbett Medal
March	Commences work on *Autumn's Legacy*

28 June	Writes about "The Sound of Words" in *The Times*
6 July	*Autumn's Legacy* first performed at the Cheltenham Festival
26 July	William Glock commissions a 20-minute work for the 1963 season of Promenade concerts. Berkeley unkeen
31 July	*Five Pieces for Violin and Orchestra* first performed at a Promenade concert
16 September	BBC talk ("Music Magazine") for Nadia Boulanger's 75th birthday. Composes the *Sonatina for oboe and piano* which is completed in October

1963

9 January	Attends a performance of Britten's *War Requiem* at the Royal Albert Hall
March	Obituary of Francis Poulenc for the *Musical Times*
24 April	Attends the wedding of Princess Alexandra in Westminster Abbey
May	Juror (until 1984) for the Prix de Composition Musicale, Foundation Prince Pierre de Monaco
12 May	Celebrates his 60th birthday
31 May	Travels to Ireland and visits Cork
June	Composes *Counting the Beats*
August	Writes *Automne* at Mouton in memory of Francis Poulenc
September	Visits Germany, Poland and Czechoslovakia
December	Starts to compose *Songs of the Half-Light* which are completed in January 1964

1964

31 March	Tells Douglas Gibson that he has rewritten the last movement of the *Oboe Sonatina*

April	At Morston, working on the *Mass for Five Voices* which is completed in October
5 May	Visits Monte Carlo with Freda
13 July	First performance of the *Diversions* at the Cheltenham Festival
August–10 September	At Morston
December	Starts to compose *Partita for Chamber Orchestra*

1965

February	Completes his *Partita*, and commences work on *Castaway* which is completed in 1966
June	Attends the Aldeburgh Festival. *Songs of the Half-Light* first performed on 22 June
2 August–10 September	Rewrites the last part of the last movement of the *Diversions* whilst at Morston
21 September	In Geneva, on the jury of the piano section of the International Competition for executants
12 November	Conducts a BBC recording of the *Partita*

1966

20 January	Receives a letter from Cardinal Heenan about Latin Masses
3 March	Writes about "Truth in Music" for the *Times Literary Supplement*
Mid-March	Goes to Norfolk
April	Writes *Aubade* for organ
3 April	Works on *Castaway*
1 May	Goes to Monte Carlo
17 June	First performance of *Aubade* for organ by Simon Preston from the Aldeburgh Festival
August–September	At Morston, scoring *Castaway* and writing the first and last movements of the *Oboe Quartet*

CHRONOLOGY · 33

5 November	Flies to Paris
7 November	Roland-Manuel's funeral
9 November	To Geneva, on jury of Queen Marie-José Composition Prize
24 November	Finishes *Castaway*
December	Revising *Ronsard Sonnets* (Set 1), and starts to compose *Signs in the Dark*

1967

1 May	To Monte Carlo. Awarded the Ordre National du Mérite Culturel de Monaco
31 May	Attends rehearsals of *Castaway* at Aldeburgh. Works on *Signs in the Dark*
3 June	First performance of *Castaway* at Aldeburgh
10 June	First BBC broadcast performance of *Castaway*
12 July	First London performance of *Castaway* at Sadler's Wells. Finishes *Signs in the Dark* on 31 July at Mouton
August	Holiday in France (Orléans, Ambert and Le Puy). Scores *Signs in the Dark*
September	Starts composition of his *Oboe Quartet*
22 October	First performance of *Signs in the Dark* at Stroud
30 November	Finishes the *Oboe Quartet*
December	Starts work on his setting of the *Magnificat* for the 1968 City of London Festival

1968

30 April	Finishes his setting of the *Magnificat*
1 May	Goes to Monte Carlo by train
21 May	Returns to London
22 May	Lunches with HM Queen at Buckingham Palace

	First performance of the *Oboe Quartet* at the Wigmore Hall
7 June	Resigns from the staff of the Royal Academy of Music
25 June	Attends the Lord Mayor of London's Banquet at the Mansion House. Writes *The Windhover: To Christ Our Lord*
4 July	Writes about his setting of the *Magnificat* in *The Listener*
8 July	Conducts the first performance of the *Magnificat* in St Paul's Cathedral which is broadcast by the BBC (Very unsatisfactory, says his diary)
10 July	*Automne* first performed at the Cheltenham Festival
19 August	Takes Michael and Julian to Berkeley Castle for the first time
27 August	First London performance of *Signs in the Dark*
10 October	Holiday in Ireland. Composes his *Theme and Variations for piano duet* which is completed in December
21 November	Article about "Lili Boulanger" in *The Listener*
December	Starts work on *Symphony No.3*

1969

January–February	Composes his first setting of *Ubi Caritas*
April	Completes *Symphony No.3*
28 April–9 May	In Monte Carlo and then on to Toulouse
14–18 May	In Paris
June–July	Composes his *Windsor Variations*
9 July	First performance of *Symphony No.3* at the Cheltenham Festival
End of August	Finishes the *Windsor Variations* (diary: July on the score)

CHRONOLOGY · 35

18 September	First performance of the *Windsor Variations*, conducted by Yehudi Menuhin
October	Encounters problems with *String Quartet No.3*
27 November	Attends a dinner at Gray's Inn
4 December	Guest at a supper for Artur Rubinstein

1970

January–April	Composes the first three movements of *String Quartet No.3*. The fourth movement is written between June and July
Early February	Attends lunches at the French Embassy for Cardinal Danielou and Pierre Boulez
5 March	Writes about Charles Burney in *The Listener*
31 March	Asked by the Performing Right Society to contribute to *Music for a Prince*
April	Composes his *Andantino (Music for a Prince)* for cello and piano
16 April	Attends a performance of Richard Rodney Bennett's opera *Victory* at Covent Garden
20 April	Travels to Monte Carlo with Freda, and then on to Naples, Amalfi and Ischia
13 May	Goes to stay with Sir William and Lady Walton in Forio, Ischia
6 June	Receives an honorary D.Mus from Oxford University
14 June	First London performance of the *Windsor Variations*
1 July	Attends the PRS Annual Luncheon when *Music for a Prince* is presented to the Prince of Wales by Sir Arthur Bliss
August	Lunches with the Queen Mother at Sandringham
1 September	Finishes the *Theme and Variations* for guitar

6–23 September	Lennox and Freda in Majorca
28 November	First performance of *String Quartet No.3*. Starts to compose the *Five Chinese Songs* which are completed in January 1971
3–8 December	Flies to Guernsey

1971

20 January	Attends Pierre Bernac's talk on Francis Poulenc at the British Institute of Recorded Sound
22 March	First performance of the *Five Chinese Songs*
23 March	First London performance of *String Quartet No.3*
9 April	Receives a copy of the libretto of *Faldon Park* from Winton Dean
31 May	Attends Sir Arthur Bliss's 80th birthday celebrations at the Royal Festival Hall
July	Composes *In Memoriam I.S.*
8 July	First performance of *A Grace*
30 July	First performance of *Dialogue* at King's Lynn
August–September	Composes his *Introduction and Allegro for double bass and piano*
October–November	Composes his *Duo for cello and piano*
2 November	Composes his *Canon for String Trio*
24 November	Attends the Alan Rawsthorne memorial concert
14 December	Celebrates his Silver Wedding. John Betjeman wrote a poem and Paul Dehn an acrostic sonnet in which the initial letters of the fourteen lines spell LENNOX AND FREDA

1972

26 January	Attends a dinner party given by C. Day Lewis and his wife for Paul Dehn and James Bernard

11 February	First London performance of *Dialogue*
21 February	Attends a performance of Arthur Bliss's opera *The Olympians* at the Royal Festival Hall
February–March	Composes his *Four Concert Studies* for piano
April	Completes the first of *Three Latin Motets*. The other two are composed in May–June
12 April	Invited by HM Queeen to a reception at Windsor Castle for the Queen of the Netherlands
16 April	Travels to Monaco
26 May	BBC commissions a work for the 1973 season of Promenade concerts
24 August	Working on the *Sinfonia Concertante* which is completed in March 1973
28 September	First performance of *Three Latin Motets* at St Asaph
1–10 October	Goes with Freda to Italy. Return home via Paris
25 October	Attends a memorial service for C. Day Lewis at St Martin in the Fields, London
15–21 November	Starts work on, and encounters "terrible struggles" with the *Sinfonia Concertante*

1973

19 January	Attends a reception at the Polish Embassy for Witold Lutoslawski
17 February	Finishes a sketch of *Sinfonia Concertante* before starting to orchestrate the work. This is completed in March
22 February	Begins to compose *Antiphon*
March–April	Works every day on *Antiphon*
12 May	Celebrates his 70th birthday. Talks to Colin Mawby and introduces the first broadcast of the *Mass for Five Voices* and the *Three Motets*

22 May	Attends a J.&W. Chester birthday concert with Nadia Boulanger
8 June	Attends a luncheon party held by Edward Boyle. Starts to compose *Voices of the Night* which is completed in July
16 June	Attends the first performance of Britten's *Death in Venice*. Unmoved by the opera
5 July	Papal Knighthood of St Gregory conferred by Cardinal Heenan
7 July	First performance of *Antiphon* at Cheltenham
10 July	70th birthday celebrations at the Cheltenham Festival
3 August	First performance of *Sinfonia Concertante* at the Royal Albert Hall, London
22 August	First performance of *Voices of the Night* at Hereford
6–26 September	To Italy and Corfu
22 October	First London performance of *Antiphon*
November	Starts work on his *Suite for String Orchestra* which is completed in January 1974
9 November	Richard Rodney Bennett and Susan Bradshaw suggest a Concerto for Piano Duet
14 November	Attends the wedding of Princess Anne in Westminster Abbey
1 December	Composers' Guild Composer of the Year Award

1974

February	Starts work on the *Guitar Concerto* which is completed in May
6 March	Declines a commission from the Havant Symphony Orchestra
13/14 March	Records the *Concerto for two Pianos* and *First Symphony* in Walthamstow Town Hall for Lyrita

18 April	Encounters problems with the *Guitar Concerto*
May	Visits Monte Carlo, returning to London on 24 May
15 June	Knighthood announced in Queen's Birthday Honours
25 June–1 July	On Carl Flesch jury
4 July	First performance of the *Guitar Concerto*
17 July	Receives knighthood at Buckingham Palace
2–6 September	To Guernsey
17 September–5 October	To France (Lyon, Basle and Paris). Starts work on the *Oboe Quintet* which is completed in March 1975
6 November	Elected Honorary Fellow of Merton College, Oxford
21 November	Conducts *Symphony No.3* at the Royal Festival Hall
28 December	Revises the *Guitar Concerto* with Julian Bream

1975

	Appointed Master of the Worshipful Company of Musicians. Awarded an honorary fellowship of the Royal Northern College of Music
15 January	Hears Arnold Cooke's 4th Symphony and complains in his diary of Peter Heyworth's criticisms
2 February	Signs a card of the Latin Mass Society, requesting a Requiem according to the old rite
April	Completes *The Lord is My Shepherd*
21 April	Flies to Monte Carlo, and returns 11 May
20 May	Attends the memorial service at Westminster Abbey for Sir Arthur Bliss
24 May	Begins to compose *The Hill of the Graces*

18 June	Attends the memorial service for Professor Jack Westrup
26 June	Elected president of the Performing Right Society (deputy is Vivian Ellis) in succession to Sir Arthur Bliss
9 July	Finishes *The Hill of the Graces*
July–September	Writes comments for *Radio Times* about each Promenade concert
4 September	*Voices of the Night* performed at a Promenade concert
1 October	Attends a reception for Alan Frank (OUP)
10–14 October	To Guernsey
12 November	Installed as Master of the Musicians' Company
1–12 December	Visits Bali and Bangkok on his way to Australia. Rewrites *Symphony No.2* on his return to London

1976

	Elected President of the Composers' Guild of GB
24 January	Visits USA for the first time
30 January	First performance of the *Quintet* in New York
3–5 February	Visits Minneapolis
5 February	Returns to New York
8 February	Visits Philadelphia
10 February	Visits Washington DC
11 February	Returns to New York
16 February	Returns to London
18 February	Receives an honorary degree at the Royal Northern College of Music in Manchester
8 March	Attends a reception at Buckingham Palace
April–May	Revises *Symphony No.1*

10 May	Flies to Monte Carlo
June–July	Completes *Fantasia for organ*
30 July	Asked by John Manduell to be President of the Cheltenham Festival
3–4 August	Recording of *Symphony No.2*. Starts to orchestrate the Poulenc Flute Sonata
25 September–1 October	Travels to Paris, and then south
1 October	Appointed Honorary Professor at the University of Keele for three years
11 October	Returns to London and starts work on *Symphony No.4*
5 November	David Willcocks asks for a work for the Bach Choir
6 November	Stays with Winton Dean and discusses the libretto for *Faldon Park*
1 December	First performance of *Fantasia for organ* by Nicholas Kynaston at the Royal Festival Hall
4 December	Death of Benjamin Britten
28 December	To Guernsey

1977

23 February	Finds suitable texts for de la Mare songs
10 March	Attends Britten memorial service in Westminster Abbey
24 March	First performance of the orchestration of Poulenc's Flute Sonata at the Royal Festival Hall by James Galway. Completes work on *Another Spring*
3 May	Flies to Nice
21 May	Returns to London
26 May	Attends Elizabeth Maconchy's 70th birthday concert

1 June	Attends the Lord Mayor of London's Midsummer Banquet
17 June	Attends the Aldeburgh Festival
20 June	First performance of the *Three Latin Motets* at Westminster Cathedral
20 July	Attends an Evening Reception at Buckingham Palace given by HM Queen and the Duke of Edinburgh to mark the Silver Jubilee of The Queen
26 July	Attends a performance of Michael Tippett's opera *The Ice Break* and is unimpressed
1 August	Rewriting *Ronsard Sonnets* (Set 1) for Peter Pears
15 August	Alun Hoddinott, Professor of Music at UCW (Cardiff) commissions *Prelude and Capriccio*
19 September–1 October	Works on the *Sonnets* and *Symphony No.4* at Darby House, Dorset
3 October	Returns to London
2 November	Monte Carlo

1978

January	Composes his *Prelude and Capriccio* for piano
April	Works on the *Elegy for String Orchestra* (Op.33, no.2b)
7–18 April	Finishes *Flute Sonata* at Darby House, Dorset
May	Composes *Judica Me*
1 May	Records "Desert Island Discs" with Roy Plomley
10 May	Asked to be a Vice President of the Bach Choir
12 May	75th birthday concert broadcast by the BBC on R3. Michael's arrangement of the *Stabat Mater* is included in the programme
13 May	"Desert Island Discs" broadcast by the BBC on

	R4. Requests include music by Mozart, Bach, Verdi, Debussy, Britten and Ravel
30 May	First performance of *Symphony No.4* at the Royal Festival Hall, London
14 June	First performance of the *Ronsard Sonnets* (Set 1) in the revised version
21–27 July	On the Carl Flesch jury for a second time
3–17 August	Finishes the third movement of the *Flute Sonata* at Darby House, Burton Bradstock, Dorset
18 August	*Symphony No.4* performed at a Promenade concert
24 August	Visits Edinburgh
30 August	James Galway gives the first performance of the *Flute Sonata* at the Edinburgh Festival
2 September	First performance of *Judica Me* at Worcester
7 September	Visits Norway (Oslo for *Symphony No.4*)
22 September	Travels to Canada
November	Starts to compose *Una and the Lion* which is completed in January 1979
21 November	Unveils Britten's memorial in Westminster Abbey at a special memorial service

1979

	President of the Oxford and Cambridge Musical Club
8–19 February	Visits Salzburg and Munich
27 February–1 March	To Manchester: teaching at the RNCM
22 March	First performance of *Una and the Lion* at the Wigmore Hall
7 May	To Monte Carlo
10 May	Reported at the London Coliseum that Berkeley had written to say that he was now engaged on

	composing *Faldon Park*, but that he did not think that the score would be ready before the beginning of 1981. Lord Harewood had approached the Arts Council to seek their help in commissioning fees both for the composer and the librettist
5 June	Attends Robert Mayer's 100th birthday concert
21 June	Attends a Supper Party and Concert at Windsor Castle
5 July	Receives a letter from Lord Harewood setting out the terms for *Faldon Park*
August	Spends the month mostly at Darby House, then Spetchley
11 September	Attends Alun Hoddinott's 50th birthday supper at Dover Street
25 September	Lord Harewood reported to the Opera Committee of the English National Opera that Sir Lennox was a third through the first act of *Falden Park*
October	Meets Paul Sacher at St James's Square, London
20 October	Attends the first AGM of the newly-formed British Music Society
22 October	Nadia Boulanger dies in Paris
7 November	Visits Paris
19 November	*Ubi caritas et Amor* is commissioned

1980

	Foreign Honorary Member, American Academy and Institute of Arts and Letters
4–5 February	Teaching at the RNCM
February–March	Composes his second setting of *Ubi caritas et amor*
April–May	Composes his *Magnificat and Nunc Dimittis*
10 June	It was reported to the Opera Committee that

	there had been a playthrough of Act 1 of *Faldon Park* which was progressing well
25 June	Lennox joins Charles Groves, Lady Barbirolli and Geraint Evans in a picket outside Broadcasting House (Photo in *The Times* of 26 June)
11 July	First performance of *Ubi caritas and Amor* in Westminster Cathedral
26 July	First performance of *Magnificat and Nunc Dimittis* in Chichester Cathedral
7 August	Filming of Jim Berrow's programme on "Composers" starts
16 October	*A Dinner Engagement* is given at the Guildhall School of Music and Drama in the presence of the Prince of Wales
1–12 November	To Senegal
4 November	Elected Honorary Member of the Guildhall School of Music and Drama
17 November	Asked by the Hallé Orchestra for a work to celebrate its 125th Anniversary and Lennox Berkeley's 80th birthday
25 November	OUMCU present a concert of his music

1981

1 April	To Paris
14 May	Jim Berrow's film "Composers" first shown on television
7 December	Agrees to write a short piano piece to mark Haydn's 150th birthday

1982

	Elected a Vice-President of the National Music Council
2 February	Nicholas Daniel tries to commission a work for oboe and piano

28 February	Attends a reception at St James's Palace and service at Westminster Abbey to mark the centenary of the Royal College of Music
31 March	First performance of *Mazurka*, written to celebrate Haydn's 150th birthday on BBC radio
6 May	Lunches at Buckingham Palace
28 May	Attends a Papal Mass at Westminster Cathedral
29 May	Attends a reception at Archbishop's House, Westminster in the presence of His Holiness Pope John Paul II
25 September	Flies to Paris, and then on to Rome
19 December	Unanimously elected Honorary Member of the Royal Society of Musicians

1983

29 January	Attends the Poulenc Anniversary Concert at the Wigmore Hall
2 February	Resigns from the Performing Right Society
28 April	Lunches at Buckingham Palace
1 May	First performance of the *Bagatelle*
5 May	Elected Membre associe de l'Academie Royale des Sciences, des Lettres et des Beaux-Arts de Belgique
12 May	Celebrates his 80th birthday with a lunch at the Royal Festival Hall organized by J. & W. Chester Ltd
17 June	*A Dinner Engagement* and *Castaway* are performed together for the first time at the Bloomsbury Theatre
2 July	80th birthday concert given in Cheltenham Town Hall when *Variations on a theme by Lennox Berkeley* (the Reapers' chorus from *Ruth*) was performed as a tribute. Each variation (lasting one minute) was written by former pupils: John Manduell, Brian Chapple, Roy Teed, Sally

	Beamish, Michael Berkeley, Christopher Headington, Christopher Brown, Richard Stoker, David Bedford, Rory Boyle, John McLeod, William Mathias, Richard Rodney Bennett, Jonathan Rutherford, John Tavener and Nicholas Maw
13 July	President of Honour, Performing Right Society
17 July	Attends a lunch given in his and Lady Berkeley's honour in Cheltenham Town Hall. The *Cello Concerto* is performed for the first time
20 July	Attends the Walton memorial service in Westminster Abbey
9 October	Concert of his chamber music at the RNCM
23 October	*Nelson* broadcast on BBC R3
27 October	*A Dinner Engagement* and *Castaway* broadcast on R3
24 December	First performance of *In Wintertime* from King's College, Cambridge

1984

	Honorary Doctor of Music, City University
13 April	*Serenade for Strings* used for the ballet *Common Ground*
29 June	Attends a Service of Thanksgiving at Westminster Abbey for the life and work of Sir John Betjeman (1906–1984)
25 October	Attends a reception at the French Embassy in honour of the President of France and Mme Mitterand

1986

3 May	Ohio ballet choreographs *Serenade for Strings*
24 May	Resigns the Presidency of the Composers' Guild

4 July	Attends a memorial service for Peter Pears in Westminster Abbey
July	First signs of illness appear
1988	
7 April	Concert performance of *Nelson* at QEH, London
22 May	85th Birthday Concert held at St Mary's Church, Paddington Green
6 June	Geraldine, Lennox's sister, dies in the Cheadle Royal Hospital
1989	
26 July	Lennox in hospital
21 December	Taken ill at midnight
26 December	Dies (at 8.50) at St Charles Hospital, Kensington
1990	
4 January	Funeral and cremation at St John's Wood
20 March	Memorial Requiem Mass held in Westminster Cathedral, celebrated by Cardinal Basil Hume. Included were performances of the *Mass for Five Voices*, *Judica Me* and *Ubi Caritas* by the choir of Westminster Cathedral (see *The Daily Telegraph*, 21 March 1990, p.23 for details of those attending the Requiem Mass)

Catalogue raisonné

Compositions are arranged chronologically and then numerically by opus number. The information supplied about each includes, wherever possible, the following:

(1) The title of the work with opus number
(2) Date of composition
(3) Text(s) used and details about the authors of the texts
(4) The body or person responsible for a work's commission
(5) The required instrumentation
(6) Dedication
(7) Duration
(8) First performance(s)
(9) Publisher
(10) Notes

Further details about autographs and publisher information can be found in the section on *Manuscripts and First Editions*.

The firm of J. & W. Chester Ltd was founded in 1874 and has specialized in the music of contemporary foreign composers (Falla, Poulenc, Lutoslawski and Stravinsky) and English composers such as Bantock, Bax, Lord Berners and John Ireland. Lennox Berkeley, John Tavener and Geoffrey Burgon were added later. It published the journal, *The Chesterian*, from 1915 to 1961. The firm was linked with Hansen and other Scandinavian publishers in 1957. In some published works the company's name is given as Chester Music or Chester/Hansen.

1924

La Belle Dame sans Merci
Song for voice and piano

Text: John Keats (1795–1821)
First performance: Oxford, University Musical Club and Union, 16 June 1924.
Unable to trace the performers

Les Dimanches
Song for voice and piano
Text: Anon
First performance: Oxford, University Musical Club and Union, 4 December 1924.
Unable to trace the performers

Minuet
for two recorders

March
for harpsichord (or piano)
Written for and dedicated to Vere Pilkington
Duration: c. 2 minutes
First performance: London, BBC Radio 3, 12 May 1988. Anthony Legge (piano)

Sonette de Ronsard
Song for voice and piano
Text: Pierre de Ronsard (c. 1524–1585)
First performance: Oxford, University Musical Club and Union, 4 December 1924.
Unable to trace the performers

Three Early Songs
for mezzo soprano or tenor voice and piano

1. D'un vanneur de blé aux vents (Moderato/Andante)
Text: Joachim du Bellay (1522–1560). Translated into English (as "The Thresher") by M.D. Calvocoressi
Dedication: To John Greenidge
Duration: 1'30"
First performance: Oxford, University Musical Club and Union, 12 March 1925. C. Day Lewis (tenor) and Lennox Berkeley (piano)
Publication: OUP (after revision in 1927)

2. Pastourelle (Allegretto, naïf)
Text: Anonymous (13th century)
Duration: c. 1 minute

First performance: Oxford University Musical Club and Union, 16 June 1924.
Unable to trace performers
Publication: J. & W. Chester Ltd

3. Rondeau (Joyeux et animé)
Text: Charles d'Orléans (1391–1465)
Dedication: To G.M.B. [Geraldine Berkeley]
Duration: 1'30"
Publication: J. & W. Chester Ltd

1925

Toccata
for piano
Dedication: To J.F. Waterhouse [later music critic of *The Birmingham Post*]
Duration: 3 minutes
First performance: Oxford, University Musical Club and Union, 6 March 1926.
Unable to trace the pianist

Two Dances
for piano duet
First performance: Oxford, University Musical Club and Union, 12 March 1925.
Unable to trace the pianists

Four Pieces for Organ
Duration: *c.* 10 minutes

Four Pieces for Flute, Oboe and Piano
Duration: *c.* 10 minutes

1926

Mr Pilkington's Toye
for harpsichord (or piano)
Written for and dedicated to Vere Pilkington

Two Songs
for voice and piano

1. Bank Holiday

Text: W.H. Auden (1906–1973)

2. ? Text: W.H. Auden (1906–1973)
First performance: Oxford, University Musical Club and Union, 1926. C. Day Lewis (tenor) and Lennox Berkeley (piano)

Introduction and Dance
for small orchestra
Written for Anthony Bernard and the London Chamber Orchestra
1.1.2.1/2.0.0.0/percussion, harp and strings
First performance: London, New Chenil Galleries (Chelsea), 26 April 1926 (Broadcast by the BBC)
The London Chamber Orchestra, conducted by Anthony Bernard

Four Pieces
for small orchestra
Probably written for Anthony Bernard and the London Chamber Orchestra
No. 3 is marked 'Lento'

Tombeaux
Five French songs for voice and piano
Text by Jean Cocteau (1889–1963)
1. Le Tombeau de Sapho (Très lent)
2. Le Tombeau de Socrate (Moderato)
3. D'un Fleuve (Con moto)
4. De Narcisse (Triste et lent)
5. De Don Juan (Vif)
Duration: c. 8 minutes
First performance: London, British Music Information Centre, 4 November 1987. Meriel Dickinson (mezzo soprano) and Peter Dickinson (piano)
Publication: J. & W. Chester Ltd

Other versions
Berkeley later prepared a version of this work for voice and chamber orchestra which he dedicated to Anthony Bernard
First performance: Paris, Spring 1928. Jane Bathori (soprano)
First broadcast performance: London, BBC, 11 March 1929. Sophie Wyss (soprano) and the London Chamber Orchestra (leader: Samuel Kutcher), conducted by Anthony Bernard
First concert performance: London, Aeolian Hall, 10 February 1931. Jeanne Dusseau (soprano) and the London Chamber Orchestra, conducted by Anthony Bernard

1927

Piece for Vere
for piano (or harpsichord)
Written for Vere Pilkington
Duration: *c.* 1 minute
First performance: London, BBC Radio 3, 19 May 1988. Anthony Legge (piano)

Three Short Pieces
for piano
Duration: *c.* 6 minutes
First performance: London, unable to trace a date in 1929 or venue
Jan Smeterlin (piano)

Sonatina
for violin
Allegro moderato – Allegretto (Tango) – Presto
Note: See P. Dickinson *The Music of Lennox Berkeley* (Thames, 1988), p.227

Concertino for Chamber Orchestra
in three movements
Written for Anthony Bernard and the London Chamber Orchestra
First performance (private): London, the Court House, Marylebone Lane, 6 April 1927. The London Chamber Orchestra, conducted by Anthony Bernard (A London Contemporary Music Centre and British Music Society Concert)
First performance (public): Harrogate Music Festival, 22 September 1927. Orchestra conducted by Basil Cameron

Prelude, Intermezzo (Blues) and Finale
for flute, violin, viola and piano
1. Prelude (Animato)
2. Intermezzo (Blues) (Andante)
3. Finale (Allegro)
Dedication: To Gordon Bryan
First performance: London, unable to trace a venue, October 1927. Aeolian Players with Gordon Bryan (piano)
Repeated on 1 November in Oxford (Holywell Music Room) by the Aeolian Players and Gordon Bryan

Petite Suite
for oboe and violoncello

1. Prelude (Moderato)
2. Allegro moderato
3. Boureé (Allegro con moto): solo cello
4. Aria (Lento): solo oboe
5. Gigue

Duration: 13'30"
First performance: London Contemporary Music Centre, 1928
First broadcast performance: London, BBC Radio 3, 12 May 1988. Sarah Francis (oboe) and Rohan de Saram (cello)

Suite
for orchestra
1. Sinfonia
2. Bourée
3. Aria
4. Gigue

2.2.2.2/4.3.3.1/timpani, percussion, harp and strings
Duration: 18 minutes
First performance: Paris, Salle Pleyel, 16 February 1928. The Straram Orchestra, conducted by Walter Straram
First British performance: London, Queen's Hall, 12 September 1929. The Henry Wood Symphony Orchestra, conducted by Lennox Berkeley

1928

Sonatine pour clarinette et piano
1. Moderato
2. Largo lento
3. Vivace allegro

Note: This sonatina was submitted by the British jury for a competition in Geneva but rejected

1929

Pièce pour flute, clarinette et basson
in one movement (Allegro)
Duration: *c.* 3 minutes
First broadcast performance: London, BBC Radio 3, 2 September 1984. Richard Adeney (flute), Thea King (clarinet) and William Waterhouse (bassoon)

Serenade
for flute, oboe, violin, viola and cello
1. Lento
2. Allegro moderato
3. Allegretto con moto

Trois Poèmes de Vildrac
Three songs for voice and piano
Text by Charles Vildrac (1882–1971)
1. Sur quel arbre du ciel (Lento tranquillo)
2. Ce caillou chaud de soleil (Andante con moto)
3. Cet enfant de jadis (Andante)
Dedication: "à Mademoiselle Nadia Boulanger en toute admiration et gratitude"
Duration: 4'30"
First UK performance: Hampstead, Rosslyn Hill Chapel, 21 May 1983. Sylvia Eaves (soprano) and Courtney Kenny (piano)
Publication: J. & W. Chester Ltd

Sonatina
for piano

Sinfonietta
for chamber orchestra
Written for Anthony Bernard and the London Chamber Orchestra

1930

Suite for flute, oboe, violin, viola and cello
1. Introduction (Lento) and Pastorale (Allegretto)
2. Galliard (Moderto)
3. Passepied (Allegro)
4. Aria (Andante)
5. Hornpipe (Allegro)

Two Pieces for String Quartet
for two violins, viola and cello
First performance: Paris, Société Musicale Independante, 2 May 1930

Suite
for oboe and cello

First performance: Paris, 31 May 1930

Suite
for harpsichord
1. Lento
2. Allegro moderato
3. Sarabande (Lento)
4. Allegretto (Tranquillo)
5. March (Introduction: Moderato quasi tempo di marcia)
Written for and dedicated to Vere Pilkington
Note: A *Piece for Harpsichord/Clavichord* may have also been intended as part of this suite

1930–31

Symphony for String Orchestra
1. Allegro
2. Andante
3. Scherzo
4. Fugue
First performance: London, Queen's Hall, 14 December 1931. The London Chamber Orchestra, conducted by Anthony Bernard. A New English Music Society Concert
Note: See P. Dickinson, *The Music of Lennox Berkeley* (Thames, 1988), p.227

1931

La Poulette Grise
Song for children's voices ("Enfants I and II"), two pianos and trumpet in C
Duration: 3 minutes
First performance: London, St James's, Piccadilly, 30 October 1993. The New London Children's Choir, the New London Orchestra with Alexander Wells (piano), conducted by Ronald Corp

Sonata No.1 for Violin and Piano
1. Lento, ma non troppo
2. Adagio
3. Allegro con brio
Dedication: To Gladys Bryans

First performance: Paris, Société Musicale Independante, 4 May 1932

1932

Ode (Partition)
for mixed choir (SATB), trumpet in C and string orchestra

Untitled Ballet Score
May have been a commission from the Ballets Russes de Monte Carlo, the manuscript of which is dated Paris: May/June 1932
Sections include:
Introduction
L'Auba
Sortie des Infants (Allegro non troppo)
Le Camelot (Vivace)
Les Enfants
Le Vieux (Andante)
Retour du Camelot (Allegro)
Scene du Bistot (Allegro)
Java (Allegro)
Les Amoreux (Andante tranquillo)
Danse à trois (Allegro)
1.1+1.1.1/0.1.1.sax./timpani, percussion, piano and strings

Other versions
Andante ("Blues"), arranged for piano by Peter Dickinson (1988)
First performance: London, BBC Radio 3, 19 May 1988. Anthony Legge (piano)

1933

Sonata No.2 in D (Opus 1)
for violin and piano
1. Allegro risoluto
2. Andante
3. Rondo: Allegro moderato
Dedication: à Mademoiselle Nadia Boulanger
Duration: 15 minutes
First performance: London, Contemporary Music Centre, 1928
Publication: J. & W. Chester Ltd

Other versions
1. Arranged for oboe and orchestra

1934

Overture for Chamber Orchestra (Opus 8)
2+1.2+1.2.2+1/4.3.2+1.1/timpani and strings
Duration: 8 minutes
First performance: London, Queen's Hall, 1 October 1935. BBC Symphony Orchestra, conducted by Lennox Berkeley
Note: The Overture was performed in Barcelona at the Palau de la Musica Catalana on 23 April 1936 as part of the 14th ISCM Festival. Orchestra conducted by the composer

1935

How Love Came In
Song for voice and piano
Text: Robert Herrick (1591–1674)
Duration: 1'30"
First performance: London, Decca Recording Studios, September/October 1955. Peter Pears (tenor) and Benjamin Britten (piano). The recording of the Decca LP LW 5241 (10")
Publication: Boosey & Hawkes

Three Pieces for Piano (Opus 2)
1. Etude (Allegro moderato)
2. Berceuse (Allegretto)
3. Capriccio (Allegro)
Dedications:
1. To Miss Harriet Cohen
2. To Alan Searle
3. To Vere Pilkington
Duration: 8 minutes
First broadcast performance: London, BBC Radio 3, 26 May 1988. James Walker (piano)
Publication: Augener/Stainer & Bell

Jonah (Opus 3)
Oratorio for tenor and baritone soli, mixed chorus (SATB), boys' voices and orchestra

Text from The Bible (Book of Jonah, chapters 1 & 2, and Psalm 139)

Part I

Orchestral Introduction (Moderato)

1. *Recitative* (baritone solo): Now the word of the Lord (Un poco più lento) and *Chorus*: Arise go to Nineveh
2. *Recitative* (baritone solo): But Jonah rose up (Moderato)
3. *Chorus*: But the Lord sent out (Allegro vivace) and *Sinfonia* (Piu Vivo)
4. *Duet* (tenors and basses): Then the mariners (Andante) and *Recitative* (baritone solo): But Jonah was gone
5. *Chorus*: And they said ev'ry one (Vivo)
6. *Recitative* (tenor solo): And he said unto them (Andante) and *Chorus*: Then were the men (Allegro)
7. *Chorus*: Then said they unto him (Allegro)
8. *Recitative* (baritone solo): And he said unto them (Lento) and *Air*: For I know
9. *Chorus*: Nevertheless the men rowed hard (Allegro)
10. *Chorus*: We beseech thee O Lord (Lento)
11. *Chorus*: So they took up Jonah (Moderato)

Part II

Orchestral Introduction (Andante)

12. *Recitative* (baritone solo): Now the Lord had prepared
13. *Air* (tenor solo): I cried by reason of mine affliction (Moderato)
14. *Air* (tenor solo): For Thou didst cast (Allegro moderato)
15. *Solo* (tenor) with *Chorus*: I am cast out (Andante)
16. *Chorus*: The waters compassed me about (Moderato)
17. *Chorus*: Yet hast Thou brought up my life (Allegro)
18. *Air* (tenor solo): When my soul fainted (Allegretto)
19. *Recitative* (tenor solo): They that observe lying vanities (Moderato)
20. *Chorus*: Alleluia. I will sing of the Lord (Lento-Andante)

2+1.2.2.2+1/4.3.2+1.1/timpani, percussion and strings

Dedication: To the memory of my parents

Duration: 70–75 minutes

First performance: London, Concert Hall – Broadcasting House, 19 June 1936. Jan van der Gucht (tenor), William Parsons (baritone), BBC Chorus (Section A) and Orchestra (Section F), conducted by Clarence Raybould. *Note*: Joan Cross (soprano) sang the part allotted to the boys' voices

First public performance: Leeds, Town Hall, 7 October 1937. Parry Jones (tenor), Roy Henderson (baritone), Leeds Festival Chorus, a choir of boys' voices from Leeds Parish Church/Leeds Grammar School and the London Philharmonic Orchestra, conducted by Lennox Berkeley

First London performance (with organ): St Michael's Church, Cornhill, 31 March

1990. Martyn Hill (tenor), David Wilson-Johnson (baritone), St Michael's Singers with Matthew Morley (organ), conducted by Jonathan Rennert
Publication: J. & W. Chester Ltd

Polka, Nocturne and Capriccio (Opus 5)
for two pianos
1. Polka (Con brio)
2. Nocturne (Andante)
3. Capriccio (Vivace)
Dedication: For Ethel Bartlett and Rae Robertson
Duration:
1. 1'30"
2. 3'30"
3. 2 minutes
First broadcast performance: London, BBC Radio 3, 26 May 1988. Anthony Legge and James Walker (pianos)
Publication: J. & W. Chester Ltd

Other versions
1. *Polka*: arranged for solo piano by the composer (Opus 5, no.1)
Publication: J. & W. Chester Ltd
2. *Polka*: arranged for two pianos, trompette, cymbal, tambour de Basque and triangle by the composer (Opus 5, no.1)
3. *Polka*: arranged for orchestra by the composer
4. *Nocturne*: arranged for solo piano by the composer
Publication: J. & W. Chester Ltd
5. *Capriccio*: arranged for solo piano by the composer
Publication: J. & W. Chester Ltd

Trio
for flute, oboe and piano
Written for the Sylvan Trio
Duration: c. 10 minutes
First performance: The Sylvan Trio, 1935
First broadcast performance: London, BBC Radio 3, 2 June 1988. Graham Mayger (flute), Sarah Francis (oboe) and Gordon Stewart (piano)

Quartet for Strings No.1 (Opus 6)
in four movements
1. Allegro moderato
2. Andante (Non troppo lento)
3. Scherzo (Vivace)

4. [Theme and Variations]:
   Tema (Moderato)   19 bars
   Variation 1 (Allegro)   38 bars
   Variation 2 (Allegretto) 33 bars
   Variation 3 (Allegro)   27 bars
   Variation 4 (Andante)   23 bars
   Variation 5 (Presto)   51 bars
   Variation 6 (Lento)   27 bars
Dedication: To the Pro Arte String Quartet
Duration: 20 minutes
First performance: London, Contemporary Music Centre, November 1935. The Pro Arte String Quartet
Publication: Boosey & Hawkes

Three Impromptus (Opus 7)
for piano
1. Moderato
2. Andantino
3. Allegro
Duration: 7 minutes
First broadcast performance: London, BBC Radio 3, 2 June 1988. Anthony Legge (piano)
Publication: Boosey & Hawkes

1936

Five Short Pieces (Opus 4)
for piano
1. Andante
2. Allegro moderato
3. Moderato
4. Andante
5. Allegro
Dedication: To N. José Rafaelli
Duration: 8 minutes
First performance: unable to trace
Publication: J. & W. Chester Ltd

Deux Poèmes de Pindar
for soloists, mixed chorus (SATB) and small orchestra

Text: Pindar (c. 522–438 BC), translated by Poyard
1. Dithyramb
2. Hymn (Allegro)
1.1.1.1/1.1.1.0/percussion, piano and strings
Dedication: à Madame la Princess Edmund de Polignac
Duration: 7 minutes
First performance: London, Queen's Hall, 24 November 1936
The Oriana Madrigal Society Choir and A Cappella Singers with the London Symphony Orchestra, conducted by Nadia Boulanger

1937

Mont Juic (Opus 9)
Suite of Catalan dances for orchestra, written in collaboration with Benjamin Britten (Op.12)
1. Andante maestoso [LB]
2. Allegro grazioso [LB]
3. Lament (Barcelona, July 1936) (Andante moderato) [BB]
4. Allegro molto [BB]
2.2.2.2+2 sax/4.2.2+1.1/timpani, percussion (2), harp and strings
Dedication: In memory of Peter Burra [d. April 1936]
Duration: 12 minutes
First performance: London, Broadcasting House, 8 January 1938. BBC Orchestra (Section C), conducted by Joseph Lewis
First concert performance: London, Queen's Hall, 5 September 1939. Cancelled owing to the outbreak of World War II
Publication: Boosey & Hawkes
Note: In a letter to the present author, dated 26 September 1986, Miss Rosamunde Strode, former Keeper of Manuscripts and Archivist at the Britten-Pears Library, confirmed that the Library held a full manuscript score of this work, entirely written in Britten's hand. She also confirmed that Britten had told her that he and Berkeley had both sworn a solemn oath never to divulge his own particular share in the composition of the piece. Berkeley agreed that they had made such a decision.

Domini est Terra (The Earth is the Lord's) (Opus 10)
Psalm for mixed chorus (SATB) and orchestra
Text from The Vulgate
2.2.0.2/0.2.2.0/timpani, piano, harp and strings
Dedication: To Mdlle. Nadia Boulanger [at whose suggestion it was written]

Duration: 9 minutes
First performance: London, Queen's Hall, 17 June 1938. London Select Choir and the BBC Orchestra, conducted by Arnold Fulton (The opening concert of the 16th ISCM Festival)
The Psalm was also performed at the Three Choirs Festival (in Worcester Cathedral) on 8 September 1938
Publication: J. & W. Chester Ltd

The Judgement of Paris (Opus 10, no.2)
Ballet in one act with choreography by Frederick Ashton
Introduction (Andante)
1. Allegro
2. Andante
3. Moderato
4. Allegro
5. Lento
1.2.2.2/4.3.3.0/timpani, harp and strings
Duration: 15 minutes
First performance: London, Sadler's Wells Theatre, 10 May 1938
The Vic-Wells Ballet: cast included Robert Helpman and Pearl Argyle. The Vic-Wells Orchestra, conducted by Constant Lambert
Costumes and decor by William Chappell

Night Covers up the Rigid Land (Opus 14, no.2)
Song for medium voice and piano
Text: W.H. Auden (1907–1973)
Dedication: To B.B. [Benjamin Britten]
Duration: 2'40"
First broadcast performance: London, BBC Radio 3, 21 February 1977. Meriel Dickinson (mezzo soprano) and Peter Dickinson (piano)
Publication: Boosey & Hawkes

Lay Your Sleeping Head, My Love (Opus 14, no.2)
Song for medium voice and piano
Text: W.H. Auden (1907–1973)
Dedication: To Benjamin [Britten]
Duration: 4'40"
First broadcast performance: London, BBC Radio 3, 2 June 1988. Margaret Cable (mezzo soprano) and Anthony Legge (piano)

1938

Three Poems by Mary Webb
for voice and piano
Text: Mary Webb (1881–1927)

The Beacon Barn (Opus 14, no.2)
Song for medium voice and piano
Text: Patrick O'Malley
Dedication: To Ursula Nettleship
Duration: 1'25"
Publication: J. & W. Chester Ltd

Incidental Music for a Puppet Play (The Seven Ages of Man) and Farce (The Station Master)
by Montague Slater
Commissioned by Helen and Margaret Binyon
Instrumentation: singer, clarinet, violin, piano and dulcitone
First performance: London, Mercury Theatre, 22 June 1938. Music played by Eileen Tranmer (clarinet), Cecile Kennard (violin and dulcitone) and Frank Kennard (piano)
Unable to trace the singer

Eleven-Fifty (Opus 14, no.2)
Song for medium voice and piano
Text: Patrick O'Malley

Introduction [Lento] and Allegro (Opus 11)
for two pianos and orchestra
2.2.2.2/4.3.3.1/timpani, percussion (1), harp and strings
Dedication: To Benjamin Britten
Duration: 14 minutes
First performance: London, Queen's Hall, 6 September 1940. Lennox Berkeley and William Glock (pianos) with the London Symphony Orchestra, conducted by Henry Wood

Bells of Cordoba (Opus 14, no.2)
Song for medium voice and piano
Text: Federico Garcia Lorca (1898–1936), trans. Stanley Richardson
Dedication: Mrs J.L. Behrend
Duration: 1'40"
Publication: J. & W. Chester Ltd

1939

Three Pieces for Clarinet [in A]
1. Moderato
2. Lento
3. Allegro
Dedication: To Thea King (added later by the composer)
Duration: c. 5 minutes
First London performance: Hampstead, Rosslyn Hill Chapel, 21 May 1983. Thea King (clarinet)
Publication: J. & W. Chester Ltd (edited by Thea King)

Concerto for Cello and Orchestra
in two movements
1. Allegro moderato
2. Adagio – Allegro moderato
Written for Maurice Eisenberg
2.2.2.2/4.2.2.1/timpani, percussion (1) and strings
Duration: 20 minutes
First performance: Cheltenham, Town Hall, 17 July 1983. Moray Welsh (cello) and the Hallé Orchestra, conducted by James Loughran
First London performance: Royal Festival Hall, 23 October 1983. Moray Walsh (cello) and the London Symphony Orchestra, conducted by Richard Hickox (The "Great British Music Festival")

Mazurka
for piano

Serenade for String Orchestra (Opus 12)
in four movements
1. Vivace
2. Andantino
3. Allegro moderato
4. Lento
Dedication: To John and Clement Davenport
Duration: 14 minutes
First performance: London, Aeolian Hall, 30 January 1940. Boyd Neel Orchestra, conducted by Boyd Neel (A London Contemporary Music Centre concert)
Publication: J. & W. Chester Ltd

Other versions
Used for the ballet *Common Ground* with choreography by Jennifer Jackson. Designed by Ella Huhne
First performance: London, Sadler's Wells Theatre, 13 April 1984. Sadler's Wells Royal Ballet

Sonatina (Opus 13)
for treble recorder (or flute) and piano
in three movements
1. Moderato
2. Adagio
3. Allegro moderato
Commissioned by Carl Dolmetsch
Dedication: To Sybil Jackson
Duration: 11 minutes
First performance (private): London, Contemporary Music Centre. Carl Dolmetsch (recorder). Unable to trace other details
First public performance: London, Wigmore Hall, 18 November 1939. Carl Dolmetsch (recorder) and Christopher Wood (harpsichord)
Publication: Schott

Other versions
Arrangement for Flute and String Orchestra by Rodney Newton
First public performance: Cheltenham, Pittville Pump Room, 17 July 1990, Elena Duran (flute) and the Scottish Ensemble, conducted by Jonathan Rees

Four Concert Studies (Opus 14, no.1)
for solo piano
1. Presto (dedicated to David Ponsonby)
2. Andante (dedicated to Bep Gever)
3. Allegro (dedicated to Marc Chatellier)
4. Allegro (dedicated to Claude Berkeley)
Duration: 10 minutes
Publication: Schott

1940

Tant Que Mes Yeux (A Memory) (Opus 14, no.2)
Song for medium voice and piano
Text: Louise Labé (1525–1565), trans. M.D. Calvocoressi

Dedication: To Sophie Wyss
First performance: London, Fyvie Hall, 20 February 1945. Sophie Wyss (soprano) and Lennox Berkeley (piano)
Publication: Oxford University Press
Note: This song was written 8–10 May 1940, possibly in Paris

Other versions
1. Arranged for voice and string orchestra

Ode du Premier Jour de Mai (Opus 14, no.2)
Song for medium voice and piano
Text: Jean Passerat (1534–1602)
First performance: London, Fyvie Hall, 20 February 1945. Sophie Wyss (soprano) and Lennox Berkeley (piano)
Publication: J. & W. Chester Ltd

Five Housman Songs (Opus 14, no.3)
for high voice and piano
Text by A.E. Housman (1859–1936)
1. The half-moon westers low, my love (*Last Poems*, XXVI) Andante
2. The street sounds to the soldiers' tread (*A Shropshire Lad*, XXII) Allegro, alla Marcia
3. He would not stay for me (*Additional Poems*, VII) Lento
4. Look not in my eyes (*A Shropshire Lad*, XV) Andante con moto
5. Because I liked you better (*More Poems*, XXXI) Andantino
Dedication: To Peter Fraser
Duration: *c.* 10 minutes

Revised version: The first four songs were written in January 1940 and then revised, and the fifth song added
First broadcast performance: London, BBC Radio 3, 25 September 1978. Ian Partridge (tenor) and Jennifer Partridge (piano)
Publication: J. & W. Chester Ltd

Quartet for Strings No.2 (Opus 15)
in three movements
1. Allegro moderato
2. Lento
3. Allegro
Duration: *c.* 20 minutes
First performance: London, Cambridge Theatre, 5 June 1941. The Stratton Quartet
Publication: J. & W. Chester Ltd

1941

Impromptu
for organ
Written for Colin Gill "on the occasion of his translation from Holborn to Brighton"

Westminster Abbey
Incidental music for the BBC radio feature by Louis MacNeice
Commissioned by the BBC
Produced by Malcolm Baker-Smith
Alto saxophone/2 horns/2 trumpets/timpani, percussion and strings
The music consists of the following sections:
I – Moderato
II – Allegretto
III – ----
IV – ----
   Fanfare I
    Più Vivo
   Fanfare II
   Fanfare III
Duration of the programme: 45 minutes
First performance: London, Broadcasting House, 7 September 1941
Cast included Laidman Browne, James McKechnie and Robert Speight
Music played (and recorded) by a section of the BBC Northern Orchestra

Sarawak National Anthem
arranged for (a) orchestra [but not used] and (b) military band
Commissioned by the BBC
First performance: London, BBC, 18 September 1941. The BBC Scottish Military Band. Cast included Hubert Gregg, James McKechnie and Laidman Browne
This recording was subsequently broadcast on the BBC's Home Service on 23 September 1941 in the programme *White Rajah – Sarawak Centenary Programme*, by Robert Gittings and produced by Malcolm Baker-Smith, celebrating the centenary of Sarawak

1942

The Sword of the Spirit
Music for the film
Commissioned and produced by the Catholic Film Society

Symphony No.1 (Opus 16)
in four movements
1. Allegro moderato
2. Allegretto
3. Lento
4. Allegro
2.2.2.2/4.2.3.1/timpani, percussion, harp and strings
Duration: 33 minutes
First performance: London, Royal Albert Hall, 8 July 1943. London Philharmonic Orchestra, conducted by Lennox Berkeley
First broadcast performance: Bedford, Corn Exchange, 20 March 1944. BBC Symphony Orchestra, conducted by Clarence Raybould
Publication: J. & W. Chester Ltd

The Midnight Murk
Song for unaccompanied mixed chorus (SATB)
Text by Sagittarius (1896–1987)
Duration: 3'25"
First performance: Bedford, BBC Studios, 20 June 1942. The BBC Singers, conducted by Trevor Harvey. Broadcast on the BBC Home Service

Sonatina for violin and piano (Opus 17)
in three movements
1. Moderato
2. Lento
3. [Theme: Allegretto (17 bars) and Variations:
    1. Un poco piu vivo (32 bars)
    2. Allegro (L'istesso tempo) (40 bars)
    3. Allegro moderato (Tempo rubato) (20 bars)
    4. Tempo di Valse (55 + 10 bars solo)
    5. Andante (34 bars)]
Dedication: To Gladys Bryans
Duration: 14 minutes
First performance: Hampstead (London), 25 September 1944. Max Rostal (violin) and Lennox Berkeley (piano)
Publication: J. & W. Chester Ltd
Note: The original manuscript was sold at Sotheby's in aid of Oxfam

Yesterday and Today
Incidental music for the BBC Radio Theatre production
Written by Philippa Stewart Craig, and produced by Robert Speaight

Cast included Carleton Hobbs, Leon Quartermaine and Charles Lamb
First performance: Evesham, BBC Studios, 19 April 1942. Music (pre-recorded on 15 April) sung by the Wireless Singers under the direction of Father J.B. McElligott

1943

Lullaby
Song for low voice and piano
Text: W.B. Yeats (1865–1939)
Dedication: To Peter Pears

The Ecstatic
Song for high voice and piano
Text: C. Day Lewis (1904–1972)
Dedication: To Peter Pears

Legacie
Song for unaccompanied mixed voices (SSATBB)
Text: John Donne (?1572–1631)

Divertimento in B flat (Opus 18)
for chamber orchestra in four movements
1. Prelude (Moderato)
2. Nocturne (Andante)
3. Scherzo (Allegro vivace)
4. Finale (Allegro)
Commissioned by the BBC for Section C of the BBC Orchestra
2.2.2.2/2.2.1.0/timpani and strings
Dedication: To Nadia Boulanger
Duration: 18 minutes
First performance: Bedford, Corn Exchange, 1 October 1943. BBC Orchestra (Section C), conducted by Clarence Raybould
Publication: J. & W. Chester Ltd

Trio (Opus 19)
for violin, viola and cello in three movements
1. Moderato
2. Adagio
3. Allegro

Dedication: To Frederick Grinke, Watson Forbes and James Phillips
Duration: 17 minutes
First performance: London, Wigmore Hall, August 1944. Frederick Grinke (violin), Watson Forbes (viola) and James Phillips (cello)
Publication: J. & W. Chester Ltd

1944

Hotel Reservé
Music for the feature film
Adapted from the novel *Epitaph for a Spy* by Eric Ambler. Directed by Victor Hanbury, Lance Comfort and Max Greene
Production company: RKO British Productions Ltd
Music composed for the following episodes: Opening titles; Beach Sequence; Dinner Sequence Parts 1 and 2; Schimler's Bedroom; Terrace Sequence; Fishing Sequence; Cannes Sequence; Billboard Sequence; Duclos Sequence; Vedassey in Office; Vedassey and Schimler in Bedroom (Passport Sequence); Roux and Odette in Bedroom Quarrel (3); Roux and Vedassey in Hall (2); Garage, Police Station and Chase Sequence; Vedassey Roof Sequence; Mary and Vedassey in Playout
Cast included James Mason, Raymond Lovell, Julian Mitchell, Herbert Lom and Valentine Dyall
Music played by: The BBC Northern Orchestra, conducted by Muir Mathieson. Recorded 28 October 1944

Out of Chaos
Music for the documentary film
Directed by Jill Craigie
Production company: Verity Films Ltd for Two Cities Ltd
2.2.2.2/2.2.3.0/timpani, percussion (1), piano and strings
The music consists of the following sections:
I – Moderato
II – Shipyard Sequence (Stanley Spencer)
III – Allegro (Battle of Britain)
Kenneth Clark, Eric Newton, Henry Moore, Graham Sutherland, Paul Nash and Leonard Roseman took part in the film
Music played by: The London Symphony Orchestra

Lord, when the sense of Thy sweet grace (Opus 21, no.1)
Anthem for mixed chorus (SATB) and organ
Text by Richard Crashaw (1612/13–1649)

Commissioned by the BBC
Dedication: To Trevor Hardy
Duration: *c*. 7 minutes
Publication: J. & W. Chester Ltd

Paysage [de France]
for piano
Contribution to an album of ten works "in honour of a redeemed France, and dedicated to Raymond Mortimer" (July 1944)
First performance: London, Fyvie Hall, 20 February 1945. Lennox Berkeley (piano)

There was neither grass nor corn
Song for unaccompanied mixed chorus (SATB)
Text by Frances Cornford (1874–1943)
Commissioned by the BBC
Dedication: To Edward Sackville-West
Duration: 4 minutes
First performance: Pre-recording made in Bedford, BBC Studios, 5 December 1944. The BBC Singers, conducted by Leslie Woodgate. Subsequently broadcast in the BBC Home Service, 24 December 1944 as part of the programme *Poet's Christmas*, produced by Edward Sackville-West. Performances of Michael Tippett's *The Weeping Babe* and Benjamin Britten's *Shepherd's Carol* and *Chorale* were also featured

1945

Esterel
Suite for orchestra
Unable to trace any details except that, according to a BBC memo, it was offered as "a novelty" for the 1945 season of Henry Wood Promenade Concerts

Sonata in A (Opus 20)
for piano in four movements
1. Moderato
2. Presto
3. Adagio
4. Introduction [moderately slow] – Allegro
Dedication: To Clifford Curzon
Duration: 25 minutes

First performance: London, unable to trace a venue, 28 July 1946. Clifford Curzon (piano)
Publication: J. & W. Chester Ltd

Sion's Daughters, Sons of Jerusalem (Opus 21, no.2)
A Festival Anthem for mixed chorus (SATB) and organ
Texts – Sequence: Jerusalem et Sion filiae (Lento)
   The Flower (George Herbert: 1593–1633) (Andantino)
   Easter Hymn (Henry Vaughan: 1621/2–1695)
Commissioned by: the Rev. Walter Hussey for St Matthew's Church, Northampton
Dedication: For the Rev. Walter Hussey and the Organist and Choir of St Matthew's Church, Northampton
Duration: 15 minutes
First performance: Northampton, Parish Church of St Matthew, 21 September 1945 (St Matthew's Day). The Parish Church Choir, conducted by Lennox Berkeley with Charles Barker (organ)
Publication: J. & W. Chester Ltd (as *A Festival Anthem*)

Other versions
1. *Andantino*
An arrangement of the aria (for treble solo) from the *Festival Anthem*, for cello and piano
Duration: 3 minutes
Publication: J. & W. Chester Ltd
2. *Andantino*
Commissioned by and arranged for organ by Jennifer Bate for her Hyperion recording (A 66061)
Recorded and first performed on 10/11 May 1982 by Jennifer Bate at the organ of St James Church, Muswell Hill, London
Duration: 3 minutes
Publication: J. & W. Chester Ltd

Sonata in D minor (Opus 22)
for viola and piano in three movements
1. Allegro ma non troppo [with slower sections]
2. Adagio
3. Allegro
Dedication: for Watson Forbes
Duration: 17 minutes
First performance: London, Contemporary Music Centre, 3 May 1946. Watson Forbes (viola) and Denise Lassimonne (piano)
Publication: J. & W. Chester Ltd (viola part edited by Watson Forbes)

Six Preludes for Piano (Opus 23)
1. Allegro
2. Andante
3. Allegro Moderato
4. Allegretto
5. Allegro
6. Andante

Commissioned by: The BBC, originally to be used as interludes in under-running programmes '
Dedication: To Val Drewry
Duration: 10–11 minutes
First broadcast performance: London, BBC, 13 July 1947. Albert Ferber (piano). (A recording made in the Concert Hall of Broadcasting House on 7 July 1947)
Publication: J. & W. Chester Ltd

1946

A Glutton for Life
Incidental music for the radio feature about Guy de Maupassant (1850–1893), written by Audrey Lucas and produced by Louis MacNeice
Music written for 16 sections
Commissioned by the BBC
1.1.1.1/1.1.1.0/timpani, percussion (1), harp and strings
Duration of programme: 45 minutes
Duration of music: 14'20"
First performance: London, Broadcasting House, 15 February 1946. Cast included Howard Marion-Crawford, Norman Shelley, Marjorie Westbury, Charles Lamb and Molly Rankin. Music played by an ad hoc orchestra, conducted by Walter Goehr

The Tempest
Incidental music for the play by William Shakespeare (1564–1616)
Produced by Eric Crozier
Music written for: unable to trace although existing records show that it included a setting of the song "Where the Bee Sucks" (for voice and orchestra in Bb major: see BBC MS 20325) and a "Peoples' Dance".
Instrumentation: 2.2.2.2/2.1.3.0 and strings
First performance: Stratford upon Avon, Shakespeare Memorial Theatre, 20 April 1946. Cast included James Raglan, Robert Harris, Donald Sinden and Hugh Griffith. Music played by the National Symphony Chamber Orchestra. Unable to

trace any conductor. Songs sung by the BBC Singers. (Recorded by the Decca Record Company)

Introduction [Lento] and Allegro (Opus 24)
for violin
Dedication: For Ivry Gitlis
Duration: 6'30"
First performance: London, Wigmore Hall, June 1947. Ivry Gitlis (violin)
Publication: J. & W. Chester Ltd

Nocturne (Opus 25)
for orchestra
2.2.2.2/4.2.3.0/timpani, percussion (1), harp and strings
Dedication: To Peter
Duration: 11 minutes
First performance: London, Royal Albert Hall, 28 August 1946. BBC Symphony Orchestra, conducted by Adrian Boult
Publication: J. & W. Chester Ltd

Five Songs (Opus 26)
for medium voice and piano
Text by Walter de la Mare (1873–1956)
1. The Horseman (Moderato)
2. Mistletoe (Andante tranquillo)
3. Poor Henry (Lento)
4. The Song of the Soldiers (Allegro. Tempo di marcia)
5. Silver (Lento man non troppo)
Dedication: To Pierre Bernac and Francis Poulenc
First performance: Unable to trace. Pierre Bernac (tenor) and Francis Poulenc (piano) may have included these songs in one of their recitals in the winter of 1946
Publication: J. & W. Chester Ltd

The Wall of Troy
Incidental music for the BBC radio play – a transcription of *The Iliad*, Book 3 by Patric Dickinson. Produced by Val Gielgud
Music written for 14 sections
Commissioned by the BBC
1.1.1.1/1.0.0.0/timpani, percussion (2), harp and strings
Duration of the programme: 60 minutes
Duration of the music: 15'49"

First performance: London, Broadcasting House, 21 November 1946 – pre-recording made which was subsequently broadcast on the 3rd Programme later that day

Cast included Leon Quartermaine, Francis de Wolff, David Kossoff, Margaret Leighton and Laidman Browne. Music played by an ad hoc orchestra, conducted by Lennox Berkeley

1947

La Fête Etrange
Ballet in one Act and two Scenes. Choreography by Andrée Howard
Music by Gabriel Fauré and selected by Ronald Crichton:
- Barcarolle No.6 (Op.66)
- Impromptu No.2 (Op.31)
- "Mandoline" (words by Verlaine)
- Nocturne No.6 (Op.63)
- Nocturne No.7 (Op.74)
- Prelude No.5 (Op.103)
- Prelude No.8 (Op.103)
- "Soir" (words by Albert Samain). Henri Rabaud's orchestration of "Le Jardin de Dolly" (from Op.36) was also used

Decor and Costumes by Sophie Fedorovitch
Libretto by Ronald Crichton (after an episode in Alain-Fournier's *Le Grand Meaulnes*)
First performance (music played on two pianos): London, Arts Theatre, 23 May 1940
First performance (with Berkeley's orchestrations): London, Sadler's Wells Theatre, 25 March 1947. Sadler's Wells Theatre Ballet (cast included Donald Britton, June Brae and Anthony Burke). [Music played by the Sadler's Wells Ballet Orchestra, conducted by Constant Lambert (?)]. Songs performed by Patricia Hughes
Note: the ballet was revived in December 1958 when new orchestrations by Guy Warrack were used

Overture
for chamber orchestra
Written for Anthony Bernard and the London Chamber Orchestra, but was later withdrawn
2.2.2.2/2.0.0.0/timpani, percussion and strings
Duration: 8 minutes

First performance: Canterbury, the Cathedral Cloisters, 27 June 1947. The London Chamber Orchestra, conducted by Anthony Bernard

The Low Lands of Holland
Old English ballad arranged for mezzo/baritone and piano
Text: Anonymous, from "Love's Helicon" (Duckworth, 1940)
Written for Sophie Wyss
Duration: 7 minutes
First performance: London, Broadcasting House, 13 July 1947. Sophie Wyss (soprano) and Lennox Berkeley (piano)
Publication: J. & W. Chester Ltd

Four Poems of St Teresa of Avila (Opus 27)
for contralto and string orchestra
Text by St Teresa of Avila (1515–1582), translated from the Spanish by Arthur Symons
1. If Lord, Thy Love for me is strong (Moderato)
2. Shepherd, Shepherd hark that calling! (Allegro)
3. Let mine eyes see Thee (Andante)
4. Today a shepherd and our kin (Allegro moderato)
Written at the request of Gerald Cooper
Dedication: To John Greenidge
Duration: 12/14 minutes
First performance: London, Broadcasting House, 4 April 1948. Kathleen Ferrier (contralto) and the Goldsborough String Orchestra, conducted by Arnold Goldsborough
First concert performance: London, Royal Festival Hall, 6 April 1952. Kathleen Ferrier (contralto) and London Symphony Orchestra, conducted by Hugo Rignold
Publication: J. & W. Chester Ltd

Stabat Mater (Opus 28)
for six solo voices: two sopranos, contralto, tenor, baritone and bass solo voices and chamber orchestra
Latin text attributed to Jacopone da Todi (*c.* 1236–1306)
1. Stabat Mater dolorosa (Lento)
2. O quam tristis et afflicta (Andante con moto)
3. Quis est homo (Adagio)
4. Pro peccatis suae gentis (Allegro)
5. Eia Mater, fons amoris (Andantino)
6. Sancta Mater (Maestoso)
7. Fac me tecum (Moderato)

8. Virgo virginum (Andante)
9. Fac me plagis (Allegro moderato)
10. Christe cum sit hinc exire (Andante)
1.1.1+1.1/1.0.0.0/percussion, harp and string quintet
Dedication: To Benjamin Britten
Duration: 33 minutes
First performance: Zurich, Tonhalle, 19 August 1947. Members of the English Opera Group (Margaret Ritchie, Lesley Duff, Nancy Evans, Peter Pears, Frederick Sharp and Norman Lumsden) and instrumentalists, conducted by Lennox Berkeley
First British performance: London, Concert Hall (Broadcasting House), 27 September 1947. Members of the English Opera Group and Orchestra, conducted by Benjamin Britten
First British concert performance: Aldeburgh, Jubilee Hall, 22 June 1953. Members of the English Opera Group and orchestra, conducted by Benjamin Britten
Publication: J. & W. Chester Ltd

Other versions
1. Rescored for full orchestra by Michael Berkeley as Opus 28a (1978)
1.1.1+1.2/2.0.0.0/percussion, harp and strings
First performance: London, Queen Elizabeth Hall, 12 May 1978. Teresa Cahill (soprano), Diana Montagu (mezzo-soprano), Meriel Dickinson (contralto), Brian Burrows (tenor), Richard Jackson (tenor) and Stephen Varcoe (baritone) with the Park Lane Music Group Players, conducted by Nicholas Braithwaite
2. Arrangement by Christopher Headington
3. Arrangement by Roy Teed

1947–48

The First Gentleman
Music for the feature film
Adapted from the play by Norman Ginsbury. Directed by Cavalcanti
Production company: Columbia
Music composed for the following episodes: Title music (arranged Berkeley) which follows through the Regent's line "Sweet grief is most profound"; Reaction to Leopold's line "Goodbye"; Quadrilles Scene; Waltz Scene; First Fanfare; Second Fanfare; Repeat Fanfare; Music off from Ballroom; Retiring Room; Regent's Study; Charlotte's line "I know where I'm not going"; Regent singing "Gather ye Rosebuds" (traditional, arranged Berkeley); Musical Box: old-fashioned (origin unknown, arranged Berkeley); Waltz number; Charlotte running (arranged Berkeley); Miss Knight resigning; Charlotte running to cab; Charlotte leaving cab; Charlotte

decides to go back; Charlotte at Windsor; Paris restaurant; Charlotte apologizing; Leopold arriving in pavilion; Wedding group on stairs to Queen's line "Wait"; Regent advised about the baby; Charlotte's conversation to "Hurry" tempo; End titles
Cast included Cecil Parker, Jean-Pierre Aumont, Joan Hopkins, Margaretta Scott, Jack Livesey, Ronald Squire, Athene Seyler and Hugh Griffith
Music played by: The Royal Philharmonic Orchestra, conducted by Thomas Beecham
Film first shown 15 March 1948 (trade), and 31 May 1948 (general release)

Concerto for Piano and Orchestra (Opus 29)
in three movements
1. Allegro Moderato
2. Andante
3. Vivace (Alla breve)
2.2.2.2/2.2.1.0/timpani and strings
Dedication: To Colin Horsley
Duration: 25 minutes
First performance: London, Royal Albert Hall, 31 August 1948. Colin Horsley (piano) and the London Symphony Orchestra, conducted by Basil Cameron
Note: This concerto was selected for performance at the 23rd ISCM festival at Palermo (26 April 1949) when it was again played by Colin Horsley and the Rome Radio Orchestra, conducted by Constant Lambert
Publication: J. & W. Chester Ltd

1948

Jigsaw and Venus Anadyomene
Jigsaw was written in 1948, *Venus Anadyomene* in 1945. Both ballets (for two pianos) were included in "Oranges and Lemons", an Intimate Revue, devised and directed by Laurier Lister
Decor by William Chappell who also arranged the dances
First performance: London, Globe Theatre, 29 January 1949. Cast included John Heawood, Sylvia Rye, Elizabeth Cooper, Nigel Burke and Ulla Söderbaum. Musical direction by John Pritchett who played one of two pianos with Betty Robb and Chris Blades (drums)

Concerto for Two Pianos and Orchestra (Opus 30)
in two movements
1. Molto moderato
2. Theme (Moderato): 34 bars and eleven Variations:
    1. Allegro ma non troppo (41 bars)

2. L'istesso tempo (36 bars)
3. Allegro (83 bars)
4. Adagio (49 bars)
5. Vivace (79 bars)
6. Andante (37 bars)
7. Tempo di Valse (113 bars)
8. Allegro (36 bars)
9. Lento (28 bars)
10. Andante con moto (26 bars)
11. L'istesso tempo (46 bars)

(*Note*: the above may have been revised as there were only ten variations in the original)
Commissioned by: The Henry Wood Concert Society
2+1.2.2.2/4.3.3.0/timpani, percussion, harp and strings
Dedication: To Phyllis Sellick and Cyril Smith
Duration: 30 minutes
First performance: London, Royal Albert Hall, 13 December 1948. Phyllis Sellick and Cyril Smith (pianos) and the London Symphony Orchestra, conducted by Malcolm Sargent
Publication: J. & W. Chester Ltd

Other versions
1. Arrangement for three pianos

1949

Colonus' Praise (Opus 31)
Cantata for mixed chorus (SATB) and orchestra
Text: W.B. Yeats (1865–1939)
Commissioned by: The BBC for the 21st birthday of the BBC Choral Society
2+1.2.2.2/4.2.3.1/timpani, percussion and strings
Duration: 14 minutes
First performance: London, Royal Albert Hall, 13 September 1949. The BBC Choral Society and BBC Symphony Orchestra, conducted by Leslie Woodgate
Publication: BBC/J. & W. Chester Ltd

Three Mazurkas (Hommage à Frederic Chopin) (Opus 32, no.1)
for piano
1. Allegro
2. Allegretto
3. Allegro

Commissioned by: "In reply to UNESCO's urgent request, 11 eminent composers have written, in tribute to Chopin, chamber music which will be performed for the first time with the co-operation of the French Broadcasting Company"
Duration: 7 minutes
First performance (no.3 only): Paris, Salle Gaveau, 3 October 1949. Helene Pignari (piano). The full programme was as follows:
1. Mazurka No.3 for piano: Lennox Berkeley (UK)
2. Etude for piano: Carlos Chavez (Mexico)
3. Sonate espagnole pour piano: Oscar Espla (Spain)
4. Pastorale for oboe and piano: Howard Hanson (USA)
5. Etude-Caprice for cello: Jacques Ibert (France)
6. Hommage à Chopin for piano: G.F. Malipiero (Italy)
7. Mazurka-Nocturne for oboe, 2 violins and cello: B. Martinů (Czechoslovakia)
8. Suite polonaise for soprano and piano: A. Panufnik (Poland)
9. Ode à Frederic Chopin for SATB and piano: F. Schmitt (France)
10. Tombeau de Chopin for string quartet: A. Tansman (Poland)
11. Hommage à Chopin for piano: H. Villa-Lobos (Brazil)
First British performance: London, BBC, 23 March 1950 (pre-recorded 22 March 1950). Colin Horsley (piano)
Publication: J. & W. Chester Ltd

Scherzo for Piano (Opus 32, no.2)
Commissioned by: Colin Horsley for his 1950 tour of Australia and New Zealand
Dedication: For Colin Horsley
Duration: 2'30"
First performance: Australia/New Zealand, 1950. Colin Horsley (piano)
First British performance: London, BBC, 23 March 1950 (pre-recorded 22 March 1950). Colin Horsley (piano)
Publication: J. & W. Chester Ltd

1950

Theme and Variations (Opus 33, no.1)
for violin
Tema (Moderato) (6 bars)
  Variation 1 (L'istesso Tempo) (12 bars)
  Variation 2 (Leggiero) (8 bars)
  Variation 3 (Andante) (15 bars)
  Variation 4 (Allegro) (21 bars)
  Variation 5 (Lento) (16 bars)

Variation 6 (Vivace) (42 bars)
Variation 7 (Moderato – Tempo primo) (19 bars)
Variation 8 (Allegro moderato) (21 bars)
Commissioned by: Frederick Grinke
Dedication: To Frederick Grinke
Duration: 7'30"
First performance: Zurich, Tonhalle, 8 September 1950. Frederick Grinke (violin)
First British performance: London, Broadcasting House, 27 September 1950. Frederick Grinke (violin)
Publication: J. & W. Chester Ltd

Elegy (Opus 33, no.2a)
for violin and piano
Commissioned by: Frederick Grinke
Dedication: For Frederick Grinke
Duration: 3 minutes
First performance: London, Broadcasting House, 27 September 1950. Frederick Grinke (violin) and Ernest Lush (piano)
Publication: J. & W. Chester Ltd (with Toccata (Opus 33, no.3))

Other versions
1. Arranged for string orchestra (Opus 33, no.2b) (April 1978) by the composer
Dedication: In memory of Essie Craxton and to the Craxton family
First performance: London, St John's Smith Square, 26 April 1978. St John's Smith Square Orchestra, conducted by John Lubbock (Essie Craxton's memorial service)
2. Arranged for violin and string orchestra

Toccata [in E minor] (Opus 33, no.3)
Commissioned by Frederick Grinke
Dedication: For Frederick Grinke
Duration: 2 minutes
First performance: London, Broadcasting House, 27 September 1950. Frederick Grinke (violin) and Ernest Lush (piano)
Publication: J. & W. Chester Ltd
Note: The *Elegy* and *Toccata* are usually played together

Sinfonietta (Opus 34)
for chamber orchestra in two movements
1. Allegro
2. Lento–Allegro non troppo
2.2.2.2/2.0.0.0/timpani and strings
Dedication: To Anthony Bernard

Duration: 13 minutes
First performance: London, Wigmore Hall, 1 December 1950. The London Chamber Orchestra, conducted by Anthony Bernard
Publication: J. & W. Chester Ltd

1951

Variations on a hymn-tune of Orlando Gibbons (Opus 35)
for tenor solo, mixed chorus (SATB), organ and string orchestra
The hymn tune used is *Song 20* (no.442 in The English Hymnal) with the text based on verses by Isaac Watts (1674–1748): "My Lord, my Life, my Love":
   Theme (Moderato)
   Variation 1 (Allegro Moderato)
   Variation 2 (L'istesso Tempo)
   Variation 3 (Allegretto)
   Variation 4 (Allegro Moderato)
   Variation 5 (Andante)
   Variation 6 (Moderato)
Commissioned by: The English Opera Group for the 5th Aldeburgh Festival
Dedication: To Dorothy, Dowager Countess of Cranbrook
Duration: 18 minutes
First performance: Aldeburgh, Parish Church of St Peter and St Paul, 21 June 1952. Peter Pears (tenor), the Aldeburgh Festival Choir and Orchestra with Ralph Downes (organ), conducted by Lennox Berkeley
Publication: J. & W. Chester Ltd

Three Greek Songs (Opus 38)
for medium voice and piano
1. Epitaph of Timas (Text: Sappho *c.* 612 BC) (Andante)
2. Spring Song (Text: Antipater 398–319 BC) (Allegro)
3. To Aster (Text: Plato *c.* 429–347 BC) (Lento)
Duration: *c.* 5 minutes
First performance: London, Morley College, 15 March 1951. Iris Kells (soprano) and John Gardner (piano)
Publication: J. & W. Chester Ltd

1952

Ask me no more (Opus 37, no.1)
Part-song for unaccompanied male chorus (TTBB)

Text by Thomas Carew (c. 1595–1640)
First performance: unable to trace
Publication: J. & W. Chester Ltd

Four Ronsard Sonnets (Set 1) (Opus 40)
for two tenor soli and piano
Texts by Pierre de Ronsard (1524–1585)
1. Marie levez-vous (Allegro con brio)
2. Comme un void sur la branche (Andante)
3. Ôtez votre beauté (Allegro Appassionato)
4. Adieu, cruelle, adieu (Lento)
Commissioned by: Peter Pears to sing with Hughes Cuenod
Dedication: To Peter Pears
First performance: London, Victoria and Albert Museum, 8 March 1953. Peter Pears and Hughes Cuenod (tenors) with George Malcolm (piano)

Revised version
This set of sonnets were rewritten in 1977 for Peter Pears
First performance: Snape, The Maltings, 14 June 1978. Peter Pears and Ian Partridge (tenors) with Steuart Bedford (piano)

Concerto for Flute and Chamber Orchestra (Opus 36)
in four movements
1. Allegro moderato
2. Presto
3. Adagio
4. Allegro vivace
Commissioned by: John Francis
0.2.0.2/2.0.0.0/timpani and strings
Dedication: To John Francis
Duration: 21 minutes
First performance: London, Royal Albert Hall, 29 July 1953. John Francis (flute) and BBC Symphony Orchestra, conducted by Malcolm Sargent
Publication: J. & W. Chester Ltd

1953

Spring at this Hour (Opus 37, no.2)
Part song for unaccompanied mixed chorus (SSATBB)
Text by Paul Dehn (1912–1976)

Written as a contribution [No.5] to *A Garland for the Queen*, the other nine contributors being Arthur Bliss (Henry Reed), Arnold Bax (Clifford Bax), Michael Tippett (Christopher Fry), R.Vaughan Williams (Ursula Wood), John Ireland (James Kirkup), Herbert Howells (Walter de la Mare), Gerald Finzi (Edmund Blunden), Alan Rawsthorne (Louis MacNeice) and Edmund Rubbra (Christopher Hassall)
Commissioned by: The Arts Council of Great Britain, to mark the occasion of the Coronation of HM Queen Elizabeth II
Dedication: Dedicated by gracious permission to Her Majesty Queen Elizabeth II
Duration: 3'09"
First performance: London, Royal Festival Hall, 1 June 1953. Augmented choir of the Cambridge University Madrigal Society and the Golden Age Singers, conducted by Boris Ord
Publication: Stainer & Bell/J. & W. Chester Ltd

Suite
for orchestra in six movements
1. Intrada (Lento ma non troppo)
2. Courante (Allegro)
3. Sarabande (Lento)
4. Gavotte (Allegro vivace)
5. Air (Adagio)
6. Hornpipe (Allegro con brio)
Commissioned by: The BBC Third Programme for Coronation Week, 1953
2+1.2+1.2+1.2+1/4.3.3.1/timpani, percussion, harp and strings
Duration: 21 minutes
First performance: London, BBC Studios, 6 June 1953. BBC Symphony Orchestra, conducted by Malcolm Sargent

Variation on an Elizabethan Theme (Sellinger's Round)
for string orchestra
No.3 (Andante) of a work to which seven composers: Arthur Oldham, Michael Tippett, Lennox Berkeley, Benjamin Britten, Humphrey Searle and William Walton, at Benjamin Britten's invitation, contributed variations. Imogen Holst transcribed Byrd's version of the theme to preface the variations
Duration: *c.* 3 minutes
First performance: Aldeburgh, Parish Church of St Peter and St Paul, 20 June 1953. The Aldeburgh Festival Orchestra, conducted by Benjamin Britten
First London performance (except Tippett's contribution): Wigmore Hall, 29 May 1957. Collegium Musicum Londinii, conducted by John Minchinton

Trio (Opus 44)
for horn, violin and piano in three movements
1. Allegro
2. Lento
3. Theme (Moderato) (16 bars) and Variations
    1. Allegro vivace (44 bars)
    2. Allegretto (24 bars)
    3. Lento (22 bars)
    4. Vivace (26 bars)
    5. Andante (30 bars)
    6. Moderato (37 bars)
    7. Adagio (36 bars)
    8. Moderato (27 bars)
    9. Allegro vivo (59 bars)
    10. Moderato (15 bars)

Commissioned by: Colin Horsley
Dedication: To Sheila Robertson
Duration: 27 minutes
First performance: London, Raphael Cartoon Gallery (Victoria and Albert Museum), 28 March 1954. Manoug Parikian (violin), Dennis Brain (horn) and Colin Horsley (piano)
Publication: J. & W. Chester Ltd
Note: Berkeley wrote his *Trio* for the same combination as the Brahms Trio (Op.40), and intended it to be used as a companion piece to the work

1954

Sonatina [in E flat major] (Opus 39)
for piano duet in three movements
1. Allegro moderato
2. Andante
3. Allegro (alla breve)

Duration: 8 minutes
First performance: Stoke on Trent, College of Art, 8 July 1954
Michael Linsey and Sybil Jones (piano)
First London performance: Wigmore Hall, 18 January 1955. Liza Fuchsova and Paul Hamburger (piano)
Publication: J. & W. Chester Ltd

Iphigenia in Taurus
Incidental music for the play by Goethe (1749–1832) in a new translation by Roy Pascal. Adapted for broadcasting by Helena Wood and produced by Val Gielgud
Unable to trace details of music written
Commissioned by the BBC
1.1.1.0/2.1.0.0/percussion, harp and strings
Duration of programme: 89'08"
Duration of music: 12'30"
First performance: London, Broadcasting House, 3 October 1954
Cast included Maria Becker, Norman Claridge, Donald Wolfit and Marius Goring. Music played by the Welbeck Orchestra (17 musicians), conducted by Lennox Berkeley

Nelson (Opus 41)
Opera in three acts (five scenes), with libretto by Alan Pryce-Jones (1908–2000)
Synopsis
Act I: The Palazzo Sessa in Naples, September 1798
Act II *Scene 1*: A drawing room at 17 Dover Street, November 1800
    Scene 2: The Garden at Merton
Act III *Scene 1*: Portsmouth – the yard of the George Inn, 21 October 1805
    Scene 2: The Cockpit of the Victory
    Scene 3: The Garden at Merton
3.2.2.2/4.3.3.1/timpani, percussion, harp and strings
Duration: Act I   49'05"
          Act II   46'20"
          Act III 44'20"
First performance: London, Wigmore Hall, 14 February 1953
Cast:

Mrs Cadogan	Catherine Lawson (mezzo-soprano)
Emma, Lady Hamilton	Arda Mandikian (soprano)
Sir William Hamilton	Thomas Hemsley (baritone)
Horatio, Lord Nelson	Peter Pears (tenor)
Lady Nelson	Nancy Evans (mezzo-soprano)
Hardy	Trevor Anthony (bass)

Two other characters, the Fortune-teller (contralto) and Lord Minto (baritone) were not included in this reading, nor was any chorus
A concert reading presented by the English Opera Group Association, introduced by the librettist and directed by the composer with Robert Keys at the piano
First staged performance: London, Sadler's Wells Theatre, 22 September 1954 (Broadcast by the BBC)

Original cast:

Mrs Cadogan	Sheila Rex
Lady Hamilton	Victoria Elliott
Sir William Hamilton	Arnold Matters
Major Domo	Charles Draper
Nelson	Robert Thomas
A guest	Cecil Lloyd
Madame Serafin	Olwen Price
Lady Nelson	Anna Pollak
Captain Hardy	David Ward
Lord Minto	Stanley Clarkson
A Surgeon	John Probyn
Three Sailors	Ereach Riley
	Peter Glossop
	Harold Blackburn
A Wounded Man	Gwent Lewis

Sadler's Wells Chorus and Orchestra, conducted by Vilem Tausky. Produced by George Devine

Subsequent performances of *Nelson* were given by the Sadler's Wells Opera Company in Birmingham and Manchester in October 1954 (conducted by Vilem Tausky), and on 22, 26 and 29 March 1955 in London, the first performances of the revised version (conducted by Tausky), alterations having been made particularly to Act 1. An 85th birthday concert performance was given by the Chelsea Opera Group under Grant Llewellyn at the Queen Elizabeth Hall, London on 7 April 1988. A new recording of the opera was made by the BBC with David Johnston, Eiddwen Harrhy and Brian Raynor Cook in the main parts and the BBC Singers and Symphony Orchestra conducted by Elgar Haworth. This was broadcast on Radio 3 on 23 October 1983 and repeated at the time of Berkeley's 85th birthday celebrations on 18 May 1988

Other versions

1. Nelson: Suite from the Opera (Opus 42)
Arranged for orchestra by the composer
1. The Sailing of the Victory [Interlude i, Act III]
2. The Cockpit [Interlude ii, Act III]
3. Portsmouth [based on themes in Act III]
2.2.2.2/4.3.3.1/timpani, percussion, celesta, harp and strings
Duration: 16 minutes
First performance: Cheltenham, Town Hall, 29 July 1955. The Hallé Orchestra, conducted by John Barbirolli
First London performance: Royal Albert Hall, 30 August 1956. The Hallé Orchestra, conducted by Basil Cameron

2. Interlude from Nelson
Arranged for orchestra by the composer
2.2+1.2.2/4.3.3.1/timpani, percussion, harp and strings
Duration: 5 minutes
Publication: J. &. W. Chester Ltd

Crux Fidelis (Opus 43, no.1)
Motet (a setting of a hymn for Good Friday) for tenor solo and unaccompanied mixed chorus (SATB)
Written at the request of Peter Pears
Dedication: To Imogen Holst [1907–1984]
First performance: London, Victoria and Albert Museum, 6 March 1955. Peter Pears (tenor) and the Purcell Singers, conducted by Imogen Holst

Look up, Sweet Babe (Opus 43, no.2)
Anthem for treble solo, mixed chorus (SATB) and organ
Text by Richard Crashaw (1612/3–1649)
Composed for the Christmas Carol Services at Westminster Abbey
First performance: London, Westminster Abbey, December 1954. Abbey choir and organ conducted by William McKie
Publication: J. & W. Chester Ltd

A Dinner Engagement (Opus 45)
A One-Act Opera in two scenes with libretto by Paul Dehn (1912–1976)

Synopsis: The Chelsea kitchen of the Earl and Countess of Dunmow
1+1.1.1+1.1/1.0.0.0/percussion (1), piano and strings (1/1/1/1)
Dedication: To Basil Douglas
Duration: 60 minutes
First performance: Aldeburgh, Jubilee Hall, 17 June 1954.
Original cast:

An Errand Boy	John Ford (tenor)
The Earl of Dunmow	Frederick Sharp (bass)
The Countess of Dunmow	Emelie Hooke (soprano)
Susan, their daughter	April Cantelo (soprano)
Mrs Kneebone, a hired "help"	Catherine Lawson (contralto)
H.R.H. The Grand Duchess of Monteblanco	Flora Nielsen (contralto)
H.R.H. Prince Philippe, her son	Alexander Young (tenor)

The English Opera Group Chamber Orchestra, conducted by Vilem Tausky. Designed by Peter Snow. Produced by William Chappell
First London performance: Sadler's Wells Theatre, 7 October 1954. Artists as above (First of three performances)

Publication: J. & W. Chester Ltd (vocal score)

The opera was first broadcast by the BBC on 1 July 1954. Further performances were broadcast on 1 May 1966 (conducted by Maurice Handford) and 27 October 1983 with *Castaway* (Op.68). Both operas had been performed together for the first time at the Bloomsbury Theatre in London on 17 June 1983

1955

Concert Study in E-flat major (Opus 48, no.2)
for piano
Dedication: For Colin Horsley
Duration: 3 minutes
First performance: London, Broadcasting House, 20 January 1955. Colin Horsley (piano)
Publication: J. & W. Chester Ltd

Sextet (Opus 47)
for clarinet [in A], horn [in F], 2 violins, viola and cello in three movements
1. Allegro moderato
2. Lento
3. Allegro
Commissioned by: The BBC for the opening concert of 11th Cheltenham Music Festival (1955)
Dedication: To Alvilde [Lees-Milnes]
Duration: 17 minutes
First performance: Cheltenham, College Hall, 11 July 1955. The Melos Ensemble: Gervase de Peyer (clarinet), Neil Sanders (horn), Eli Goren and Ivor McMahon (violins), Patrick Ireland (viola) and Bernard Richards (cello)
First London performance: Victoria and Albert Museum, 11 December 1955. The Melos Ensemble
Publication: J. & W. Chester Ltd

Allegro
for two treble recorders
Publication: Boosey & Hawkes

Other versions
1. Revised and adapted for two oboes by the composer
Publication: Boosey & Hawkes

Salve Regina (Opus 48, no.1)
Motet for unison chorus and organ
Dedication: For the Society of St Gregory
Publication: J. & W. Chester Ltd

Concertino (Opus 49)
for recorder (or flute), violin, cello and harpsichord (or piano) in four movements
1. Allegro moderato
2. Aria I: Lento
3. Aria II: Andantino
4. Rondo: Vivace [originally Allegro]
Commissioned by: Carl Dolmetsch
Duration: 13 minutes
First performance: London, Broadcasting House, 24 January 1956. Carl Dolmetsch (recorder), Jean Pougnet (violin), Arnold Ashby (cello) and Joseph Saxby (harpsichord)
Publication: J. & W. Chester Ltd

1956

Ruth (Opus 50)
Lyrical opera in one act (three scenes) with libretto by Eric Crozier (1914–1994)

Synopsis
Scene 1: A mountain place near Bethlehem
Scene 2: A harvest field belonging to Boaz
Scene 3: A threshing floor, at night
2+1.0.0.0/1.0.0.0/percussion (1), piano and strings
Dedication: To Freda [Berkeley]
Duration: 80 minutes
First performance: London, Scala Theatre, 2 October 1956
Original cast:
Ruth	Anna Pollak (mezzo soprano)
Boaz	Peter Pears (tenor)
Naomi	Una Hale (soprano)
Orpah	April Cantelo (soprano)
Head Reaper	Thomas Hemsley (baritone)

English Opera Group Chorus and Orchestra, conducted by Charles Mackerras. Scenery and costumes by Ceri Richards. Produced by Peter Potter

Publication: J. & W. Chester Ltd (vocal score)
Note: The opera was given its first broadcast performance on 12 December 1967

The Seraphina
or "Round the Heart in Any Year"
Incidental music for the morality play by George Barker. Produced by Douglas Cleverdon
Music written for 28 sections
Commissioned by the BBC
0.0.sax.0/0.0.2+1.0/timpani, percussion (1), harp, strings and musette accordion. In addition, parts were written for three solo voices: soprano (the voice of the Seraphina), counter tenor (the head of Orpheus) and bass (Jimmy)
First performance: London, Broadcasting House, 4 October 1956, having been pre-recorded earlier that day. Cast included Cyril Cusack, Denis Quilley, Marjorie Westbury, Diana Maddox and Norman Shelley. Music played by 17 members of the Sinfonia of London, Marjorie Westbury (soprano), Alfred Deller (counter tenor), Denis Quilley (bass) and Albert Delroy (musette accordion), conducted by Lennox Berkeley

1957

Sweet was the Song (Opus 43, no.3)
Carol for mixed chorus (SATB) and organ
Text by William Ballet (seventeenth century)
Dedication: To Alvilde [Lees-Milnes]
Publication: J. & W. Chester Ltd

Sonatina for Guitar (Opus 52, no.1)
in three movements
1. Allegretto
2. Lento
3. Rondo: Allegro non troppo
Commissioned by: Julian Bream
Dedication: For Julian Bream
Duration: 11 minutes
First performance: London, Morley College, 9 March 1958. Julian Bream (guitar)
Publication: J. & W. Chester Ltd (edited with fingering by Julian Bream)

Look back to Lyttletoun
Incidental music for the play by Carl Brahms. Produced by Charles Lefeaux.

Originally called *Quiet City*
Music written for 53 sections
Commissioned by the BBC
1.1.1.1/1.0.0.0/timpani, percussion, harp and strings. In addition, parts were written for a chamber choir (SSAATTBB)
First performance: London, Broadcasting House, 8 July 1957, the play having been pre-recorded the previous day; and the music on 2 July and 6 July in Studio A at the BBC's Transcription Service. Cast included Barbara Couper, James McKechnie, Beryl Calder, Gretchen Franklin, Simon Lack and Joan Sanderson. Music played by 14 members of the English Opera Group Orchestra and a section of the Ambrosian Singers, conducted by Norman del Mar. Jack Macintosh played (and recorded) several ad lib fanfares (00'42"), specially composed by Berkeley

Youth in Britain
Music for the film
1+1.1.1.1/1.0.0.0/timpani, percussion (1), piano and strings
Music written for the following sections:
I M 1 – Moderato/Allegro Moderato (Titles)/Lento/Allegretto
I M 2 – Allegro
I M 3 – Allegro
I M 4 – Lento
I M 5 – Allegro Moderato
I M 6 – Moderato
I M 7 – Allegro (Tempo di Marcia)

1958

Concerto for Piano and Double String Orchestra (Opus 46)
in three movements
1. Allegro moderato
2. Lento
3. Capriccio: Allegro
Commissioned by: Colin Horsley
Dedication: To Colin Horsley
Duration: 26 minutes
First performance: London, Royal Festival Hall, 11 February 1959. Colin Horsley (piano) and the BBC Symphony Orchestra, conducted by Lennox Berkeley (A Royal Philharmonic Society Concert, the remainder of which was conducted by Rudolf Schwarz)
First broadcast performance: 14 February 1959 with the same artists

Symphony No.2 (Opus 51)
in four movements
1. Lento – Allegro Moderato
2. Scherzando ma non troppo vivo
3. Lento
4. Allegro Moderato

Commissioned by: The Feeney Trust for the City of Birmingham Symphony Orchestra
2+1.2+1.2+1.2+1/4.3.3.1/timpani, percussion, celesta, harp and strings
Duration: 29 minutes
First performance: Birmingham, Town Hall, 24 February 1959. City of Birmingham Symphony Orchestra, conducted by Andrzej Panufnik
First London performance: Royal Albert Hall, 9 September 1959. BBC Symphony Orchestra, conducted by Lennox Berkeley

Revised version (1972; 1976)
1. Lento
2. Allegro Vivace
3. Lento
4. –

2+1.2.2.2+1/4.2.2.1/timpani, percussion (2), harp and strings
First performance: unable to trace

Five Poems by W.H. Auden (Opus 53)
for medium voice and piano
1. Lauds (Among the leaves the small birds sing) (Allegretto)
2. O lurcher-loving collier, black as night (Andante)
3. What's in your mind, my dove, my coney? (Moderato)
4. Eyes look into the well (Lento)
5. Carry her over the water (Moderato)

Four of the five poems are taken from Auden's *Songs and other musical pieces* included in his collected poems (1930–44), but the first, *Lauds*, is taken from a later collection *The Shield of Achilles*
Commissioned by: Alice Esty
Dedication: To Mrs Alice Esty
Duration: 10'20"
First performance: New York, March 1959. Alice Esty
First British performance: London, RBA Galleries, 23 October 1959. Nancy Evans (contralto) and Norman Franklin (piano)
Publication: J. & W. Chester Ltd

1959

So Sweet Love Seemed
Song for medium voice and piano
Text by Robert Bridges (1844–1930)
Duration: 1'55"
First performance: Manchester, Friends Meeting House, 30 October 1975. Meriel Dickinson (mezzo-soprano) and Peter Dickinson (piano)

Overture [in B flat]
for light orchestra
Commissioned by: The BBC for the 1959 BBC Light Music Festival
2.2.2.2/4.2.3.0/timpani, percussion, harp and strings
Dedication: To Vilem and Peggy Tausky
Duration: 7 minutes
First performance: London, Royal Festival Hall, 4 July 1959. BBC Concert Orchestra, conducted by Vilem Tausky

Sonatina (Opus 52, no.2)
for two pianos/four hands in three movements
1. Moderato
2. Andante
3. Rondo: Allegro con brio
Commissioned by: Sir Ashley Clarke for a concert of British music given in Rome in 1959
Dedication: To Ashley Clarke
Duration: 12 minutes
First performance: Rome, Villa Wolkonsky, 26 May 1959. Ashley Clarke and Nini Straneo (pianos)
First British performance: London, BBC, 12 May 1963. Joan and Valerie Trimble (pianos)
Publication: J. & W. Chester Ltd

1960

Hail, Gladdening Light
Hymn tune: Melfort
for unaccompanied mixed voices (SATB)
Words from the Greek, translated by John Keble (published in 1834)

A Winter's Tale
Incidental music for the play by William Shakespeare (1564–1616). Directed by Peter Wood
Music written for: unable to trace although it may have consisted of the numbers included in the orchestral suite, together with Autolycus's songs including "Daffodils" (see discography)
Commissioned by: The Royal Shakespeare Company
2.2.0.2/2.2.1.0/percussion, harp, double bass and harpsichord
First performance: Stratford-upon-Avon, Shakespeare Memorial Theatre, 30 August 1960. Cast included Roy Dotrice, Ian Richardson, Peter Jeffrey, Dennis Waterman, Eric Porter, Patrick Allen, Peggy Ashcroft, Ian Holm, Diana Rigg and Dinsdale Lansden. Music played by the Shakespeare Memorial Theatre Wind Band, conducted by Brian Priestman

Other versions
1. Suite: A Winter's Tale (Opus 54)
Re-scored for orchestra, in eight movements, by the composer
1. Prologue (Lento)
2. The Banquet (Allegro vivace)
3. Nocturne (Andante)
4. Mamillius (Allegretto)
5. The Storm (Andante)
6. Florizel and Perdita (Andante)
7. Shepherd's Dance (Allegro moderato)
8. The Statue (Andante)
2+1.2.2.2/4.2.3.1/timpani, percussion, harp and strings
Duration: 16'30"
First performance: Norwich, St Andrew's Hall, 27 May 1961. BBC Symphony Orchestra, conducted by Rudolf Schwarz
Publication: J. & W. Chester Ltd

Thou Hast Made Me (Opus 55, no.1)
Anthem for mixed chorus (SATB) and organ
Text by John Donne (1572–1631)
Written for the St Cecilia's Day Service (1960) of the Musicians' Benevolent Fund
Duration: 5'40"
First performance: London, Church of St Sepulchre (Holborn Viaduct), 22 November 1960. The choir, consisting of children of HM's Chapel Royal and choristers from St Paul's Cathedral, Westminster Abbey and Canterbury Cathedral, together with gentlemen of St.Paul's Cathedral and Westminster

Abbey, and O.H. Peasgood (organ), conducted by J. Dykes Bower
Publication: J. & W. Chester Ltd

Improvisation on a theme of Manuel de Falla (Opus 55, no.2)
for piano
Written for inclusion in a volume of five piano solos by different composers (Berkeley, Eugene Goossens, John Ireland, Gian Francesco Malipiero and Francis Poulenc) to commemorate the centenary (in 1960) of the founding of the firm of J. & W. Chester
The improvisation alludes to the languorous 7/8 movement in Falla's ballet *El Amor Brujo*
Dedication: To [R.] Douglas Gibson [1894–1985] [Managing Director at J. & W. Chester]
Duration: 4 minutes
First performance: unable to trace
Publication: J. & W. Chester Ltd (The House of Chester, 1860–1960. Centenary Album)

Prelude and Fugue (Opus 55, no.3)
for clavichord
Duration: 3'30"

Missa Brevis (Opus 57)
for mixed chorus and organ
1. Kyrie (Lento)
2. Gloria (Andante)
3. Sanctus (Lento)
4. Benedictus (Andante)
5. Agnus Dei (Lento)
Text from the Latin Missal
Dedication: To Michael and Julian [Berkeley] and the boys of Westminster Cathedral Choir
Duration: 11 minutes
First performance: London, Westminster Cathedral, 12 March 1960 (Feast of St Gregory). The Cathedral Choir and organist, conducted by Francis Cameron
Publication: J. & W. Chester Ltd

Other versions
1. Version for the Anglican Communion Service (SATB and organ)
2. Arrangement for woodwind instruments and mixed voices

1961

Five Pieces for Violin and Orchestra (Opus 56)
1. Lento
2. Allegro
3. Allegro scherzando
4. Aria (Andante)
5. Finale (Allegro)

Commissioned by: Frederick Grinke
2+1.2.2.2/2.0.0.0/timpani, percussion(1) and strings
Dedication: To Frederick Grinke
Duration: 20 minutes
First performance: London, Royal Albert Hall, 31 July 1962. Frederick Grinke (violin) and the BBC Symphony Orchestra, conducted by Lennox Berkeley
Publication: J. & W. Chester Ltd

Concerto for Violin and Chamber Orchestra (Opus 59)
in three movements
1. Moderato
2. Passacaglia: Lento
3. Lento–cadenza–Allegro moderato

Commissioned by: The Bath Festival Society for the 1961 Bath Music Festival
0.2.0.0/2.0.0.0/strings
Dedication: To Yehudi Menuhin
Duration: 22 minutes
First performance: Bath, the Abbey, 1 June 1961. Yehudi Menuhin (violin) and the Festival Chamber Orchestra, conducted by Lennox Berkeley
Publication: J. & W. Chester Ltd

1962

Autumn's Legacy (Opus 58)
Seven songs for high voice and piano
1. The Mighty Thoughts of an Old World (Allegro moderato)
   Text: Thomas Lovell Beddoes (1803–1849)
2. All Night a Wind of Music (Vivace)
   Text: Thomas Lovell Beddoes (1803–1849)
3. Lesbos (Andante)
   Text: Lawrence Durrell (1912–1990)
4. Tonight the Winds Begin to Rise (Allegro)

Text: Alfred, Lord Tennyson (1809–1892)
5. Hurrahing in Harvest (Moderato)
   Text: Gerard Manley Hopkins (1844–1889)
6. Rich Days (Allegretto)
   Text: W.H. Davies (1871–1940)
7. When We Were Idlers With Loitering Rills (Andante)
   Text: Hartley Coleridge (1796–1849)
Commissioned by: The 1962 Cheltenham Festival
Dedication: To Lord Edward Sackville who helped with the choice of poems. *Lesbos* is dedicated to Wallace Southam
First performance: Cheltenham, Town Hall, 6 July 1962. Richard Lewis (tenor) and Geoffrey Parsons (piano)
Publication: J. & W. Chester Ltd

Batter my heart, three person'd God (Opus 60, no.1)
Cantata for solo soprano, mixed chorus (SATB), oboe, horn in F, cellos, double basses and organ
Text by John Donne (1572–1631) from the *Holy Sonnets*
Commissioned by: The Riverside Church Choir of New York and Director Richard Weagley
Dedication: To the Riverside Church Choir of New York and its Director Richard Weagley
Duration: 13 minutes
First performance: New York, Riverside Church, unable to trace any date. Church Choir and ensemble, conducted by Richard Weagley
First British performance: Leeds, University Hall, 1963. BBC Northern Singers and Orchestra, conducted by Lennox Berkeley
First London performance: Holy Trinity Church, 14 November 1963. London Bach Group and Collegium Musicum Londinii, conducted by John Minchinton
Publication: J. & W. Chester Ltd

Other versions
1. Arranged for soprano, mixed voices (SATB) and string orchestra

1963

Christ is the World's Redeemer
Hymn tune: Gartan
Words attributed to St Columba (521–597) and translated from the Latin by Rev. Duncan MacGregor

Written to celebrate the fourteenth centenary of the death of St Columba
Dedication: To Derek Hill who commissioned the music for the St Columba's open air Centenary at Gartan in June 1963
Duration: 4 minutes
First performance: Ireland, Garton (Co. Donegal), 2 June 1963. Four local choirs and the Britannia Band of Derry, conducted by Lennox Berkeley
Publication: Novello (*The Musical Times* 104, July 1963, p.497)

Justorum Animae: For All Saints and Feasts of Martyrs (Opus 60, no.2)
Motet for four unaccompanied mixed voices (SATB)
Text from *Wisdom* III.vv.1–3
Dedication: To Margaret Ritchie
Duration: 5 minutes
Publication: J. & W. Chester Ltd

Automne (Opus 60, no.3)
Song for medium voice and piano
Text by Guillaume Apollinaire (1880–1918)
Written in memory of Francis Poulenc [1899–1963]
Duration: 3 minutes
First performance: unable to trace
First British performance: Cheltenham, Town Hall, 10 July 1968. Nigel Wickens (baritone) and Peter Croser (piano)
Publication: J. & W. Chester Ltd

Counting the Beats (Opus 60, no.4)
Song for high voice and piano
Text by Robert Graves (1895–1985)
One of four settings of Robert Graves's poems, commissioned by Patric Dickinson (the others having been composed by Richard Arnell, Nicholas Maw and Humphrey Searle), written for the 1963 Festival of Poetry and organized by the Poetry Book Society
First performance: London, Royal Court Theatre, 16 July 1963. Gerald English (tenor) and John Constable (piano)

Revised version (1971)
Publication: Thames

Sonatina (Opus 61)
for oboe and piano in three movements
1. Molto moderato

2. Andante
3. Allegro
Dedication: To Janet and John Craxton
Duration: 12 minutes
Publication: J. & W. Chester Ltd

Revised version
Unable to trace any details

Four Ronsard Sonnets (Set 2) (Opus 62)
for tenor voice and orchestra
Texts by Pierre de Ronsard (1524–1585) from his *Sonnets pour Helène*
1. Ce première jour de Mai
2. Je sens une douceur
3. Ma fièvre croist toujour (Allegro con fuoco)
4. Yeux, qui versez en l'âme (Lento)
Commissioned by: The BBC for the 1963 season of Promenade Concerts
2+1.2.2.2/4.2.3.1/timpani, percussion (2), harp and strings
Dedication: To the memory of Francis Poulenc
Duration: 19 minutes
First performance: London, Royal Albert Hall, 9 August 1963. Peter Pears (tenor) and the BBC Symphony Orchestra, conducted by Lennox Berkeley

Other versions
1. Arrangement for chamber orchestra (Opus 62a)
1.1.1.1/2.0.0.0/timpani, harp and strings
Publication: J. & W. Chester Ltd

1964

Diversions (Opus 63)
for eight instruments (oboe, clarinet in B flat, bassoon, horn in F, piano, violin, viola and cello) in four movements
1. Adagio – Allegro
2. Vivace
3. Lento
4. Allegro
Commissioned by: The Delphos Ensemble for the 1964 Cheltenham Music Festival
Duration: 18 minutes
First performance: Cheltenham, Town Hall, 13 July 1964. David Cowsill (oboe),

Michael Saxton (clarinet), Michael Whewell (bassoon), Frank Downes (horn), James Walker (piano), Meyer Stolow (violin), Kenneth Page (viola) and Oliver Brookes (cello)
Publication: J. & W. Chester Ltd

Adeste Fideles
An arrangement of the Christmas carol ("O Come All Ye Faithful"), in Latin, for treble solo (verses 1 and 3) and mixed chorus (SATB) (verses 2 and 4) with piano or organ

Mass (Opus 64)
for five unaccompanied voices (SSATB)
Text from the Latin Missal
1. Kyrie (Lento)
2. Gloria (Andante)
3. Sanctus (Lento)
4. Benedictus (Andante)
5. Agnus Dei (Lento)
Commissioned by: His Eminence Cardinal Heenan, Archbishop of Westminster
Dedication: To Colin Mawby and the Choir of Westminster Cathedral
Duration: c. 12 minutes
First performance: London, Westminster Cathedral, unable to trace any date. Cathedral Choir conducted by Colin Mawby
Publication: J. & W. Chester Ltd

Songs of the Half-Light (Opus 65)
for high voice and guitar
Texts by Walter de la Mare (1873–1956). Guitar part edited by Julian Bream
1. Rachel (Allegro moderato)
2. Full Moon (Lento)
3. All that's past (Allegretto)
4. The Moth (Lento)
5. The Fleeting (Andante)
Commissioned by: Peter Pears for the 1965 Aldeburgh Festival
Dedication: To Peter Pears
Duration: 13 minutes
First performance: Aldeburgh, Jubilee Hall, 22 June 1965. Peter Pears (tenor) and Julian Bream (guitar)
Publication: J. & W. Chester Ltd (guitar part edited and fingered by Julian Bream)

1965

Partita (Opus 66)
for chamber orchestra in four movements
1. Prelude (Allegro moderato) and Fugue (Allegro)
2. Aria 1 (Andante)
3. Aria 2 (Lento)
4. Rondo (Allegro)
Commissioned by: Crosby & Co. Ltd for the Farnham Festival
1.1.2.1/2.1.1.0/timpani, percussion and strings
Duration: 13 minutes
First performance: Farnham, Parish Church of St Andrew, 17 May 1965. Frensham Heights School Orchestra, conducted by Edward Rice
Publication: J. & W. Chester Ltd

Other versions
1. Arrangement for piano by the composer

Three Songs (Opus 67, no.1)
for four unaccompanied male voices (TTBB)
1. Fair Daffodils (Andante con moto)
2. Spring goeth all in white (Lento)
3. Kissing Usurie (Allegro)
Texts (1 and 3) by Robert Herrick (1591–1674) and (2) by Robert Bridges
Commissioned by: The University of California, Santa Barbara
First performance: University of California, 15 March 1966. The Schubertians, conducted by Carl Zytowski (no.3 was first performed in Santa Barbara by The Schubertians on 20 November 1965)
First British performance: Cheltenham, Pittville Pump Room, 13 July 1986. The Schubertians, conducted by Carl Zytowski
Publication: J. & W. Chester Ltd

1965–66

Castaway (Opus 68)
An opera in one act (four scenes) with libretto by Paul Dehn (1912–1976), designed as a companion-piece to "A Dinner Engagement" (Opus 45)

Synopsis
Scene 1: The sea shore – night and stormy
Scene 2: A corridor in the Palace

Scene 3: As Scene 1, but in bright sunshine
Scene 4: The palace banquet-hall – night
1+1.1+1.2+1.1/2.1.1.0/percussion (2), harp, piano and strings
Dedication: To Paul [Dehn]
Duration: 60 minutes
First performance: Aldeburgh, Jubilee Hall, 3 June 1967
Original cast:

Odysseus, shipwrecked King of Ithaca	Geoffrey Chard (baritone)
Nausicaa, Princess of Scheria	Patricia Clark (soprano)
Queen Arete, her mother	Jean Allister (contralto)
Praxinoe, Handmaiden	Patricia Blans (soprano)
Briseis, Handmaiden	Verity Ann Bates (soprano)
Ismene, Handmaiden	Carolyn Maia (mezzo soprano)
King Alcinous	James Atkins (bass)
Laodamas, Nausicaa's brother	Malcolm Rivers (baritone)
Demodocus, a blind minstrel	Kenneth MacDonald (tenor)

English Opera Group Chorus and Orchestra, conducted by Meredith Davies. Scenery and costumes designed by Peter Rice. Produced by Anthony Besch
First London performance: Sadler's Wells Theatre, 12 July 1967. Artists as above
Publication: J. & W. Chester Ltd (vocal score)

Castaway and *A Dinner Engagement* were performed together for the first time at the Bloomsbury Theatre, London on 17 June 1983. They were also broadcast together on 27 October 1983 by the BBC

1967

Hears't thou, my soul
Hymn tune: Boar's Hill
Words by Richard Crashaw (c. 1613–1649)
Commissioned by: The Cambridge Hymnal
Publication: CUP (No.40)

I sing of a maiden
Words: Fifteenth century
Commissioned by: The Cambridge Hymnal
Publication: CUP (No.152)

Lord, by whose breath
Hymn tune: Wiveton

Words by Andrew Young (1885–??)
Commissioned by: The Cambridge Hymnal
Publication: CUP (No.61)

Nocturne (Opus 67, no.2)
for harp
Commissioned by: Hannah Francis
Dedication: For Hannah Francis
Duration: 3 minutes
Publication: Stainer & Bell (edited by David Watkins)

Signs in the Dark (Opus 69)
Four songs for mixed chorus (SATB) and string orchestra
Text by Laurie Lee (1914–1997)
1. Day of these Days (Allegro moderato)
2. Twelfth Night (Un poco piu lento)
3. The Three Winds (Allegro vivace)
4. Poem for Easter (Andante)
Commissioned by: The 1967 Stroud Festival
Dedication: To Freda [Berkeley]
Duration: 23 minutes
First performance: Stroud, Parish Church of St Lawrence, 22 October 1967. The Festival Choir and Orchestra, conducted by Eric Sanders
First London performance: Royal Albert Hall, 27 August 1968. The BBC Chorus and BBC Northern Singers, and the strings of the BBC Northern Symphony Orchestra, conducted by Lennox Berkeley
Publication: J. & W. Chester Ltd

Quartet (Opus 70)
for oboe and string trio in three movements
1. Moderato – Allegro
2. Presto
3. Andante
Commissioned by: Lady Norton, on behalf of the Institute of Contemporary Arts, with a grant from the Norton Foundation
Dedication: To Lady Norton
Duration: 15 minutes
First performance: London, Wigmore Hall, 22 May 1968. The London Oboe Quartet: Janet Craxton (oboe), Perry Hart (violin), Brian Hawkins (viola) and Kenneth Heath (cello)
Publication: J. & W. Chester Ltd

1968

Magnificat (Opus 71)
for mixed chorus (SATB), organ and orchestra
Text from the Latin Missal
Commissioned by: The City Arts Trust for the opening concert of the 1968 Festival of the City of London
2+1.2+1.2+1.2+1/4.3.3.1/timpani, percussion, harp, organ and strings
Dedication: To Michael [Berkeley]
Duration: 25'25"
First performance: London, St Paul's Cathedral, 8 July 1968. The combined choirs of St Paul's Cathedral, Westminster Abbey and Westminster Cathedral, and the London Symphony Orchestra, conducted by Lennox Berkeley
Subsequent performances were given on 4 August 1969 from the Henry Wood Promenade Concerts (conducted by Adrian Boult) and the Three Choirs Festival, Hereford (conducted by Roy Massey) on 27 August 1970
Publication: J. & W. Chester Ltd (vocal score)

Three Pieces for Organ (Opus 72, no.1)
1. Aubade (Allegro moderato)
This *Aubade* for organ was composed for the Edith Sitwell Memorial Concert at the 1966 Aldeburgh Festival and first performed by Simon Preston in Aldeburgh Parish Church on 17 June 1966
2. Aria (Andante)
3. Toccata (Allegro)
Commissioned by: The 1968 Cheltenham Festival
Dedication: To Julian [Berkeley]
Duration: 9 minutes
First complete performance: Cheltenham, College Chapel, 5 July 1968. Simon Preston (organ)
Publication: J. & W. Chester Ltd

The Windhover: To Christ our Lord (Opus 72, no.2)
Part-song for unaccompanied mixed chorus (SATB)
Text by Gerard Manley Hopkins (1844–1889)
First performance: Stonyhurst, Chapel of Stonyhurst College, 13 December 1971. BBC Northern Singers, conducted by Stephen Wilkinson. (Broadcast by the BBC on Radio 3 as the second of two programmes of contemporary settings of poems by Hopkins)
Publication: Novello (*The Musical Times* 109, November 1968 – supplement)

Theme and Variations (Opus 73)
for piano duet
Theme (Moderato) – 15 bars
   Variation 1 (Allegro)   45 bars
   Variation 2 (Lento)   16 bars
   Variation 3 (Allegro)   39 bars
   Variation 4 (Lento)   16 bars
   Variation 5 (Andante)   20 bars
   Variation 6 (Allegro)   19 bars
   Coda (Moderato)   17 bars
Dedication: To Annie Alt and Gerald Stofsky
Duration: 8 minutes
First performance: unable to trace
First British performance: Stroud, Parish Church of St Lawrence, 20 October 1971. Annie Alt and Gerald Stofsky (pianos)

1969

Symphony No.3 (Opus 74)
in one movement
Commissioned by: The 1969 Cheltenham Festival (25th)
3+1.2+1.2.2+1/4.3.2+1.1/timpani, percussion (2), harp and strings
Dedication: To Anthony and Lili Hornby
Duration: 15 minutes
First performance: Cheltenham, Town Hall, 9 July 1969. L'Orchestre National de L'Office de Radiodiffusion Television Française, conducted by Jean Martinon
First London performance: Royal Albert Hall, 3 August 1973. BBC Northern Symphony Orchestra, conducted by Raymond Leppard
Publication: J. & W. Chester Ltd (miniature score)

Ubi Caritas et Amor
Motet for four solo male voices (counter-tenor, tenor, baritone and bass)

Windsor Variations (Opus 75)
for chamber orchestra
Tema (Moderato)   23 bars
   Variation 1 (Allegro)   31 bars
   Variation 2 (Adagio)   20 bars
   Variation 3 (Allegretto)   23 bars
   Variation 4 (Andante con moto) 16 bars

Variation 5 (Allegro)   59 bars
Variation 6 (Allegro)   41 bars
Variation 7 (Lento)   25 bars

Commissioned by the Windsor Festival Society with funds from the Arts Council of Great Britain
1.2.0.2/2.0.0.0/strings
Duration: 13 minutes
First performance: Windsor, St George's Chapel (Windsor Castle), 18 September 1969. The Menuhin Festival Orchestra, conducted by Yehudi Menuhin
First London performance: Southwark, Cathedral Church of St Saviour and St Mary Overie, 14 July 1970. The Menuhin Festival Orchestra, conducted by Yehudi Menuhin
Publication: J. & W. Chester Ltd

1970

Hail Holy Queen
Song for solo voice or unison voices and organ
Dedicated to Black Prince, the composer's dog, and dated 6 March 1970
This setting may have received its first performance by the Jeffreys Consort of Voices, conducted by Michael Berkeley, at St Mary's Church, Paddington Green. Unable to trace any date.

Andantino
for cello and piano
A contribution to *Music for a Prince*, dedicated to the Prince of Wales by the contributors who, besides Lennox Berkeley, were Arthur Bliss, Ronald Binge, Vivian Ellis, John Gardner, Joseph Horovitz, Mitch Murray, Steve Race, Ernest Tomlinson, William Walton, Guy Warrack, Brian Willey, Grace Williams and David Wynne
Commissioned by: The Performing Right Society
Dedication: To HRH The Prince of Wales
Note: When all the manuscripts were assembled, they were bound into a red leather volume, handsomely tooled in gold and bearing the gold-blocked inscription: "Music for a Prince". Sir Arthur Bliss presented the album to the Prince of Wales at the PRS Annual Luncheon, held at the Hilton Hotel, on 1 July 1970

Quartet for Strings No.3 (Opus 76)
in four movements
1. Allegro moderato

2. Allegro vivace
3. Lento
4. Molto vivace
Commissioned by: Lord Chaplin for the Dartington String Quartet
Dedication: To Anthony Chaplin
Duration: 20 minutes
First performance: Dartington, 28 November 1970. The Dartington String Quartet.
First London performance: Purcell Room, 23 March 1971. The Alberni Quartet

Theme and Variations (Opus 77)
for guitar
Theme (Moderato)   19 bars
   Variation 1 (Allegro)   18 bars
   Variation 2 (Allegretto)   16 bars
   Variation 3 (Lento)   16 bars
   Variation 4 (Andante)   23 bars
   Variation 5 (Allegro)   15 bars
   Epilogue (Lento)   14 bars
Commissioned by: Written at the request of the Italian guitarist Angelo Gilardino
Dedication: To Angelo Gilardino
Duration: c. 7 minutes
First performance: Italy, Tronzano-Vercelli, Salone della Regola, 19 December 1971. Angelo Gilardino (guitar)
Publication: J. & W. Chester Ltd/Berben (edited and fingered by Angelo Gilardino)

i carry your heart
Song for voice and piano
Text: e.e. cummings

1971

Five Chinese Songs (Opus 78)
for medium voice and piano
1. People hide their love (Andante con moto)
Text: Wu-Ti, Liang dynasty AD 464–549, translated by Arthur Waley
2. The Autumn Wind (Allegretto, gently flowing)
Text: Wi-Ti, Han dynasty 157–87 BC, translated by Arthur Waley
3. Dreaming of a Dead Lady (Slow, sustained and intense)
Text: Shen-Yo, AD 441–513, translated by Arthur Waley

4. Late Spring (Moderato)
Text: Yang Knang, translated by R. Kotewell and N.L. Smith
5. The Riverside Village (Calm and slow – Andante tranquillo)
Text: Ssu-K'ung Shu, translated by R. Kotewell and N.L. Smith
Commissioned by: The Park Lane Group
Dedication: To Meriel and Peter Dickinson
Duration: 8 minutes
First performance: London, Purcell Room, 22 March 1971. Meriel Dickinson (mezzo-soprano) and Peter Dickinson (piano)
Publication: J. & W. Chester Ltd
Note: An additional song "Releasing a Migrant Yen" remains in manuscript (BL)

Dialogue (Opus 79)
for cello and chamber orchestra in three movements
1. Andante (Allegro)
2. Lento
3. Allegro moderato
Commissioned by: The King's Lynn Festival
1.2.0.2/2.0.0.0/strings
Duration: 17 minutes
First performance: King's Lynn, St Nicholas Chapel, 30 July 1971. Maurice Gendron (cello) and the English Chamber Orchestra, conducted by Raymond Leppard
First London performance: Queen Elizabeth Hall, 11 February 1972. Thomas Igloi (cello) and the English Chamber Orchestra, conducted by Raymond Leppard

Revised version
Revisions were made to the score for the 1981 Cheltenham Music Festival

In Memoriam Igor Stravinsky
Canon for string quartet (1.1.1.1)
Duration: 2 minutes
First performance: London, Broadcasting House, 8 April 1972 (having been previously recorded on 20 March 1972). John Tunnell (violin), Peter Carter (violin), Brian Hawkins (viola) and Charles Tunnell (cello)
Publication: Boosey & Hawkes (*Tempo, no. 97 (1971)*: the Berkeley composition appeared in Set 1 of the Canons and Epitaphs. A total of 16 composers – eight of them British – contributed short pieces in memory of Stravinsky to *Tempo*)

Introduction [Andante] and Allegro (Opus 80)
for double bass and piano

Commissioned by: Rodney Slatford with the aid of a grant from the Arts Council of Great Britain
Dedication: For Rodney Slatford
Duration: c. 7 minutes
First performance: London, 1971. Rodney Slatford (double bass) and Clifford Lee (piano)
Publication: Yorke Edition

A Grace
for unaccompanied mixed chorus (SATB)
Written for the Merchant Taylors' Company
Dedication: To John Reigate
First performance: London, Merchant Taylors' Hall, 8 July 1971.
The Linden Singers

Duo
for oboe and cello
Duration: 10 minutes

Diana and Actaeon Waltz (Opus 81, no.2)
for orchestra
Written at the request of Richard Buckle for "The Greatest Show on Earth", held in aid of the "Save The Titian" Fund and the Museum of Theatre Arts
2+1.2.2.2/4.2.3.1/timpani, percussion, harp and strings
Dedication: For Dicky Buckle
Duration: 7 minutes
First performance: London, the Coliseum, 22 June 1971.
The Welsh Philharmonia Orchestra, conducted by Lennox Berkeley

Other versions
1. Arranged for piano duet as the *Palm Court Waltz* (**Opus 81, no.2a**)
Dedication: for Burnet [Pavitt] with love and gratitude
Duration: 4 minutes
Publication: J. & W. Chester Ltd

Canon
for string trio
Written for and dedicated to Sir Arthur Bliss on the occasion of his 80th birthday [August 1971].
One of a collection of original works (*Greetings to Sir Arthur Bliss*) presented to Sir Arthur Bliss by the Composers' Guild of Great Britain [in manuscript] and dated 2 November 1971

Duo (Opus 81, no.1)
for cello and piano
Commissioned by: The Park Lane Group for their Young Artists and 20th Century Music Series, London, January 1972
Dedication: To George Rizza
Duration: 9 minutes
First performance: London, Purcell Room, 11 January 1972. Elizabeth Wilson (cello) and Kathleen Sturrock (piano)
Publication: J. & W. Chester Ltd

1972

Fanfare
for E flat trumpet, 4 B flat trumpets 2 tenor trumpets, bass trumpet and timpani
Commissioned by: The Royal Academy of Music for the 150th Anniversary Banquet
Dedication: To the Royal Academy of Music
Duration: 1 minute
First performance: London, Savoy Hotel, 14 July 1972. Trumpeters of the Band of the Royal Marines, conducted by Major Paul Neville

Four Concert Studies (Opus 82)
for piano
1. Allegro moderato
2. Allegro
3. Lento
4. Presto leggiero
Commissioned by: Lord Chaplin for Margaret Bruce
Dedication: To Anthony Chaplin
Duration: 8 minutes
First performance: London, Purcell Room, 9 December 1975. Margaret Bruce (piano)
Publication: J. & W. Chester Ltd

Three Latin Motets (Opus 83, no.1)
for five unaccompanied voices (SSATB)
1. Eripe me, Domine (Lento)
2. Veni sponsa Christi (Andantino)
3. Regina coeli laetare (Allegro)
Texts from Psalm 140 (1), and the Antiphon for the BVM (2 and 3)

Commissioned by: The North Wales Music Festival with funds provided by the Welsh Arts Council
Dedication: To Alec Robertson
Duration: 12 minutes
First performance: St Asaph, the Cathedral Church, 28 September 1972. The Choir of St John's College, Cambridge, conducted by George Guest
First London performance: Westminster Cathedral, 20 June 1977. Cathedral choir, conducted by Colin Mawby
Publication: J. & W. Chester Ltd

Hymn for Shakespeare's Birthday (Opus 83, no.2)
for mixed chorus (SATB) and organ
Text by C. Day Lewis (1904–1972)
Commissioned by: Sam Wannamaker (the Globe Theatre Trust)
First performance: Southwark, Cathedral Church of St Saviour and St Mary Overie, 23 April 1972. Exultate Singers, conducted by Garrett O'Brien

1973

Air and Recitative from *Ruth*, an oratorio by George Tolhurst first performed in 1864
Specially orchestrated for performance by Lennox Berkeley
Other composers involved were Timothy Baxter, Eric Fenby, John Gardner, Michael Head, Joseph Horovitz, John Joubert, Anthony Lewis, Malcolm Macdonald, Robin Orr, Paul Patterson, Humphrey Searle, Richard Stoker and Roy Teed
First performance: London, Royal Albert Hall, 6 March 1973. Norma Burrowes (soprano), Marjorie Thomas (contralto), Kenneth Bowen (tenor) and Eric Shilling (bass) with Alan Harverson (organ) and the First Orchestra and Chorus of the Royal Academy of Music, conducted by Antony Hopkins. (A Grand Musical Entertainment in aid of the 150th Anniversary Appeal of the Royal Academy of Music)

Sinfonia Concertante (Opus 84)
for oboe and chamber orchestra in five movements
1. Lento
2. Allegro vivace
3. Aria: Adagio
4. Canzonetta: Andantino
5. Allegro

Commissioned by: The BBC for a 1973 Henry Wood Promenade Concert to celebrate Lennox Berkeley's 70th birthday
2.0.2.2/2.2.0.0/timpani, piano and strings
Dedication: To Janet [Craxton]
Duration: 24 minutes
First performance: London, Royal Albert Hall, 3 August 1973. Janet Craxton (oboe) and the BBC Northern Symphony Orchestra, conducted by Raymond Leppard
Publication: J. & W. Chester Ltd (piano reduction)

Other versions
1. Canzonetta: arranged for oboe and piano by the composer
Publication: J. & W. Chester Ltd

Antiphon (Opus 85)
for string orchestra in two movements
1. Lento
2. Theme (Andante) – a plainsong melody "Laetamini in Domino" from the Antiphonale Romanum: 12 bars, and five variations
   Variation 1 (L'istesso tempo)   19 bars
   Variation 2 (Allegro moderato)   43 bars
   Variation 3 (Andante)   16 bars
   Variation 4 (Allegro)   47 bars
   Variation 5 (Lento, very slow)   19 bars
Commissioned by: The 1973 Cheltenham Music Festival with funds provided by the Arts Council of Great Britain
Dedication: To John Manduell
Duration: 13 minutes
First performance: Cheltenham, Town Hall, 7 July 1973. The Academy of St Martin's in the Fields, conducted by Neville Marriner
First London performance: Queen Elizabeth Hall, 22 October 1973. The Fine Art Orchestra, conducted by Lennox Berkeley
Publication: J. & W. Chester Ltd

Voices of the Night (Opus 86)
for orchestra
Commissioned by: The 1973 Three Choirs Festival with funds provided by the Arts Council of Great Britain
2.2.2.2+1/4.3.3.1/timpani, percussion (1), harp and strings
Dedication: To Charlotte Bonham Carter
Duration: 10 minutes

First performance: Hereford, Cathedral Church of Our Lady and St Ethelbert, 22 August 1973. The City of Birmingham Symphony Orchestra, conducted by Lennox Berkeley
First London performance: Royal Albert Hall, 4 September 1975. BBC Symphony Orchestra, conducted by Adrian Boult
Publication: J. & W. Chester Ltd

1974

Suite (Opus 87)
for string orchestra in four movements
1. Introduction (Lento) and Fugue (Allegro)
2. Air (Andantino)
3. Scherzo
4. Epilogue (Lento sostenuto)
Commissioned by: The Westminster Cathedral String Orchestra with funds from the Arts Council of Great Britain
Duration: 11 minutes
First performance: London, St John's Smith Square, 1 June 1974. The Westminster Cathedral String Orchestra, conducted by Colin Mawby

Five Herrick Poems (Opus 89)
for high voice and harp
1. Now is your turne, my dearest (Andante)
2. Dearest of thousands (Lento)
3. These springs were maidens once that lov'd (Allegretto)
4. My God! Look on me with eye of pitie (Slow but freely)
5. If nine times you your bridegroom kisse (Allegro)
Written for Peter Pears
First performance: Snape, The Maltings, 19 June 1974. Peter Pears (tenor) and Osian Ellis (harp)

Revised version
The songs were revised in 1976 as the "definitive" version

Concerto for Guitar and Small Orchestra (Opus 88)
in three movements
1. Andantino
2. Lento
3. Allegro con brio

Commissioned by: The Festival of the City of London, 1974
1.1.1.1/2.0.0.0/strings
Dedication: For Julian Bream
Duration: 22 minutes
First performance: London, Church of St Bartholomew the Great, 4 July 1974. Julian Bream (guitar) and the English Chamber Orchestra, conducted by Andrew Davis
Publication: J. & W. Chester Ltd (edited by Julian Bream)
Note: After the first performance, Berkeley revised the concerto with help from Julian Bream

1975

Quintet (Opus 90)
for oboe, clarinet, horn, bassoon and piano in four movements
1. Andante
2. Scherzo (Allegro vivace)
3. Intermezzo (Andante)
4. Theme (Allegretto) 18 bars, and five variations

Variation 1 (Allegro moderato)	46 bars
Variation 2 (Allegro)	27 bars
Variation 3 (L'istesso tempo)	40 bars
Variation 4 (Andante)	17 bars
Variation 5 (Allegro moderato)	53 bars
(Coda – Allegretto)	17 bars

Commissioned by: The Chamber Music Society of Lincoln Center, New York
Dedication: To Frank Taplin
Duration: 26 minutes
First performance: New York, Alice Tully Hall, 30 January 1976. Members of the Chamber Music Society
First British (private) performance: London, Houseman Room (University College), 1 May 1976. Members of the Oxford and Cambridge Musical Club
First British (public) performance: London, Wigmore Hall, 4 December 1976. Members of the Melos Ensemble
Publication: J. & W. Chester Ltd

The Lord is my Shepherd (Opus 91, no.1)
Anthem for treble solo, mixed chorus (SATB) and organ
Text from Psalm 23
Commissioned by: Walter Hussey, Dean of Chichester, for the Cathedral's 900th anniversary

Dedication: To the Very Rev. Walter Hussey, Dean of Chichester
Duration: 4'50"
First performance: Chichester, Cathedral Church of the Holy Trinity, 14 June 1975. The Choir of Chichester Cathedral and Ian Fox (organ), conducted by John Birch
Publication: J. & W. Chester Ltd

The Hill of the Graces (Opus 91, no.2)
Motet for unaccompanied mixed double chorus (SSAATTBB)
Text taken from *The Faerie Queene*: Book VI, Canto X, by Edmund Spenser (*c*. 1552–1599)
Commissioned by: The BBC to celebrate the 50th anniversary of the BBC Singers' first unaccompanied recital
Dedication: To Nicholas [Berkeley]
Duration: 13'45"
First performance: London, St John's Smith Square, 20 October 1975. The BBC Singers, conducted by John Poole
Publication: J. & W. Chester Ltd

1976

Flute Sonata by Francis Poulenc (Opus 93, no.2)
Orchestrated by Lennox Berkeley in three movements
1. Allegro malinconico
2. Cantilena
3. Presto grazioso

Commissioned by: James Galway
1.2.2.2/2.0.0.0/timpani and strings
Duration: 14 minutes
First performance: London, Royal Festival Hall, 24 March 1977. James Galway (flute) and the Royal Philharmonic Orchestra, conducted by Charles Dutoit

Fantasia (Opus 92)
for organ
Commissioned by: The Organ Club for its Golden Jubilee recital, with funds provided by the Arts Council of Great Britain
Dedication: To Julian [Berkeley]
Duration: 10 minutes
First performance: London, Royal Festival Hall, 1 December 1976. Nicholas Kynaston (organ)
Publication: J. & W. Chester Ltd

1977

Another Spring (Opus 93, no.1)
Three songs for medium voice and piano
Texts by Walter de la Mare (1873–1956) from "Inward Companion" (Faber, 1950)
Commissioned by: The Chichester 902 Festivities as a tribute to the Very Rev. Walter Hussey, marking his retirement as Dean of Chichester Cathedral
1. Poetry (Lento)
2. Another Spring (Allegretto)
3. Afraid (very slow, in strict time throughout)
Dedication: To Janet Baker
Duration: 7 minutes
First performance: Chichester, Cathedral Church of the Holy Trinity, 20 July 1977. Janet Baker (mezzo-soprano) and Geoffrey Pratley (piano)
Publication: J. & W. Chester Ltd

Four Score Years and Ten
for voice and piano (two versions were composed, one in 3/4 time, the other in 6/8 time)
Text by Vivian Ellis
Written as a tribute to Leslie Boosey on his 90th birthday and first performed on 26 July 1977. Unable to trace further details

1978

Prelude [Andante] and Capriccio in A major (Opus 95)
for piano
Commissioned by Alun Hoddinott (Professor of Music at UCW, Cardiff) for the 24 February 1978 concert with funds provided by the Welsh Arts Council
First performance: Cardiff, New Hall (Corbett Road), 24 February 1978. Roger Woodward (piano)

Symphony No.4 (Opus 94)
for orchestra in three movements
1. Lento
2. [Theme] Andante 27 bars [and five Variations]
　　　Variation 1 (Allegretto)　　　30 bars
　　　Variation 2 (Allegro)　　　　 51 bars
　　　Variation 3 (Lento)　　　　　 41 bars
　　　Variation 4 (Allegro moderato) 51 bars

Variation 5 (Adagio) 38 bars
3. [Allegro]: ending later revised and amended to Meno vivo
Commissioned by: The Royal Philharmonic Orchestra, with funds provided by the Arts Council of Great Britain
2+1.2+1.2+1.2+1/4.3.3+1.1/timpani, percussion (2), harp and strings
Dedication: To Burnet Pavitt
Duration: 30 minutes
First performance: London, Royal Festival Hall, 30 May 1978. Royal Philharmonic Orchestra, conducted by Charles Groves

Judica Me (Opus 96, no.1)
Motet for unaccompanied mixed chorus (SSATBB)
Text from the Roman Missal
Commissioned by: The 1978 Three Choirs Festival
Dedication: To Sheila MacCrindle
Duration: 7 minutes
First performance: Worcester, Cathedral Church of Christ and St Mary, 2 September 1978. Festival Chorus, conducted by Donald Hunt
Publication: J. & W. Chester Ltd

Sonata (Opus 97)
for flute and piano in three movements
1. Allegro moderato
2. Adagio
3. Allegro vivace
Commissioned by: The Edinburgh International Festival for James Galway
Dedication: To James Galway
Duration: 12 minutes
First performance: Edinburgh, Leith Theatre, 30 August 1978. James Galway (flute) and Phillip Moll (piano)
Publication: J. & W. Chester Ltd

1979

Una and the Lion (Opus 98)
Cantata concertante for soprano voice, soprano recorder, viola da gamba and harpsichord
Texts by Edmund Spenser (c. 1552–1599) from *The Faerie Queene*, Canto III
1. If fortuned out of the thicket wood (Moderato)
2. Sarabande [instrumental] (Andante)

3. The Lion Lord of every beast (Allegro moderato)
4. Redowning tears did choke (Allegro moderato)
5. Still when she slept (Andante con moto)

Commissioned by: Carl Dolmetsch, with funds provided by the Arts Council of Great Britain
First performance: London, Wigmore Hall, 22 March 1979. Elizabeth Harwood (soprano), Jeanne Dolmetsch (soprano recorder), Marguerite Dolmetsch (viola da gamba) and Joseph Saxby (harpsichord)

1980

Ubi Caritas et Amor (Opus 96, no.2)
Motet for unaccompanied mixed chorus (SSATB)
Commissioned to celebrate the 1500th anniversary of the birth of St Benedict (480–1980)
Dedication: To the Benedictine Order
Duration: c. 5 minutes
First performance: Westminster Cathedral, 11 July 1980. The Cathedral Choir, conducted by Stephen Cleobury
Publication: J. & W. Chester Ltd

Magnificat and Nunc Dimittis (Opus 99)
for mixed chorus (SATB) and organ
Text from the Book of Common Prayer
Commissioned by: The Southern Cathedrals Festival with funds from the Southern Arts Association
Dedication: For John Birch
Duration: 9 minutes
First performance: Chichester, Cathedral Church of the Holy Trinity, 26 July 1980. The combined choirs of Chichester, Salisbury and Winchester Cathedrals with Ian Fox (organ), conducted by John Birch
Publication: J. & W. Chester Ltd

1981

Bagatelle (Opus 101, no.1)
for two pianos (4 hands)
Allegro – quick waltz time [based on a melody from A Dinner Engagement] (Opus 45)

Dedication: To (Lady) Helen Dashwood
First performance: London, Purcell Room, 1 May 1983. Margaret Bruce and Jennifer Bowring (pianos)
Publication: J. & W. Chester Ltd

1982

Mazurka (Opus 101, no.2)
for piano
A contribution to *Homage to Haydn* (1982): six pieces by George Benjamin, Richard Rodney Bennett, Berkeley, Robert Sherlaw Johnson, John McCabe and Edmund Rubbra, written to celebrate Haydn's 250th birthday
Commissioned by: The BBC
Duration: 2 minutes
First performance: London, BBC Studios, 18 March 1982. John McCabe (piano). This recording was subsequently played on the BBC's Radio 3 on 31 March 1982.
Publication: J. & W. Chester Ltd (An 80th birthday tribute to Lennox Berkeley, it contains a facsimile of the composer's manuscript)

Sonnet (Opus 102)
for high voice and piano
Text by Louise Labé (1525–65) Written for and dedicated to Hugues Cuenod with "love and admiration"
Duration: 2 minutes
First performance: privately performed by Peter Pears
First public performance: London, Wigmore Hall, 26 June 1990. Jane Watson (soprano)
Publication: J. & W. Chester Ltd

1983

In Wintertime (Opus 103)
Carol for mixed chorus (SATB) and organ
Text by Betty Askwith
Commissioned by: Stephen Cleobury and the choir of King's College, Cambridge for the 1983 Festival of Nine Lessons and Carols
Dedication: to the memory of Keith Miller-Jones
Duration: 2'48"
First performance: Cambridge, King's College Chapel, 24 December 1983. The

Choir of King's College, conducted by Stephen Cleobury
Publication: J. & W. Chester Ltd

Faldon Park (Opus 100)
Opera in two acts with libretto by Winton Dean
Commissioned by: Lord Harewood for English National Opera with funds provided by the Arts Council of Great Britain
Unfinished at the time of Lennox Berkeley's death in 1989
A tenor aria from *Faldon Park*, "You married couples are all the same", was given its first performance at St Mary's Church, Paddington Green on 22 May 1988 by Edward Byles (tenor) and orchestra, conducted by Victor Morris (Lennox Berkeley's 85th birthday concert)

Manuscripts and first editions

Prepared by Joan Redding

Most of the Berkeley manuscripts are in the LOAN collection deposited in the British Library (London) by Lady Berkeley in 1990. This collection is made up of the manuscripts formerly held at the Berkeley home in Warwick Avenue, and those from J. & W. Chester Ltd.

The descriptions of each fall into two sections: one giving details of the physical layout, the other the textual contents. Included are such facts as the manuscript size, its binding, a transcription of the title page, the number of pages, and whether it is signed and dated by the composer.

Details of printed first editions of Lennox Berkeley's published scores follow, also with transcriptions of each title page, the number of pages, size, description of the cover, full date of publication and print run, wherever possible, given.

This list is a continuation or amalgamation of the work of the following people who should be acknowledged: Prof. Peter Dickinson, Prof. Stewart Craggs, Curators Arthur Searle and Chris Banks from the British Library, and Andrea Steadman who undertook the painstaking work of identifying and sorting the sketches. My thanks also go to those who privately hold Berkeley manuscripts for allowing me access to them during my work.

Glossary

Holograph: manuscript written in Lennox Berkeley's hand
MS, MSS: manuscript, manuscripts
[ ]: indicates editorial omissions; unnumbered pages

ADESTE FIDELES
Holograph in black ink with text typed between staves
The score is written on one side of one double sheet and on both sides of a single

sheet of 16-stave paper measuring 34.1 × 27.1 cm
The manuscript paper printer's mark is shown as WH Nr.5.F.16
Pages bound together with sellotape
No title page
6 pages:
p. [i]   Blank with some sketches
pp. 1–4   Music
p. [5]   Blank
No date, place, dedication or signature is apparent
Present location: British Library: LOAN 101.97c
No printed first edition

AIR (Orchestration of Air from "Ruth" by George Tolhurst)
Holograph in black and blue ink with overlays
The score is written on three double sheets of 24-stave paper measuring 40.3 × 26.8 cm
No manuscript paper printer's mark is apparent
No title page
12 pages:
p. [i]   Ruth Nos 20–21 [autograph in pencil]
p. [ii]   Blank
pp. [1–6]   ARIA | from Ruth by Tolhurst | Orch:by Lennox Berkeley
pp. [7–10] Blank
No date, dedication or location is apparent
Signed by composer on page 1
Present location: Royal Academy of Music: RAM MS NO. 440
No printed first edition

ALLEGRO FOR TWO TREBLE RECORDERS
Holograph in blue ink with some autograph annotations in blue ink and pencil
The unbound score is written on one side of a double sheet of 14-stave paper measuring 26.2 × 35.5 cm
The manuscript paper printer's mark is shown as [encircled galleon] | A. L. No 41 | Printed in England
No title page: p. [1]: Allegro for Two Recorders | Lennox Berkeley
4 pages:
p. [i]   Blank
pp. [1–2]   Music "Allegro" [both parts on same staff system]
p. [3]   Blank

The manuscript is dated 1955 by the composer at bottom of page [1]
No place or dedication is apparent
Signed by composer on upper right hand corner of page [1]
Present location: British Library: LOAN 101.86d
First edition
Recorder Pieces | From the 12th to the 20th Century | Benjamin Britten and Imogen Holst, editors | RP7 also includes Purcell: Six Rounds – Holst: Gavotte – Aichinger: Two Motets – Anon. (col. Petrie): Seven Traditional Irish Tunes – Walther: Two Chorales
4 pages. 168 × 264 mm
Contained in light orange paper folder with other works in the Recorder Pieces series, No. 7. Lettered in black. Trimmed edges
Publication: © 1955 by Hawkes and Son (B&H 17771) at 9d. each or 3/6 for set
Other versions
"Allegro" by Lennox Berkeley revised and adapted for two oboes by the composer for Contemporary Music for Oboe, ed. Peter Wastall
Publication: © 1981 by Boosey and Hawkes (B&H 20500) @ £2.25 [Exploring music series]

ANDANTINO FOR CELLO AND PIANO (Opus 21/2)
Holograph in blue ink with production annotations in blue-black ink, red ink and pencil
The unbound score is written on two double sheets of 12-stave paper measuring 31.2 × 24 cm. The manuscript has been torn in half
The manuscript paper printer's mark is shown as Keith Prowse | UV12
Title page [not autograph]: Andantino | for Cello & Piano | by | Lennox Berkeley | [autograph] (original manuscript)
8 pages:
p. [i]   Title page
p. [ii]   Blank
pp. [1–3]   Music "Andantino"
pp. [4–6]   Blank
No date, place and dedication is apparent
Signed by composer on upper right hand corner of page [1]
Present location: British Library: LOAN 101.86c
First edition (Score and Part)
LENNOX BERKELEY | ANDANTINO | for CELLO & PIANO | PRICE 2/6 NET* | J. & W. CHESTER, LTD. | 11, Great Marlborough Street, London, W.1

8 pages: score, 6 pages; part, 2 pages. 305 × 228 cm
Buff paper covers. Lettered in black. Trimmed edges
Publication: © 1955 by J. & W. Chester Ltd (J.W.C.945) @ 2/6

Arrangement for Organ

Andantino (Opus 21, no. 2b)
Version for organ arranged by Jennifer Bate from Opus 21/2
First edition
Lennox Berkeley | ANDANTINO | arranged for Organ by | Jennifer Bate | [Preface] | Duration: 3 minutes | [photocopy notice] | CHESTER MUSIC | J & W Chester/Edition Wilhelm Hansen London Ltd | Eagle Court London EC1M 5QD
4 pages. 305 × 228 mm
White stiff paper wrappers. Lettered in blue. Trimmed edges
Publication: © 1982 by J. & W. Chester Ltd (J.W.C.55446). Unpriced

ANDANTINO FOR CELLO AND PIANO (Music for a Prince)
Holograph in pencil
The score is written on a single sheet of 12-stave music paper
It was later bound with the other manuscripts in red leather for presentation to the Prince of Wales
2 pages:
p. [1]   Music
p. [2]   Blank
Signed by the composer below the double bar line. [Dated March–April 1970; no place apparent]
Present location: The Prince of Wales
No printed first edition

ANOTHER SPRING (Opus 93, no.1)
Holograph in black ink with autograph annotations in pencil, including page numbers. Publication annotations in blue ink bottom page 1, including copyright date © 1977
The score is written on four double sheets of 16-stave paper measuring 36.5 × 27 cm
Bound in light blue stiff paper wrappers stapled at the spine. Square yellow label on front cover
No manuscript paper printer's mark is apparent

Title page: [autograph in black ink] THREE SONGS | LENNOX BERKELEY. | POEMS BY WALTER DE LA MARE

16 pages:

p. [i]	Title page
p. [ii]	[autograph in black ink] These songs were written for performance in Chichester Cathedral	on the occasion of Dean Walter Hussey's retirement.	L.B.
pp. 1–3	I.	Poetry	Lento "In stagnant gloom"
pp. 4–8	II.	Another Spring	Allegretto "What though the first pure snow-drop wilt and die"
pp. 9–[10]	III.	Afraid	Very slow, in strict time throughout "Here lies, but seven years old"
pp. [11–14]	Blank

The manuscript is dated "Feb–March 1977" after double bar page [10] and dedicated "To Janet Baker" on top of page 1 by the composer

No location is apparent

Signed by the composer on upper right hand corner of page 1

Present location: West Sussex Record Office: Hussey Papers (H290)

Also: annotated photocopy of holograph bound with clear tape. Annotations include autograph sketch

Title page [autograph]: Another Spring | Three Songs | LENNOX BERKELEY | (Three POEMS BY WALTER DE LA MARE)

Revised version

Details taken from photocopy of holograph [above] annotated by composer; also production annotations in pencil

The score is written on eleven pages

Title page [autograph]: Another Spring | T̶h̶r̶e̶e̶ ̶S̶o̶n̶g̶s̶ | LENNOX BERKELEY | (Three POEMS BY WALTER DE LA MARE)

16 pages:

pp. [i–ii]	Blank
p. [1]	Title page
pp. 2–4	I. Poetry: Lento
pp. 5–9	II. Another Spring: Allegretto
pp. 10–11	III. Afraid: Very slow, in strict time throughout
pp. [12–14]	Blank

Present location: British Library: LOAN 101.94f

Afraid (no.III) with fragments of other songs

Holograph [incomplete] in black ink with pencil annotations and overlays. Entire score crossed out in pencil

The score is written on one double sheet of 16-stave paper measuring 36.5 × 26.8 cm

No manuscript paper printer's mark is apparent

4 pages:
p. 3   end of I
p. 4   II. Another Spring Allegro moderato [first 12 bars]
pp. 9–10   III. Afraid

No date, dedication, location or signature is apparent
Present location: British Library: LOAN 101.94f with photocopies of a different version

First edition
Another Spring was commissioned by the Chichester 902 Festivities and first performed | in Chichester Cathedral by Janet Baker and Geoffrey Pratley on 20th July, 1977. It is | a tribute to the Very Reverend Walter Hussey, marking his retirement as Dean of | Chichester. | LENNOX BERKELEY | Another Spring | Op.93 | Three songs to poems by | WALTER DE LA MARE | CHESTER MUSIC | J. & W. Chester/Edition Wilhelm Hansen London Ltd. | Eagle Court, London EC1M 5QD
Stiff white paper wrappers. Lettered in blue. Trimmed edges
10 pages. 300 × 223 cm
Publication: © 1978 by J. & W. Chester Ltd (J.W.C.55181). Unpriced

ANTIPHON (Opus 85)
Holograph in black ink with some pencil bar lines and autograph overlays
The score is written on seven double sheets of 18-stave paper measuring 36.6 × 26.3 cm
Bound together with other Macnaghten Concerts scores in hard-covered red folio volume
Title page [autograph]: ANTIPHON | For String Orchestra | LENNOX BERKELEY
28 pages:
p. [i]   Title page
p. [ii]   Blank
pp. 1–11   I. Lento
                pp. 1–3   Lento
                pp. 3–10   Allegro
                p. 11   Lento
pp. 12–[24]   II. Theme and 5 variations; there are two pages numbered 23
                pp. 12–13   Theme: Andante
                pp. 13–14   Var. I: L'istesso tempo
                pp. 14–17   Var. II: Allegro moderato
                pp. 17–18   Var. III: Andante
                pp. 18–22   Var. IV: Allegro

pp. 22–[24]   Var. V: Lento; there are two pages numbered 23
pp. [25–26]   Blank

The manuscript is dated "March, April 1973" by the composer after the double bar on p. [24] and dedicated "To John Manduell" at the upper centre of page 1
The score is signed by the composer on the upper right hand corner of page 1
Present location: British Library ADD MS 59810.475b (Macnaghten Concerts Collection), leaves 32–52

First edition (Miniature score)
LENNOX BERKELEY | ANTIPHON | J. & W. CHESTER LTD LONDON [text encircling JWC emblem] | EDITION WILHELM HANSEN, LONDON
22 pages. 190 × 141 mm
White stiff paper wrappers. Lettered in blue and grey. Trimmed edges
Publication: © 1974 by J. & W. Chester Ltd (J.W.C. 484). Unpriced

ASK ME NO MORE (Opus 37, no.1)
Holograph in black ink with autograph annotations in pencil and production annotations in black ink
The score is written on both sides of two single sheets of 28-stave paper measuring 37.8 × 27 cm
The manuscript paper printer's mark is shown on bottom right of page as "Margarita Friedemann – Moneda 1027, Santiago"
Spine bound with sellotape
No title page; page 1 [autograph]: Ask me no more | Thomas Carew | Lennox Berkeley
4 pages:
pp. 1–4   Music: Lento
No date, dedication or location is apparent
Signed by composer on upper right hand corner of page 1
Present location: British Library: LOAN 101.95e

First edition
[Lyre & panpipes border] CHESTER LIBRARY | LENNOX BERKELEY | ASK ME NO MORE | MALE VOICES | (T.T.B.B.) | PRICE 1/- NET | J. & W. CHESTER LTD
8 pages. 242 x 194 cm
Buff paper wrappers. Lettered in black. Trimmed edges
Publication: © 1952 by J. & W. Chester Ltd (J.W.C.8783) @ 1/-

AUTOMNE (Opus 60, no.3)
Location of holograph unknown

Details taken from a photocopy
The score is written on one double sheet of 18-stave paper
No manuscript paper printer's mark is apparent
Title page: AUTOMNE | LENNOX BERKELEY | POEM BY | GUILLAUME APOLLINAIRE
4 pages:

p. [i] Title page
pp. [1–3] Music

The manuscript is dated "Mouton, August 1963." by the composer after double bar on p. [3]
The manuscript is dedicated "In memory of Francis Poulenc" on top of page [1]
Signed by composer on upper right hand corner of page [1]

First edition
AUTOMNE in collection: LENNOX BERKELEY (1903–1989) | THE COMPLETE FRENCH SONGS | SOLO VOICE & PIANO | CHESTER MUSIC
3 pages (pp. 50–52). 304 × 229 mm
Glossy stiff paper wrappers with full colour portrait of Berkeley in Paris. Lettered in black. Trimmed edges
Publication: © 1992 by J. & W. Chester Ltd (CH55985) @ £12.95

AUTUMN'S LEGACY (Opus 58)
Holograph (incomplete) in black ink with autograph sketches and annotated dyeline pages
The unbound score is written on one double sheet of 32-stave paper measuring 36.7 × 27.1 cm, two double sheets and six single sheets of 18-stave paper measuring 36.5 × 27 cm
Title page [autograph]: AUTUMN'S LEGACY | SONG CYCLE | LENNOX BERKELEY
24 pages:

p. [i] Title page
p. [ii] Blank
p. 1 I. The Mighty Thoughts of an Old World
[pp. 2–3 Missing]
p. 4 I. continued to end
[pp. 5–7 Missing; should be II. All Night a wind of music]
[pp. 8–9] Missing; should be III. Lesbos
p. 10 III. Lesbos [final section]
pp. 11–16 IV. Tonight the winds begin to rise
pp. 16–21 V. Hurrahing in the harvest [two p. 16s; should be pp. 17–22]

pp. 22–24   VI. Rich days [should be pp. 23–25]
pp. 25–27   [dyeline] VII. When we were idlers with loitering rills [pp. 27–28]
The manuscript is dated "Mar–May 1962" after double bar on p. 27[28]
No dedication, location or signature is apparent
Present location: British Library: LOAN 101.93d with annotated dyeline copies of complete holograph

Other versions

Lesbos (no.III)
Holograph in black ink with autograph annotations in pencil and overlays
The score is written on one double sheet of 18-stave paper measuring 35.4 × 26.1 cm
The manuscript paper printer's mark is shown as [encircled galleon] | A. L. No 2 | Printed in England.
No title page
4 pages:
p. [i]   pencil sketches
pp. 7–9   Music with annotations in blue ink
The manuscript is dedicated "To Wallace Southam" on page 7 with annotation in blue ink: "So grateful to you dear Wallace for introducing me to this lovely poem, Lennox" on page 9. No date and location apparent
Signed by composer on upper right hand corner of page 7
Present location: British Library: LOAN 101.93d with two annotated dyelines

First edition
Commissioned by the Committee of the Cheltenham Festival 1962 | First performed by Richard Lewis and Jeffrey[sic] Parsons | AUTUMN'S LEGACY | Op. 58 | for High Voice and Pianoforte | by | LENNOX BERKELEY | Cover Design by Doreen Roberts
28 pages. 305 × 241 cm
Stiff off-white paper wrappers with design on front cover by Doreen Roberts. Lettered in black and white. Trimmed edges
Publication: © 1963 by J. & W. Chester Ltd (J.W.C.4064) @ 10/-

BAGATELLE for two pianos (4 hands) (Opus 101, no.1)
A: Draft
Holograph in black ink with autograph sketches, additions, corrections and bar numbers in pencil; overlays
The score is written on two double sheets of 18-stave paper measuring 36.8 × 27.2 cm
The manuscript paper printer's mark is shown as [note and globe motif] B&H at lower left hand corner of page [1]

No title page; page [1] [Autograph]: To Helen Dashwood.| Bagatelle | Allegro (Quick Waltz time) d = 138; Lennox Berkeley
8 pages:
pp. [1–7]   Allegro
p. [8]   Blank
The manuscript is dedicated "To Helen Dashwood" on top page [1]
No date or location is apparent
Signed by composer on upper right hand corner of page [1]
B: Fair copy corrected
Holograph in black ink with autograph sketches, additions and corrections in pencil, bars crossed out, overlays
The score is written on three double sheets of 18-stave paper measuring 36.8 × 27.2 cm with one side of a single sheet of 18-stave paper measuring 36.8 × 27.2 cm
The manuscript paper printer's mark is shown as [note and globe motif] B&H at lower left hand corner of page [1]
No title page; page [1] [Autograph]: To Helen Dashwood.| Bagatelle | Allegro (Quick Waltz time); Lennox Berkeley
12 pages:
pp. [i–ii] Blank
pp. 1–5   Allegro [incorporates corrections from (A)]
pp. [6–10] Blank
1 page:
p. [1]   Pencil sketch of corrected ending
p. [2]   Blank
Present location: British Library: LOAN 101.90e

First edition
Lennox Berkeley | BAGATELLE | for two pianos | Op.101a | [copyright warning] | CHESTER MUSIC | J & W Chester/Edition Wilhelm Hansen London Ltd. | Eagle Court, London EC1M 5QD
Two scores, 6 pages each. 303 × 229 mm
White stiff paper wrappers. Lettered in dark and light blue. Trimmed edges
Publication: © 1982 by J. & W. Chester/Edition Wilhelm Hansen London Ltd (J.W.C.55448). Unpriced

BALLET (no title): 1932
Location of holograph: unknown
Dyeline copy of the original manuscript (105 pages in brown paper wrappers) with rehearsal/performance annotations (not autograph) in blue and red pencil. Consists of some 17 numbers with an introduction
No title page. Dated: "Paris. May/June 1932"

Present location: Chester Music, London
No printed first edition

BATTER MY HEART, THREE PERSON'D GOD (Opus 60, no.1)
Holograph in black ink with editorial corrections in pencil; extensive autograph overlays in pencil and blue ink. Ink spilled on pp. 9, 22
The unbound score is written on one double sheet and on both sides of fifteen single sheets of 18-stave paper measuring 36.6 × 27 cm
Contained in buff folder
Cover: [not autograph] BERKELEY | MSS | BATTER MY HEART | Sop. Solo, Choir, Ob. Hns. 'Celli + Bassi | + Organ
Title page: [autograph in pencil] BATTER MY HEART, THREE PERSONED GOD | (John Donne) | CANTATA | [FOR | SOPRANO SOLO | CHOIR, | OBOE, HORN, 'CELLOS + BASSES | and | organ] | L.B.
[with pencil annotation indicating how title information to appear on publication]
34 pages:

p. [i]	Title page
pp. [ii–iii]	Blank
pp. 1–3	Andante maestoso [instr]; Green slip of paper attached to the bottom of page 1 contains publication information, © 1962
pp. 3–9	"Batter my heart three-person'd God"
pp. 9–13	Allegretto "I like a userp'd town"
pp. 13–14	Andante Moderato "Reason your viceroy in mee"
pp. 15–18	Andante con moto "Yet dearly I love you"
pp. 18–19	Moderato
pp. 20–22	Allegro molto "Take me to Thee"
pp. 22–25	Largamente "Take me to you"
pp. 25–29	Andante "except you enthrall me"
p. [30]	Blank
p. [31]	[autograph in pencil] Should there be a version just for voices & organ? Or wd it be better to print [arrow to organ]

No date, dedication, location or signature is apparent; composer initials on title page
Present location: British Library: LOAN 101.77 with incomplete holograph of string orchestra version

Version with String Orchestra
Solo soprano, SATB, oboe, horn in F, timps, strings
Holograph (incomplete) in black ink with autograph additions, corrections and sketches in pencil
The unbound score is written on two double sheets and on both sides of two single sheets of 22-stave paper measuring 36.8 × 27 cm

No title page
12 pages:
pp. [1–3]   [Instrumental introduction]
pp. [3–4]   Largamente "Batter my heart" (pages 1–4 of original holograph)
pp. [5–8]   "... and stand" (pages 6–13 of original holograph)
pp. [8–12]   "I like a userpt'd town"
pp. [12]   "Reason your viceroy" (incomplete)
No date, dedication, location or signature is apparent
Present location: British Library: LOAN 101.77 with original holograph

First edition
"Batter my heart, three person'd God" | for soprano solo, choir, oboe, horn, cellos, double-basses and organ | Words by JOHN DONNE | Music by | LENNOX BERKELEY | J. & W. CHESTER, LTD. | 11 GREAT MARLBOROUGH STREET, | LONDON, W.1
35 pages. 272 × 191 mm
Blue paper wrappers. Lettered in black. Trimmed edges
Publication: © 1962 by J. & W. Chester Ltd (J.W.C.9757) @ 10/-

THE BEACON BARN (Opus 14, no.2)
Holograph in black ink with one autograph annotation in pencil
The score is written on one double sheet of 20-stave paper measuring 32.8 × 27 cm
The manuscript paper printer's mark is shown as Néocopie Musicale, Paris (No.7) in lower left hand corner of paper
No title page; p.[1]: Words by | Patrick O'Malley; THE BEACON BARN | [pencil] Rather a slow Andante; Lennox Berkeley
4 pages:
p. [i]   Blank
pp. [1–2]   Music
p. [3]   Unidentified pencil sketches: three lines of instrumental short score
The manuscript is dated "Oct 1938" after double bar on p. [2]
No dedication or location is apparent
Signed by the composer in upper right hand corner of p. [1]
Present location: British Library: LOAN 101.92d

First edition
LENNOX BERKELEY | THE BEACON BARN | WORDS BY PATRICK O'MALLEY | VOICE AND PIANOFORTE | PRINTED IN ENGLAND | | [decorative border featuring Pan playing pipes] J.&W. CHESTER LTD. | LONDON: 11, Great Marlborough Street, W.1. | [international distributors]
3 pages. 334 × 259 mm

Brown paper wrappers. Lettered in black. Trimmed edges
Publication: © 1940 by J. & W. Chester Ltd (J.W.C.4027) @ 1/6
Printed in England

BELLS OF CORDOBA (Opus 14, no.2)
Holograph in black ink with production annotations (not autograph) in red ink and pencil
The score is written on one double sheet of 20-stave paper measuring 32.8 × 27 cm
The manuscript paper printer's mark is shown as Néocopie Musicale, Paris. (No.7)
No title page; p.1: Words by F.G.Lorca | (Trans. Stanley Richardson); Bells of Cordoba; Lennox Berkeley | Allegretto
4 pages:
p. [i]   Blank
pp. [1–3]   Music: Allegretto
The manuscript is dated "December 1938" after double bar on page [3]
No location or dedication apparent
Signed by composer upper right hand corner of page [1]
Present location: British Library: LOAN 101.92d

First edition
No title page; cover: CHESTER LIBRARY | LENNOX BERKELEY | BELLS OF CORDOBA | SONG | PRICE 2/- NET | | [decorative border featuring Pan playing pipes] J.&W. CHESTER LTD.
4 pages. 335 × 260 mm
Brown paper wrappers. Lettered in black. Trimmed edges
Publication: © 1940 by J. & W. Chester Ltd (J.W.C.4026) @ 2/-

CANON FOR STRING TRIO
Holograph in black ink
The score is written on one side of a single sheet of 16-stave paper measuring 300 × 231 mm
No title page
2 pages:
p. [1]   Music
p. [2]   Blank
The manuscript is dated 2 November 1971, dedicated to Sir Arthur Bliss on his 80th birthday and signed by the composer
Present location: Lady Bliss
No printed first edition

CASTAWAY (Opus 68)
Full score
A: Holograph in black and blue ink with performance annotations in pencil in unknown hand. Extensive autograph overlays. Black ink spilled on pp. 141–66

The score is written on 19 double sheets and on both sides of 11 single sheets of 24-stave paper measuring 35.5 × 25.4 cm and on 18 double sheets and on both sides of seven single sheets of 24-stave paper measuring 34.2 × 26.9 cm with one blank single sheet of 24-stave paper measuring 37.1 × 27.3 cm wrapped in one double sheet of 26-stave paper measuring 36.8 × 27.3 cm

The manuscript paper printer's mark is shown as [encircled galleon] | A. L. No 18 | Printed in England; WH Nr.9.F.24 on lower left hand side of page; and [design] G | & | T on lower left hand side of page

Some pages sellotaped together, otherwise unbound

Cover [not autograph]: BERKELEY | Castaway

Title page [autograph in black ink]: CASTAWAY | Opera in ONE ACT | LENNOX BERKELEY | LIBRETTO BY PAUL DEHN | [FULL SCORE.]

190 pages:

p. [i]	Cover page
p. [ii]	Blank
p. [iii]	Title page
p. [iv]	Orchestration and roles
pp. 1–15	SCENE I [The sea shore. Night and storm]: Allegro moderato
pp. 15–26	SCENE II [Before Tabs: A Corridor in the Palace]: Andante
pp. 26–91	SCENE III [Tabs part to reveal same decor as Scene I in bright sunshine]; Nausicaa and her Maidens sing as they dry the washing: Allegro
pp. 92–142	SCENE II [stet]	The Palace Banquet Hall. Night.	Piu Lento
[No p. 143 continues on:]	
pp. 144–71	Scene continued
p. "171A"	Blank except for "Over" and horizontal arrow in centre of page in pencil pointing to right hand side of page
pp. 172–181	Continued to end of opera
pp. [182–6]	Blank

The manuscript is dated "1965–66" after double bar page 181 and signed by composer on upper right corner of page 1

No dedication or location is apparent

Present location: British Library: LOAN 101.56

Other versions

Dyeline of A with autograph annotations and sketches in blue ink and pencil,

many overlays and one additional autograph page to replace p. 71. Autograph annotation on page 1: "Full Score Original MS"
Present location: British Library: LOAN 101.58
B: Holograph [incomplete] in pencil; very rough and in bad condition
The unbound score is written on five double sheets and on both sides of 11 single sheets of 24-stave paper measuring 35.5 × 25.4 cm; on one double sheet and on both sides of two sheets of 24-stave paper measuring 36.8 × 27.1 cm; on both sides of one single sheet of 22-stave paper measuring 36 × 26.4 cm; on one double sheet of 24-stave paper measuring 34.1 × 27 cm; and on two double sheets of 24-stave paper measuring 34.1 × 26.8 cm [wrapped in cover sheets with my writing on front]
The manuscript paper printer's mark is shown as [encircled galleon] | A. L. No 18 | Printed in England; WH Nr.9.F.24 on lower left hand side of page
No title page; untitled
64 pages:

pp. 1–8	[Scene I]
pp. 8–12	[Scene II]
pp. 17–18	Scene continued
pp. [21]–35	Scene continued
p. [36]	Crossed out
p. 36[new]	
p. [37]	Crossed out
pp. 37[new]–54	
pp. 57–68	
p. 73	
p. [73]	Old sketch of ending

The manuscript is dated Nov 24th 1966 after double bar p.73
No dedication, location or signature is apparent
Present location: British Library: LOAN 101.56
No printed first edition
Publication: © 1966 by J. & W. Chester Ltd; score and parts housed in hire library
Vocal score
Holograph in black ink with autograph additions in black and blue ink and pencil; bars and pages crossed out; rehearsal numbers in blue ink; overlays. Some pages are not autograph
The score is written on ten double sheets and both sides of five single sheets of 14-stave paper measuring 34 × 27.2 cm and on 12 double sheets and one side of one single sheet and both sides of one single sheet of 16-stave paper measuring 34 × 27 cm
The manuscript paper printer's mark is shown as "WH Nr.4.F.14." and "WH Nr.5.F.16." paper

No title page; page 1 [autograph in black ink]: CASTAWAY | Paul Dehn; SCENE I [The sea shore, night and storm]; Lennox Berkeley
102 pages:
pp. 1–15   Scene I: Allegro moderato; autograph annotation in blue ink: "Piano Reduction Original MS"
pp. 6–15   Scene II: "[A corridor in the palace]": Andante
[No page 16]
pp. 17–25
p. [26 or i]   Blank crossed X with pencil
pp. 26–37
[No page 38]
pp. 39–54
pp. 54–58   "Scene II" [stet] "The palace banquet hall – night": Andante
[No page 59]
pp. 60–102
pp. [103–104]   Blank
No date, dedication or location apparent
Signed by the composer on upper right hand of page 1
Present location: British Library: LOAN 101.55 with sketch
Other versions
Dyeline of copyist vocal score with autograph pencil annotations and sketches and pages crossed out. On cover [not autograph]: Repetiteur | Berkeley | Castaway | (Temporary Reduction) | [Chester Hire Library stamp] | Vocal Score
Present location: British Library: LOAN 101.57
First edition (Vocal score)
CASTAWAY | An Opera in one act, four scenes designed as a | companion-piece to "A Dinner Engagement" | * | MUSIC BY | LENNOX BERKELEY | LIBRETTO BY | PAUL DEHN | J. & W. CHESTER LTD LONDON [text encircling JWC emblem] | EDITION WILHELM HANSEN, LONDON
96 pages. 255 × 179 mm
White stiff paper wrappers. Lettered in dark and light blue. Trimmed edges
Publication: © 1970 by J. & W. Chester Ltd (J.W.C.8876). Unpriced
Printed by Halstan & Co. Ltd., Amersham, Bucks

COLONUS' PRAISE (Opus 31)
Full score
Holograph in black and blue ink with minimal autograph additions and corrections; overlays. Corrections in orange for production or performance
The score is written on both sides of 21 single sheets of 20-stave paper measuring 36.5 × 26.8 cm and on one side of a single sheet of 18-stave paper

measuring 36.5 × 26.8 cm
Bound with three string ties
The manuscript paper printer's mark is shown as [encircled] J&W | Chester | Ltd. | London | No. 20
Title page: [not autograph in pencil] Colonus' Praise | (Full Score). | L. Berkeley
44 pages:

p. [i]	Title page
p. [ii]	Blank
pp. 1–3	Moderato [orch]
pp. 3–7	Meno vivo "Come praise Colonus' horses"
pp. 7–12	Tempo primo [orch]
pp. 13–17	Andante tranquillo "And yonder in the gymnast's garden thrives"
pp. 18–24	Allegro [orch]
pp. 24–32	"Who comes into this country"
pp. 32–38	Largamente "Who finds a bounding Cephisus"
pp. 39–42	Allegro "Every Colonus lad and lass discourses"

The manuscript is dated "1949" after double bar page 42
There is no place or dedication apparent
Signed by the composer on upper right hand corner of page 1
Present location: British Library : LOAN 101.75 with copyist score pp. 7–30 (one minimal annotation p. 29)
Also: Copyist full score used for performance with annotation [not autograph]: "Control score" 13.9.49 1st performance Leslie Woodgate 9'40". Copy dated 1949
Present location: BBC Music Library (BBC MSS 19497)
No printed first edition

Vocal score

Holograph in black and blue ink with autograph additions, corrections and sketches in pencil; overlays. Production annotations in blue crayon
The unbound score is written on four double sheets of 20-stave paper measuring 36.6 × 27 cm
The manuscript paper printer's mark is shown as [encircled] J&W | Chester | Ltd. | No. 20 [upside down on all pages]
No title page; p. 1: [autograph] W.B. Yeats; Colonus' Praise; Lennox Berkeley
16 pages:

p. 1	Moderato [orch]
pp. 1–3	A tempo "Come Praise"
pp. 3–4	Un poco più vivo [orch.]
pp. 4–6	Andante tranquillo "And yonder in the gymnast's garden thrives"
pp. 6–10	Allegro [orch.]
pp. 10–13	Meno mosso "Who finds abounding Cephisus"

pp. 14–15   Allegro ma marcato "Every Colonus lad and lass discourses"
p. [16]   Blank
The manuscript is dated "Jan:Feb: 1949" after double bar on page 15
No location or dedication is apparent
Signed by the composer on upper right hand corner of page 1
Present location: British Library: LOAN 101.75 with vocal score produced by BBC containing autograph annotations, corrections; overlays
First edition (Piano score)
Piano Score | COLONUS' PRAISE | W.B. YEATS | FOR CHORUS AND ORCHESTRA | LENNOX BERKELEY
19 pages. 305 × 251 mm
Cream covers. Lettered in black. Trimmed edges
Publication: no date. British Broadcasting Corporation (BBC 109)
Available from Chester Music

CONCERT STUDY IN Eb for piano (Opus 48, no.2)
Location of holograph in private hands
First edition
Cover: Lennox Berkeley | Concert Study | in E flat | J & W Chester Ltd 11 Great Marlborough St London W1 | Wilhelm Hansen Musik-Forlag Copenhagen | Wilhelmiana Musikverlag Frankfurt a M | Norsk Musikforlag A/S Oslo | A B Nordiska Muskforlaget Stockholm
7 pages. 304 × 241 mm
White stiff paper wrappers. Lettered in blue and grey. Trimmed edges
Publication: © 1956 by J. & W. Chester Ltd (J.W.C.2336). Unpriced
Printed in England. Cover and advertisement designed by John Hall. Printed by Lowe and Brydone (Printers) Limited, London

CONCERTINO FOR FLUTE (RECORDER), VIOLIN, CELLO AND HARPSICHORD (Opus 49)
Location of holograph unknown
First edition (Score and parts)
Lennox Berkeley | CONCERTINO | for recorder (or flute), violin, cello and harpsichord (or piano). | Op.49 | Duration c. $12^{1}/_{2}$ minutes | CHESTER MUSIC | J.&.W. Chester/Edition Wilhelm Hansen London Ltd. | Eagle Court, London EC1M 5QD
Score, 36 pages; Parts, 8 pages, 8 pages, 8 pages. 298 × 222 mm
White stiff paper wrappers. Lettered in dark and light blue. Trimmed edges
Publication: © 1961 by J. & W. Chester Ltd (J.W.C.279) @ 20/-
Printed by Caligraving Ltd, Thetford, Norfolk

CONCERTO FOR CELLO AND ORCHESTRA (1939)

Holograph in black ink with autograph pencil annotations, overlays and notes scratched out. Outside sheets are ripped and in poor condition

The unbound score is written on 24 double sheets of 28-stave paper measuring 36.5 × 27 cm

Title page [autograph]: LENNOX BERKELEY | Cello Concerto

96 pages:

p. [i]	Title page
pp. [ii–iv]	Blank
pp. 1–49	I. Allegro moderato
pp. 50–87	II. Adagio – Allegro moderato
pp. [88–92]	Blank

The manuscript is dated 1939 after double bar on page 87

No location or dedication is apparent

Signed by the composer on title page and on upper right hand corner of page 1

Present location: British Library: LOAN 101.4

Other versions

Dyeline (Comb-bound in stiff blue paper covers from Chester Hire Library) with autograph annotations and additions in pencil and red ink, especially at the beginning and on p. 75

Present location: British Library: LOAN 101.4

No printed first edition

Publication: © 1983 by J. & W. Chester Ltd; score and parts housed in hire library

CONCERTO FOR FLUTE AND [CHAMBER] ORCHESTRA (Opus 36)

Holograph in pencil with pencil annotations; page 55 is torn

The score is written on 29 sheets of 28-stave paper measuring 35.8 × 27 cm

No manuscript paper printer's mark is apparent

No title page

58 pages:

pp. 1–16	I. Allegro moderato (p. 14 Cadenza; pp. 14–16 Andante)
pp. 17–28	II. Presto
pp. 28–34	III. Adagio
pp. 35–58	IV. Allegro vivace

The score is dated "1951–52" after double bar page 58 and dedicated to John Francis on upper centre of page 1

No location apparent

Signed by composer on upper right hand corner of page 1

Present location: British Library: LOAN 101.15 with two annotated [not autograph] dyeline copies; BL LOAN 101.16

First edition (Piano reduction)
LENNOX BERKELEY | CONCERTO | FOR FLUTE AND ORCHESTRA | J. & W. CHESTER, Ltd. | 11 Great Marlborough Street, London, W.1
Score, 35 pages; part, 10 pages. 30 × 238 mm
Blue paper wrappers. Lettered in black. Trimmed edges
Publication: © 1956 by J. & W. Chester Ltd (J.W.C.1591) @ 20/-
Printed in England

CONCERTO FOR GUITAR AND SMALL ORCHESTRA (Opus 88)
Full score
Holograph in black ink with pencil annotations by composer; extensive overlays
The unbound score is written on 19 double sheets of 20-stave paper measuring 36.8 × 27 cm
Title page [autograph]: LENNOX BERKELEY | CONCERTO for GUITAR | & | CHAMBER ORCHESTRA | (Op:89) [sic]
76 pages:

p. [i]	Title page
p. [ii]	Blank
pp. 1–32	I. Andantino; large yellow sheet of blotting paper inserted between pp. 26 & 27 for no apparent reason
pp. 33–43	II. Lento
pp. 44–72	III. Allegro con brio
p. 63	Cadenza
pp. [73–74]	Blank

The manuscript is dated "Feb:-May 1974" after double bar page 72
No location or dedication is apparent
Signed by the composer on upper right hand corner of page 1
Present location: British Library: ADD MS 59539

Short score
Holograph draft (incomplete) in pencil with extensive annotations in pencil and one in blue ink. Bars crossed out. Tattered condition
The unbound score is written on four double sheets and on both sides of nine single sheets of 24-stave paper measuring 40.6 × 26.5 cm
No manuscript paper printer's mark is apparent
In grey Chester Music Hire folder
Cover: [autograph in black ink] Guitar Concerto. | 1st rough copy | [pencil] 1 page missing
No title page
34 pages:

pp. 1–34	Music

[missing pp. 18–19]
p. [22a]   Blank
p. [35]   Blank
No date, dedication, location or signature is apparent
Present location: British Library: LOAN 101.35 with other sketches
Sketches
Sketches include pages of short score in pencil and rejected pages of full score in ink; old title page: CONCERTINO | FOR | GUITAR + CHAMBER ORCH: | LENNOX BERKELEY
Present location: British Library: LOAN 101.36 with short score draft in pencil
Also: Photocopy of printed proofs (piano reduction score and part) with autograph annotations in pencil. Production annotation top left corner in red ink: L.B. | First Proofs
Title: [not autograph, blue ink] LENNOX BERKELEY | Guitar Concerto | Piano Reduction | L.B.'s FIRST PROOFS
Present location: British Library: LOAN 101.36
First edition (Score)
81 pages, octavo
Publication: © 1977 by J. & W. Chester Ltd. Unpriced [Opus 88 – BCM]
Edited by Julian Bream
First edition (Piano reduction score and part)
Score: 31 pages; part: 13 pages
Publication: © 1977 by J. & W. Chester Ltd/Edition Wilhelm Hansen London Ltd. Unpriced

CONCERTO FOR PIANO AND DOUBLE STRING ORCHESTRA (Opus 46)
Movements II and III (incomplete)
Holograph [incomplete] in black and blue ink with autograph pencil additions and corrections; blue pencil performance annotations; overlays on pages 24 and 31
The score is written on both sides of a single sheet and on 13 double sheets of 22-stave paper measuring 36.8 × 27.1 cm
No manuscript paper printer's mark is apparent
No title page
II. Lento
14 pages:
pp. 3–16   [untitled; incomplete]
III. Capriccio
40 pages:
pp. 1–40   Music

No date, dedication, location or signature is apparent
Present location: British Library: LOAN 101.18 with two annotated dyelines of copyist manuscript with autograph annotations, BL LOAN 101.23
No printed first edition
Publication: © 1958 by J. & W. Chester Ltd; score and parts housed in hire library

CONCERTO FOR PIANO AND ORCHESTRA (Opus 29)
Full score
Holograph in blue ink with autograph annotations in pencil; overlays. Performance annotations in red and blue pencil
The score is written on both sides of 56 sheets of 20-stave paper measuring 36.3 × 26.8 cm
The manuscript paper printer's mark is shown as [encircled] J & W | CHESTER | LTD | LONDON No.20
Bound in grey boards with cloth spine. Pages sewn into spine. Some pages loose
Title page [autograph]: [26284 stamped on cover] | To Colin Horsley | CONCERTO IN B flat | for | Piano & Orchestra | Lennox Berkeley | [Chester copyright stamp]
116 pages:

p. [i]	Title page
p. [ii]	Blank
pp. 1–48	I. Allegro Moderato; p. 13 is numbered p. 11
pp. [48–50], 50–55	Cadenza
pp. [iii–iv]	Blank
p. [v]	Pencil sketch
pp. 56–67	II. Andante
pp. 68–107	III. Vivace (Alla breve)

Opus number not noted on manuscript
The manuscript is dated 1947–48 after double bar p. 107 and dedicated "To Colin Horsley" upper centre of page 1
Signed by the composer on title page and on upper right hand corner of page 1
Present location: British Library: LOAN 101.9
Piano reduction
Second movement only
Holograph in pencil with annotations in orange pencil
The score is written on two double sheets of 18-stave paper measuring 36.5 × 27 cm
The manuscript paper printer's mark is shown as [encircled] J & W | CHESTER | LTD | LONDON No.18
No title page

8 pages:
pp. 1–6   Music: Andante
pp. [7–8]   Blank
Present location: British Library: LOAN 101.9
Annotated printed copy
Contains annotation: "Corrections as approved by LB 31/8/75"
Also performance annotations in pencil
with sheet of corrections:
Holograph in pencil in poor condition
The correction score is written on both sides of one page of 24-stave paper measuring 36.8 × 27 cm
No manuscript paper printer's mark is apparent
2 pages:
pp. [1–2]   Corrections linked to printed full score by bar numbers
Present location: British Library: LOAN 101.10
First edition (Piano reduction)
Cover: LENNOX BERKELEY | CONCERTO in B flat | for PIANO and ORCHESTRA | PRICE 12/6 NET* | J. & W. CHESTER, Ltd. | 11, Great Marlborough Street, London W.1
64 pages. 308 × 248 mm
Stiff blue paper wrappers. Lettered in black. Trimmed edges
Publication: © 1951 by J. & W. Chester Ltd (J.W.C.2941) @ 12/6
Printed in England

CONCERTO FOR TWO PIANOS AND ORCHESTRA (Opus 30)
Full score
Holograph in blue and black ink with autograph corrections, additions and sketches in pencil; overlays. Performance annotations in blue and orange crayon and green, purple and pink pencil. An ink stain covers the middle of p. 85
The score is written on both sides of 54 single sheets of 28-stave paper measuring 43.7 × 30.4 cm
Bound in grey boards; sewn and taped spine; in tattered condition
The manuscript paper printer's mark is shown as [encircled] J & W | CHESTER | LTD | LONDON
No title page; cover: [not autograph in pencil] N.B. PIANO PARTS ARE INCORRECT IN | THIS SCORE | [black ink] CONCERTO | for 2 Pianos [pencil] & Orch | [black ink] Lennox | Berkeley
108 pages:
pp. 1–30   [autograph in blue ink] Concerto – Lennox Berkeley
            I | Molto Moderato

pp. 31–101   II. | THEME & VARIATIONS
              p. 31   TEMA – Andante Moderato
              pp. 32–37   VAR: I. Allegro ma non troppo
              pp. 37–43   VAR: II Allegro [crossed out in pencil] [pencil & blue ink] (L'Istesso Tempo) [pencil] (Allegro)
              pp. 44–51   VAR: III Allegro
              pp. 52–57   VAR: IV Adagio
              pp. 57–66   VAR: V Vivace
              pp. 66–73   VAR: VI Andante
              pp. 73–84   VAR: VII Tempo di Valse
              pp. 85–87   VAR: VIII Allegro [blue crayon] Pianos only
              pp. 87–90   VAR: IX Andante Lento
              pp. 91–92   VAR: X | Andante Con Moto
              pp. 93–101   VAR: XI (L'Istesso Tempo)
p. [102]   Blank
p. [103]   [not autograph in blue crayon]: L. Berkeley | 2 Piano Concerto | 2nd MVT | Variations VI–X
p. [104]   Blank
p. [105]   [not autograph in pencil]: Lennox Berkeley | Concerto for 2 Pianos | Full Score 2nd movement (incomplete)
p. [106]   Blank
p. [107]   Autograph 2-bar pencil sketch
p. [108]   Blank

The manuscript is dated "1948" after double bar page 101
No dedication or location is apparent
Signed by the composer on upper right hand corner of page 1
Present location: British Library: LOAN 101.11
Also: Correction to Piano II: autograph 9-bar pencil sketch for Piano II, Var. V figure 26
Present location: British Library: LOAN 101.12b
Copyist version of full score
Incomplete dyeline of copyist version of full score with some stray autograph annotations made late in life
pp. 24–113 (end of 1st movement and entire 2nd movement)
Present location: British Library: LOAN 101.13

Piano reduction
2nd movement
Holograph (incomplete) in black ink with autograph annotations and sketches in pencil
The unbound score is written on both sides of thirteen single sheets of 20-stave paper measuring 36.5 × 27 cm

Contained in buff folder
The manuscript paper printer's mark is shown as [encircled] J & W | CHESTER | LTD. | LONDON No. 20
No title page; Cover of buff folder: [not autograph] MS. MIDEM | CONCERTO for 2 Pianos | 2nd mvmt | arr 3 pianos | (pp. 16–40)
26 pages:

p. 16	II. Theme & Variations	Tema – Moderato
pp. 17–19	Var: I
pp. 19–21	Var: II
pp. 22–25	Var: III
pp. 25–29	Var: IV Adagio
pp. 29–32	Var: V Vivace
pp. 32–36	Var: VI Andante
pp. 36–40	Var: VII Tempo di Valse
p. [41]	Blank

No date, dedication or location is apparent
Signed by the composer on upper right hand corner of page 16
Present location: British Library: LOAN 101.12
First edition (Piano reduction)
Cover: LENNOX BERKELEY | CONCERTO | FOR | TWO PIANOS | AND ORCHESTRA | PRICE 20/- NET* | J. & W. CHESTER, Ltd. | 11, Great Marlborough Street London, W.1
84 pages. 310 × 248 mm
Blue still paper wrappers. Lettered in black. Trimmed edges
Publication: © 1948 by J. & W. Chester Ltd (J.W.C.2943) @ 20/-
Printed in England

CONCERTO FOR VIOLIN AND CHAMBER ORCHESTRA (Opus 59)
Original version
Holograph in black ink with autograph corrections, addition and sketches in pencil; overlays
The score is written:
I&II: on ten double sheets and both sides of two sheets of 22-stave paper measuring 356 × 26.3 cm
III: on four double sheets of 22-stave paper measuring 35.9 × 26.5 cm and two double sheets of 18-stave paper measuring 35.5 × 26.2 cm
The manuscript paper printer's mark is shown as:
I&II: [encircled galleon] | A. L. No 16 | Printed in England
III: no mark; [encircled galleon] | A. L. No 12 | Printed in England
Unbound score is covered in grey paper and stapled at spine. Cover [autograph]:

V'n Concerto | Original
Title page: CONCERTO | for | Violin & Chamber Orchestra | LENNOX BERKELEY | MVTS I &II Full Score [pencil] (also III)
68 pages:

p. [i]	Title page
p. [ii]	Blank
pp. 1–22	I. Moderato
pp. 23–35	II. Passacaglia: Lento
pp. [36–42]	Blank
p. 36	III. Introduction: Lento – Cadenza
pp. 37–56	Allegro moderato
pp. [57–59]	Blank

The manuscript is dated 1961 and dedicated "To Yehudi Menuhin" by the composer. Signed by the composer on upper right hand corner of page 1
Present location: British Library: LOAN 101.22 with pencil sketches of short score and letter to Lennox Berkeley from Manoug Parikian regarding corrections dated 21.v.74

Revised version
Annotated dyeline with new ending, see p. 56 last four bars
Present location: British Library: LOAN 101.23
First edition (Miniature score)
Cover: Lennox Berkeley | Concerto | for Violin and | Chamber | Orchestra | J & W Chester Ltd Eagle Court London EC1 | [Distributors]
55 pages. 190 × 138 mm
White stiff paper wrappers. Lettered in blue and grey. Trimmed edges
Publication: © 1962 by J. & W. Chester Ltd (J.W.C.9904) @ 10/-
First edition (Piano reduction)
CONCERTO | FOR | VIOLIN AND CHAMBER ORCHESTRA | (Opus. 59) | Arranged for violin and piano | by | LENNOX BERKELEY | Orchestration: 2 oboes, 2 horns in F and strings | Duration: Approx. 15 mins. | J. & W. CHESTER LTD LONDON [text encircling JWC emblem] | [sister companies listed around emblem
Score, 28 pages; Part, 8 pages. 304 × 242 mm
White stiff paper wrappers. Lettered in green and grey. Trimmed edges
Publication: © 1962 by J. & W. Chester Ltd (J.W.C.432) @ 10/-
Printed by Lowe and Brydone (Printers) Limited, London

COUNTING THE BEATS (Opus 60, no.4)
A: Draft
Holograph in black ink with corrections in pencil and editorial notes [not

autograph] in blue pencil, overlays

The score is written on two double sheets of 14-stave paper measuring 34.2 × 27.1 cm

The manuscript paper printer's mark is shown as [vertical along spine] WH Nr.4. F.14

No title page; page [1] [autograph]: Robert Graves | Andante | Counting the Beats | Lennox Berkeley

8 pages:

pp. [1–6]   Music
pp. [7-8]   Blank

No date, dedication or location is apparent

Signed by the composer on the upper right hand of page [1]

Present location: British Library: LOAN 101.94a with annotated photocopy of (B)

Note: Autograph annotations in pencil on photocopy of (B) were incorporated into first printed edition

B: Fair copy

Holograph in black ink with pencil annotations and overlays

The score is written on two double sheets and both sides of one single sheet of 18-stave paper measuring 35.6 × 26.2 cm

The manuscript paper printer's mark is shown as [encircled galleon] | A. L. No 12 | Printed in England

Bound together in red cloth folio "Presented by the Poetry Book Society" with other manuscript scores commissioned by Patric Dickinson for the 1963 Festival of Poetry: scores by Humphrey Searle and Nicholas Maw

Title page [autograph]: COUNTING THE BEATS | (Robert Graves) | Lennox Berkeley

10 pages:

p. [i]   Title page
p. [ii]   Blank with autograph pencil annotation bottom of page
pp. 1–6   Music: Counting the Beats | Robert Graves | Lennox Berkeley | Lento
pp. [7–8]   Blank

The manuscript is dated "June 1963" after the double bar on page 6

No location is apparent

Signed by the composer on title page and on upper right hand corner of page 1

Present location: British Library ADD MS 52464C

See also British Library LOAN 101.94a for annotated photocopy of this score. Annotations were incorporated into first printed edition.

Note: In 1973 the MS was used for the Britain in the Twentieth Century Exhibition.

First edition
Publication: © 1972 by Thames (Revised edition, 1971). Unpriced

CRUX FIDELIS (Opus 43, no.1)
Location of holograph unknown
Original copyist manuscript at Westminster Cathedral
No autograph annotations
13 pages; written on paper with printer's mark "W & Co."
No date, location or signature is apparent. Dedicated "To Imogen Holst" on top of page 1
Present location: Chester Music
No printed first edition

DEUX POÈMES DE PINDARE
Holograph in black ink with autograph corrections in pencil; overlays. Performance annotations in red and blue pencil. Bar lines in pencil
The score is written on 11 double sheets of 24-stave paper measuring 32.8 × 27 cm
The manuscript paper printer's mark is shown as on Néocopie Musical, Paris (No. 8) paper
Bound: sewn at spine, cover pages covered in waxy paper
Title page: Deux Poèmes de Pindare | Lennox Berkeley
[with "N.B. 36 rue Ballu, Paris-9o" stamp on title page]
44 pages:

p. [i]	Title page
p. [ii]	Blank
pp. 1–24	I. DITHYRAMBE
pp. 25–38	II. HYMNE: Allegro
pp. [39–42]	Blank

The manuscript is dedicated "A Madame la Princesse Edmond de Polignac" by the composer in upper centre of page 1
There is no date or place apparent
Signed by composer on title page on upper right hand corner of page 1
Present location: British Library: LOAN 101.70
No printed first edition

DIALOGUE FOR CELLO AND CHAMBER ORCHESTRA (Opus 79)
Full score
Location of holograph is unknown; description taken from dyeline copy

MANUSCRIPTS AND FIRST EDITIONS · 151

The score is written on 18-stave paper measuring 37 × 25.5 cm (approximately)
73 pages:
pp. 1–28   Andante
pp. 29–42   Lento
pp. 43–73   III. Allegro moderato
No date, dedication or location is apparent
Signed by composer upper right hand corner of page 1
Present location (dyelines): British Library LOAN 101.27. Two annotated copies of dyeline. One copy: "Revisions for Cheltenham Festival July '81 marked in red"; new pages added pp. 65–66
No printed first edition
Publication: © 1971 by J. & W. Chester Ltd; score and parts housed in hire library

Piano reduction

Holograph in black ink with minimal pencil annotations; overlays. Orchestration and performance rehearsal numbers in blue ink
The score is written on six double sheets and on both sides of two single sheets of 18-stave paper measuring 37 × 27.2 cm
No manuscript paper printer's mark is apparent
Title page [autograph]: C52a [pencil] | DIALOGUE | For | 'Cello & Orchestra | (Piano Reduction) | LENNOX BERKELEY
30 pages:
p. [i]   Title page
pp. [ii–iv]   Blank
pp. 1–3   I. Andante
pp. 3–11   Allegro
pp. 12–15   II. Lento
pp. 16–24   III. Allegro moderato
pp. [25–26]   Blank
No date, dedication or location is apparent
Signed by composer upper right hand corner of page 1
Present location: British Library: LOAN 101.26 with incomplete sketches in full score
No printed first edition
Publication: © 1971 by J. & W. Chester Ltd

A DINNER ENGAGEMENT (Opus 45)
Full score
Holograph fair copy in blue ink with large sections by copyist; autograph corrections in blue ink; performance annotations in blue crayon and lead pencil; extensive autograph overlays

The score is written on 19 double sheets of 22-stave paper measuring 35.8 × 26.5 cm and on 43 double sheets and both sides of two single sheets of 24-stave paper measuring 36.8 × 27 cm. Also single sheet of flyleaf at back

The manuscript paper printer's mark is shown on some sheets as [encircled] J & W | CHESTER | LTD | LONDON No.24

Bound in grey boards with green cloth spine; pages sewn together in spine, some pages have come away from binding.

Cover: A DINNER | ENGAGEMENT | OPERA | in | ONE ACT | by | Lennox Berkeley | Libretto by | Paul Dehn | [copyright]

Title page [autograph]: To Basil Douglas | A DINNER ENGAGEMENT | OPERA | IN | ONE ACT | BY | LENNOX BERKELEY | LIBRETTO BY | PAUL DEHN | [FULL SCORE]

250 pages:

p. [i]	Title page
p. [ii]	Orchestration (autograph): 1(pic&bfl).1.1(bcl).1/1000/hp/perc (only one player) for: timp (chromatic), Side Drum, Tenor Drum, Bass Drum, Cymbals, Triangle, Tambourine, Gong, Chinese Block/1.1.1.1.1
pp. 1–138	Music: A Dinner Engagement	SCENE I.	Allegro moderato; Lennox Berkeley; (Op:45)
pp. 139–204	Scene II: Molto Moderato [The formal presentations have been made.	The Duchess is peering through her lorgnettes] [cuts pp. 160–161]
pp. [203–204]	Duplicate page numbers follow original p. 204; numbering continues from there
pp. 205–231	Scene II continued
p. [231]	Duplicate page number
pp. 232–40	Scene II continued – end
p. [241]	Blank
p. [242]	Autograph four-bar sketch in pencil
p. [243]	Blank
pp. [244–5]	Blank endpapers – no staves

The manuscript is dated "1954" after double bar page 240 and dedicated "To Basil Douglas" on the title page by the composer

Signed by composer on upper right hand corner of page 1

Present location: British Library LOAN 101.50

No printed first edition

Publication: © 1954 by J. & W. Chester Ltd; score and parts housed in hire library

Vocal score

Holograph in black and blue ink with autograph pencil annotations and extensive overlays; rehearsal numbers in blue pencil

The score is written on one side of one single sheet of 20-stave paper measuring 34.2 × 24.8 cm; on two double sheets and both sides of 30 single sheets of 22-stave paper measuring 35.5 × 26.1 cm; on both sides of six single sheets of 18-stave paper measuring 36.5 × 27 cm; on both sides of four single sheets of 24-stave paper measuring 36 × 26.3 cm

The manuscript paper printer's mark is shown as:
[lyre motif] B.C.; No.6 (20 Staves).; Made and Printed in England by BOSWORTH & CO., LTD.; [encircled galleon] | A. L. No 16 | Printed in England; [encircled] J & W | CHESTER | LTD | LONDON No.18

No title page; page 1 [autograph]: To Basil Douglas | "A DINNER ENGAGEMENT" | Paul Dehn; SCENE I; Lennox Berkeley

93 pages:

p. 1	Scene I: Allegro Moderato
p. [2]	Blank
pp. 2–48	Scene I continued
pp. 48–59	Scene II: Molto moderato
	[The formal presentations have been made.	The Duchess is peering through her lorgnettes]
pp. [60–63]	Missing
pp. 64–93	Scene II continued

The manuscript is dated "Nov 1953 – March 1954" after the double bar on page 93 and dedicated "To Basil Douglas" upper centre page 1
Signed by the composer on the upper right hand of page 1
Present location: British Library: LOAN 101.49 with autograph pencil sketches

First edition (Vocal score)
A DINNER ENGAGEMENT | AN OPERA IN TWO SCENES | MUSIC BY | LENNOX BERKELEY | LIBRETTO BY | PAUL DEHN | Cover design by Peter Snow
99 pages. 297 × 223 mm
Stiff white paper wrappers. Lettered in grey with design by Peter Snow. Trimmed edges
Publication: © 1955 by J. & W. Chester Ltd (J.W.C.9752). Unpriced
Other versions
Printed vocal score used by English Opera Group: "Master Copy" with extensive annotations in pencil by composer and copyist; certain sections recomposed; typescript of synopsis inside front cover dated 9/4/54
Present location: Britten-Pears Library: 5H1 / 2-9104528; formerly in English Opera Group collection

Libretto
Typescript libretto with Paul Dehn's address typed on with annotations in blue ink possibly by Paul Dehn to do with either orchestration generally or with a

particular performance. For example, some lines are described as "inaudible" and pauses are suggested

Present location: British Library: LOAN 101.48 with annotated photocopy

DIVERSIONS FOR EIGHT INSTRUMENTS (Opus 63)

Holograph in black ink; queries in pencil by editor and autograph responses/additions in blue ink and pencil; bars crossed out; extensive overlays. Rehearsal numbers in blue ink and crayon

The score is written on three double sheets and on both sides of 12 single sheets of 20-stave paper measuring 36.5 × 27.1 cm and on two double sheets and on both sides of one single sheet of 24-stave paper measuring 35.5 × 25.4 cm

Bound with clear tape

No manuscript paper printer's mark is apparent for 20-stave paper; for 24-stave paper, the manuscript paper printer's mark is shown as: [encircled galleon] | A.L. No18 | Printed in England

Title page: [autograph] DIVERSIONS. | For | Oboe, Clarinet, Horn, Piano, Violin, Viola + 'Cello. | LENNOX BERKELEY | (1964)

46 pages:

p. [i]	Title page
p. [ii]	Blank
pp. 1–9	I. Adagio-Allegro
	pp. 8–9 Revised ending; overlay for last 15 bars
	p. [9a] "ending" [pencil autograph] crossed out
pp. 10–24	II. Vivace
	p. 18 Tempo I [pencil autograph] "see corrections"
	p. 23 Pencil sketch
p. [24a]	Blank
pp. 25–28	III. Lento
pp. 29–40	IV. Allegro
	pp. 32–34 completely rewritten using overlays
p. [41]	Blank
p. [42]	Pencil annotation [not autograph] "César Franck	Chorale No.3 in A minor

The manuscript is dated 1964 on title page and signed by the composer on upper right hand corner on page 1

There is no location or dedication apparent

Present location: British Library: LOAN 101.87a with dyeline of earlier version of holograph (before overlays applied); Errata sheet and sketch

Errata sheet

Holograph in pencil with red ink annotations

The errata pages are written on one double sheet of 24-stave paper measuring 36.4 × 27.1 cm
The manuscript paper printer's mark is shown as: [encircled galleon] | A.L. No18 | Printed in England
4 pages:
pp. [1–3]   Corrections for all movements
p. [4]   Blank
No date, location, dedication or signature apparent
Location: British Library: LOAN 101.87a with holograph
First edition (Score)
Lennox Berkeley | Diversions | Four Pieces for Eight Instruments | Chester Music
41 pages. 30 × 227 mm
White stiff paper wrappers. Lettered in dark and light blue. Trimmed edges
Publication: © 1983 by J. & W. Chester/Edition Wilhelm Hansen London Ltd (J.W.C.55313). Unpriced
Printed in England

DIVERTIMENTO IN Bb (Opus 18)
Location of holograph unknown
Copyist version
Manuscript copy by P.W. Tilbrook dated Dec. '43. No autograph annotations
Present location: British Library: LOAN 101.7
First edition (Miniature score)
DIVERTIMENTO | in B Flat | for ORCHESTRA | by | LENNOX BERKELEY | I Prelude | II Nocturne | III Scherzo | IV Finale | J. & W. CHESTER LTD LONDON [text encircling JWC emblem] | EDITION WILHELM HANSEN, LONDON
94 pages. 190 × 137 mm
White stiff paper wrappers. Lettered in blue and grey. Trimmed edges
Publication: © 1946 by J. & W. Chester Ltd (J.W.C.84)
Printed by Halstan & Co. Ltd, Amersham, Bucks

DOMINI EST TERRA (Opus 10)
Full score
Location of holograph unknown, details taken from dyeline copies
The score is written on 21 pages of 18-stave paper; cannot determine measurements
Title page [autograph]: Lennox Berkeley | Domini est terra

24 pages:
p. [i]   Title page
p. [ii]   Blank?
pp. 1–18   Moderato [2 x pp. 2, 3, 4]
                  [Sequence: 1, 2, 3, 2, 3, 4, 4, 5, 6, 7, 8 …]
p. [19]   Blank

The manuscript is dated "1937" after double bar p. 18 and dedicated "To Mdlle. Nadia Boulanger" by the composer in upper centre of page 1
Signed by the composer on upper right hand corner of page 1
Annotations to dyeline: minimal autograph additions in pencil. Also a pencil sketch of the Latin chant at the end of the manuscript on both copies, p. [19]. Inside cover stamped "N.B. 36 rue Ballu Paris-9o". Also "Op.10" added in pencil by composer
Present location: British Library: LOAN 101.71 with two dyeline copies
First edition (Choral score)
DOMINI EST TERRA | PSALM | FOR | CHORUS AND ORCHESTRA | MUSIC BY | LENNOX BERKELEY | Time of performance 9 minutes | J. & W. CHESTER, Ltd. | 11 Great Marlborough Street, London W.1
11 pages. 274 × 194 mm
Buff paper covers. Lettered in black. Trimmed edges
Publication: © 1938 by J. & W. Chester Ltd (J.W.C.9738). Unpriced

DUO FOR CELLO AND PIANO (Opus 81, no.1)

Holograph in black ink with autograph corrections and additions in pencil; overlays. Other performance annotations in pencil
The unbound score is written on six double sheets of 16-stave paper measuring 30.1 × 24.2 cm
No manuscript paper printer's mark is apparent
No title page; p. 1: [autograph] DUO
24 pages:
p. [i]   "Kathron Sturrock" in red felt tip pen; pencil markings, address rubbed out
p. [ii]   Blank
pp. 1–18   Allegro moderato
pp. [19–22]   Blank

The manuscript is dated "October–November 1971" after double bar page 18
No location or dedication is apparent
Signed by the composer on upper right hand corner of page 1
Present location: British Library: LOAN 101.87f with incomplete pencil draft and sketches

First edition
Commissioned by the Park Lane Group for their Young Artists and 20th Century Music Series, London, January 1972 | LENNOX BERKELEY | DUO | for cello and piano | Duration 9 minutes | [JWC intertwined logo] with words: J.&W. CHESTER LTD LONDON in circle on outside | [international publishers]
Score: 14 pages; Part: 8 pages. 304 × 238 mm
White stiff paper wrappers. Lettered in blue and grey. Trimmed edges
Publication: © 1973 by J. & W. Chester Ltd (J.W.C.476). Unpriced

DUO FOR OBOE AND CELLO
Manuscript in private hands
No printed first edition

THE ECSTATIC
Holograph in blue ink with title information in black ink and correction in pencil p. [2], bar 23
The score is written on both sides of one double sheet of 18-stave paper, measuring 36.5 × 27 cm
The manuscript paper printer's mark is shown as (encircled) J&W | CHESTER | LTD | LONDON | No.18
No title page; p. [1]: The Ecstatic | Cecil Day Lewis; Lennox Berkeley
4 pages:
pp. [1–4]   Music
The manuscript is dated "1943" by the composer
No place or dedication apparent
Signed on upper right hand corner of p. [1]; dated by composer after double bar line on p. [4]
Present location: Britten-Pears Library 5H1 / 2-9104519; formerly in Benjamin Britten's collection
No printed first edition

ELEGY FOR VIOLIN AND PIANO (Opus 33, no.2a)
Location of holograph unknown
First edition
LENNOX BERKELEY | ELEGY | for | Violin and Piano | Price 2s. 6d. net* | J. & W. Chester, Ltd. | 11, Great Marlborough Street, | London, W1
4 pages. 309 × 242 (no separate violin part)
Light blue paper wrappers. Lettered in black. Trimmed edges

Publication: © 1951 by J. & W. Chester Ltd (J.W.C.395) @ 2/6. (Later published with Toccata Op.33 no.3)

Other versions
Elegy for String Orchestra (Opus 33, no.2b)
Two holographs
A: Holograph draft in pencil with extensive autograph corrections and additions in pencil
The unbound score is written on one double sheet of 16-stave paper measuring 36.4 × 27 cm
No manuscript paper printer's mark is apparent
No title page; p. [1]: [autograph in pencil] Violin + String Orch:
4 pages:
pp. [1–4]   [draft]
No date, dedication, location or signature apparent
Present location: British Library: LOAN 101.39b with (B)
B: Holograph in black ink; minimal overlays
The unbound score is written on one double sheet of 20-stave paper measuring 36.7 × 27 cm and wrapped in one double sheet of 24-stave paper measuring 37.9 × 27.1 cm
No manuscript paper printer's mark apparent for first double sheet, for second double sheet it is shown as B&H [incorporated into music globe design]
Title page: ELEGY for Strings. | Lennox Berkeley | April 1978
8 pages:
p. [i]   Title page
p. [ii]   Blank
pp. [1–3]   Elegy | Andante
pp. [4–6]   Blank
The manuscript is dated "April 1978" on title page and dedicated "In memory of Essie and to the Craxton family" by the composer on top of page [1]
No location is apparent
Signed by the composer on title page and on upper right hand corner of page [1]
Present location: British Library: LOAN 101.39b with (A)
No printed first edition
Publication: © 1978 by J. & W. Chester Ltd; score and parts housed in hire library

ELEVEN-FIFTY (Opus 14, no.2)
Holograph in black ink with minimal autograph additions and corrections in pencil; pencil sketch of alternative ending following double bar page [3]
The score is written on both sides of one double sheet of 20-stave paper measuring 32.7 × 26.9 cm

The manuscript paper printer's mark is shown as Néocopie Musicale, Paris (No. 7)

No title page; p. [1]: ELEVEN-FIFTY | Words by | Patrick O'Malley | Lennox Berkeley

4 pages:

pp. [1–3]   Music "Allegro"
p. [3]   Autograph pencil sketch of alternative ending
p. [4]   Blank

The manuscript is dated "Oct 1938" by composer after double bar on page [3]
No location or dedication is apparent
Signed on upper right hand corner of page [1]
Present location: British Library: LOAN 101.92d
No printed first edition

FALDON PARK [Incomplete] (Opus 100)
Full score

Holograph [incomplete] in black ink with autograph annotations in pencil and additions [not autograph] in blue ink

The score is written on 14 double sheets and both sides of two single sheets of 20-stave paper measuring 37.4 × 26.6 cm and on one side of one single sheet of 18-stave paper measuring 36.7 × 27.4 cm

The manuscript paper printer's mark is shown as B&H [incorporated into music globe design]

Title page: (FULL SCORE) [black ink] | ACT 1 [blue ink] with non-autograph pencil annotation with title and one-bar sketch in pencil which could be autograph

62 pages:

p. [i]   Title page
p. [ii]   Blank
pp. 1–6   Winton Dean; Faldon Park; Lennox Berkeley | Lento
pp. 6–20   Allegro "Enter removal men"
pp. 20–22   "The Park, my lovely park" (Barbara)
pp. 23–30   "We live today" (Lord Digby) incomplete, end "richest moment of your ... [life.]"
p. [31]   Blank
pp. [32–34]   Sketches in black ink – unidentified
pp. [35–60]   Blank

No date, dedication or location is apparent
Signed by the composer on upper right hand corner of page 1
Present location: British Library: LOAN 101.61

Vocal score
Holograph [incomplete] in black ink with annotations in black ink and pencil and extensive overlays
The score is written on 12 double sheets and on both sides of 15 single sheets of 18-stave paper measuring 36.8 × 27.2 cm
The manuscript paper printer's mark is shown as B&H [incorporated into music globe design]
Not bound but wrapped loosely inside buff foolscap folder. Cover: FALDON PARK [autograph]; Piano Score | First Drafts Only | Act I to Entry of Colonel (March) [the entire aria] | + Xerox of same [moved to BL LOAN 101.63] | All copied by S.B. [Susan Bradshaw]
No title page; Page 1: FALDON PARK | ACT ONE | Scene I | Lento Lennox Berkeley
78 pages:

pp. 1–2	Act One, Scene one, Lento
pp. 2–7	Allegro (Enter two removal men)
pp. 8–11	Andantino "Sad to see an old place go" (2nd man)
pp. 11–12	Lento, Barbara and Sir Digby "The Park my lovely park"
pp. 12–14	Allegretto "We live today" (Barbara and Sir Digby)
pp. 14–17	Andante "Give me the golden age" (Barbara)
pp. 17–19	Andante Quartet (B, Sir D, 2 men)
pp. 19–24	Allegro moderato "Come Barbara" (Sir Digby)
pp. 25–29	Allegro moderato Chorus "Have you heard the latest news?"
pp. 30–37	Tempo I: Enter Sir Bartholomew and Lady Skipton
pp. 37–41	Lento "Oh please be merciful" (Lady Skipton)
pp. 41–46	Allegro "You married couples are all the same" (Martin)
pp. 46–50	Allegretto "I'm sorry Mother" (Martin)
pp. 51–54	Andantino Trio (Lady S, Martin, Sir Bartholomew)
pp. 54–55	Allegro vivace (Fothergill and Eleana) "We've heard the news"
pp. 55–57	Allegro "A Serpent at my table"
pp. 57–58	Lento [Andante crossed out] "Good Sir Bartholomew"
pp. 59–62	Allegro "Oh really Sir this is too mych" (Fothergill)
pp. 62–70	Lento: "The unbroken colt"
pp. 70–77	Enter Colonel and Militia Band; Interlude followed by "On Blenheim Field" (Colonel) incomplete, stops after "When England's manhood to itself was … [true]"
p. [78]	Blank, back of photocopied page

No date, location or dedication apparent
The manuscript is signed by the composer on upper right hand corner of page 1
Present location: British Library: LOAN 101.61; with annotated photocopies LOAN 101.63/64; sketches LOAN 101.62

Other versions
Notebook containing partial autograph vocal score draft in pencil
Spiral bound with grey mottled cover, twenty-six sheets of 12-stave paper measuring 33.8 × 24.5 cm
32 pages:

pp. 11–24	from beginning of duet Barbara with Sir D "The Park my lovely park"
pp. [25–52]	ends with duet Lady and Sir B "He's a scoundrel and a wastrel – Good Sir remember your salad days"

Present location: British Library: LOAN 101.60
Copyist version (Vocal score)
Photocopy of vocal score copied by Susan Bradshaw, comb-bound (white) in stiff blue paper wrappers; with autograph corrections in pencil. From beginning to middle of Colonel's aria
Present location: British Library: LOAN 101.64
No printed first edition
Publication: © 1982 by J. & W. Chester Ltd; score and parts housed in hire library
Libretto
Typescript of synopsis with autograph annotations in black ink (5 single sheets)
Two photocopies of complete libretto, with some autograph annotations in pencil; one incomplete copy with extensive annotations; replacement typescript pages with autograph annotations in blue ink; one notebook page with autograph corrections in black ink
Letter from Lord Harewood, Managing Director ENO (28 March 1979) regarding commissioning of opera with Winton Dean 2½ years before
Present location: British Library: LOAN 101.59

FANFARE FOR THE ROYAL ACADEMY OF MUSIC BANQUET
Holograph in black ink with pencil barlines and overlays
The score is written on one double sheet of 12-stave paper measuring 29.4 × 23.4 cm
No manuscript paper printer's mark is apparent
Title page: FANFARE | for the | Royal Academy of Music Banquet. | 1972
4 pages:

p. [i]	Title page
pp. 1–3	Music: Moderato

The manuscript is dated 1972 and dedicated to the Royal Academy of Music by composer on title page
Signed by composer on upper right hand corner of page 1
Present location: Royal Academy of Music: RAM MS No.448

Other versions
Photocopy of copyist manuscript
Present location: British Library: LOAN 101.39a
No printed first edition
Publication: © 1972 by J. & W. Chester Ltd; score and parts housed in hire library

FANTASIA FOR ORGAN (Opus 92)
Location of holograph unknown
Sketches
Substantial number of sketches and partial drafts
Present location: British Library: LOAN 101.91d
First edition
Lennox Berkeley | Fantasia for Organ | CHESTER MUSIC | J. & W. Chester/Edition Wilhelm Hansen London Ltd
17 pages. 298 × 222 mm
White stiff paper wrappers. Lettered in blue. Trimmed edges
Publication: © 1977 by J. & W. Chester/Edition Wilhelm Hansen London Ltd (J.W.C.55090). Unpriced

A FESTIVAL ANTHEM (Opus 21, no.2)
Holograph in alternating black and blue ink with autograph pencil annotations, some partially erased. Pencil sketch on page 13 of organ solo. Publication details in blue ink on bottom page 1
The unbound score is written on five double sheets of 24-stave paper measuring 36.8 × 27.2 cm
The manuscript paper printer's mark is shown as [encircled] J & W | CHESTER | LTD. | LONDON | No.24
No title page; p. 1: [autograph in black ink] Festival Anthem
20 pages:

pp. 1–5	Lento (organ)
	p. 1 "Sion's daughters"
	p. 4 "Splendid and terrible"
pp. 5–7	L'Istesso Tempo (organ)
	p. 6 "Christ whose joys"
pp. 7–10	Andantino "O that I once past changing were"
pp. 11–13	Moderato "Death and darkness"
	p. 11 "Piu Lento "Graves are beds now"
	p. 12 [pencil] Tempo "The weak and aged"
pp. 13–15	Andante Maestoso "Then unto him"

p. [16]	Blank
p. [17]	Autograph sketch in pencil of last bars of music
pp. [18–20]	Blank

The manuscript is dated "May–June 1945" after double bar page 15 and dedicated "For the Rev: Walter Hussey + the Choirs of St. Matthews Northampton" on top of page 1 by the composer

No location is apparent

The manuscript is signed by the composer on the upper right hand corner of page 1
Present location: West Sussex Record Office: Hussey papers (H288) with note on half sheet (torn): [autograph in blue ink] Dear Walter Hussey. | Here is, at last, my MS. | with many apologies for having taken so long to send it | Yrs Sin [stet] | Lennox Berkeley

First edition
A | FESTIVAL ANTHEM | FOR | CHORUS AND ORGAN | MUSIC BY | LENNOX BERKELEY | [Chester logo]
31 pages. 272 × 191 mm
Blue paper wrappers. Lettered in black. Trimmed edges
Publication: © 1945 by J. & W. Chester Ltd (J.W.C.9741). Unpriced
Printed by Bradford & Dickens Ltd

Andantino from A Festival Anthem
Andantino "O that I once past changing were" was arranged by the composer for cello and piano; arranged by Jennifer Bate for organ. See separate entries

FIVE CHINESE SONGS (Opus 78)

Location of complete holograph unknown
Details taken from dyeline
The score is written on 16 sheets of 16-stave paper
The manuscript paper printer's mark is shown as WH Nr.5.F.16 [perpendicular bottom left]
Title page [autograph]: Chinese Songs | Lennox Berkeley
16 pages:

p. [i]	Title page
pp. 1–3	I. People Hide Their Love	Wu-Ti, Liang Dynasty (AD 464–549). Trans. Arthur Waley	Andante con moto
pp. 4–7	II. The Autumn Wind	Wu-Ti (157–87 BC Han Dynasty)	Trans: Arthur Waley	Allegretto	Gently flowing
pp. 8–9	III. Dreaming of A Dead Lady	Shen-Yo (AD 441–513)	Trans. Arthur Waley	Slow. Sustained and intense
pp. 10–13	IV. Late Spring	Yang Knang	Trans: R. Kotewall + N.L. Smith	Moderato

pp. 14–15   V. The Riverside Village | Ssu-K'ung Shu | Trans: Kotewall + Smith. | Calm and Slow (Andante tranquillo)

The manuscript is dated "Nov. 1970 – Jan. 1971" after double bar on page 15 and dedicated "To Meriel and Peter Dickinson" upper centre page 1
Signed by the composer on title page and on upper right hand corner of page 1
Present location: British Library: LOAN 101.94c with sketches and annotated proof copies of II & III

Amongst sketches:
Releasing a Migrant Yen [not used in final version]
Incomplete rough draft holograph in pencil
The score is written on one double sheet of 16-stave paper measuring 34 × 27 cm
The manuscript paper printer's mark is shown as [vertical along spine] WH Nr.5.F.16
No title page
4 pages:
pp. 1–4   Music
No date, dedication, location or signature is apparent

Dreaming of a Dead Lady (no. III)
Holograph in black ink
The score is written on one double sheet of 16-stave paper measuring 34 × 27 cm
The manuscript paper printer's mark is shown as [vertical along spine] WH Nr.5.F.16
No title page
4 pages:
pp. 1–3   Slow. Sustained and intense
p. 4   4-bar pencil sketch
No date, dedication, location or signature is apparent
Present location: British Library LOAN 101.94c with sketches of other songs

First edition
LENNOX BERKELEY | Five Chinese Songs | Op.78 | for medium voice and piano | CHESTER MUSIC | J.&W. Chester/Edition Wilhelm Hansen London Ltd. | Eagle Court, London EC1M 5QD
16 pages. 298 × 221 mm
White stiff paper wrappers. Lettered in blue and grey. Trimmed edges
Publication: © 1975 by J. & W. Chester Ltd (J.W.C.8903) @ £3.99

FIVE HERRICK POEMS (Opus 89)
Three holographs
A: Holograph in black and blue ink with autograph additions and corrections in pencil; extensive overlays. Songs 1–3, 5 in black ink; song 4 in blue ink
The score is written on two double sheets and on both sides of four sheets of 16-stave paper measuring 36.6 × 26.8 cm wrapped inside one double sheet of

20-stave paper measuring 36.8 × 26.8 cm

Title page [autograph]: FIVE HERRICK POEMS, | FOR | VOICE & HARP | LENNOX BERKELEY | [pencil, not sure if autograph] Op 88 Op. 89

18 pages:

p. [i]	Title page
p. [ii]	Blank
pp. 1–3	I. Moderato
	Pencil annotation [not autograph] "23.21.76 Definitive version"
pp. 4–6	II. Lento (Slow and sombre) Adagio (Very slow and sombre)
pp. 7–9	III. Allegretto. Smooth & flowing
pp. 10–12	IV. Andante (Slow but freely)
pp. 13–15	V. Allegretto ["Love, love begets"]
pp. [16–18]	Blank

The manuscript is dated [not autograph] "23.1.76 Definitive version" and dedicated "For Peter Pears" by the composer on top of page 1

No location is apparent

Signed by the composer on upper right hand corner of page 1

B: Holograph [incomplete] in black ink with autograph corrections and additions in pencil; overlays

The score is written on one double sheet and two single sheets of 20-stave paper measuring 36.9 × 26.8 cm

No manuscript paper printer's mark is apparent

Spine formerly bound together with clear tape

No title page

18 pages:

pp. 1–2	I. Andante (♩=76)
pp. 3–4	II. Lento, ♩=54
[p.5	end of II missing]
[p.6	beginning of III missing]
pp. 7–8	end of III
pp. 8–10	IV. Slow but freely (about ♩=60)

No date, dedication or location is apparent

Signed by the composer on upper right hand corner of page 1

C: Holograph in pencil

The score is written on four double sheets and on both sides of ten single sheets of 16-stave paper measuring 29.1 × 26.8 cm

36 pages:

pp. 1–3	[II]
pp. 4–6	[I]
pp. 7–9	[III]
p. [10]	Sketches

pp. 10–11   [IV]
pp. [12–17]   [IV]
pp. [18–20]   [V] "If nine times you"
pp. [23–24]   sketches
pp. [25–27]   [IV]
pp. [28–35]   sketches

No date, dedication, location or signature is apparent

Present location: British Library: LOAN 101.94d with sketches, drafts of songs, two annotated photocopies

Note: Song V in (A) "Love, love begets" was abandoned in favour of "If nine times you your bridegroom kisse" (see holograph below)

Also: Two annotated photocopies of holograph

A: Photocopy of holograph bearing annotation in red ink "CORRECTED COPY AS PER L.B. & O.E. [Osian Ellis]. ORIGINAL VERSION (1973–74)"

Title page: | Op. 88 | Property of Osian Ellis, | 90, Chandos Ave., | London.N.20. Original probably with Osian Ellis (90 Chandos Avenue, London N20)

B: Photocopy (incomplete) of holograph which has been annotated: contains missing title page and pages 5–6 but is itself missing page 1

Present location: British Library: LOAN 101.94d with holograph and drafts

If Nine Times you your bridegroom kisse (no. V)

Holograph in black ink with annotations in black and red ink

The score is written on both sides of a single sheet of 20-stave paper measuring 36.6 cm

No manuscript paper printer's mark is apparent

2 pages:

pp. [1–2]   V Allegro moderato

No date, dedication, location or signature is apparent

Present location: British Library: LOAN 101.94d with holograph, drafts, sketches and annotated photocopies

Also: Photocopy of this holograph is attached to photocopy (A) of entire holograph bearing annotation in red ink "CORRECTED COPY AS PER L.B. & O.E. [Osian Ellis]. ORIGINAL VERSION (1973–74)"

No printed first edition

Publication: © 1974 by J. & W. Chester/Edition Wilhelm Hansen (copyist score in Chester archive), 12 pages

FIVE HOUSMAN SONGS (Opus 14, no.3)

First version

Entitled **Four Songs,** incorporating songs I–IV

Holograph in black ink with minimal autograph corrections in pencil; included with score, on blue notepaper, are French translations of poems by composer (6 leaves; 12.8 × 6.2 cm)

The score is written on two double sheets of 16-stave paper measuring 35.1 × 27.1 cm wrapped inside one double sheet of 28-stave paper measuring 36.5 × 27.1 cm

No manuscript paper printer's mark apparent

Title page [autograph in black ink]: FOUR SONGS | Lennox Berkeley | (Poems by A.E. Housman)

12 pages:

p. [i]	Title page
p. [ii]	Blank
pp. [1–2]	A.E. Housman; Lennox Berkeley	I	Andante [The half moon westers low, my love]
pp. [2–5]	II. Allegro-alla marcia [The street sounds to the soldiers tread]
p. [5]	III. Lento ma non troppo [He would not stay for me]
pp. [6–7]	IV. Andante con moto [Look not in my eyes]
pp. [8–10]	Blank

The manuscript is dated "Jan 1940" after double bar p. [7]

No dedication or location is apparent

Signed by composer on title page and on upper right hand corner p. [1]

Present location: British Library: LOAN 101.92e

No printed first edition in this version

Revised version

Holograph in black ink with some pencil annotations, all autograph

Score is written on one side of one double sheet of 12-stave paper measuring 35 × 27 cm and both sides of three double sheets of 18-stave paper measuring 35.5 × 25.5 cm

No manuscript printer's mark apparent

Title page: LENNOX BERKELEY | Five Songs | (A.E. HOUSMAN) | op.14/3 [pencil annotation] | P.P. Inventory No. 34

16 pages

p. [i]	Title page
p. [ii]	Blank
pp. 1–2	To Peter Fraser	A.E. Housman; Lennox Berkeley	I. Andante
pp. 3–6	II. Allegro, alla marcia
p. 6	III. Lento
pp. 7–8	IV. Andante con moto
pp. 9–11	IV [sic] Andantino [Because I liked you better]
pp. [12–14]	Blank

The manuscript is dated "London, 1940" by the composer after the double bar on p. 11

The manuscript is signed and dedicated "To Peter Fraser" on upper right hand corner of p. 1
Present location: Britten-Pears Library 5H1 / 2-9104522; formerly in Peter Pears' collection
Also: Edited version
Photocopy of holograph of revised version with annotations: On title page in pencil: "Manuscript at Aldeburgh Britten-Pears Library"; note on pink paper: "Corrections made by composer 1980". Autograph pencil sketches on pp. 1, 2, 9. Numbering of songs corrected by composer; second IV made V
Present location: British Library: LOAN 101.92e
First edition
Lennox Berkeley | Five | Housman Songs | Chester Music
13 pages. 304 × 229 mm
White stiff paper wrappers. Lettered in blue. Trimmed edges
Publication: © 1983 by J. & W. Chester/Edition Wilhelm Hansen London Ltd (J.W.C.55160). Unpriced
Printed in England

FIVE PIECES FOR VIOLIN AND ORCHESTRA (Opus 56)

Holograph [incomplete] in black ink with pencil annotations
The unbound score is written on both sides of 28 single sheets of 22-stave paper measuring 36.8 × 27 cm
No manuscript paper printer's mark is apparent
No title page
56 pages:
pp. 11–12, 15 [I. Lento incomplete]
pp. 16–24 II. "Allegro"
pp. 30–47 [III. Allegro scherzando incomplete]
pp. 47–50 IV. "Andante"
pp. 51–75 V. "Allegro"
The manuscript is dated "Dec. 28th 1961"
No dedication, location or signature is apparent
Present location: British Library: LOAN 101.21b
First edition (Piano reduction and part)
Lennox Berkeley | FIVE PIECES | for violin and orchestra | Op. 56 | Piano reduction by | the composer | [photocopy warning] | CHESTER MUSIC | J & W Chester/Edition Wilhelm Hansen London Ltd. | Eagle Court, London EC1M 5QD
Score, 35 pages; part 13 pages. 304 × 229 mm
White stiff paper wrappers. Lettered in light and dark blue. Trimmed edges

Publication: © 1988 by J. & W. Chester/Edition Wilhelm Hansen London Ltd (CH55778). Unpriced

FIVE POEMS by W.H. Auden (Opus 53)
Holograph in black and blue ink with production annotations in pencil; overlays
The score is written on both sides of nine single sheets of 14-stave paper measuring 36.7 × 27.1 cm wrapped inside one double sheet of 18-stave paper measuring 35.9 × 26.6 cm
The manuscript paper printer's mark is shown as [encircled] J.&.W. | Chester | Ltd. | LONDON
No title page; p. 1 [autograph]: To Mrs. Alice Esty | Op.53; W.H. Auden | Lennox Berkeley
18 pages:

pp. 1–4	I. Lauds: Allegretto
[pp. 5–6	Missing]
pp. 7–9	II. O lurcher-loving collier: Andante
pp. 10–13	III. What's in your mind: Moderato
pp. 14–16	IV. Eyes look into the well: Lento
pp. 17–20	V. Carry her over the water: Leggiere [crossed out]; Allegro moderato [crossed out] and "Moderato" added in another hand

The manuscript is dated "April–June 1958" after the double bar p. 20 and dedicated "To Mrs. Esty" [crossed out; replaced with] "Mrs. Alice Esty" on upper left of p. 1
Signed by composer on upper right hand corner of p. 1
Other versions
Annotated dyeline of holograph with dyeline of missing autograph title page [autograph]: FIVE POEMS | BY | W.H. AUDEN | LENNOX BERKELEY and autograph annotations in blue ink, especially tempo markings; performance annotations in pencil
Present location: British Library: LOAN 101.93b
Also: Sketches of pages 1–3 (I.) with pencil holograph complete for II
First edition
Cover: LENNOX BERKELEY | FIVE POEMS | (W. H. AUDEN) | J. & W. Chester, Ltd. | 11 Great Marlborough Street, London, W.1
16 pages. 309 × 244 mm
Blue paper wrappers. Lettered in black. Trimmed edges
Publication: © 1960 by J. & W. Chester Ltd (J.W.C.4060) @ 7/6
Printed by kind permission of Messrs Curtis Brown Ltd, London
Engraved by Lowe and Brydone (Printers) Ltd, London. Printed in England

FIVE SHORT PIECES FOR PIANO (Opus 4)
Location of holograph unknown
First edition
FIVE SHORT PIECES | Lennox Berkeley | J. & W. CHESTER, Ltd. | 11 Great Marlborough Street, London W.1
11 pages. 308 × 244 mm
Blue paper wrappers. Lettered in black. Trimmed edges
Publication: © 1937 by J. & W. Chester Ltd (J.W.C.2238). Unpriced

FIVE SONGS (Walter de la Mare) (Opus 26)
Holograph in black and blue ink with minimal autograph annotations in pencil; overlays
The score is written on four double sheets of 12-stave paper measuring 30.5 × 24 cm wrapped in one double sheet of 12-stave paper measuring 31.5 × 25 cm
No title page; p. 1 [autograph]: To Pierre Bernac and Francis Poulenc [pencil autograph] | I | Walter de la Mare; The Horseman; Lennox Berkeley | BER-2 [on masking tape covers]: To Pierre & Francis; Lennox 1946 [blue/black ink autograph]
20 pages:

pp. [i–ii]	Blank
pp. 1–3	I. The Horseman Moderato
pp. 3–6	II. Mistletoe Andante tranquillo
pp. 6–8	III. Poor Henry Lento
pp. 8–12	IV. The Song of the Soldiers Allegro
pp. 12–16	V. Silver Lento ma non troppo
pp. 17–18	Blank

The manuscript is dated June 1946 after double bar p. 16
Signed by composer and dedicated "To Pierre Bernac and Francis Poulenc" by the composer on top of p. 1
Present location: British Library: LOAN 101.92g
First edition
FIVE SONGS | For Medium Voice | Words by | Walter de la Mare | The Horseman | Mistletoe | Poor Henry | The Song of the Soldiers | Silver | Music by | LENNOX BERKELEY | J. & W. CHESTER, Ltd. | 11, Great Marlborough Street, London, W.1
15 pages. 305 × 241 mm
Buff stiff paper wrappers. Lettered in black. Trimmed edges
Publication: © 1948 by J. & W. Chester Ltd (J.W.C.4042) @ 6/-
Printed in England

FOUR CONCERT STUDIES FOR PIANO (Opus 14, no.1)
Location of holograph unknown
Annotated printed copy
Present location: British Library ADD MS 64984 (Curzon Collection)
First edition
LENNOX BERKELEY | FOUR | CONCERT STUDIES | FOR PIANO | Schott & Co. Ltd., 48 Great Marlborough Street, London W.1
18 pages. 303 × 228 mm
Stiff buff paper wrappers. Lettered in black. Trimmed edges
Publication: © 1940 by Schott (S. & Co. 5076) @ 3/-
Printed in England

FOUR CONCERT STUDIES FOR PIANO (Opus 82)
Holograph in black ink with autograph corrections in pencil and black ink, some final bars changed; overlays
The unbound score is written on five double sheets of 14-stave paper measuring 34.2 × 27 cm
The manuscript paper printer's mark is shown as WH Nr.4.F.14
Title page: FOUR PIANO STUDIES | LENNOX BERKELEY
20 pages:

p. [i]	Title page
p. [ii]	COMMISSIONED BY	LORD CHAPLIN	for	MARGARET BRUCE
pp. 1–4	I. Allegro Moderato
pp. 5–7	II. Allegro
p. [7a]	Blank
pp. 8–11	III. Lento
	p. 9 Allegretto
	p. 10 Lento
	p. 11 Ending is changed – last two bars
pp. 12–15	IV. Presto leggiero
pp. [16–17]	Blank

The manuscript is dated "Feb.-March 1972" after double bar page 15
No location or dedication is apparent
Signed by the composer on upper right hand corner of page 1
Present location: British Library: LOAN 101.89g with pencil and ink drafts, sketches, and annotated dyeline (minimal annotations for fingering, page 1)
First edition
Lennox Berkeley | FOUR PIANO STUDIES | CHESTER MUSIC | J. & W. Chester/Edition Wilhelm Hansen London Limited

15 pages. 298 × 223 mm
White stiff paper wrappers. Lettered in blue. Trimmed edges
Publication: © 1976 by J. & W. Chester Ltd (J.W.C.55076). Unpriced
Printed in England

FOUR PIECES FOR SMALL ORCHESTRA
Location of complete holograph unknown
No. 3
Holograph in black/brown ink
The unbound score is written on three double sheets of 16-stave paper measuring 35.5 × 26.3 cm
The manuscript paper printer's mark is shown as [encircled galleon] A. L. No 10 | Printed in England
No title page; page [1]: [autograph] Four Pieces for Small Orch
12 pages:

| pp. [1–6] | III. Lento |
| pp. [7–12] | Blank |

No date, dedication, location or signature apparent
Present location: British Library: LOAN 101.39c
No printed first edition

FOUR POEMS OF ST TERESA OF AVILA (Opus 27)
Full score
Holograph in black ink with corrections in pencil; overlays
The score is written on six double sheets of 20-stave paper measuring 36.5 × 27 cm
The manuscript paper printer's mark is shown as [encircled] J&W | CHESTER | LTD | LONDON No.20
Bound in orange paper covers with spine sewn and taped
Title page: [stamp] 26267 | LENNOX BERKELEY | FOUR POEMS | BY | St TERESA | FOR | CONTRALTO | AND | STRING ORCHESTRA | [Chester library stamp] | [pencil] 3.2.2.2.1
24 pages:

p. [i]	Title page
p. [ii]	Orchestrations, annotations [black ink] 4 2 2 2 1 [pencil] 6 4 4 3 1	"More strings may be used, but the same proportion should be maintained. The work cannot be played with less."
pp. 1–6	I. If Lord Thy love for me is strong: Moderato
pp. 7–10	II. Shepherd, shepherd hark that calling: Allegro
pp. 11–13	III. Let mine eyes see Thee: Andante

pp. 14–20   IV. Today a shepherd and our kin: Allegro moderato
pp. [21–22] Blank

The manuscript is dated by composer "Feb–May 1947" afer double bar page 20
Dedicated by composer "To John Greenidge" upper centre of page 1
Signed by the composer on title page and on upper right hand corner of page 1
Present location: British Library: ADD MS 59538

Shepherd, Shepherd

Autograph rough draft in pencil of Shepherd, Shepherd [incomplete] on both sides of one single sheet of 26-stave paper measuring 37 × 27.5 cm
Present location: British Library: LOAN 101.72

Other versions

Copyist score with minimal autograph annotations in pencil, including changing tempo of No. 2 from Allegro Moderato to Allegretto and No. 3 from Andante to Andantino. Dated 1947 on Title page of score
Location: LOAN 101.72

Vocal score (or piano reduction)
Holograph in blue and blue/black ink with autograph annotations in pencil
The score is written on four double sheets of 20-stave paper measuring 36.5 × 26.6 cm
The manuscript paper printer's mark is shown as [encircled] J & W | CHESTER | LTD | LONDON No.20
Bound in stiff orange paper wrappers with tape, not sewn and pages loose
No title page; untitled; front cover gives title and "Piano Reduction" on Chester's Circulating Music Library label
16 pages:

pp. 1–4   I. Moderato [If Lord, Thy love for me is strong]
pp. 4–7   II. Allegro [Shepherd, shepherd, hark that calling!]
pp. 7–9   III. Andante [Let mine eyes see Thee]
pp. 10–[14] IV. Allegro moderato [Today a shepherd and our kin]
pp. [15–16] Blank

The manuscript is dated "Feb–April 1947" after double bar page [14]
No dedication or location apparent
Signed by composer upper right hand corner of page 1
Present location: British Library: LOAN 101.72/73 and ADD MS 59538

Original copyist manuscript

Minimal additions and corrections in pencil, possibly autograph; one-page typescript of programme notes by "O.T" accompanying manuscript (two pages of draft in full score per BRITISH LIBRARY CAT.)

First edition

FOUR POEMS | of | St. TERESA of AVILA | for Contralto and String Orchestra | Music by | LENNOX BERKELEY | Full Score | (with Piano reduction) | String parts available on hire | [decorative border featuring Pan playing pipes] J.&W. CHESTER LTD. | LONDON: 11, Great Marlborough Street, W.1. | [international distributors]

42 pages. 306 × 239 mm

Grey paper wrappers. Lettered in black. Trimmed edges

Publication: © 1949 by J. & W. Chester Ltd (J.W.C.116). Unpriced

Other versions

String parts, each with the name Kathleen Ferrier added on the first page

No autograph annotations

Present location: British Library: LOAN 101.D.73

FOUR RONSARD SONNETS (SET 1) (Opus 40)

Original version

A: Holograph in black ink with overlays

The score is written on both sides of 12 single sheets of 14-stave paper measuring 34 × 27 cm and wrapped in one double sheet of 14-stave paper measuring 34 × 27 cm

The manuscript paper printer's mark is shown as WH Nr.4 F.14 on lower left hand corner of page

Title page: FOUR RONSARD SONNETS | (Set 1) | for Two Tenors and Piano | Op.40 | LENNOX BERKELEY

28 pages:

p. [i]	Title page
p. [ii]	Blank
pp. 1–6	I. Allegro con brio [Marie levez-vous]
pp. 7–10	II. Andante [Comme un void sur la branche]
pp. 11–15	III. Allegro appassionato [Ôtez votre beauté]
pp. 16–23	IV. Lento [Adieu, cruelle, adieu]
p. [24]	Blank
p. [25]	Old title page crossed out [autograph blue ink]: RONSARD SONNETS ["Four" added in blue ink, not autograph]	Set 1, for TWO TENORS & Piano	LENNOX BERKELEY
p. [26]	Blank

No date, dedication or location is apparent

Signed by composer on upper right hand corner of page 1

Present location: British Library: LOAN 101.93a with annotated dyeline and sketches

B: Holograph in blue ink with extensive pencil annotations by Berkeley and Peter Pears

The score is written on both sides of seven single sheets and two double sheets of

22-stave paper, measuring 36.5 × 27 cm
Sellotape binding pp. 1–23 and encased in two double sheets of 22-stave paper
No manuscript printer's mark apparent
P.P. Inv.No.35 | FOUR | RONSARD | SONNETS | FOR | TWO TENORS | & | PIANO | Lennox Berkeley | Op.40 [pencil, not autograph] | 9104523
34 pages:

p. [i]	"P.P.Inv.No.35" [Peter Pears Inventory No.35] in pencil
pp. [ii–iv]	Blank
p. [v]	Title page
p. [vi]	"NB There is no page 9 in this MS" in ink
pp. 1–6	I. Allegro con brio
pp. 6–8	II. Andante (no page 9)
p. [9]	Missing
pp. 10–11	II. continued
pp. 12–23	III. Allegro Appassionato
p. 23	IV. Lento
pp. [24–29]	Blank

The manuscript is dated "December 1952" and dedicated "To Peter Pears" by composer
No place of composition is apparent
Signed on title page, p. [v] and on upper right hand corner of p. 1
Present location: Britten-Pears Library 5H1 / 2-9104523; formerly in Peter Pears' collection
No printed first edition
Publication: © 1955 by J. & W. Chester Ltd

Revised version (1977)
Holograph in black ink with pencil annotations and overlays
The score is written on five double sheets and on both sides of a single sheet of 18-stave paper measuring 36.5 × 27 cm, wrapped in one double sheet of 16-stave paper measuring 36.4 × 27 cm
No manuscript paper printer's mark is apparent
Title page: RONSARD SONNETS | (Set 1) | for | TWO TENORS & PIANO | LENNOX BERKELEY
26 pages:

p. [i]	Title page
p. [ii]	Blank
pp. 1–6	I. Allegro con brio [Marie levez-vous]
pp. 7–10	II. Andante [Comme un void sur la branche]
pp. 10–15	III. Allegro appassionato [Ôtez votre beauté]
pp. 15–21	IV. Lento [Adieu, cruelle, adieu]
pp. [22–24]	Blank

The manuscript is dated "2nd version August–October 1977" after double bar on page 21
No location or dedication is apparent
Signed by composer on upper right hand corner of p. 1
Present location: British Library: LOAN 101.93a with drafts, sketches and annotated photocopy
No printed first edition
Publication: © 1977 by J. & W. Chester Ltd

FOUR RONSARD SONNETS (SET 2) (Opus 62)
Full score
Holograph [incomplete] in black and blue ink with autograph annotations in pencil, overlays, and non-autograph annotations in blue biro (to complete orchestration). Page numbers in blue ink. Pages in bad condition
The unbound score is written on two double sheets and on both sides of 20 single sheets of 24-stave paper measuring 36.8 × 27 cm
No title page; untitled because first pages are missing
48 pages:

pp. 3–6	[I. Ce premier jour de Mai]
pp. 9–18	continued
p. 21	last two bars
pp. 22–28	II. [Je sens une douceur] – incomplete
pp. 33–36	III. Allegro con fuoco [Ma fièvre croist toujours]
pp. 45–52	continued to end
pp. 53–66	IV. Lento [Yeux, qui versez en l'âme]

No date, dedication, location or signature is apparent
Present location: British Library: LOAN 101.78A
Also: Two dyeline copies
A: Dyeline copy [incomplete] with autograph annotations in pencil and overlays
Contains pp. 1–50 with following exceptions:
I. Complete pages [including 7–8, 19–20 missing from holograph]
II. Missing pp. 23–24 [these pages exist in holograph]
III. Missing pp. 37–38 [also missing in holograph]; autograph overlays pp. 43–44
IV. Missing entirely
B: Dyeline copy [fragment] pp. 31–44 with autograph sketches in pencil. Contains pp. 37–38 missing both in holograph and in first dyeline copy
Present location: British Library: LOAN 101.78B
Reduced version for chamber orchestra
Holograph in black ink with autograph annotations in pencil and overlays

The unbound score is written on 16 double sheets of 24-stave paper measuring 36.8 × 27 cm

No title page; page 1 [autograph]: FOUR RONSARD SONNETS | (Reduced Version for Chamber Orchestra) | I. | Lennox Berkeley

64 pages:

pp. 1–20	I. Allegro [Ce premier jour de Mai]
pp. 21–31	II. Andante tranquillo [Je sens une douceur]
pp. 32–51	III. (no tempo) [Ma fièvre croist toujours]
pp. 52–64	IV. Lento [Yeux, qui versez en l'âme]

No date, dedication or location is apparent

Signed by composer upper right hand of page 1

Present location: British Library: LOAN 101.78A

Also two dyeline copies

A: Later version: autograph annotations and overlays, mostly for performance purposes but some changes in overlays two pages before the end in first dyeline copy (pp. 62–63), also including adding "Allegro in blue biro to opening of III." Corrected page on pp. 42–43

B: Earlier version: Autograph annotations with two "correction pages" pp. 42–43 but without correction of first dyeline on pp. 62–63.

Present location: LOAN 101.78B/a & b

Vocal score

Holograph in pencil

The score is written on nine double sheets of 12-stave paper measuring 30.5 × 23.8 cm

Title page: FOUR RONSARD SONNETS | FOR | TENOR & ORCHESTRA. | LENNOX BERKELEY. | (Piano reduction)

36 pages:

p. [i]	Title page
p. [ii]	Blank
pp. 1–10	I [Ce premier jour de Mai]
pp. 11–16	II. Andante [Je sens une douceur]; blotches of black ink after double bar p. 16
pp. 17–25	III. Allegro con fuoco [Ma fièvre croist toujours]
pp. 26–33	IV. [Yeux, qui versez en l'âme]
p. 34	Blank

No date, dedication, location or signature is apparent

[Name all in caps – autograph]

Present location: British Library: LOAN 101.78A

First edition (Miniature score)

FOUR RONSARD | SONNETS | (Set 2) | *for Tenor and Orchestra* | Music by | LENNOX BERKELEY | 1. Ce premier jour de Mai | 2. Je sens une douceur |

3. Ma fièvre croist toujours | 4. Yeux, qui versez en l'âme | J. & W. CHESTER, LTD. | 11 Great Marlborough Street London, W.1.
66 pages. 189 × 132 mm
White stiff paper wrappers. Lettered in dark pink and grey. Trimmed edges
Publication: © 1964 by J. & W. Chester Ltd (J.W.C. 130) @ 15/-
Printed in England

Vocal scores

Manuscript consists of five separate parts: Title page, typescript of text, piano reduction score, piano reduction score of IV, extra title page

Holograph in black ink with annotations in black and blue ink by composer and in lead and red pencil by Peter Pears; typescript of texts with annotations in pencil and red ink

The title page is written on one side of a double sheet of 18-stave paper measuring 35.5 × 52.3 cm; the typescript of text is written on one side each of four single sheets of thin typing paper, measuring 25.5 × 20.3 cm; the piano reduction score is written on both sides of seven double and one single sheet of 18-stave paper measuring 30.5 × 26.1 cm (cut down from larger paper); the piano reduction score of IV is written on both sides of two double sheets of 18-stave paper measuring 36.5 × 27 cm; final title page is written on one side of a single sheet of 18-stave paper measuring 31 × 27 cm (cut down from larger paper)

Sellotape binding score of complete piano reduction, the rest inside double sheets of music paper

No manuscript printer's mark apparent except for first title page which is shown as A.L. No.12 | Printed in England with galleon logo

RONSARD SONNETS | I and II | "complete" [pencil annotation] | (Piano reduction) | Lennox Berkeley | op.62 | P.P. Inventory No.36 | 9104524

54 pages:

p. [i]	Title page
p. [ii]	Blank
pp. [iii–x]	Typescript of poems
pp. 1–9	I. Ce premier jour de Mai Allegro
pp. 10–15	II. Je sens une douceur Andante
p. [16]	Blank
pp. [17–24]	III. Ma fièvre croist toujours Allegro con fuoco
pp. [25–32]	IV. Yeux, qui versez Lento
p. [33]	Title page (holograph): Ronsard	IV	Piano score
p. [34]	Blank
pp. [35–41]	IV. Lento, Yeux, qui versez
pp. [42–44]	Blank

No date, place or dedication is apparent
Signed on title page p. [i]

Present location: Britten-Pears Library 5H1 / 2-9104524; formerly in Peter Pears' collection
Vocal part (voice only with cues specifically for Peter Pears)
Holograph in blue ink with black and blue ink and pencil annotations by the composer and blue ink and pencil annotations by Peter Pears
The score is written on both sides of two double sheets of 18-stave paper measuring 36.5 × 27 cm
No manuscript printer's mark apparent
8 pages:
pp. 1–2   I
pp. 3–4   II
pp. 4–5   III
pp. 6–7   IV
p. 8   Blank
No date, place, dedication or signature is apparent
Present location: Britten-Pears Library: 5H1 / 2-9104525
No printed first edition

FOUR SCORE YEARS AND TEN
Two holograph drafts in pencil
A: 3/4 Version
The score is written on both sides of a single sheet of 13-stave paper measuring 31 × 22.8 cm which has been cut in half
The manuscript paper printer's mark is shown as BBC MUSIC MSS PAPER 26 Stave
No title page
2 pages:
pp. [1–2]   Music
No date, dedication, location or signature is apparent
B: 6/8 Version
The score is written on both sides of a single sheet of 13-stave paper measuring 31 × 22.8 cm which has been cut in half
The manuscript paper printer's mark is shown as BBC MUSIC MSS PAPER 26 Stave
No title page
2 pages:
pp. [1–2]   Music
No date, dedication, location or signature is apparent
Present location: British Library: LOAN 101.94e
No printed first edition

A GLUTTON FOR LIFE

Holograph in black ink with rehearsal numbers and performance annotations in black pencil. Some queries and clarifications in orange pencil. Notes scratched out and autograph overlays. Autograph sketch in pencil on top bar p. 23. Outer pages are torn and soiled

The unbound score is written on twelve double sheets of 18-stave paper measuring 36.6 × 27 cm

The manuscript paper printer's mark is shown on bottom left of page as [encircled] J. & W. Chester Ltd. | London No.18

No title page; page 1: [Untitled] Maupassant [pencil] Lennox Berkeley

48 pages:

pp. 1–3	I. Lento – Andante
pp. 4–7	II. Allegro Moderato
p. 8	III.A. Moderato – FADE OUT
	III.B. Allegro (tpt solo) four bars
pp. 9–10	III.C. Allegretto (full orch)
p. 11	IV. Andante [cut in BBC parts]
pp. 12–17	V. Allegro [cut in BBC parts]
pp. 18–22	VI. Vivace
pp. 23–25	VII. Allegro
p. 26	VIII. Lento [cut in BBC parts]
pp. 27–32	IX. Allegro moderato
p. 33	X. Andante
	XI. [Instruction]: "Repeat No. I from figure 1" [cut in BBC parts]
pp. 33–35	XII. Moderato
p. 36	XIII. Lento
pp. 37–38	Allegro Moderato
pp. 38–39	Andante
pp. 40–43	Allegro
pp. 44–45	Adagio
p. 46	XIV. Lento
pp. 47–48	Allargando – FADE OUT [final page is partially ripped away losing several bars pp. 47–48]

The manuscript is dated "Painsuiello Jan 14th–Feb:2nd 1946" after double bar p. 48

No dedication is apparent

Signed by composer on upper right hand corner of page 1

Present location: British Library: LOAN 101.65

Location of parts: BBC Music Library (BBC MSS 20219) copied by Annelle R, London 1946 & "Eusdem"

Order of performance as indicated by parts: I–IIIC, 10, 6, 7, 9, 12–14. (4, 5, 8 & 11 cut)
No printed first edition

A GRACE for the Merchant Taylors' Company
Holograph in black ink with queries about accidentals in pencil
The score is written on one double sheet of 16-stave paper measuring 37 × 28 cm
No manuscript paper printer's mark is apparent
Title page: [autograph]: GRACE | For the Merchant Taylors' Company. | LENNOX BERKELEY
4 pages:
p. [i]   Title page
pp. [1–2]   Lento – Piu Vivo
p. [3]   Blank
The manuscript is dedicated by composer to John Reigate on top of p. [1]
Signed by the composer on upper right hand corner of p. [1]
Present location: British Library: LOAN 101.96e
No printed first edition

HAIL GLADDENING LIGHT (MELFORT)
Location of holograph unknown
No printed first edition

HAIL HOLY QUEEN
Holograph in black ink
The score is written on one double sheet of 16-stave paper measuring 34.1 × 27.1 cm
The manuscript paper printer's mark is shown as [vertical along spine] WH Nr 5.F.16
Title page [autograph]: MS | HAIL HOLY QUEEN | L. BERKELEY
4 pages:
p. [i]   Title page
pp. 1–2   Music
p. [3]   Blank
The manuscript bears autograph annotation "B.P. 6.III.70" which means it is dated 6 March 1970 and dedicated to Black Prince, the composer's dog
Signed by the composer on upper right hand corner of page 1
Present location: British Library: LOAN 101.94b with pencil sketch
No printed first edition

THE HILL OF THE GRACES (Opus 91, no.2)
Two holographs
A: Fair copy
Holograph in black ink with autograph sketches and corrections in pencil; overlays
Extensive production annotations in blue and lead pencil – original tempo markings all changed. Bar lines in pencil. The unbound score is written on five double sheets of 20-stave paper measuring 36.7 × 27 cm
No manuscript paper printer's mark is apparent
No title page; p. 1: [autograph] To Nicholas | Edmund Spenser. The Hill of the Graces | Lennox Berkeley | [pencil, not autograph] (Op.91 No.2)
20 pages:

pp. 1–5	Lento "Unto this place"
pp. 5–11	Allegro Moderato "There did he see that pleased much his sight"
pp. 11–13	Tempo Primo "Looke how the Crowne which Ariadne wore"
pp. 13–17	Allegretto "Such was the beauty of that goodly band"
pp. 17–20	Lento "But that fair one"

The manuscript is dated "Summer 1975" after double bar on page 20 and dedicated "To Nicholas" [Berkeley] by the composer on top of page 1
No location is apparent
Signed by the composer on upper right hand corner of page 1
Present location: British Library: LOAN 101.96d with pencil draft and sketches
B: Pencil draft
Holograph in pencil with extensive corrections and bars crossed out
The score is written on one double sheet, on both sides of seven single sheets, and on one side of one-half of a single sheet of 24-stave paper measuring 40.2 × 26.5 cm
No manuscript paper printer's mark is apparent
No title page
20 pages:

pp. 1–4	"Unto this place"
pp. 4–9	Allegro Moderato "There did he see that pleased much his sight"
p. [10]	Blank (half page)
pp. 10–13	Andante Maestoso "Looke how the Crowne which Ariadne wore"
pp. 13–15	"Those were the graces"
pp. 15–19	Lento (Tempo del Principio) "But that fair one"

The manuscript is dated "July 9./75" by composer after double bar page 17
No location, dedication or signature is apparent
Present location: British Library: LOAN 101.96d with holograph fair copy and sketches

First edition
Contemporary Choral Series | THE HILL OF THE GRACES | for unaccompanied chorus SSAATTBB | text by | EDMUND SPENSER | music

by | LENNOX BERKELEY | Op.91 no.2 | CHESTER MUSIC
24 pages. 254 × 177 mm
White paper wrappers. Lettered in black. Trimmed edges
Publication: © 1977 by J. & W. Chester Ltd (J.W.C.55062). Unpriced
Printed by Halstan & Co. Ltd, Amersham, Bucks

HOW LOVE CAME IN
Location of holograph unknown
First edition
Published in A Heritage of 20th Century British Song | VOLUME 2, pp. 6–8
HOW LOVE CAME IN
3 pages. 253 × 178 mm
Green stiff paper wrappers. Lettered in white. Trimmed edges
Publication: © 1936 by Boosey & Co. Ltd. (WINTHROP ROGERS EDITION)
B.&H.20352 @ £9.25 for collection
Printed in USA

HYMN FOR SHAKESPEARE'S BIRTHDAY (Opus 83, no.2)
Holograph in black ink with minimal autograph annotations; overlays
The unbound score is written on three double sheets of 16-stave paper measuring 29.1 × 26.5 cm
No manuscript paper printer's mark is apparent
Title page: [autograph in black ink in top right corner] MS | [not autograph in black ink] BERKELEY | [autograph in pencil] Hymn for SHAKESPEARE'S | BIRTHDAY
12 pages:

p. [i]	Title page
p. [ii]	Blank
pp. 1–6	[autograph] Hymn for Shakespeare's Birthday	C. Day Lewis Lennox Berkeley
pp. [7–10]	Blank

The manuscript is dated 1972 by the composer after double bar page 6
No location or dedication is apparent
Signed by the composer on upper right hand corner of page 1
Present location: British Library: LOAN 101.96b
No printed first edition
Publication: © 1972 by J. & W. Chester/Edition Wilhelm Hansen London Ltd (copies of manuscript available from Chester archive; BBC 19181)

i carry your heart
Holograph draft in pencil with pencil corrections
The score is written on one double sheet of 16-stave paper measuring 29.1 × 26.5 cm
No manuscript paper printer's mark is apparent
4 pages:
pp. [1–4]   Music
No date, dedication, location or signature is apparent
Present location: British Library: LOAN 101.94h with pencil sketches

I SING OF A MAIDEN
Holograph in black ink; on verso: "Lord By Whose Breath"
The score is written on one side of a single sheet of 12-stave paper measuring 30.3 × 23.9 cm
No date, dedication, location or signature is apparent
Present location: British Library: LOAN 101.97a
First edition
Publication: Cambridge University Press 1967 The Cambridge Hymnal No. 152

IMPROMPTU FOR ORGAN
Holograph in blue/black ink with minimal autograph corrections in pencil; autograph sketch at end of manuscript. Extensive pencil annotations for performance by organist. Manuscript is torn
The unbound score is written on two double sheets of 20-stave paper measuring 36.6 × 27 cm
The manuscript paper printer's mark is shown as [encircled] J & W | CHESTER | LTD. | LONDON | NO. 20
Title page: [autograph in blue ink] IMPROMPTU | For Organ | by | Lennox Berkeley | Written for Colin Gill, on the occasion of his translation | from Holborn to Brighton. (October 1941)
8 pages:
p. [i]   Title page
p. [ii]   [not autograph in pencil]: "RAM" & registrations
pp. [1–4]   Allegro
pp. [5–6]   Blank
The manuscript is dated "October 1941" and dedicated to Colin Gill by the composer on title page
No location is apparent
Signed by the composer on upper right hand corner of page [1]

Present location: British Library: LOAN 101.91a
No printed first edition

IMPROVISATION ON A THEME BY MANUEL DE FALLA (Opus 55, no.2)
Holograph in black ink with minimal annotations; overlays. Green typescript sheet containing details for publication stapled to bottom page 1
The unbound score is written on one double and on one side of a single sheet of 12-stave paper measuring 37.9 × 25.2 cm
No manuscript paper printer's mark is apparent
No title page
6 pages:
p. [i]   Blank
pp. 1–[4] Andante
           p. 1   Piu Vivo (Tempo II) – Rit
           p. [3] Tempo II
           p. [3] Tempo I
p. [5]   Blank
The manuscript is dedicated "To Douglas Gibson" by the composer on top of page 1
No date or location is apparent
Green typescript sheet stapled to bottom page 1: "NOTE: This work was written for the Centenary Album issued by the House of Chester, 1960"
Signed by the composer on upper right hand corner of page 1
Present location: British Library: LOAN 101.89f with copy of CENTENARY ALBUM containing facsimile of holograph with minimal annotations in pencil by composer

First edition
LENNOX BERKELEY | IMPROVISATION | on a theme of Manuel de Falla | PIANO SOLO | J.&W. CHESTER LTD LONDON [encircling JWC logo] | EDITION WILHELM HANSON [other International Distributors]
5 pages. 311 × 239 mm
White paper wrappers. Lettered in black. Trimmed edges
Publication: © 1960 by J. & W. Chester Ltd (J.W.C.2345A) @ 2/6
Printed by Lowe and Brydone (Printers) Ltd, London

IN WINTERTIME (Opus 103)
Holograph in pencil with corrections
The score is written on one side of a single sheet of 18-stave paper measuring 35.8 × 26.7 cm
No manuscript paper printer's mark is apparent

No title page
2 pages:
p. [1]   In Wintertime
p. [2]   Blank
No date, location, dedication or signature apparent
Location: British Library: LOAN 101.96 with:
1) Printed copy with autograph corrections in pencil
2) Photocopy with autograph annotations and sketch
3) Holograph in pencil of first two verses (same paper as complete holograph)
4) Copyist manuscript without corrections (same paper as complete holograph); organ part. Four staves attached with staples

First edition
This work was commissioned by Stephen Cleobury and the choir of | Kings College, Cambridge who gave the first performance as part of | A Festival of Nine Lessons and Carols on 24th December, 1983. | IN WINTERTIME | for SATB Choir and Organ | words by | BETTY ASKWITH | music by | LENNOX BERKELEY | CHESTER MUSIC | J&W Chester/Edition Wilhelm Hansen London Ltd | Eagle Court, London EC1M 5QD
4 pages. 253 × 177 mm
White paper covers. Lettered in black. Trimmed edges
Publication: © 1983 by J. & W. Chester Ltd (J.W.C.55634). Unpriced
Printed by Halstan & Co. Ltd, Amersham, Bucks, England

INTRODUCTION AND ALLEGRO FOR DOUBLE BASS AND PIANO (Opus 80)
Location of holograph unknown
Sketches
Present location: British Library: LOAN 101.87g

First edition
lennox | berkeley | introduction | and allegro | for | double bass | and piano | yorke edition
10 pages. 304 × 228 cm
White stiff paper wrappers. Lettered in black. Trimmed edges
Publication: © 1972 by Rodney Slatford | Yorke Edition (Y E 0021). Unpriced
Printed in England by West Central Printing Co. Ltd

INTRODUCTION AND ALLEGRO FOR TWO PIANOS AND ORCHESTRA (Opus 11)
Holograph in black ink with autograph annotations in pencil and blue pencil;

overlays. Holograph of cadenza in pencil inserted into original holograph score
The score is written on 18 double sheets of 28-stave paper measuring 36.1 × 27 cm and an insert (cadenza) written on one double sheet of 28-stave paper measuring 36.3 × 26 cm
Bound in stiff light brown wrappers; stapled spine
On front cover: "C.36" "Chester Library"
Title page [autograph]: To Benjamin Britten | Introduction & Allegro | for | 2 pianos & Orchestra | Lennox Berkeley | [orchestration information] | Time of Performance, 14 Minutes | [Chester Library stamp]
76 pages:

p. [i]	Title page
p. [ii]	Blank
pp. 1–10	Music: Introduction "Lento"
pp. 11–49	Allegro
pp. 50–51	Blank; Separate insert "CADENZA":
	pp. [1–3] Music
	p. [4] Blank
pp. 52–61	Music continued to end
pp. [62–70]	Blank

The manuscript is dated 1938 and dedicated "To Benjamin Britten" on title page
Signed by the composer on upper right hand corner of page 1
No opus number noted on holograph
Present location: British Library: LOAN 101.2
No printed first edition
Publication: © 1938 by J. & W. Chester Ltd; score and parts housed in hire library

INTRODUCTION AND ALLEGRO FOR VIOLIN (Opus 24)
Location of holograph unknown
First edition
Cover: CHESTER LIBRARY | LENNOX BERKELEY | INTRODUCTION and ALLEGRO | for | SOLO VIOLIN | PRICE 3/- NET [all within lyre motif featuring Pan playing pipes] | J & W CHESTER L.TD [stet] | [surrounded by decorative border with top text: DOMINE DIRIGE NOS [within encircled fastened belt with castle tower on top]] and at bottom text: IN DEO FIDEMUS [also within encircled fastened belt with star and 2 fish motif]
3 pages. 339 × 260 mm
Grey-blue paper wrappers. Lettered in black. Trimmed edges
Publication: © 1949 by J. & W. Chester Ltd (J.W.C.1304) @ 3/-
Edited by Ivry Gitlis. Printed in England

JONAH (Opus 3)
Full score
First version

Holograph in black ink with extensive autograph additions, corrections, and sketches in pencil; some overlays

The unbound score is written on 42 double sheets of 32-stave paper measuring 39.8 × 28.8 cm

No title page; page 1 [autograph]: JONAH | Prelude | Lennox Berkeley

168 pages:

	pp. 1–7	Prelude: Andante
[Part I not indicated on holograph]	pp. 8–23	I. Recitative & Chorus: "Now the word of the Lord came to Jonah"
	pp. 24–25	II. Recitative: Moderato: "But Jonah rose up to flee"
	pp. 26–36	III. Chorus and Sinfonia: Allegro "But the Lord sent out a great wind"
	pp. 37–40	IV. Duo and Recitative: Andante "Then the mariners were afraid"
	pp. 40–52	V. Chorus: Vivo "And they said every one to his fellow"
	pp. 53–54	VI. Recitative & Chorus: Moderato "And he said unto them"
	pp. 54–62	Allegro "Then were the men exceedingly afraid"
	pp. 63–67	VII. Chorus: Moderato "Then said they unto him"
	p. 68	VIII. Recitative and Aria: Andante "And he said unto them"
	pp. 68–75	Lento (Aria) "Take me up and cast me forth" (Jonah)
	pp. 76–78	IX. Chorus: "Nevertheless the men rowed hard"
	pp. 79–94	X. Chorus: Moderato "Wherefore they cried"
	pp. 95–103	XI. Chorus: Allegro moderato "So they took up Jonah"
Part II	pp. 104–5	XII. Introduction and Recitative: Andante "Now the Lord had prepared a great fish"
	pp. 106–14	XIII. Aria: "I cried by reason of my affliction" (Jonah)
	pp. 115–23	XIV. Aria: Allegro moderato "For thou did'st cast me" (Jonah)
	pp. 124–25	XV. Quintet: "I am cast out"
	pp. 126–30	XVI. Chorus: "The waters compassed me about"
	pp. 131–43	XVII. Chorus: Allegro "Yet hast thou brought up my life"

pp. 144–49	XVIII. Aria: Allegretto "When my soul fainted within me"(Jonah)
pp. 150–51	XIX. Recitative: "They that observe lying vanities" (Jonah)
pp. 152–56	XX. Chorus: Lento (ma non troppo)
pp. 156–64	[2 x p.156]
pp. [165–67]	Blank

The manuscript is dated "1933" after the double bar p. 164
No dedication or location is apparent
Signed by the composer on upper right hand of page 1
Present location: British Library: LOAN 101.67

Second version

Holograph in black ink with autograph additions, corrections and sketches in pencil; overlays; pencil bar lines; performance annotations in lead pencil and blue and red pencil; notes/sketches on last page of score

The score is written on 39 double sheets and both sides of two single sheets of 26-stave paper measuring 34.9 × 27 cm

The manuscript paper printer's mark is shown as "LARD ESNAULT Superieur 251–26" at lower left against spine (vertical)

Bound in stiff orange paper wrappers with sewn and taped spine. Chester's Circulating Music Library label on front cover

Title page [autograph]: JONAH | Lennox Berkeley

160 pages:

	p.[i]	Title page
	p.[ii]	JONAH	Oratorio for Soli Chorus + Orchestra
Part I	pp. 1–16	I. Recitative and chorus: Moderato "Now the word of the Lord came to Jonah"
	pp. 17–19	II. Recitative: Moderato "But Jonah rose up to flee"
	pp. 20–28	III. Chorus & Sinfonia: Allegro Vivace "But the Lord sent out a great wind"
	pp. 29–33	IV. Duo and Recitative: Andante "Then the mariners were afraid"
	pp. 33–43	V. Chorus: Vivo "And they said every one to his fellow"
	pp. 44–45	VI. Recitative & Chorus: Andante "And he said unto them"
	pp. 45–52	Allegro "Then were the men exceedingly afraid"
	pp. 53–56	VII. Chorus: Allegro "Then said they unto him"
	p. 57	VIII. Recitative and Aria: Lento "And he said unto them"
	pp. 57–65	Più lento (Aria) "Take me up and cast me forth" (Jonah)

	pp. 66–69	IX. Chorus: Allegro "Nevertheless the men rowed hard"
	pp. 70–84	X. Chorus: Lento "Wherefore they cried"
	pp. 84–91	XI. Chorus: Moderato "So they took up Jonah"
Part II	pp. 92–94	XII. Introduction & Recitative: Andante "Now the Lord had prepared a great fish"
	pp. 94–101	XIII. Aria: Moderato "I cried by reason of my affliction" (Jonah)
	pp. 102–8	XIV. Aria: Allegro moderato "For thou did'st cast me" (Jonah)
	pp. 109–10	XV. Quintet (Solo & chorus): Andante "I am cast out"; annotation: "*The Chorus must sing 'sotto voce' throughout accompanying the Tenor Solo"
	pp. 110–14	XVI. Chorus: Moderato "The waters compassed me about"
	pp. 114–22	XVII. Chorus: Allegro "Yet hast thou brought up my life"
	pp. 122–25	Continued = 2 x p. 122
	pp. 126–32	XVIII. Aria: Allegretto "When my soul fainted within me"(Jonah)
	pp. 133–34	XIX. Recitative: Moderato "They that observe lying vanities" (Jonah)
	pp. 135–41	XX. Chorus: Lento "Alleluia"
	pp. 141–51	Andante "Whither shall I go"
	p. [152]	Four-bar autograph sketch in pencil headed "Queries"
	pp. [153–60]	Blank

No date, dedication or location is apparent
Signed by the composer on title page and on upper right hand corner of page 1
Present location: British Library: LOAN 101.68
Vocal score (revised version?)
Holograph in black ink with minimal autograph additions and corrections in pencil; overlays. Score leaves out soloist's arias
The unbound score is written on 15 double sheets of 16-stave paper measuring 33 x 26.8 cm
The manuscript paper printer's mark is shown as Néocopie Musicale, Paris (No. 6) on lower left hand corner of paper
Title page [autograph]: LENNOX BERKELEY | JONAH (Oratorio) | (Chorus – Score); "Vandyke" appears in pencil on upper left hand corner of title page
60 pages:

	p. [i]	Title page
	p. [ii]	Blank
Part I	p. 1	Introduction: Andante [Cue]
	pp. 1–10	I. Recitative & chorus: Moderato

	[No p. 8]	
	p. 10	II. Recitative (Chorus tacit)
	pp. 10–11	III. Chorus: Allegro "But the Lord sent out a great wind"
	p. 11	Sinfonia: Chorus tacit
	pp. 11–12	IV. Duo & Recitative: Andante–allegro "Then the mariners were afraid"
	pp. 13–17	V. Chorus: Vivo "And they said every one to his fellow"
	pp. 18–20	VI. Recitative & Chorus: [Cues for solos and orchestra] – (no tempo) "Then were the men exceedingly afraid"
	pp. 21–22	VII. Chorus: Allegro "Then said they unto him"
	p. 22	VIII. Recit. and Aria (Chorus tacit)
	pp. 22–23	IX. Chorus (Tenors only): Allegro "Nevertheless the men rowed hard"
	pp. 23–31	X. Chorus: Lento "Wherefore they cried"
	pp. 31–34	XI. [Chorus]: L'istesso tempo "So they took up Jonah"
Part II	p. 34	XII. Introduction & Recitative (Chorus tacet)
	p. 34	XIII. Aria (Tenor solo) (Chorus tacet)
	p. 34	XIV. Aria (Tenor solo) (Chorus tacet)
	pp. 34–37	XV. Quintet (Tenor solo & chorus): Moderato "I am cast out";
	pp. 38–39	XVI. Chorus: Moderato "The waters compassed me about"
	pp. 40–43	XVII. Chorus: Allegro "Yet hast thou brought up my life"
	p. 44	XVIII. Aria (Chorus tacet)
	p. 44	XIX. Recitative (Chorus tacet)
	pp. 44–51	XX. Chorus
	pp. [52–59]	Blank

No date, dedication or location is apparent
Signed by the composer on upper right hand corner of page 1
Present location: British Library: LOAN 101.69
Other versions
Sketches:
Three pages of autograph sketches of choruses, XVI & XX. in pencil in LOAN 101.102
First edition (vocal score)
Cover: JONAH | Oratorio | for | Soli, Chorus and Orchestra | LENNOX BERKELEY | Price 20/- | J. & W. CHESTER LTD. | 11, GREAT MARLBOROUGH STREET | LONDON, W.1 | PRINTED IN ENGLAND
113 pages. 308 × 245 mm
Brown paper wrappers. Lettered in black. Trimmed edges
Publication: © 1936 by J. & W. Chester Ltd (J.W.C.9735) @ 20/-

THE JUDGEMENT OF PARIS
Full score
Location of holograph unknown
Microfilm of holograph: British Library: Mus.Mic.H.2.(1.)[1988]
Piano score
Holograph (incomplete) in black and blue ink with autograph additions in pencil and black ink; overlays. Bars crossed out. Annotations for choreography in pencil
The unbound score is written on four double sheets and on one side of a single sheet of 12-stave paper measuring 32.8 × 26.8 cm
The manuscript paper printer's mark is shown as [horizontal bottom left] Néocopie Musicale, Paris (No.3)
Title page: [stamp] PROPERTY OF | SADLER'S WELLS FOUNDATION | [autograph in pencil] L. Berkeley | Judgement of Paris | (Piano Score)
18 pages:

p. [i]	Title page
p. [ii]	Blank
p. 1	[No title details] Introduction	Andante
pp. 1–4	I.	Allegro
pp. 5–8	Pas de Deux	Andantino
pp. 9–12	III.	Moderato – Allegretto
pp. 12–15	IV. Allegro Vivace
p. 16	V.	Lento (incomplete)

No date, dedication or location apparent
Signed by the composer on title page and on upper right hand corner of page 1
Present location: British Library: LOAN 101.41a
No printed first edition
Publication: © 1938 by Boosey & Hawkes

JUDICA ME (Opus 96, no.1)
Holograph in black ink with minimal autograph clarifications in pencil; minimal production annotations in pencil; overlays; "Hire Material" stamp
The score is written on three double sheets of 14-stave paper measuring 37 × 27 cm
No manuscript paper printer's mark apparent
No title page; p. 1: [autograph] Judica me | (Motet). | Lennox Berkeley
12 pages:

pp. 1–11	Lento – Un poco piu mosso – Allegro – Lento
p. [12]	Blank

The manuscript is dated May 1978 after double bar p. 11
No location or dedication is apparent

Signed by the composer on upper right hand corner of p. 1
Present location: British Library: LOAN 101.96f (score and sketches)
First edition
CONTEMPORARY CHURCH MUSIC SERIES | LENNOX BERKELEY | JUDICA ME | Op.96 | for unaccompanied chorus | SSATBB | CHESTER MUSIC
12 pages. 298 × 223 mm
Cream paper wrappers. Lettered in black. Trimmed edges
Publication: © 1978 by J. & W. Chester/Edition Wilhelm Hansen London Ltd (J.W.C.55166). Unpriced
[Contemporary Church Music Series]
Printed in England

JUSTORUM ANIMAE (Opus 60, no.2)
Holograph in pencil with black ink marks on p. [2], bars crossed out
The score is written on both sides of a single sheet and on one side of a single sheet of 24-stave paper measuring 36.8 × 27.1 cm
No manuscript paper printer's mark apparent
No title page
4 pages:
pp. [1–3]   Music
p. [4]   Blank
No date, location, dedication or signature is apparent
Present location: British Library: LOAN 101.95i
First edition
CONTEMPORARY CHURCH MUSIC SERIES | Justorum Animae | MOTET FOR FOUR VOICES | FOR ALL SAINTS AND FEASTS OF MARTYRS | by | LENNOX BERKELEY | J.&W. CHESTER LTD. LONDON [encircling JWC logo] | International distributors
7 pages. 254 × 180 mm
White paper wrappers. Lettered in black. Trimmed edges
Publication: © 1965 by J. & W. Chester Ltd (J.W.C.8842). Unpriced
Printed by Lowe and Brydone (Printers) Ltd, London

LAY YOUR SLEEPING HEAD, MY LOVE (Opus 14, no.2)
Holograph in black ink with autograph clarifications in pencil; overlays
The score is written on two double sheets of 16-stave paper measuring 32.9 × 27 cm
The manuscript paper printer's mark is shown as Néocopie Musicale, Paris (No. 6)

No title page; p.[1]: [autograph] To Benjamin | Words by W.H. Auden. | Lay your sleeping head, my love | Lennox Berkeley
8 pages:
pp. [1–6]   Lento
pp. [7–8]   Blank
The manuscript is dedicated "To Benjamin" [Britten] by the composer on top p. [1]
No date or location is apparent
Signed by the composer on upper right hand corner of p. [1]
Present location: Private collection but due to go to the British Library as LOAN 101.92j
No printed first edition

LEGACIE
Holograph in blue ink
The unbound score is written on one double sheet of 18-stave paper measuring 36.5 × 27 cm
The manuscript paper printer's mark is shown as [encircled] J&W | CHESTER | LTD. | LONDON NO.18
No title page; page 1 [Untitled]
4 pages:
pp. [1–4]   Music "When I died last"
The manuscript is dated 1943 after the double bar page [4]
No dedication, location or signature is apparent
Present location: British Library: LOAN 101.95b
No printed first edition

LOOK BACK TO LYTTLETOUN
Holograph [incomplete] in blue ink with autograph annotations and additions in pencil. Timings and page numbers in blue pencil. Some autograph overlays
The unbound score is written on 17 double sheets and both sides of one single sheet of 22-stave paper measuring 36.8 × 27.2 cm; on three double sheets of 28-stave paper measuring 36 × 26.5 cm; and on one double sheet of 28-stave paper measuring 36.6 × 27.1 cm
No title page; page 1: [Untitled] Lennox Berkeley
94 pages:
p. 1   I.A.
pp. 1–2   I.B.   Andante
pp. 2–3   II.   Allegretto

p. 4	III. Allegro (3 bars)
	IV. Andante con moto (4 bars)
	V.A. violin pizzicato (1 bar)
	V.B. Moderato (1 bar)
	V.C. Vivo (1 bar)
	V.D. Lento (1 bar)
p. 5	VI.A. Allegretto (3 bars)
	VI.B. Andante (7 bars)
pp. 5–7	VII.A. Maestoso
p. 7	VII.B. Moderato (3 bars)
pp. 8–9	VIII. Andante
pp. 9–10	IX. "And royalty has seen fit"
p. 11	X. (4 bars)
pp. 11–12	XI.
pp. 12–17	XII. Allegro vivace "Open the windows"
pp. 18–19	XIII. Allegretto
p. 20	XIV. Lento
	XV.A. (2 bars) [Altered in dyeline of holograph]
p. 21	XV.B. (6 bars)
p. 22	XVI.A. Moderato "His Lordship is coming here for Easter"
	XVI.B. Andante "His Lordship's brougham
	XVII. Andante "[crossed out in dyeline of holograph; replaced by 2-bar pencil sketch "Moderato" inserted into dyeline score]
p. 23	XVIII.A. Allegro moderato "This is the moment"
pp. 24–26	XVIII.B. Allegro "Welcome, Welcome"
p. 27	XIX.A. Allegro moderato – Lento
p. 28	XIX.B. Moderato "Home"
pp. 29–31	XX. Andante
p. 32	XX.B. Moderato (4 bars)
	XXI. Andante "Peace to your building"
	XXII. Andante "Firmness and delight"
pp. 33–34	XXIII. Andante
p. 34	XXIV.A. Moderato "In the Old Days"
	XXIV.B. "In the Country"
p. 35	XXIV.C. "In the old days"
	XXV.
pp. 36–37	XXVI. Lento, p. 37: autograph pencil sketch and annotation
pp. 38–55	XXVII. Tempo di Valse – Meno mosso – Piu Lento (Molto moderato)
p. 56	XXVIII. (3 bars)
pp. 57–59	XXIX. Allegretto

pp. 60–65	XXX. Allegro
	[Missing pp. 61–68 in holograph; details added from dyeline]
p. 66	XXX.B. Lento (1 bar)
	XXX.C. Vivo (1 bar)
	XXXI.A. Andante (2 bars)
pp. 67–68	XXXI.B. Andante "Lyttletoun"
p. 69	XXXI.C. Lento
	XXXII. Allegretto (3 bars)
p. 70	XXXIII. Allegretto "Cometh green and leafy thing"
p. 71	XXXIV.A. Lento (2 bars)
	XXXIV.B. Lento (3 bars)
	XXXIV.C. Lento (3 bars)
	[XXXIV.D. (4 bars) added as pencil holograph inserted into dyeline copy – a late addition in copied parts]
p. 72	XXXIV.D̶.E. Lento (5 bars) ["D" changed on holograph]
	XXXV. Allegro "Summer is icumen in"
p. 73	XXXVI.A. Allegro Moderato
	XXXVI.B. (5 bars)
p.74	XXXVI.C. Allegro Moderato (4 bars)
	XXXVI.D. Moderato (3 bars)
	XXXVI.E. "Repeat C"
p. 75	XXXVII.A. Lento (5 bars)
	XXXVII.B. Moderato (6 bars)
p. 76	XXXVII.C. "Repeat B"
pp.76–77	XXXVII.D. Moderato
p. 77	XXXVIII. Lento "How to choose between rose and rose"
p.78	XXXIX. Andante
	XL. Moderato "Time is a word without a meaning"
pp. 79–82	XLI. Allegro [spoken] "The Heavens opened and the rain came"
p. 83	XLII. Lento (3 bars) clarinet solo
	XLIII. Allegretto (7 bars)
	XLIV.A. Andante (4 bars)
	XLIV.B (3 bars)
p. 84	XLV. Andante "Here life hath death"
	XLVI Andante
	XLVII.A. Lento (1 bar)
	XLVII.B. Lento (2 bars)
	XLVII.C. Lento (3 bars)
pp. 85–86	XLVIII. Andante con moto "The Lord gave"
p. 86	XLIX.A. Lento (2 bars)
	XLIX.B. Lento (2 bars)

p. 87	XLIX.C. Moderato (2 bars)
	XLIX.D. "Repeat I.B."
	L. Lento
p. 88	LI. Andante
p. 89	LII.A. Allegretto "Lyttletoun"
p. 90	LII.B. Allegretto "Lyttletoun"
pp. 91–92	LIII. Andante "The Lord gave"
pp. [93–94]	Blank

No date, dedication or location is apparent
Signed by the composer on upper right hand corner of page 1
Present location: British Library: LOAN 101.65
Also BBC Music Library (BBC MS 31204): Dyeline of complete holograph with many autograph additions in pencil, including new XVII and additional XXXIV.D. Also has performance annotations. Also auto-positive negatives of holograph. With vocal scores and parts
No printed first edition

LOOK UP, SWEET BABE (Opus 43, no.2)

Holograph in blue ink with production annotations in black ink and pencil; overlays on p. 6. Autograph pencil sketches on inside pages of both outer sheets, presumably from Nelson, crossed out in pencil

The score is written on one double sheet and on both sides of three single sheets of 18-stave paper measuring 34.4 × 25.8 cm; and on one side of one single sheet of 18-stave paper measuring 35.5 × 26.3 cm

The manuscript paper printer's marks are shown on bottom left of page as [lyre motif] B.C. No. 5 (18 staves) Made and Printed in England by Bosworth & Co., Ltd. and as [encircled galleon] | A. L. No 12 | Printed in England

Title page [not autograph]: Music 800/8 pages | Look up Sweet Babe | Anthem | for | Choir & Organ | Lennox Berkeley | Dec./'54

12 pages:

p. [i]	Title page
p. [ii]	Pencil sketch [Nelson?]
pp. 1–7	Music: Andante
	production annotation "1956 differs from printed score"
p. [8]	Blank
pp. [9–10]	Pencil sketch, continuation of p.[ii]

The manuscript is dated December 1954 [not autograph]
No location or dedication is apparent
Signed by composer on upper right hand corner of p. 1
Present location: British Library: LOAN 101.95g

First edition
No title page
8 pages. 253 × 177 mm
White paper. Lettered in black. Trimmed edges
Publication: © 1957 by J. & W. Chester Ltd (J.W.C.7740) @ 1/-
Printed by Halstan & Co. Ltd, Amersham, Bucks

LORD, BY WHOSE BREATH (Wiveton)
Holograph in black ink; on verso: "I Sing of a Maiden"
The score is written on one side of a single sheet of 12-stave paper measuring 30.3 × 23.9 cm
No date, dedication, location or signature is apparent
Present location: British Library: LOAN 101.97a
First edition
Publication: Cambridge University Press 1967 The Cambridge Hymnal No. 61

THE LORD IS MY SHEPHERD (Opus 91, no.1)
Two holographs
A: Holograph in black ink with autograph corrections and additions in pencil. Queries from editor in pencil. One bar line in red ink
The unbound score is written on three double sheets of 20-stave paper measuring 36.7 × 27 cm
No manuscript paper printer's mark is apparent
Title page: [autograph in black ink] THE LORD IS MY SHEPHERD. | Anthem for treble solo, choir + organ. | LENNOX BERKELEY
12 pages:

- p. [i]   Title page
- p. [ii]   Blank
- pp. 1–6   Andante "The Lord is my Shepherd"
- pp. [7–9]   Blank
- p. [10]   autograph pencil sketches rubbed out

The manuscript is dated "April 1975" after double bar page 6
No location or dedication is apparent
Signed by the composer on upper right hand corner of page 1
Present location: British Library: LOAN 101.96c with pencil draft and sketches
B: Holograph in pencil
The score is written on both sides of two single sheets of 24-stave paper measuring 40.1 × 26.5 cm
No manuscript paper printer's mark apparent

No title page
4 pages:
pp. [1–4]   "The Lord is my Shepherd"
No date, location, dedication, signature is apparent
Present location: British Library: LOAN 101.96c with holograph in ink and sketches
Also: Photocopy of holograph without any annotations
Present location: West Sussex Record Office: Hussey Papers (H.289)
First edition
Contemporary Church Music Series | LENNOX BERKELEY | The | Lord is my Shepherd | Op.91 No.1 | This anthem was written for the 900th anniversary of the | foundation of Chichester Cathedral, and is dedicated to | the Very Rev. Walter Hussey, Dean of Chichester. | CHESTER MUSIC | J & W Chester/ Edition Wilhelm Hansen London Ltd | Eagle Court, London EC1M 5QD
7 pages. 253 × 178 mm
White paper wrappers. Lettered in black. Trimmed edges
Publication: © 1976 by J. & W. Chester/Edition Wilhelm Hansen Ltd (J.W.C. 55057). Unpriced. Contemporary Church Music Series

LORD, WHEN THE SENSE OF THY SWEET GRACE (Opus 21, no.1)
Holograph [incomplete] in black ink with rehearsal numbers in blue pencil and autograph overlays
The score is written on two double sheets of 22-stave paper measuring 37 × 27.4 cm
The manuscript paper printer's mark is shown as [encircled] J & W | CHESTER | LTD | LONDON & GENEVA No. 22
No title page; page 1 [autograph]: To Trevor Hardy | Poem by Richard Crashaw Lord, when the sense of Thy sweet grace Lennox Berkeley
8 pages:
pp. 1–8   Andante [missing final pages]
The manuscript is dedicated "To Trevor Hardy"
No date or location is apparent
Signed by composer on upper right hand corner of p. 1
Present location: British Library: LOAN 101.95c
First edition
LORD, WHEN THE SENSE | OF THY SWEET GRACE | ANTHEM FOR MIXED VOICES AND ORGAN | WORDS BY | RICHARD CRASHAW | MUSIC BY | LENNOX BERKELEY | J. & W. CHESTER LTD. | 11, GREAT MARLBOROUGH STREET | LONDON, W.1
12 pages. 253 × 178 mm

White paper wrappers. Lettered in black. Trimmed edges
Publication: © 1945 by J. & W. Chester Ltd (J.W.C.7737) @ 10d

THE LOW LANDS OF HOLLAND
Location of holograph unknown
Annotated copyist manuscript
Copyist manuscript in black ink with autograph corrections and additions in pencil; bars crossed out. One page of autograph corrections and sketches; one sketch is the definitive version of ending
The copyist score is accompanied by a sheet of autograph corrections written on both sides of a single sheet (cut from larger paper) of 14-stave paper measuring 21.6 × 30.4 cm
The manuscript paper printer's mark is shown as J & W | CHESTER | LTD. | LONDON
The manuscript is dated 1947 and tempo Moderato by the copyist
No location, dedication or signature is apparent
Present location: British Library: LOAN 101.92h
No printed first edition
Publication: © 1952 by J. & W. Chester Ltd (J.W.C.4049)

LULLABY
Holograph in blue ink with minimal additions in pencil p. [3], bar 82; typescript of poem pasted on p. [3]
The score is written on three sides of one double sheet of 18-stave paper measuring 36.5 × 27 cm
The manuscript paper printer's mark is shown as [encircled] J&W | CHESTER | LTD | LONDON | No.18
No title page; p. [1]: Lullaby | W.B. Yeats; Lennox Berkeley
4 pages:
pp. [1–3]   Music "Lento"
p. [4]   Blank
The manuscript is dated 1943 by the composer after double bar on page [3]
No location or dedication is apparent
Signed on upper right hand corner of page [1]
Present location: Britten-Pears Library 5H1 / 2-9104520; formerly in Benjamin Britten's collection
Other versions
Holograph [probably] in black ink, bar lines and text in pencil. A blank section is cut out of pp. [3–4]

The score is written on one double sheet of 16-stave paper measuring 34.2 × 26.9 cm
The manuscript paper printer's mark is shown as W.H.Nr.5.F.16 in lower left hand corner
No title page
4 pages:
pp. [1–2]   Music
pp. [3–4]   Blank
No date, dedication, location or signature is apparent
Present location: British Library: LOAN 101.92f
No printed first edition

MAGNIFICAT (Opus 71)
Full score
Holograph in black ink with autograph corrections and additions in pencil; overlays. Some performance annotations
The unbound score is written on 20 double sheets of 30-stave paper measuring 35.5 × 25.7 cm. One half of one sheet is glued down to another sheet, reducing the number of pages by two
The manuscript paper printer's mark is shown as [galleon] A.L. No. 29 | Printed in England lower left hand corner of paper
No title page; page 1 [autograph]: To Michael | MAGNIFICAT | Allegro moderato; Lennox Berkeley [annotation in blue ink: Full Score | Original MS] in upper left hand corner of page 1
81 pages:
pp. 1–25   Allegro moderato "Et exultavit spiritus meus"
pp. 26–43   Lento "Et misericordia ejus"
pp. 43–45   Lento "Esurientes implevit bonis"
pp. 45–51   [2 × p. 45]; Allegro "Et divites dimisit inanes?"
pp. 51–53   Lento "Esurientes implevit bonis"
pp. 53–58   Moderato "Suscepit Israel"
pp. 58–60   Moderato "Sicut locutus est"
pp. 60–64   Allegretto "Abraham et semine ejus"
pp. 64–79   Allegro "Gloria"
pp. [80–81] Blank
The manuscript is dated "Dec. 1967–April 1968" after double bar page 79 and dedicated "To Michael [Berkeley]" in upper centre of page 1
Signed by the composer on upper right hand corner of page 1
Present location: British Library: LOAN 101.80 (with annotated dyeline and corrected proof of vocal score)

Other versions

1. Autograph pencil ROUGH draft, pp. 1–32 [2 × p. 26] dated April 10th 1968
Pages crossed out

The unbound score is written on eight double sheets and on both sides of one single sheet of 24-stave paper measuring 34.2 × 27 cm

The manuscript paper printer's mark is shown as WH Nr.9.F.24 vertical lower left hand of page

No title page; untitled

34 pages:

pp. 1–26

p. 26   [repeated]

pp. 26–32   pp. 31 & 32 crossed in pencil

p. [33]   upside-down verso of p. 32, numbered p. 35 contains last 9 bars of Magnificat

The manuscript is dated "April 10th 1968" after double bar p. 32

No dedication, location or signature is apparent

2. Dyeline of holograph showing original title page: MAGNIFICAT | LENNOX BERKELEY | FULL SCORE

Performance annotations in green pencil

Present location: British Library: LOAN 101.81

Vocal score

Location of holograph unknown

3. Proof copy of printed vocal score with autograph annotations in pencil and production queries in red and blue ink

Present location: British Library: LOAN 101.81

First edition (vocal score)

LENNOX BERKELEY | Magnificat | for chorus and orchestra | Vocal Score | (Orchestral parts on hire) | J.&W.CHESTER.LTD.LONDON [circled round JWC logo] | EDITION WILHELM HANSEN, LONDON

Publication: © 1968 by J. & W. Chester Ltd (J.W.C.8864). Unpriced

Printed by Halstan & Co. Ltd, Amersham, Bucks

MAGNIFICAT AND NUNC DIMITTIS (Opus 99)

Holograph in black ink with autograph clarifications in pencil; extensive overlays

The unbound score is written on five double sheets of 18-stave paper measuring 36.9 × 27.2 cm

The manuscript paper printer's mark is shown as B&H [incorporated into music globe design]

Title page: [pencil – not autograph] Lennox Berkeley | MAGNIFICAT AND | NUNC DIMITTIS

20 pages:
p. [i]	Title page
p. [ii]	Blank
pp. 1–12	Magnificat
pp. 1–4	Moderato "My soul doth magnify the Lord"
pp. 5–8	Allegro "He hath showed strength with his arm"
pp. 8–10	Meno Vivo "He remembering"
pp. 10–12	Gloria
pp. 10–12	Andante con moto "Glory be to the Father"
pp. 13–15	Nunc Dimittis
	Moderato "Lord now lettest thou thy servant"
pp. [16–18]	Blank

The manuscript is dated "April–May 1980" after double bar on page 15
No location or dedication is apparent
Signed by the composer on upper right hand corner of page 1
Present location: British Library: LOAN 101.96h with sketches, photocopy of holograph and annotated publisher proofs

Sketches
A: Sketches with holograph
Present location: British Library: LOAN 101.96h
B: Sketches within Faldon Park material
Present location: British Library: LOAN 101.62

First edition
CONTEMPORARY CHURCH MUSIC SERIES | LENNOX BERKELEY | MAGNIFICAT | AND | NUNC DIMITTIS | SATB AND ORGAN | CHESTER MUSIC
16 pages. 253 × 178 mm
White paper wrappers. Lettered in black. Trimmed edges
Publication: © 1980 by J. & W. Chester Ltd (J.W.C.55306). Unpriced.
Contemporary Church Music Series
Printed by Caligraving Ltd, Thetford, Norfolk

MARCH FOR PIANO
Holograph in black ink, no annotations
The score is written on one double sheet of 14-stave paper measuring 35.5 × 26 cm
The manuscript paper printer's mark is shown as [encircled masted ship] | A L | No. 8
Bound together with Mr. Pilkington's Toye etc.
No title page; p. [1] (autograph): To Vere Pilkington | March | Lennox Berkeley | Piano

4 pages:
pp. [1–3]   Music
p. [4]   Blank

The manuscript is dedicated "To Vere Pilkington" on upper left page [1] and signed by the composer on upper right hand corner of page [1]
No date or location is apparent
Present location: British Library: ADD MS 63847, leaves 6 & 7
Copyist score
Appears to be faithful copy of holograph with addition of date and location: "April 1924 Beaulieu"
Bound with holograph
Present location: British Library: ADD MS 63847, leaves 8 & 9
No printed first edition

MASS FOR FIVE VOICES (Opus 64)

Holograph in black ink with minimal autograph sketches and corrections in pencil; bars crossed out in black ink; overlays. Production annotations and queries in pencil and blue ink
The score is written on four double sheets of 20-stave paper measuring 36.5 × 27 cm
No manuscript paper printer's mark is apparent
No title page; sheets contained inside orange foolscap folder with autograph title information on cover in black ink: Berkeley | MASS FOR | FIVE VOICES | (1964) | (Op.64) [pencil annotation]
16 pages:
pp. [1–3]   I. Kyrie: Lento
pp. [4–9]   II. Gloria: Andante
p. [10]   III. Sanctus: Lento
pp. [11–12]   Allegro
p. [12]   IV. Benedictus: Andante
pp. [13–14]   Allegro
pp. [14–16]   V. Agnus dei: Lento

The manuscript is dated "July–October 1964" after double bar p. [14]
No location or dedication is apparent
Signed by composer on upper right hand corner of page [1]
Present location: British Library: LOAN 101.95j with sketches of Gloria, Agnus Dei & Benedictus
First edition
CONTEMPORARY CHURCH MUSIC SERIES | MASS FOR FIVE VOICES | unaccompanied chorus SSATB | LENNOX BERKELEY | CHESTER MUSIC

31 pages. 253 × 176 mm
White paper wrappers. Lettered in black. Trimmed edges
Publication: © 1965 by J. & W. Chester Ltd (J.W.C.8845) @ 10/-

MAZURKA FOR PIANO
Holograph in black ink with autograph annotations in pencil; extensive overlays. Tattered condition
The score is written on one double sheet of 18-stave paper measuring 36.5 × 27 cm
No manuscript paper printer's mark is apparent
No title page; p. [1]: MAZURKA LB
4 pages:
p. [i]   autograph 33-bar pencil sketch
pp. [1–3]   MAZURKA
The manuscript is dated "Dec:1939." by the composer after double bar page [3]
No location or dedication is apparent
Signed by the composer on upper right hand corner of page [1]
Present location: British Library: LOAN 101.89b

MAZURKA FOR PIANO
Holograph
Present location: University of Sheffield

MAZURKA FOR PIANO (Opus 101, no.2) (101b on printed copy)
Location of holograph unknown
Details taken from published facsimile edition
The unbound score is written on 16-stave paper
No title page; p. 1: Mazurka | Lennox Berkeley
2 pages:
p. [1]   Music
p. [2]   Blank
No date, dedication or location is apparent
Signed by the composer on upper right hand corner of page [1]
First edition
Lennox Berkeley | MAZURKA | for piano | Op. 101b | The work was commissioned by the BBC as one of a group of works marking the 250th | anniversary of the birth of Haydn. The first performance was given as part of a broadcast by | John McCabe on 18th March, 1982. | Mazurka is published by Chester Music as an 80th birthday tribute to Sir Lennox Berkeley. | A facsimile of the composer's manuscript is shown on page 4. | CHESTER MUSIC

| J & W Chester/Edition Wilhelm Hansen London Ltd. | Eagle Court, London EC1M 5QD
4 pages. 304 × 229 mm
White stiff paper wrappers (inner pages not secured). Lettered in blue. Trimmed edges
Publication: © 1983 by J. & W. Chester/Edition Wilhelm Hansen London Ltd (J.W.C.55582). Unpriced
Process-engraved by Christopher Hinkins of Woodhall Spa, Lincolnshire, as a tribute to Sir Lennox Berkeley on the occasion of his eightieth birthday
Other works by Benjamin, Bennett, Sherlaw Johnson, McCabe and Rubbra
Facsimile of manuscript on page 4
Printed by Caligraving Ltd, Thetford, Norfolk

THE MIDNIGHT MURK
A: Holograph in black ink; corrections and performance annotations in pencil by another hand, including "Poem by Sagittarius" and "T.H. 20.6.42 | 5'25"" on p. [1] and "3 1/2 minutes" on p. [3]; coffee/tea stain on 4th stave on p. [1] and coffee/tea ring on p. [3]; blue stamp on p. [1]: "J&W Chester Ltd. | 11, Great Marlborough St."
The score is written on three sides of one double sheet of 20-stave paper, measuring 36.5 × 27 cm
The manuscript paper printer's mark is shown as (encircled) J&W | CHESTER | LTD | LONDON | No 20
No title page
4 pages:
pp. [1–3]   Top of page [1]: The Midnight Murk | Poem by Sagittarius (pencil) | Lennox Berkeley | Andante
            Music
p. [4]   Blank
No date, place or dedication is apparent
Signed by composer on upper right hand corner of p. [1]
Present location: Britten-Pears Library 5H1 / 2-9104521; formerly in Benjamin Britten's collection
B: Annotated photocopy of holograph with autograph corrections and additions in pencil. Bars crossed out in pencil; sketches for these bars on p. [3]
Present location: British Library: LOAN 101.95a
No printed first edition

MINUET FOR TWO RECORDERS
Location of holograph unknown

Copyist version
Two parts in black ink; no autograph annotations
The parts are written on two double sheets of 12-stave paper measuring 27 × 17.2 cm
The manuscript paper printer's mark is shown as [incorporated into decorative emblem] "B.C." | No.26 | Made and printed in England
Present location: British Library: ADD MS 63847, leaves 12 & 13
No printed first edition

MISSA BREVIS (Opus 57)
Holograph in black and blue ink with autograph performance annotations in red ink and pencil; extensive overlays. Publication and copyright information in blue ink on bottom of first page
The score is written on three double sheets and on both sides of two single sheets of 18-stave paper measuring 36.6 × 27.3 cm
The manuscript paper printer's mark is shown as [encircled] J&W | CHESTER | LTD. | LONDON
No title page; page 1: MISSA BREVIS | Lennox Berkeley
16 pages:

- pp. 1–3   Kyrie: Lento
- pp. 4–10   Gloria: Andante
- pp. 11–12   Sanctus: Lento
- pp. 12–13   Andante maestoso
- pp. 13–14   Benedictus: Andante
- pp. 14–16   Agnus dei: Lento

No date, dedication or location is apparent
Signed by composer on upper right hand corner of page 1
Present location: British Library: LOAN 101.95h
First edition
This Mass was first performed in Westminster Cathedral on the Feast of St. | Gregory (March 12th) 1960 under the direction of Mr. Francis Cameron. | MISSA BREVIS | by | LENNOX BERKELEY | for | Mixed Voices and Organ | [Photocopy notice] | [CM logo] CHESTER MUSIC
20 pages. 254 × 179 mm
White paper wrappers. Lettered in black. Trimmed edges
Publication: © 1960 by J. & W. Chester Ltd (J.W.C.8812) @ 4/-
Anglican service version
Holograph in red and green ink together with printed score of original version with extensive autograph annotations and additions in red and black ink
The score is written on one side of a single sheet of 16-stave paper measuring

36.6 × 27.3 cm which is folded in half together with original printed score measuring 19 × 27 cm

The manuscript paper printer's mark is shown as W.H.

No title page

2 pages:

p. [1]   [new version of the Kyrie with English text]; autograph annotation: in black ink: "Responses to the Commandments"
in pencil: "In type on page facing music" referring to annotation in black ink: "This work, in its original form, is a setting of the Ordinary of the Mass, omitting the Credo. This version is an adaptation to fit the words of the Anglican Holy Communion Service. L.B."

p. [2]   Blank

17 pages:

pp. 3–19   printed score with English text and organ responses added by composer

No date, dedication, location or signature is apparent

Present location: British Library: LOAN 101.95h with original version

No printed first edition

Organ part

Holograph in black ink

The score is written on one side of a single sheet of 9-stave paper [torn in half] measuring approximately 18 × 26.3 cm

The manuscript paper printer's mark is shown as [encircled galleon] | A. L. No 12 | Printed in England

No title page

2 pages:

p. [1]   autograph annotation in black ink: "organ part of Responses"

p. [2]   blank

No date, dedication, location or signature is apparent

Present location: British Library: LOAN 101.95h with original version and Anglican Service version

No printed first edition

MONT JUIC (Opus 9)

Holograph entirely Benjamin Britten autograph

Andante maestoso

Allegro grazioso

Lament (Barcelona, July 1936) – Andante moderato

Allegro molto

Present location: Britten-Pears Library 5K1 / 2-9401152; formerly in Peter Pears' collection

First edition
MONT JUIC | Suite of Catalan Dances | for | Orchestra | by | LENNOX BERKELEY | and | BENJAMIN BRITTEN | FULL SCORE | PRICE 7/6 NET | HAWKES & SON (LONDON), LTD. | [Distributors]
64 pages. 354 × 254 mm
Green paper wrappers. Lettered in darker green. Trimmed edges
Publication: © 1938 by Hawkes & Son (London) Ltd (B. & H. 8071) @ 7/6
Later publication: © 1979 by Boosey & Hawkes (HPS [Hawkes Pocket Scores], 951). Unpriced

MR PILKINGTON'S TOYE
For piano or harpsichord
Holograph in black ink with pencil annotations
The score is written on both sides of one double sheet of 12-stave paper measuring 35 × 26 cm
The manuscript paper printer's mark is shown as DURAND & Cie 4, Place de la Madeleine, PARIS
Bound in green boards with leather spine and embossed edges; poor condition. Title on front cover: LENNOX BERKELEY | COMPOSITIONS | C.V.P.
Title page with black border [not autograph]: Mr. Pilkington's Toye | [Line drawing of dancing gentleman] | from | Lennox & John | Christmass | 1926
4 pages:
p. [i]   Title page
pp. [1–2]   Music: "Vivace"
p. [3]   Pencil sketch unidentified [15 bars]
The manuscript is dated "L.B.1926" after double bar page 3
Dedicated to Vere Pilkington
No location or signature is apparent
Present location: British Library: ADD MS 63847, leaves 1–[3] (should be 1–2) with copyist manuscript, leaves [4–5]. No printed first edition

NELSON (Opus 41)
Full score in three volumes
Present location: British Library: LOAN 101.45–47
Act I
Holograph in blue and black ink with extensive autograph corrections in pencil; extensive overlays. Rehearsal numbers in black ink and performance annotations in blue ink. Rejected pages glued together rather than crossed out. Autograph list of errata on page [ii]
The score is written on 43 double sheets of 28-stave paper measuring 36 × 26.5 cm,

four double sheets of 24-stave paper measuring 36.5 × 27 cm and on both sides of one sheet of 20-stave paper measuring 36.5 × 27 cm

The manuscript paper printer's mark on the 24-stave pages is shown as [encircled] J & W | CHESTER | LTD | LONDON No.24

Bound in hard covers of dark green buckram; spine sewn but many pages detached. Tattered condition

Spine: NELSON – FULL SCORE – ACT I – BERKELEY

No title page; page 1 [not autograph]: NELSON | Opera in Three Acts. | Libretto by Alan Pryce-Jones; Music by Lennox Berkeley

194 pages:

p. [i]	Blank with Chester Music stamps
p. [ii]	Errata in pencil and orange pencil by composer
pp. 1–99	Music
pp. [100–110]	Bound together at right hand edges to be superseded by:
pp. 100–107	Music continued
p. [108]	Covered over with white sheet
pp. 108–46	Music continued
p. [147]	Covered over with white sheet
pp. 147–68	Music continued
p. [169]	Blank
pp. 169–75	Music continued – "END OF ACT I"
p. [176]	Blank
pp. [177–78]	End papers; no staves

No date, dedication, location or signature is apparent

Present location: British Library: LOAN 101.45

Act II: Volume II

Holograph in blue and black ink with rehearsal and page numbers in blue pencil, performance annotations in red ink and pencil, and autograph additions and corrections in pencil, some overlays. Page [ii] contains list of errata, some autograph The score is written on 24 double sheets and on both sides of one single sheet of 24-stave paper measuring 36.5 × 26.8 cm, on both sides of one single sheet of 18-stave paper measuring 36.8 × 26.8 cm and on 14 double sheets of 28-stave paper measuring 36 × 26.5 cm; two fly sheets without staves with annotations

The manuscript paper printer's mark on some of the 24-stave pages is shown as [encircled] J & W | CHESTER | LTD | LONDON No.24

No title page; page 1: ACT II | SCENE 1

156 pages:

p. [i]	Blank except for Chester stamps
p. [ii]	Errata list in pencil and orange pencil, some autograph
pp. 1–90	ACT II	Scene 1: "Lento"
pp. 1–48	Scene II "The Garden at Merton" Lord Minto? and Hardy

p. [48]   Insert
p. [49]   Blank
pp. 49–59   Scene II continued – "END OF ACT II"
p. [60]   Blank
pp. [61–62]   Blank endpapers, no staves

No date, dedication, location or signature is apparent
Present location: British Library: LOAN 101.46

Act III: Volume III

Holograph in blue and black ink with rehearsal and page numbers in blue pencil, performance annotations in red ink and pencil, and autograph additions and corrections in pencil and red pencil, some overlays. Page [ii] contains autograph list of errata

The score is written on seven double sheets and on both sides of 32 single sheets of 24-stave paper measuring 35.7 × 26.8 cm, and on 15 double sheets and both sides of one single sheet of 28-stave paper measuring 36 × 26.5 cm; two fly sheets without staves with annotations

The manuscript paper printer's mark on some of the 24-stave pages is shown as [encircled] J & W | CHESTER | LTD | LONDON No.24

No title page; page 1: ACT III | SCENE 1 [In front of the George Inn at Portsmouth | A crowd has assembled to bid | farewell to Nelson.]

158 pages:

p. [i]   Blank, Chester copyright stamp
p. [ii]   Autograph list of errata
pp. 1–74   Scene 1: Allegro con brio
pp. 74–98   Interlude: Piu Lento
pp. 98–131   Scene II: Meno vivo
pp. 131–135   [Interlude], p. 135 CONCERT ENDING in pencil highlighted with pink crayon box
pp. 135–154   Scene III: (The Terrace at Merton) [Emma and Hardy]
pp. [155–156]   Blank endpapers, no staves

The manuscript is dated "Full Score finished 31–VII–54"
No dedication, location or signature is apparent
Present location: British Library: LOAN 101.47
No printed first edition
Publication: © 1954 by J. & W. Chester Ltd; score and parts housed in hire library
Only libretto was printed

Vocal score

Location of complete holograph unknown

Act I

Holograph of Act I only in blue and black ink with extensive autograph annotations and additions in pencil and extensive overlays

The score is written on both sides of 40 sheets of 22-stave paper measuring 36.7 × 27.2 cm and on both sides of one sheet of 18-stave paper measuring 36.5 × 27 cm plus two sheets without staves used for binding

The manuscript paper printer's mark is shown as [embossed] J & W | CHESTER | LTD | LONDON & GENEVA No.22 and [encircled in blue ink] J & W | CHESTER | LTD | LONDON No.18

Bound in grey boards with green cloth spine, sewn with two fly leaves which the composer has partially annotated

Title page [autograph in pencil]: NELSON | ACT I | (Piano Score)

86 pages:

p. [i]	Title page
p. [ii]	Blank
pp. [1]–82	NELSON	ACT I
pp. [83]–[84]	Blank

No date, dedication or location are apparent

The manuscript is signed by the composer on upper right hand corner of page 1

Present location: British Library: LOAN 101.42

No printed first edition

Publication: © 1954 by J. & W. Chester Ltd; score and parts housed in hire library

Other versions

1. Bound dyeline of copyist manuscript of complete vocal score with minimal autograph annotations in pencil in Act III, Scene III, pp. 454–5 and 458. Some pages crossed out in pencil.

Present location: British Library: LOAN 101.43

2. Bound dyeline of copyist manuscript of Acts I & II, used for performance by Robert Keys or Mr Frederick Sharp? Both these names appear at top page 1. Performance annotations in blue ink are not autograph

Present location: British Library LOAN 101.44

Libretto

First edition (Libretto)

NELSON | OPERA IN THREE ACTS | LIBRETTO BY | ALAN PRYCE-JONES | MUSIC BY | LENNOX BERKELEY | J. & W. CHESTER LTD | 11 GREAT MARLBOROUGH STREET | LONDON W.1

56 pages. 192 x 128 mm

Blue stiff paper wrappers. Lettered in red. Trimmed edges

Publication: © 1954 by J. & W. Chester Ltd. Unpriced

Printed by Bradford & Dickens, London WC1

NIGHT COVERS UP THE RIGID LAND (Opus 14, no.2)

Holograph in black ink with minimal editorial annotations in pencil and red ink

The unbound score is written on two double sheets of 12-stave paper measuring 30.4 × 23.9 cm
No manuscript paper printer's mark is apparent
Title page: [not autograph in red pencil] WR Song – Taken | [autograph in pencil] The poem is reprinted | by permission of the Author | Night Covers up the rigid land (Auden) | Lennox Berkeley | [stamp encircled] Boosey & Hawkes Ltd. | 295 Regent Street | LONDON W.1. | MUSIC PUBLISHERS, & Co. | H15010 | Copt. Boosey + Co. Ltd
8 pages:
p. [i]   Title page
p. [ii]   Blank
pp. [1–3] Andante tranquillo "Night covers up the rigid land"
pp. [4–6] Blank
The manuscript is not dated but has © 1938 at foot of page
Dedicated To Benjamin Britten To B.B. at top of page [1]
No location apparent
Signed by the composer on title page and on upper right hand corner of page 1
Present location: Boosey & Hawkes (H15010)

First edition
Winthrop Rogers Edition | LENNOX BERKELEY | NIGHT COVERS UP THE RIGID LAND| Poem by | W. H. AUDEN | PRICE 2/6 | BOOSEY & HAWKES
4 pages. 311 × 235 mm
Buff paper covers. Lettered in green. Trimmed edges
Publication: © 1939 by Boosey & Co., Winthrop Rogers Edition (H.15010) @ 2/6
Printed in England

NOCTURNE FOR HARP (Opus 67, no.2)
Holograph in black ink with minimal autograph corrections in pencil; overlays
The score is written on four pages with cover sheets measuring 34 × 27 cm
The manuscript paper printer's mark is shown as WH Nr.5.F.16
Title page?
8 pages:
pp. [i–ii] Blank
pp. 1–4   Music "Andante con moto"
pp. [5–6]   Blank
Manuscript is dated 1967 and dedicated "For Hannah Francis" by the composer.
Signed by the composer on upper right hand corner of p. 1

Present location: British Library: LOAN 101.87b
First edition
Cover: H 144 | NOCTURNE FOR HARP | LENNOX BERKELEY | STAINER AND BELL | GALAXY MUSIC CORP | 50p Publication: Stainer & Bell 1972
4 pages. 304 × 228 mm
Blue stiff paper wrappers. Lettered in black over design in white lettering using text "MODERN HARP". Trimmed edges
Publication: © 1972 by Stainer & Bell @ 50p
Edited by David Watkins
Printed by Galliard Ltd, Great Yarmouth, Norfolk

NOCTURNE FOR ORCHESTRA (Opus 25)
Holograph in blue and black ink with autograph corrections in pencil; overlays. Production annotations in red and blue crayon and pencil
The score is written on seven double sheets of 28-stave paper measuring 43.2 × 30 cm
The manuscript paper printer's mark is shown as [encircled] J&W | Chester | Ltd. | London
Bound in grey boards with cloth spine; taped and sewn
Title page [autograph]: 26219 [stamp] | NOCTURNE | for | Orchestra | Lennox Berkeley | [CM Copyright stamp]
28 pages:

p. [i]	Title page
p. [ii]	Autograph [orchestration & duration ($10\,^1/_2$ minutes)]
pp. 1–22	Andante
pp. [23–26]	Blank

The manuscript is dated 1945–46 after double bar page 22 and dedicated "To Peter" by the composer on upper left hand corner of page 1
No location apparent
Signed by the composer on upper right hand corner of page 1
Present location: British Library: LOAN 101.8
First edition (Miniature score)
Cover: LENNOX BERKELEY | NOCTURNE | FOR ORCHESTRA | J. & W. CHESTER Ltd., | LONDON: | 11 Great Marlborough Street, W.1.
24 pages. 190 × 140 mm
Blue stiff paper wrappers. Lettered in black. Trimmed edges
Publication: © 1948 by J. & W. Chester Ltd (J.W.C.113) @ 5/-
Printed by Bradford & Dickens, London WC1

ODE (Partition)

Holograph in black ink with autograph one-line pencil sketch on last page; pencil bar lines

The score is written on four double sheets of 28-stave paper measuring 32.8 × 26.9 cm

The manuscript paper printer's mark is shown as Néocopie Musicale, Paris (No. 10) lower left hand corner

Title page [autograph]: ODE | (Partition) | Lennox Berkeley

16 pages:

p. [i]	Title page
p. [ii]	Blank
pp. 1–11	Ode "O Vous qui regnez sur les ondes"
pp. [12–14]	Blank; 6-bar unidentified pencil sketch on p. [14]

No date, dedication or location is apparent

Signed by composer on title page and on upper right hand corner of page 1

Present location: British Library: LOAN 101.66b

No printed first edition

ODE DU PREMIER JOUR DE MAI (Opus 14, no.2)

Holograph in pencil

The score is written on two double sheets of 12-stave paper measuring 31 × 23.5 cm

No manuscript paper printer's mark apparent

Title page [autograph]: Ode du Premier Jour de Mai | (Jean Passerat) | Lennox Berkeley

8 pages:

p. [1]	Title page
pp. [2–7]	Allegro
p. [8]	Blank

No date, dedication or location is apparent

Signed on title page

Present location: British Library: LOAN 101.92d

First edition

Ode du premier jour de Mai | Words by | Jean Passerat | Music by | Lennox Berkeley | J. & W. CHESTER, LTD., | LONDON: 11, GREAT MARLBOROUGH STREET, W.1.

8 pages. 306 × 240 mm

Buff paper wrappers. Lettered in black. Trimmed edges

Publication: © 1945 by J. & W. Chester Ltd (J.W.C.4035) @ 2/-

ORANGES AND LEMONS: contribution to the review (1948)

1. *Jig-saw*

Holograph (incomplete) in black ink with autograph pencil additions and corrections; overlays. Rehearsal numbers in orange crayon

The unbound score is written on one double sheet of 18-stave paper measuring 36.5 × 27 cm

The manuscript paper printer's mark is shown as [encircled] J&W | CHESTER | LTD | LONDON | No. 18

No title page or title details

4 pages:

pp. 3–5   Begins with Rehearsal No. 4
pp. 5–6   Moderato (Tempo Primo)
            p. 5, Bar 1: "[the children separate the couple.]"
            p. 5, Bar 3: "[They close the puzzle]"

The manuscript is dated "July 1948" after double bar page 6

No dedication, location or signature is apparent

Present location: British Library: LOAN 101.41b with Venus Anadyomene holograph (incomplete)

2. *Venus Anadyomene*

Holograph (fragment) in black ink with autograph pencil additions and corrections; overlays. Rehearsal numbers in orange crayon

The unbound score is written on one double sheet and on one side of a single sheet of 18-stave paper measuring 36.5 × 27 cm

The manuscript paper printer's mark is shown as [encircled] J&W | CHESTER | LTD | LONDON | No. 18

No title page or title details apparent

6 pages:

pp. 3–5   Starts one bar before Rehearsal No. 3
            p. 3, r. 3, bar 5: Allegro "[Entry of Venus]"
            Rehearsal No. 4 "[The Mermen blow on their conch shells]"
            p. 4, r. 4, bar 5: "[The Mermen blow madly]"
            p. 5, bar 1: "[Venus tells the Mermen to make less noise]"
            p. 5, r. 6: "[She approaches the boy]"
p. 5   Andante "[… He walks …]"
pp. 5–6   Pas de deux "[Venus and the Boy]" | Moderato
pp. 6–7   Allegro "[Venus carries off the boy]"
p. [8]   Blank

The manuscript is dated "July 1945" after double bar page 7

No dedication, location or signature is apparent

Present location: British Library: LOAN 101.41b with Jig-Saw holograph (incomplete)

No printed first edition

OUT OF CHAOS

Holograph in black ink with autograph pencil annotations and rehearsal numbers in blue pencil

The unbound score is written on six double sheets of 22-stave paper measuring 37 × 27.5 cm

The manuscript paper printer's mark is shown as [embossed and encircled] J&W CHESTER LTD. | LONDON & GENEVA No.22

No title page; page 1 [autograph]: OUT OF CHAOS | Lennox Berkeley

24 pages:

pp. 1–11   I. Moderato
pp. 12–20   II. Shipyard Sequence (Stanley Spencer): Allegro
pp. 20–21   III. Allegro (Battle of Britain)
pp. 21–24   Andante (Totesmeer) P. Nash

No date, dedication or location is apparent

Signed by composer on upper right hand corner of page 1

Present location: British Library: LOAN 101.65

No printed first edition

OVERTURE FOR CHAMBER ORCHESTRA (Opus 8)

Holograph in black ink with autograph performance annotations in pencil and red pencil, including "Duration approx. 8 mins"; overlays. Production annotations in red, orange and blue. Pencil bar lines

The score is written on ten double sheets of 32-stave paper measuring 39.8 × 29 cm

Bound in stiff orange paper wrappers, metal piece securing spine, pages taped; with label on front: Chester's Circulating Music Library | Full Score | No.224801 | Berkeley, Lennox | Overture (1934)

No title page; p. 1: OVERTURE | Allegro | Lennox Berkeley

40 pages

pp. 1–38   Music: Allegro
pp. [39–40]   Blank

The manuscript is dated "Cap Ferrat [France] 1934" after double bar p. 38

No dedication or opus number is apparent

Signed by composer on upper right hand corner of page 1

Present location: British Library: LOAN 101.1

No printed first edition

Publication: © 1934 by J. & W. Chester Ltd; score and parts housed in hire library

PALM COURT MUSIC: DIANA AND ACTAEON WALTZ (Opus 81, no.2)

Holograph in black ink with autograph annotations in pencil and blue ink; overlays

The score is written on six double sheets of 24-stave paper measuring 36.8 × 27 cm

No manuscript paper printer's mark is apparent

Formerly bound with sellotape

No title page; page 1: [autograph in black ink] For Dicky Buckle. PALM COURT MUSIC. Diana and Actaeon Waltz

24 pages:

pp. [i–ii]	Blank
pp. 1–10	Lento
pp. 10–16	Allegro moderato;
	Performance instruction: at end of page 16 there is an instruction to repeat from rehearsal [1] on page 1 to rehearsal [16] on page 10; then skip to rehearsal [10] page 17 (Allegro moderato) to end
pp. 17–20	(Allegro moderato)
pp. [21–22]	Blank

No location is apparent

Dedicated by the composer "For Dicky Buckle" top centre of page 1

Signed by the composer upper right hand corner of page 1

Present location: British Library, ADD MS 63066 with two letters:

A: Letter dated 18/10/82

From Roderick Lakin [SPNM]

To Sir Lennox Berkeley

"I am writing on behalf of Elizabeth Maconchy, to thank you for your donation of the MS of your Palm Court Waltz for the Francis Chagrin Fund auction...."

B: Letter dated 8/10/82

From Zoe Knott, Promotions Assistant, Chester Music

To Mrs Elizabeth Maconchy, President SPNM

"On behalf of Sir Lennox Berkeley, I have pleasure in enclosing the MS of his Palm Court Waltz [stet.] to be auctioned for the Francis Chagrin Fund. I do hope that this appeal will be successful."

Other versions

Copies of holograph – annotated

1. Dyeline with performance annotations in pencil, some autograph
2. Photocopy comb-bound in blue stiff paper wrappers with minimal annotations

Present location: British Library: LOAN 101.29b with sketches

No printed first edition

Publication: © 1971 by J. & W. Chester Ltd

PALM COURT WALTZ (Opus 81, no.2a)

Piano duet arrangement

Version A

Holograph in black ink with extensive performance annotations and corrections in pencil and blue ink, and bars crossed out; overlays. Heavily thumbed in lower right hand corner from frequent performance

The score is written on four double sheets of 16-stave paper measuring 36.8 × 27 cm

No manuscript paper printer's mark is apparent

Spine sewn with brown wool thread

Title page: PALM COURT WALTZ | Piano Duet Arrangement | LENNOX BERKELEY

16 pages:

p. [i]	Title page
pp. [ii–iii]	Blank
pp. 1–10	Lento [presented as for piano duet performance, Parts I & II on facing pages with corresponding page turns]
pp. [11–13]	Blank

The manuscript is dedicated "For Burnet [Pavitt] with love and gratitude. Lennox December 1971" by the composer on upper left hand corner of page 1

Signed by composer on title page

Present location: British Library: LOAN 101.90d with autograph sketches and annotated photocopy of fair copy score (possibly version B) with overlays

Version B

Holograph in black ink with autograph annotations in blue and red ink and pencil; pasteovers. Written with parts on facing pages to be performed as piano duet

The score is written on four double sheets of 16-stave paper measuring 36.4 × 27.2 cm

No manuscript paper printer's mark is apparent

Title page [autograph]: For Burnet with love and gratitude. | 'PALM COURT' WALTZ | [Piano Duet arrangement] | Lennox Berkeley

16 pages:

p. [1]	Title page
pp. 1/2	Introduction
pp. 1/2–5/6	Waltz: Moderato
pp. 5/6–9/10	Allegro vivace – Moderato – Largamente (Tempo del Introduzione)
pp. 9/10–11/12	Allegro vivace – Moderato
pp. 11/12	Meno Vivo – Allegro vivace
pp. [13–15]	Blank

Dedicated to Burnet [Pavitt] on title page

No date or location apparent

Signed by composer on title page

Present location: Private collection
First edition
Lennox Berkeley | PALM COURT WALTZ | Op.81 No.2 | for Piano Duet | CHESTER MUSIC | J. & W. Chester/Edition Wilhelm Hansen London Limited
12 pages. 298 × 222 mm
Blue stiff paper wrappers. Lettered in white. Trimmed edges
Publication: © 1976 by J. & W. Chester/Edition Wilhelm Hansen London Ltd (J.W.C.55067). Unpriced

PARTITA FOR CHAMBER ORCHESTRA (Opus 66)
Full score
Holograph in pencil with tempo markings in black ink and annotations in pencil. Publication information in black ink at the bottom of the first page. Inserted slip of blue paper inside front cover containing autograph notes regarding corrections in pencil. Orchestration listed inside front cover
The score is written on 14 double sheets of 24-stave paper measuring 35.3 × 26 cm plus one blue sheet measuring 17.6 × 13.3 cm
The manuscript paper printer's mark is shown as [encircled galleon] | A. L. No 18 | Printed in England
Title page: PARTITA | FOR | CHAMBER ORCHESTRA | LENNOX BERKELEY
52 pages:

p. [i]	Title page
p. [ii]	ORCHESTRA: 1,1,2,1/2110/Timp.Perc(2)/str
pp. 1–15	I. Prelude: Allegro moderato
pp.15–26	Fugue: Allegro
pp. 27–29	II. Aria I: Andante
pp. 30–34	III. Aria II: Lento
pp. 35–50	IV. Rondo: Allegro

The manuscript is dated "Dec 1964–Feb. 1965" after double bar page 50
No location or dedication is apparent
Signed by the composer on upper right hand corner of page 1
Present location: British Library: LOAN 101.24 (also two annotated dyelines British Library: LOAN 101.25)
First edition
Commissioned by Crosby and Co. Ltd., | Farnham and first performed at the | Farnham Festival, May 17th, 1965 | PARTITA | for | Chamber Orchestra | by | LENNOX BERKELEY | J. & W. CHESTER LTD. LONDON [text encircling Chester logo] | [international distributors]
48 pages. 190 × 268 mm
Blue stiff paper wrappers. Lettered in white. Trimmed edges

Publication: © 1966 by J. & W. Chester Ltd (J.W.C.289) @ 10/-
Printed by Lowe and Brydone (Printers) Ltd, London
Piano reduction [Movement I]
Holograph in pencil
The score is written on two double sheets of 24-stave paper measuring 35.3 × 26 cm
The manuscript paper printer's mark is shown as [encircled galleon] | A. L. No 18 | Printed in England
Movements I and II on A.L. No. 18 paper and III on J&W Chester Ltd. London No. 24
Title page: PARTITA | I | Prelude & Fugue | (Piano Reduction)
8 pages:
p. [i]   Title page
p. [ii]   Blank
pp. 1–3   I. Prelude: Allegro moderato
pp. 4–6   Fugue: Allegro
No date, dedication or location is apparent
Signed by composer upper right hand corner of page 1
Present location: British Library: LOAN 101.24
Piano reduction [Movements II–III]
Holograph in pencil
The score is written on one double sheet of 24-stave paper measuring 36.8 × 36.8 cm
The manuscript paper printer's mark is shown as [encircled] J&W | CHESTER | LTD | LONDON No. 24
No title page
4 pages:
p. [1]   Aria I
pp. [2–3]   Aria II: Lento
p. [4]   Blank
No date, dedication, location or signature is apparent
Present location: British Library: LOAN 101.24
No printed first edition

PAYSAGE FOR PIANO

Holograph in black ink with minimal autograph annotations in pencil; overlays
The unbound score is written on one double sheet and on both sides of a single sheet of 12-stave paper measuring 30.2 × 23.8 cm
No manuscript paper printer's mark is apparent
No title page; page 1: [autograph] To Raymond Mortimer | Paysage de France | Lennox Berkeley

6 pages:
pp. 1–5 Andante tranquillo
p. 2 Un poco piu Vivo
p. 4 Tempo Primo
p. [6] Blank except for series of notes on top barline

The manuscript is dated 1944 after double bar on page 5 and dedicated to Raymond Mortimer on top of page 1 by the composer
Signed by the composer on upper right hand corner of page 1
Present location: British Library: LOAN 101.89c
No printed first edition

PETITE SUITE FOR OBOE AND CELLO

Two copyist manuscripts – different versions
A: Copyist manuscript in black and purple ink with autograph additions and corrections in pencil, including movement titles; overlays. Blocks of black ink. Fingering and phrasing annotations in pencil
The score is written on three double sheets of 12-stave paper measuring 34.8 × 27 cm
No manuscript paper printer's mark is apparent
No title page or any title details
12 pages:
pp. 1–3 I. Moderato [additional autograph annotation in pencil, over I] "Prelude"
p. 1 [pencil annotation] "(19 rue du Mont-C-)" in upper right hand corner
pp. 3–6 II. Allegro Moderato [additional autograph annotation in pencil, over II] "Allegro Moderato"
p. 5 Trio. Meno mosso
pp. 6–7 [overlay in purple ink] III. BOUREE [Hautbois tacet] | Allegro con moto
pp. 7–8 "IV [Violoncelle tacet]" Lento. Lamentoso. [autograph addition in pencil over IV] Aria
pp. 8–10 V GIGUE
p. [11] Autograph sketch in black ink of 7 bars from V. rehearsal no. 7
p. [12] [autograph annotation in pencil] Miss Wadham | London Contemporary Music Society | 117–123 Gt. Portland Street. | B'Charon – NB | 30/29 avenue Ho Chi | D'Abrami

The copyist manuscript is dated "Paris. Mars–Avril 1927"
No dedication or signature is apparent
Present location: British Library: LOAN 101.84a with other copyist manuscript (dyeline & photocopy), oboe part

B: Copyist manuscript location unknown
Details taken from annotated dyeline copy
Title page: [typescript] LENNOX BERKELEY | PETITE SUITE | FOR | OBOE AND VIOLINCELLO
Title on page [1]: [annotated in pencil by composer] Petite Suite | Pour | [addition by composer in pencil] for | Oboe and Violoncello | Lennox Berkeley | (1928)
Dyeline copy with autograph corrections and additions in pencil
Present location: British Library: LOAN 101.84a with photocopy of same with performance annotations in pencil; other copyist manuscript, oboe part

Oboe part
Holograph in black ink with autograph annotations in pencil
The part is written on two double sheets of 12-stave paper measuring 33.1 × 26.8 cm
The manuscript paper printer's mark is shown as [horizontal lower left] Néocopie Musicale, Paris (No.3)
No title page; p.[1]: Suite pour Hautbois et Violoncelle
8 pages:
p. [1]   I. Moderato – Pio Lento – a tempo
p. [1]   [annotation in pencil under signature] "19 rue du Mont C-"
pp. [2–3]   II. Allegro Moderato. – Trio. Meno Moss. Da Capo
p. [3]   III. Bouree – Hautbois Tacet.
p. [3]   IV. ARIA – Lento
p. [4]   V. Gigue – Allo Modo
pp. [5–8]   Blank
No date, dedication or location apparent
Signed "Berkeley" on upper right hand corner of page [1]
Present location: British Library: LOAN 101.84a with two versions of copyist manuscripts
No printed first edition

PIECE FOR CLAVICHORD
Holograph in black ink
The score is written on one side of one double sheet of 12-stave paper measuring 34.4 × 26.5 cm
No manuscript paper printer's mark is apparent
No title page; page 1 [pencil not autograph]: "Piece for Clavichord"
1 page:
p. [14]   [Final page of Suite for Harpsichord]
No date, dedication, location or signature is apparent
Present location: British Library ADD MS 63848 with Suite for Harpsichord
No printed first edition

PIECE FOR VERE (for piano or harpsichord)

Holograph in black ink with pencil annotations

The score is written on one double sheet of 22-stave paper measuring 35.5 × 26 cm

The manuscript paper printer's mark is shown as [embossed]: [encircled] J&W | CHESTER | LTD | LONDON No. 22

No title page

4 pages:

p. [1]   Music
pp. [2–4]   Blank

Autograph annotation: "For Vere – Boreham, Dec. 29th 1927" after double bar page [4]

Signed by composer upper right hand corner of page [1]

Copyist manuscript

Copyist manuscript: no annotations; pencil sketch [not autograph] for keyboard 5½ bars

Title page [not autograph]: for Vere No.3 | Piece | Lennox Berkeley | Boreham 29th Dec. 1927

Present location: British Library ADD MS 63847

No printed first edition

PIECE POUR FLUTE, CLARINETTE ET BASSON

Score

Holograph in black ink with minimal annotations; initial tempo changed on full score and all parts. Blue crayon boxes surround all the rehearsal letters

The score is written on three double sheets of 12-stave paper measuring 28.1 × 22.1 cm

No manuscript paper printer's mark is apparent

Title page: [autograph in black ink] Lennox Berkeley | Piece pour Flute, Clarinette et Basson

12 pages:

p. [i]   Title page with [stamp] N.B. | 36, RUE BALLU | PARIS 9o
pp. 1–5   Allegro Moderato [Correction made to all parts]
pp. [6–11]   Blank

No date, dedication, or location is apparent

Signed by the composer on title page

Present location: British Library: LOAN 101.84b with parts

Parts

Holograph and copyist parts in black and purple ink with autograph annotations in pencil and black ink. All initial tempos corrected: Allegro Moderato

The parts are written each on one double sheet of 14-stave paper measuring 31.5 × 24 cm
All parts stamped N. B. | 36, RUE BALLU | PARIS 9o
No date, dedication, location or signature is apparent
Present location: British Library: LOAN 101.84b with score
No printed first edition

POLKA, NOCTURNE AND CAPRICCIO FOR TWO PIANOS (Opus 5)
1. Polka
Two holographs
A: Rough/performance copy:
Holograph in black ink with pencil annotations, including sketch; overlays. Poor condition with tears from spine and heavily worn on lower right hand corner probably from frequent performances
The score is written on two double sheets of 14-stave paper measuring 34.9 × 27.1 cm
No manuscript paper printer's mark is apparent
No title page; page 1 [autograph]: POLKA | Con brio; For Ethel Bartlett & Rae Robertson | Lennox Berkeley
8 pages:
pp. 1–6   Con brio; p. 6 contains autograph sketch in pencil from bar 7
pp. [7–8] Blank
The manuscript is dedicated "For Ethel Bartlett and Rae Robertson" by the composer on upper centre of page 1
No date or location is apparent
Signed by the composer on upper right hand corner of page 1
B: Fair copy:
Holograph in black ink with section of paper [one line of staff system] cut away from final page
The score is written on two double sheets of 12-stave paper measuring 33 × 26.8 cm
The manuscript paper printer's mark is shown as Néocopie Musicale, Paris. (No.4)
Bound in brown paper covers with sewn spine.
No title page; cover page: POLKA [cedilla] | Lennox Berkeley | [cedilla] 2 Pianos | [CM Copyright stamp]
8 pages:
p. [i]   "Original MS" [stamp]
pp. [1–6] Con brio; no double bar to end piece on p. [6]
p. [7]   Blank

No date, dedication or location is apparent
Signed by composer on upper right hand corner of page [1]
Note: Work incorporates corrections made in (A) but is not identical to previous rough/performance copy, particularly compare (A) first two bars p. [4] to (B) last bar p. 3 and first bar p. 4
Present location: British Library: LOAN 101.90a
Annotated printed copy
Printed copy with autograph annotations in pencil and heavily annotated for performance by Sir Clifford Curzon
Present location: British Library: CURZON ADD MS 64985

First edition
LENNOX BERKELEY | POLKA | FOR | TWO PIANOS | J. & W. CHESTER LTD LONDON [text encircling JWC emblem] | Made in Great Britain
8 pages. 336 × 260 mm
Grey paper wrappers. Lettered in black. Trimmed edges
Publication: © 1934 by J. & W. Chester Ltd (J.W.C.2924) @ 4/-

Solo piano arrangement [*Polka*] (*Opus 5, no.1*) [by composer]
Holograph in black ink with extensive editorial and production annotations in pencil and red ink by unknown hand; overlays. On page 2 the visible reverse image of the printed score of "Polka" has bled onto the page
The score is written on one double sheet and on one side of a single sheet of 12-stave paper measuring 30.3 × 24.2 cm
The manuscript paper printer's mark is shown as Paxton
Bound at spine with staples and brown tape
No title page; page 1: Polka. | Con brio; [Arrangement for Piano Solo] | Lennox Berkeley
6 pages:
pp. 1–5   Con brio
p. [6]   Blank
No date, dedication or location is apparent
Signed by composer on upper right hand corner of page 1
Present location: British Library: LOAN 101.90a

First edition
Lennox Berkeley | POLKA | Piano Solo | CHESTER MUSIC | J & W Chester/ Edition Wilhelm Hansen London Ltd | Eagle Court London EC1M 5QD
4 pages. 298 × 222 mm
White paper wrappers. Lettered in black. Trimmed edges
Publication: © 1934 by J. & W. Chester/Edition Wilhelm Hansen London Ltd (J.W.C.2221). Unpriced
"The original version of this work, for two pianos, is also available from the publishers"

Printed in England
Ensemble arrangement (*Opus 5, no.1*)
Holograph in black ink with minimal autograph additions in pencil
The score is written on two double sheets of 10-stave paper measuring 32.8 × 26.5 cm; parts are written on one side of three single sheets of 10-stave paper measuring 32.8 × 26.5 cm
The manuscript paper printer's mark is shown as Néocopie Musicale, Paris (No. 1)
No title page
Score:
8 pages:
pp. [1–6]   [autograph] Polka; Lennox Berkeley
pp. [7–8]   Blank except for crossed out heading
Parts: 1 separate page each for:
            Trompette (ut) (Con Sord: | Sempre)
            Tambour de Basque
            Triangle
No date, dedication or location apparent
Signed by composer on upper right hand corner of p. [1] and on all parts
[Pencil annotation by Peter Dickinson] "Op.5 No.1" on upper left hand corner of page [1]
Present location: British Library: LOAN 101.90a
No printed first edition
Orchestral version
Location of holograph unknown
No extant materials
No printed first edition

2. **Nocturne**

Holograph in black ink with autograph annotations in red and black ink and pencil; autograph overlays. Tattered condition, used for performance
The unbound score is written on three double sheets of 16-stave paper measuring 32.9 × 27cm
The manuscript paper printer's mark is shown as Néocopie Musicale, Paris (No.6)
Title page: [autograph] NOCTURNE | Lennox Berkeley | [purple stamp] CLIFFORD CURZON | c/o | IBBS & TILLETT | 124, WIGMORE STREET | LONDON, W.1
12 pages:
p. [i]   Title page
p. [ii]   Blank
pp. 1–8   Nocturne
pp. [9–10]   Blank
No date, dedication or location is apparent

Signed by the composer on title page and on upper right hand corner of page 1
Present location: British Library: ADD MS 64985 with annotated printed copy
First edition
LENNOX BERKELEY | NOCTURNE | FOR | TWO PIANOS | Time of Performance $3^1/_2$ minutes | [decorative border featuring Pan playing pipes] | J.&W. CHESTER LTD. | LONDON: 11, Great Marlborough Street, W.1. [international distributors]
8 pages. 335 × 260 mm
Grey paper wrappers. Lettered in black. Trimmed edges
Publication: © 1938 by J. & W. Chester Ltd (J.W.C.2929) @ 4/- complete
Printed in England

3. **Capriccio**
Location of holograph unknown
Copyist manuscript
Copyist manuscript with autograph additions in purple pencil: annotations include composer's signature, "Allegro Vivace", rehearsal numbers, and some corrections, in particular one four-bar correction after double bar
No date, dedication, location or signature is apparent
Present location: British Library: LOAN 101.90a
First edition
LENNOX BERKELEY | CAPRICCIO | FOR | TWO PIANOS | Time of Performance $1^1/_2$ minutes | Printed in England | [decorative border featuring Pan playing pipes] J.&W. CHESTER LTD. | LONDON: 11, Great Marlborough Street, W.1. | [international distributors]
12 pages. 336 × 260 mm
Grey paper covers. Lettered in black. Trimmed edges
Publication: © 1938 by J. & W. Chester Ltd (J.W.C.2928) @ 4/-
Printed in England

LA POULETTE GRISE
Full score
Holograph in black ink with minimal autograph performance annotations in pencil; durations in pencil
The score is written on three double sheets of 22-stave paper measuring 32.8 × 27.5 cm
Unbound but outer pages covered in waxy paper
Title page [autograph]: La Poulette Grise | Lennox Berkeley
Stamp on front cover, upper left: "N.B. | 36, RUE BALLU | PARIS-9o"
12 pages:
p. [i]   Title page

p. [ii]   Blank
pp. 1–7   Allegro
pp. [8–10] Blank

No date, dedication or location is apparent

Signed by composer on title page and on upper right hand corner of p. 1 [also on upper right hand corner of part]

Present location: British Library: LOAN 101.66a

Piano II part

Holograph in black ink with autograph annotations in pencil, overlays

The unbound score is written on two double sheets of 12-stave paper measuring 32.8 × 27.1 cm

The manuscript paper printer's mark is shown as Néocopie Musicale, Paris.(No.3) lower left hand side of page

8 pages:

pp. 1–[5]   Music: Allegro
pp. [6–8]   Blank

No date, dedication, location is apparent

Signed by composer upper right hand corner of p. 1

Present location: LOAN 101.66a

No printed first edition

Publication: Chester Music: score and parts housed in hire library

PRELUDE AND CAPRICCIO FOR PIANO (Opus 95)

Holograph in black ink

The unbound score is written on four double sheets of 16-stave paper measuring 30.2 × 23.6 cm

No manuscript paper printer's mark is apparent

Title page: [autograph] Prelude and Capriccio | for Piano | L. Berkeley

16 pages:

p. [i]   Title page
p. [ii]   Blank
pp. 1–3   Prelude: Andante
pp. 3–7   Capriccio: Allegro Moderato
pp. [8–14] Blank

The manuscript is dated January 1978 after double bar page 7

No location or dedication is apparent

Signed by the composer on upper right hand corner of page 1

Present location: British Library: LOAN 101.89h

No printed first edition

Publication © 1978 by J. & W. Chester/Edition Wilhelm Hansen London Ltd

PRELUDE AND FUGUE FOR CLAVICHORD (Opus 55, no.3)
Holograph in black ink with autograph annotations in blue ink and pencil; other editorial queries and fingerings. Manuscript tattered; tears repaired with discoloured clear tape

The unbound score is written on both sides of two single sheets of 16-stave paper measuring 36.4 × 27 cm

No manuscript paper printer's mark is apparent

Contained in orange folder

Cover: [not autograph in black ink] BERKELEY | Prelude for Clavichord | [pencil]: + Fugue | Op.55 No. 3

No title page

4 pages:

p. [1]	Prelude – Andantino [covered by ink blotch]
pp. [2–3]	Fugue – Lento
p. [4]	Blank

No date, dedication or location is apparent

Signed by the composer on upper right hand corner of page 1

Present location: British Library: LOAN 101.91b. No printed first edition

PRELUDE, INTERMEZZO AND FINALE FOR FLUTE, VIOLIN, VIOLA AND PIANO
Holograph in purple ink and also copyist manuscript in black ink with autograph corrections and additions in black ink and pencil; overlays. Rehearsal numbers in pencil. Bright purple ink "blocks" instead of overlays or to mark end of lines

The score is written on seven double sheets and on both sides of five single sheets of 12-stave paper measuring 31.4 × 23.4 cm

Bound in blue/grey boards (worn) in collection with "Sonatine pour clarinette et piano" and other works

No manuscript paper printer's mark is apparent

Title page of collection: [black ink, not autograph] LENNOX BERKELEY | PRELUDE. INTERMEZZO. FINALE | FOR | FLUTE. VIOLIN. VIOLA. PIANO [autograph addition in black ink] + | SONATINA for Clarinet et [stet] Piano (p.40) | [sketch in black ink of figure behind open book with musical instruments]

Title page: To | Gordon Bryan | PRELUDE, Intermezzo and FINALE | for | Flute, Violin, Viola and Piano. | Lennox Berkeley | 4 Rue du R-Paris 1928 | 8

38 pages:

pp. 1–14	Animato
p. 15	Blank
pp. 16–19	II	INTERMEZZO (Blues)	Andante

p. 20   Blank
pp. 21–36   III | FINALE | Allegro
pp. [37–38]   Blank

The manuscript is dated "Paris-Veneux les Sablons. | June–August 1927" by composer after double bar page 36

Dedicated "To Gordon Bryan" by the composer on top of page 1

Signed by the composer on title page and on upper right hand corner of page 1

Present location: British Library: LOAN 101.83a

No printed first edition

QUARTET FOR OBOE, VIOLIN, VIOLA AND 'CELLO (Opus 70)

Holograph (incomplete) in black and blue ink with autograph annotations in pencil; overlays

The unbound score is written on:

Six double sheets of 16-stave paper measuring 34.1 × 27 cm with manuscript paper printer's mark shown as [vertical left] WH Nr.5.F.16

Both sides of a single sheet of 14-stave paper measuring 34 × 27.1 cm with manuscript paper printer's mark shown as [horizontal left] WH Nr.4.F.14

One double sheet of 16-stave paper measuring 32.9 × 26.8 cm with manuscript paper printer's mark shown as Néocopie Musicale, Paris.(No.6) [upside down]

Title page [not original]: [not autograph in pencil] 2 clefs for v.c. | also Time | sig. | [autograph] L. Berkeley | String Quartet No.3. | Oboe Quartet minus first four pages [score only missing pp. 3–4]

30 pages:

p. [i]   Title page
p. [ii]   Pencil sketch
pp. 1–13   I. Moderato
                pp. 1–2 ["missing" pages]
[pp. 3–4   missing]
p. 5   I. continued
pp. 14–22   II. Presto
pp. 23–27   III. Andante
pp. [28–30]   Blank

The manuscript is dated "Sept–Nov 1967" after double bar page 27

No location or dedication is apparent

Signed by the composer on upper right hand corner of page 1

Present location: British Library: LOAN 101.87c with corrected dyeline of holograph and sketches

Dyeline "Corrected copy"

Dyeline of complete holograph with autograph annotations in pencil; overlays.

Includes dyeline copy of original title page and pages 3–4 missing from holograph. Further editorial annotations in purple and pink pencil. Editorial queries with composer's written answers

Title of dyeline copy: [stamp] Janet Craxton [autograph in pencil] Corrected Copy | to be used for | published score | L.B. | [Dyeline of original title page] QUARTET | FOR | OBOE VIOLIN VIOLA + 'CELLO. | LENNOX BERKELEY

Present location: British Library: LOAN 101.87c with incomplete holograph and sketches

First edition (Miniature score)

LENNOX BERKELEY | OBOE QUARTET | Duration: 15 minutes | J. & W. CHESTER LTD LONDON [encircling JWC logo] | EDITION WILHELM HANSEN, LONDON | [International Distributors]

20 pages. 190 × 138 mm

White stiff paper wrappers. Lettered in blue and grey. Trimmed edges

Publication: © 1970 by J. & W. Chester (J.W.C.455). Unpriced

QUARTET FOR STRINGS NO. 1 (Opus 6)

Location of holograph unknown

First edition

STRING QUARTET | By | LENNOX BERKELEY | SCORE | PRICE 7/6 NET | (Parts for hire) | HAWKES & SON | (LONDON). LTD.

36 pages. 309 × 235 mm

Brown stiff paper wrappers. Lettered in black. Trimmed edges

Publication: © 1936 by Hawkes & Son (H.14570) @ 7/6

QUARTET FOR STRINGS NO. 2 (Opus 15)

Location of holograph unknown

First edition (Miniature score)

Cover: Royal 4to | [text within lyre motif] CHESTER LIBRARY | LENNOX BERKELEY | STRING QUARTET | No. 2 | MINIATURE SCORE 4/- | PARTS 10/- | [Beneath lyre motif] J & W CHESTER LTD

24 pages. 189 × 137 mm

Brown stiff paper wrappers. Lettered in black. Trimmed edges

Publication: © 1943 by J. & W. Chester Ltd (J.W.C.257) @ 4/-

Printed in England

QUARTET FOR STRINGS NO. 3 (Opus 76)

Holograph in black ink with minimal autograph annotations in pencil; overlays

The score is written on nine double sheets of 16-stave paper measuring 35 × 27 cm
The manuscript paper printer's mark is shown as [vertical along spine] WH Nr 5.F.16
No title page; p.1: [autograph] To Anthony Chaplin | STRING QUARTET | No.3
36 pages:

pp. 1–10	I. Allegro Moderato
pp. 11–18	II. Allegro Vivace
pp. 19–24	III. Lento
pp. 24–35	IV. Molto vivace – Lento – Tempo Primo (Molto Vivace)
p. [36]	Blank

The manuscript is dated "Jan–April | June, July 1970" by composer after double bar p. 35
Dedicated to Anthony Chaplin by composer on top of p. 1
No location is apparent
Signed by composer on upper right hand corner of p. 1
Present location: British Library: LOAN 101.87d
See also autograph sketch in ink held in British Library: LOAN 101.94b
First edition
Publication: © 1970 by J. & W. Chester Ltd

QUINTET FOR OBOE, CLARINET, HORN, BASSOON, AND PIANO (Opus 90)

Holograph in black ink; overlays. Bar lines in pencil
The unbound score is written on 12 double sheets and on both sides of a single sheet of 20-stave paper measuring 36.8 × 27.1 cm
No manuscript paper printer's mark is apparent
Title page: [not autograph] Op.90 | [autograph in black ink] QUINTET | for | Oboe Clarinet Horn Bassoon | and | Piano | LENNOX BERKELEY
50 pages:

p. [i]	Title page
p. [ii]	Blank
pp. 1–13	I. Andante
pp. 13–26	II. Scherzo
pp. 37–30	III. Intermezzo: Andante
pp. 30–41	IV. Allegretto
	p. 31 Allegro Moderato (Var: I)
	p. 33 Allegro (Var: II)
	p. 35 L'istesso Tempo (Var: III)
	p. 37 Andante (Var: IV)

p. 38   Allegro Moderato (Var: V)
p. 41   Allegretto-Lento-Allegro (coda)
pp. 42–48   Blank

The manuscript is dated "October 1947–March 1975" after double bar on page 41
No dedication or location is apparent
Signed by the composer on upper right hand corner of page 1
Present location: British Library: LOAN 101.88a with pencil drafts and sketches; photocopy of holograph above with autograph annotations including "Completely Correct copy"; otherwise no major changes or corrections

First edition
Score | LENNOX BERKELEY | QUINTET | Op.90 | for | Oboe, Clarinet, Horn, Bassoon & Piano | CHESTER MUSIC | J. & W. Chester | Edition Wilhelm Hansen London Limited
49 pages. 298 × 222 mm (5 parts available separately)
White stiff paper wrappers. Lettered in light and dark blue. Trimmed edges
Publication: © 1977 by J. & W. Chester/Edition Wilhelm Hansen London Ltd (J.W.C.55072). Unpriced
Printed by Novello & Co. Ltd. Borough Green, Sevenoaks, Kent

RUTH (Opus 50)
Full score
Holograph [incomplete] in blue ink [rest of details taken from dyeline copy in BL] with autograph annotations in pencil and overlays, also non-autograph annotations in blue biro, mostly completing orchestration and other elements of score
No title page for entire work [looking at dyeline]
Scene One: A Mountainous Place near Bethlehem
The unbound score is written on nine sheets of 22-stave paper measuring 35.9 × 26.4 cm, ten double sheets of 24-stave paper measuring 36 × 26.5 cm
Title page [autograph in pencil]: Ruth | SC I | (Full Score) | [blue ink] Original MS with annotation upper left corner: Scene III [box]47 5 bars | 2nd vns.
76 pages:
p. [i]   Title page
p. [ii]   Orchestration: 2fl/hn/perc.timp=1 player for both/pf/4.2.2.2.1
pp. 1–65   RUTH | Libretto by | Eric Crozier; SCENE I; Lennox Berkeley – END OF SC:I
pp. [66–74] Blank
No date, dedication or location is apparent
The manuscript is signed by the composer on upper right hand corner of page 1

Scene Two: A Harvest Field belonging to Boaz
No title page; page 1: SCENE II | (The Harvest Field) | Allegro molto
[Title page in dyeline: RUTH | SCENE II | (Full Score)]
The score is written on both sides of eight single sheets of 22-stave paper measuring 36 × 26.4 cm and both sides of thirty single sheets of 22-stave paper measuring 36.8 × 27.2 cm
86 pages:
pp. 1–52
[Missing pp. 53–54]
pp. 55–68
[Missing pp. 69–74]
pp. 75–82   pp. 80–81 missing large chunk of upper right hand corner of page
[Missing pp. 83–84]
pp. 85–86   To END OF SCENE II
No date, dedication, location or signature is apparent

Scene Three: A Threshing-Floor, at Night
The score is written on both sides of 33 single sheets of 22-stave paper measuring 36.8 × 27.2 cm and on both sides of 20 single sheets of 24-stave paper measuring 36.8 × 27.1 cm
No title page
106 pages:
pp. 13–24
[Missing pp. 25–26]
pp. 27–28
[Missing pp. 29–30]
pp. 31–32
[Missing pp. 33–34]
pp. 35–46
[Missing pp. 47–48]
pp. 49–50
[Missing pp. 51–[52]]
Two p. 52s so sequence starts again with p.52
pp. 52–106
p. [107 or i]   Blank
pp. 107–126   incomplete
[Dyeline shows that p. 127 is missing and p. [128] Blank]
No date, dedication, location or signature is apparent
Present location: British Library: LOAN 101.52 (also autograph sketches in pencil)
Dyeline of complete Full Score comb-bound in stiff blue paper wrappers with autograph annotations in pencil and index cards with staging attached to beginning

of Scenes II and III
Present location: British Library: LOAN 101.54
Vocal score
A: Holograph in blue ink with autograph annotations in pencil, rehearsal numbers and page numbers in pencil; extensive autograph overlays
The score is written on:
one side of a single sheet of 16-stave paper measuring 36.6 × 27.1 cm
both sides of 34 single sheets of 22-stave paper measuring 36 × 26.5 cm
both sides of 21 sheets of 22-stave paper measuring 36.7 × 27.1 cm
one double and both sides of three single sheets of 18-stave paper measuring 6.6 × 27.1 cm
on both sides of eight single sheets of 20-stave paper measuring 36.5 × 27 cm
on one side of one single sheet of 28-stave paper measuring 35.9 × 26.4 cm
on one double sheet of 24-stave paper measuring 34 × 27 cm (The manuscript paper printer's mark is shown as [Lyre motif] B.C. | No.8 Printed at Leipzig)
No overall title page
144 pages:
Scene I – 36 pages:

p. [i]	Title page [autograph in pencil]: Ruth.	SCENE I.	(Piano Score)
p. [ii]	Blank
pp. 1–17	"ACT I, SCENE I	Lento	Slow and sustained"
p. [iii]	Blank
pp. 18–32	Scene I continued to end
p. [33]	Blank

Scene II – 30 pages:

	No title page
	[missing opening section of Scene II, starts after harvest choruses and just after Naomi's entrance]
pp. 43–60	Scene II, 2 bars before Rehearsal number 15 (p. 59 in printed vocal score); large sections of pp. 50–51 crossed out with autograph annotation in pencil "See correction sheet"
	[missing section from 5 bars after rehearsal number 30 (31 in printed vocal score) – duet Ruth and Boaz; starts again second bar of rehearsal number 38, p. 91 of printed vocal score]
p. [65]	Title page [autograph in pencil]: Ruth	(Pages 67–73)	Scene II; Piano reduction (original)	1 bar pencil sketch
p. [66]	Blank with pencil sketch
pp. 67–73	Scene II from 2nd bar rehearsal number 38 to end Scene II; piano reduction crossed out pp.68–69 with autograph annotation in pencil p. 69 "See correction sheet"
pp. [74–75]	Blank

p. [76]	Pencil sketch

Scene III – 78 pages:

p. [i]	Title page [Autograph in pencil]: Ruth | Scene III pages 1–28 [crossed out] and replaced with (1–24)
p. [ii]	Pencil sketch upside down
pp. 1–24	Scene III: Allegro Vivace – 9 bars into rehearsal number 26 (p. 137 of printed vocal score)
p. [iii]	Title page [pencil – not all autograph]: Ruth | Scene III | (20 pages – Piano Score) | (pp. 25–56) 32 pages inclusive | (Transfers 175–240)
p. [iv]	Blank
pp. 25–54	Continues without break from p. 24; from pp. 29–54 old numbering 1–26 crossed out; p. 35, large section of Boaz's recit crossed out
pp. [55–56 OR v–vi?]	Blank
p. [vii]	Title page [autograph in pencil]: Ruth | SC:III (Conclusion) | Piano Score
p. [viii]	Blank
pp. 55–68	Scene III, from 2 bars before rehearsal number 58 (page 196 of printed vocal score) to end
pp. [69–70]	Blank

The manuscript is dated "October 1955–July 1956" after double bar p. 68 by composer. Dedicated to Freda [Berkeley]

Present location: British Library: LOAN 101.51 (with libretto with autograph annotations in pencil including musical sketches on p. 1)

Other versions

Annotated copies of printed score (pencil, not extensive) and dyeline of copyist manuscript Scene II (timings only, not autograph)

Present location: British Library: LOAN 101.53

First edition (Vocal score)

RUTH | AN OPERA IN THREE SCENES | [star] | MUSIC BY | LENNOX BERKELEY | LIBRETTO BY ERIC CROZIER | [star] | J. & W. CHESTER, Ltd. | 11 GREAT MARLBOROUGH STREET, LONDON, W.1.

228 pages. 312 × 245 mm

Light green stiff paper wrappers. Black lettering. Trimmed edges

Publication: © 1960 by J. & W. Chester Ltd (J.W.C.9754) @ 40/-

Printed by Lowe and Brydone (Printers) Ltd, London, NW10

Libretto

Typescript with extensive autograph corrections and musical sketches

Present location: British Library: LOAN 101.51

No printed first edition

SALVE REGINA (Opus 48, no.1)
Holograph in blue ink with autograph annotations in pencil; other pencil correction and annotations in another hand
The score is written on one double sheet of 16-stave paper measuring 35.6 × 26.2 cm
The manuscript paper printer's mark is shown as [encircled galleon] | A. L. No 10 | Printed in England
No title page; p. 1: [autograph] SALVE REGINA | Lennox Berkeley
4 pages:
pp. 1–4   Moderato [blue ink] (Con moto) [autograph in pencil]
No date, dedication or location is apparent
Signed by composer on upper right hand corner of p. 1
Present location: Private collection but due to go to the British Library as LOAN 101.95m

First edition
Church Music Association of the Society of St. Gregory | [inside decorative border with lyre motif]: CHESTER | EDITION | LENNOX BERKELEY | SALVE REGINA | ANTIPHON B.V.M. | UNISON | [underneath lyre motif] CHESTER MUSIC
4 pages. 250 × 185 mm
White paper wrappers. Lettered in black. Trimmed edges
Publication: © 1955 by J. & W. Chester Ltd (J.W.C.4725). Unpriced
Printed in England

SCHERZO FOR PIANO (Opus 32, no.2)
Location of holograph: in private hands
First edition
LENNOX BERKELEY | SCHERZO | for PIANO | Price 2/6 NET* | J. & W. CHESTER, Ltd. | 11, Great Marlborough Street, London, W.1
4 pages. 307 × 248 mm
Blue stiff paper wrappers. Lettered in black. Trimmed edges
Publication: © 1950 by J. &. W. Chester Ltd (J.W.C.2315) @ 2/6

THE SERAPHINA
Location of holograph unknown; details taken from complete parts in BBC; autograph annotations in black ink (change to 3 bars) on p. 10 (No.XVIII) of Seraphina part and in pencil throughout Jimmy part
I. Moderato
II. Allegro moderato: Jimmy's first song with accordion "What sailors at sea with a fish in their hands"

III. Allegretto: Jimmy's second song with accordion "Love me, love my brother" segue to
IV. Accordion solo – not written down (ad lib) Fade Out
V. Lento
VI. Allegro moderato
VII. Allegro: trombones and strings (cello and contrabass parts cut)
VIII. Andante: Seraphina with sax and strings "There is an innocence of all created things"
IX. Moderato: Jimmy's third song with accordion "What harm could she ever do to us"
X. Solo in 5/8 for harp, triangle and strings
XI. Allegretto: Seraphina with ensemble "What is love?"
XII. Lento (Cut)
XIII. Andante con moto
XIV. Lento: sax & harp only (bars crossed out in harp part) – repeated after XXVII
XV. Andante: Seraphina with ensemble "And so slowly under the sun"
XVI. Moderato: sax solo
XVII. Allegro
XVIII. Andante tranquillo: Seraphina with sax, harp & strings "Sleep double face of troubled man"
XIX. Allegretto: sax, harp & strings (copious edits – bars crossed out in vln parts); segue to:
XX. Allegro moderato
XXI. Lento: Jimmy with accordion "O a bucket of blood and a spoon"
XXII. Moderato for sax, strings & percussion
XXIII. Andante
XXIV. Lento: Head of Orpheus (sections crossed out in parts) "I speak to you not from the tongues of the dead"
XXV. Allegro con brio: Jimmy with accordion "Now farewell my mopsey"
XXVI. Lento (parts added in for trombones)
XXVII. Andante: Harp solo
XIV. Repeated
XXVIII. Lento
Present location: BBC Music Library (BBC MS 31166); "Score with composer Lennox Berkeley"
No printed first edition

SERENADE FOR FLUTE, OBOE, VIOLIN, VIOLA AND 'CELLO (1929)
Score
Holograph in black ink with minimal autograph corrections and additions in pencil,

encircled production numbers in blue crayon

The score is written on four double sheets of 20-stave paper measuring 33.9 × 26.8 cm

Bound with clear tape

The manuscript paper printer's mark is shown as [horizontal bottom left] Néocopie Musicale, Paris (No.7)

Title page: [autograph in black ink] SERENADE | FOR | FLUTE, OBOE, VIOLA + 'CELLO | LENNOX BERKELEY

16 pages:

p. [i]	Title page
p. [ii]	Blank
pp. 1–4	Serenade	I. Lento
pp. 4–8	II. Allegro [moderato]
pp. 9–12	III. [Allegretto] con moto
p. [13]	Blank
p. [14]	[autograph in pencil] 4-bar sketch; with blue crayon sketch crossed out

No date, dedication or location is apparent

Signed by the composer on upper right hand corner of page 1

Present location: British Library: LOAN 101.84c with parts

Parts

Flute and oboe parts

Holographs in black ink with pencil annotations for performance

Each part written on one double sheet of 12-stave paper measuring 30.3 × 24.2 cm

The manuscript paper printer's mark is shown as [middle bottom] "Paxton"

Each part 4 pages

Viola and cello parts

Copyist manuscripts; no annotations

The manuscript paper printer's mark is shown as Néocopie Musicale, Paris (No.1)

Each part 7 pages

Present location: British Library: LOAN 101.84c with score

No printed first edition

SERENADE FOR STRING ORCHESTRA (Opus 12)

Holograph in black ink with autograph corrections in pencil and overlays. Queries and production annotations in pencil and blue crayon

The score is written on seven double sheets of 28-stave paper measuring 36.5 × 27 cm

Bound in orange stiff paper wrappers; spine sewn and taped. Front cover: Chester's Circulating Music Library [label] "No.22596 – MS FULL SCORE (Original)" |

Lennox Berkeley | Serenade | [copyight stamp]
Title page: SERENADE | FOR | STRING ORCHESTRA | Lennox Berkeley | 14 mins. | J. & W. Chester Ltd. | [Chester stamp]
28 pages:

p. [i]	Title page
p. [ii]	Blank
pp. 1–5	I. Vivace
pp. 6–9	II. Andantino
pp. 10–18	III. Allegro moderato
pp. 19–20	IV. Lento
pp. [21–26]	Blank

The manuscript is dated "Sept–Nov. 1939" after the double bar on page 20 and dedicated "To John and Clement Davenport" at upper centre of page 1
Signed by composer on upper right hand corner of page 1
No opus number apparent on manuscript
Present location: British Library: LOAN 101.3

First edition
Cover: LENNOX BERKELEY | SERENADE | for STRINGS | FULL SCORE 7/6 NET* | PARTS, each 2/6 NET* | J. & W. CHESTER, LTD. | 11, Great Marlborough Street, London, W.1
24 pages. 304 × 241 mm
Blue stiff paper wrappers. Lettered in black. Trimmed edges
Publication: © 1940 by J. & W. Chester Ltd (J.W.C.110) @ 7/6
Performance materials located in Hire Library

SEXTET (Opus 47)
Holograph in blue ink with autograph annotations in pencil and overlays
Manuscript in three distinct physical sections:
First Movement: I. Allegro moderato
The score of the first movement is written on two double sheets and on both sides of four single sheets of 18-stave paper measuring 35.5 × 26.3 cm
16 pages:

pp. 1–16	Music: I. Allegro moderato

Second Movement: II. Lento
The score of the second movement is written on one double sheet and on one side of a single sheet of 18-stave paper measuring 36 × 26.4 cm, bound with sellotape. An added double sheet of 12-stave paper measuring 36 × 26.4 cm covers the score
10 pages:

p. [i]	Title page [autograph] : SEXTET	2nd Movement	Lennox Berkeley

p. [ii]   Blank
pp. 1–5   II. Lento; pp. 1–3 renumbered "21–23"
Third Movement: III. Allegro
The score of the third movement is written on three double sheets of 18-stave paper measuring 34.3 × 26.1 cm
12 pages:
pp. [1]–12   III. Allegro; p. [1] annotation "See Corrected copy"
The manuscript is dated "April–June 1955" after double bar page 12, third movement and dedicated "To Alvilde [Lees-Milnes]" at the top of page 1, first movement
Present location: British Library: LOAN 101.86b
First edition (Miniature score)
Cover: LENNOX BERKELEY | SEXTET | FOR | CLARINET, | HORN & STRING QUARTET | J. & W. CHESTER Ltd., | LONDON: | 11 Great Marlborough Street, W.1.
48 pages. 191 × 138 mm
Blue stiff paper wrappers. Lettered in black. Trimmed edges
Publication: © 1957 by J. & W. Chester Ltd (J.W.C.271) @ 10/-
Printed in England

SIGNS IN THE DARK (Opus 69)
Full score
Holograph (incomplete) in pencil of movements I & II only
The score is written on three double sheets and on both sides of three single sheets of 24-stave paper measuring 35.4 × 25.2 cm
The manuscript paper printer's mark is shown as [encircled galleon] A.L. No.18 | Printed in England
No title page
18 pages:
pp. 1–8   Day of These Days "Such a morning it is when love"
pp. 9–16   Twelfth Night (Lento) "No night could be darker than this"
p. 16b   altered ending of Twelfth Night
p. 17   The Three Winds (Allegro vivace) "The hard blue winds of [March]" (first 21 bars)
            [Completely missing – Poem for Easter]
No date, location, dedication or signature is apparent
Present location: British Library: LOAN 101.79
Poem for Easter [no.4]
Two holographs
A: Holograph (incomplete) in ink with autograph annotations in pencil; overlays

The unbound score is written on two double sheets of 24-stave paper measuring 34.1 × 26.8 cm

The manuscript paper printer's mark is shown as [horizontal lower left] WH Nr.9.F.24

No title page

8 pages:

pp. 37–43   [Poem for Easter] "O Serpent in the egg"

p. [44]   Blank

The manuscript is dated "Finished July 1967 | Score written at Cla- August 1967" by composer after double bar page 43

No date or signature is apparent

B: Holograph in pencil [from rehearsal 38 of ink holograph to end]. Dates noted after double bar page 33

The unbound score is written on one double sheet of 24-stave paper measuring 34.1 × 26.8 cm

The manuscript paper printer's mark is shown as WH Nr.9.F.24 (horizontal lower left)

4 pages:

pp. 31–33   "Cold is their hope our mortal eyes"

p. 34   Blank

The manuscript is dated "Finished at Mouton July 31st 1967" by the composer after double bar page 33

No dedication or signature is apparent

Present location: British Library: LOAN 101.79

First edition (Vocal score)

LENNOX BERKELEY | Signs in the Dark | for chorus and string orchestra | Vocal Score | (Orchestral parts on hire) | [encircled] J. & W. CHESTER LTD. LONDON [logo] | [international distributors]

40 pages. 271 × 189 mm

Blue stiff paper wrappers. Lettered in white and blue. Trimmed edges

Publication: © 1968 by J. & W. Chester Ltd (J.W.C.8866) @ 12/-

SINFONIA CONCERTANTE FOR OBOE AND ORCHESTRA (Opus 84)
Full score

Holograph in black ink with autograph additions in pencil; overlays. Page numbers in blue ink. Pencil bar lines

The score is written in three distinct sections on 17 double sheets and on both sides of two single sheets of 18-stave paper measuring 36.7 × 26.5 cm and on nine double sheets of 16-stave paper measuring 36.5 × 27.2 cm

Partially bound with clear tape at the spine

No manuscript paper printer's mark is apparent

Title page: [autograph in pencil] Sinfonia | Concertante [label covering "Pf & Orch"] [autograph in black ink on top of label] Oboe & Orchestra | [pencil] I + II. [black ink] III. IV. V

108 pages:

p. [i]	Title page
p. [ii]	Blank
pp. 1–15	SINFONIA CONCERTANTE	I Lento
pp. 16–45	II Allegro Vivace
p. [45a]	Blank
p. [45b]	Title page: [autograph in pencil] Sinfonia Concertante	III&IV
p. [45c]	Blank
pp. 46–52	II.	ARIA	Adagio
pp. 53–63	IV.	CANZONETTA.	Andantino
pp. [63a–b]	Blank
p. [63c]	Title page: [autograph in pencil] Sinfonia Concertante	V
p. [63d]	Blank
pp. 64–95	V.	Allegro
	p. 84 Cadenza [see alteration on dyeline copy]
pp. [96–99]	Blank

The manuscript is dated "Nov:1972–March 1973" after double bar page 95
No dedication or location is apparent
Signed by the composer on upper right hand corner of page 1
Present location: British Library: LOAN 101.30B with index card:[not autograph] B---(L). L/A/1 | Sinfonia Concertante | Orch + Pf. | 1972–3
Also: Incomplete drafts and sketches in pencil
Present location: British Library: LOAN 101.30A
Also: Two dyeline copies of full score with extensive annotations; one complete and one incomplete.
1. Complete copy: extensive autograph pencil annotations and sketches; overlays pp. 71–72
2. Incomplete:
pp. 33–63 with editorial annotations in red ink. No autograph annotations
pp. 64–95 with autograph annotations in pencil and overlays
Present location: British Library: LOAN 101.31
First edition (Miniature score)
LENNOX BERKELEY | SINFONIA CONCERTANTE | CHESTER MUSIC | J. & W. Chester/Edition Wilhelm Hansen London Ltd.
79 pages. 190 × 139mm
White stiff paper wrappers. Lettered in blue. Trimmed edges
Publication: © 1976 by J. & W. Chester/Edition (J.W.C.55047). Unpriced
Printed in England

Piano reduction
Holograph in black ink with minimal autograph additions in pencil and black ink. Publication annotations in pencil, including "© 1975"; extensive overlays; autograph instrumentation on score in blue ink. Blue rehearsal numbers
The score is written on nine double sheets of 20-stave paper measuring 36.6 × 27 cm wrapped inside one double sheet of 24-stave paper measuring 36.8 × 26.5 cm
No manuscript paper printer's mark is apparent
Title page: [autograph in pencil] "© as used by copyist" | [autograph in black ink] BERKELEY | [autograph in blue ink] Sinfonia Concertante. | [not autograph in black ink] Op.84 (1973) | [autograph in blue ink] MVTS.1 + 2 | Reduction for Oboe and Piano. | [autograph 1-bar pencil sketch]
40 pages:

p. [i]	Title page
p. [ii]	Blank
pp. 1–4	I.	Lento
pp. 5–13	II.	Allegro
p. [13a]	Blank
pp. 14–15	III	ARIA	Adagio
pp. 16–18	IV.	CANZONETTA	Andantino
pp. 19–27	V.	Allegro
pp. [28–35]	Blank
p. [36]	Autograph 3-bar pencil sketch
p. [37]	Blank

No date, dedication or location is apparent
Signed by the composer on upper right hand corner of page 1
Present location: British Library: LOAN 101.30B
First edition (Piano reduction)
Sinfonia concertante for Oboe and Chamber Orchestra was commissioned by the B.B.C. for the 1973 | season of Promenade Concerts. It was first performed in the Royal Albert Hall on the 3rd August 1973 | by Janet Craxton with the B.B.C. Northern Symphony Orchestra conducted by Raymond Leppard. | LENNOX BERKELEY | Sinfonia Concertante | (for Oboe and Chamber Orchestra) | Piano reduction by the Composer | CHESTER MUSIC | J.&W. Chester / Edition Wilhelm Hansen London Ltd. | Eagle Court, London EC1M 5QD
Score: 36 pages; part 8 pages. 299 × 223 mm
White stiff paper wrappers. Lettered in blue. Trimmed edges
Publication: © 1976 by J. & W. Chester Ltd (J.W.C.55061). Unpriced
Canzonetta
For oboe and piano; arranged from Sinfonia Concertante by the composer
Location of holograph unknown

First edition
Cover: Lennox Berkeley | Canzonetta | from Sinfonia Concertante | for Oboe and Chamber Orchestra | [CM logo] CHESTER MUSIC
Score, 4 pages; part, 1 page. 305 × 229 mm
White stiff paper wrappers. Lettered in dark and light blue. Trimmed edges
Publication: © 1978 by J. & W. Chester/Edition Wilhelm Hansen London Ltd (CH55061a). Unpriced
Printed in England

SINFONIETTA (Opus 34)
Holograph in blue ink with annotations in pencil; overlays. Publication information in black ink at bottom of first page
The score is written on nine double pages of 24-stave paper measuring 37 × 28 cm
No manuscript paper printer's mark is apparent
Bound in light brown paper wrappers; taped and sewn. Title on cover [autograph]: "Original Score" | Full Score | Lennox Berkeley | "Sinfonietta" | for | S̶m̶a̶l̶l̶ Chamber Orchestra
Title page [autograph]: To Anthony Bernard | SINFONIETTA | for | Chamber Orchestra | Lennox Berkeley
36 pages:

p. [i]	Title page
p. [ii]	Blank
pp. 1–13	I. Allegro
pp. 14–19	II. Lento
pp. 19–30	Allegro non troppo; [pencil annotation] "13 minutes"
pp. [31–34]	Blank

The manuscript is dated August–September 1950 after double bar page 30 and dedicated "To Anthony Bernard" on title page
No location apparent
Signed by composer on title page on upper right hand corner of page 1
Present location: British Library: LOAN 101.14 with two annotated dyeline copies

First edition (Miniature score)
Cover: LENNOX BERKELEY | SINFONIETTA | FOR ORCHESTRA | J. & W. CHESTER Ltd., | LONDON: | 11 Great Marlborough Street, W.1
32 pages. 190 × 141 mm
Blue stiff paper wrappers. Lettered in black. Trimmed edges
Publication: © 1951 by J. & W. Chester Ltd (J.W.C.93) @ 7/6
Printed in England

SIX PRELUDES FOR PIANO (Opus 23)
Two holographs
A: Early version
Holograph in blue ink with extensive autograph corrections in pencil; extensive overlays. Tattered condition. Page numbers in pencil
The unbound score is written on two double sheets and on both sides of four single sheets of 12-stave paper measuring 30.1 × 23.8 cm
No manuscript paper printer's mark is apparent
No title page; p. [1]: [autograph in pencil] SIX PRELUDES LB | *see errata list
16 pages:
pp. [1]–4   I. Allegro
pp. 5–6   II. Andante
pp. 6–9   III. Allegro Moderato
pp. 10–11   IV. Allegretto
pp. 12–14   V. Allegro
pp. 15–16   VI. Andante
No date, dedication or location is apparent
Signed by the composer on upper right hand corner page [1]
Present location: British Library: LOAN 101.89d with holograph of revised version; no errata list attached
B: Revised version
Holograph in black and blue ink with title [not autograph] in pencil; autograph additions in pencil; overlays. Page numbers in orange crayon
The unbound score is written on five double sheets of 12-stave paper measuring 30.1 × 23.9 cm
No manuscript paper printer's mark is apparent
No title page
20 pages:
pp. 1–5   I. Con moto
pp. 5–6   II. Andante
pp. 7–10   III. Allegro Moderato
pp. 11–13   IV. Allegretto
pp. 13–17   V. Moderato
pp. 18–19   VI. Andantino
p. [20]   Blank
The manuscript is dated "Sept–Oct 1945" after double bar page 19 and dedicated "To Val Drewry" on top of page 1 by composer
No location is apparent
Signed by the composer on upper right hand corner of page 1
Present location: British Library: LOAN 101.89d with earlier holograph

First edition
Cover: LENNOX BERKELEY | SIX PRELUDES | for PIANO | PRICE 3/6 NET | J. & W. CHESTER, Ltd | 11, Great Marlborough Street, London, W.1
16 pages. 307 × 248 mm
Blue paper wrappers. Lettered in black. Trimmed edges
Publication: © 1948 by J. & W. Chester Ltd (J.W.C.23061–6) @ 3/6
Printed in England

SO SWEET LOVE SEEMED
Holograph in black ink with overlays
The score is written on two double sheets of 16-stave paper measuring 36.8 × 27.3 cm
No manuscript paper printer's mark is apparent
No title page; p. [1]: SO SWEET LOVE SEEMED
8 pages:

p. [i]	Blank
p. [ii]	Blank with partially erased autograph pencil sketch of piano accompaniment of first song
pp. [1–4]	Music: Allegretto
pp. [5–6]	Blank

No date, dedication or location apparent
Signed by composer on upper right hand corner of page 1
Present location: British Library: LOAN 101.93c
No printed first edition

SONATA FOR FLUTE AND PIANO (Opus 97)
Holograph in black ink with minimal autograph corrections; extensive overlays. On inside back cover sheet: "Miss S. McCrindle/ J&W Chester Ltd/Eagle Court/ London EC1." On back cover, 2-line pencil sketch
The score is written on six double sheets of 16-stave paper measuring 37 × 27 cm
No manuscript paper printer's mark is apparent
No title page; p. 1: [not autograph] SONATA | for flute and piano
24 pages:

pp. 1–10	I. Allegro moderato – Piu Lento – ancora piu lento
pp. 11–13	II. Adagio
pp. 14–22	III. Allegro vivace – Meno Vivo – Tempo I – Meno mosso – Tempo I
pp. [23–24]	Blank

The manuscript is dated by composer: "Finished 14.VIII.78 | Burton Bradstock" after double bar p. 22

No dedication is apparent
Signed by composer upper right hand corner of p. 1
Present location: British Library: LOAN 101.88b
First edition
Lennox Berkeley | SONATA | for flute and piano | Op. 97 | [copyright warning] | CHESTER MUSIC | J. & W. Chester/Edition Wilhelm Hansen London Ltd. | Eagle Court, London EC1M 5QD
Score, 22 pages; part, 6 pages. 305 × 223 mm
White stiff paper wrappers. Lettered in dark and light blue. Trimmed edges
Publication: © 1979 by J. & W. Chester/Edition Wilhelm Hansen London Ltd (CH55183). Unpriced

SONATA FOR FLUTE AND PIANO by Francis Poulenc
Arranged for flute and orchestra by Lennox Berkeley (Opus 93, no.2)
Holograph in black and blue ink and pencil with extensive autograph additions in blue ink and pencil; overlays. Bar lines in pencil. Rehearsal numbers in blue ink boxes. Page numbers in blue ink
The unbound score is written on eighteen double sheets of 20-stave paper measuring 37 × 26.8 cm
No manuscript paper printer's mark is apparent
Title page: [autograph in black ink] POULENC | FLUTE SONATA. | Orchestral Version (L. BERKELEY) | FULL SCORE
72 pages:

p. [i]	Title page
p. [ii]	Blank
pp. 1–24	SONATA	I. Allegro Moderato ["Allegro malinconico" in original]
pp. 25–35	II	Cantilena	Assez Lent
pp. 36–67	III. Presto Giocoso
	p. 67 "Alternative ending"
pp. [68–70]	Blank

No date, location or dedication apparent
Signed by the composer on title page and on upper right hand corner of page 1
Present location: British Library: LOAN 101.40 with pencil sketches
No printed first edition
Publication: © 1979 by J. & W. Chester Ltd. Unpriced

SONATA FOR PIANO IN A (Opus 20)
A: Location of holograph unknown
B: Copyist holograph with annotations by composer

Autograph annotations:
  Dated 1945 and dedication "To Clifford Curzon" upper left hand corner of page 1 [address under Lennox Berkeley: 58 Warwick Square SW1]
  II. Presto, p. 9: overlay correction for entire page in blue ink
  IV. Introduction – Allegro, p. 8: overlay for one bar in blue ink
Heavily annotated for performance by Clifford Curzon, lower right-hand edges worn from use
C: Printed score with annotations by Clifford Curzon
Minor annotations, not autograph
Present location: British Library ADD MS 64984 (Curzon Collection)

First edition
SONATA FOR PIANO | by | LENNOX BERKELEY | Duration of performance 24$^{1}/_{2}$ minutes | [decorative border featuring Pan playing pipes] J.&W. CHESTER LTD.| LONDON: 11, Great Marlborough Street, W.1. | [international distributors]
32 pages. 306 × 239 mm
Grey paper wrappers. Lettered in black. Trimmed edges
Publication: © 1947 by J. & W. Chester Ltd (J.W.C.2304) @ 7/6 (Revised price)

SONATA FOR VIOLIN AND PIANO (No. 1)

Copyist manuscript in black ink; autograph annotations in pencil and autograph overlays in black ink. Corrections and clarifications in pencil by performer
The score is written on seven double sheets of 18-stave paper measuring 36.6 × 26.4 cm inside binding sheets
The manuscript paper printer's mark is shown as [encircled] J&W | CHESTER | LTD | [outside circle] LONDON No.18
Bound in green boards with sewn spine
Cover: [gold embossed lettering] LENNOX BERKELEY | VIOLIN SONATA | 1931
Title page: VIOLIN SONATA
32 pages:

p. [i]	"7 R. B."
pp. [ii–iii]	Blank
p. [iv]	Contents page
pp. 1–12	I: Lento, ma non troppo
p. 5	[autograph addition in ink] Allegro
pp. 12–17	II: Adagio
p. 15	[autograph addition in pencil] Piu Moto
pp. 17–25	III: Allegro con bio
pp. [26–28]	Blank

The manuscript is dated "1931" after double bar page 25 and dedicated "To Gladys Bryans" on top of page 1
No location or signature is apparent
Present location: British Library: LOAN 101.85a
No printed first edition

SONATA FOR VIOLIN AND PIANO, No. 2 (Opus 1)
Holograph in black ink with production annotations in pencil; overlays
The dedication and the addition of "(No. 2)" appear on the cover sheets
The unbound score is written on one double sheet of 24-stave paper and on seven double sheets of 12-stave paper measuring 32.9 × 28 cm
The manuscript paper printer's mark is shown as Néocopie Musicale, Paris (No. 5) paper; holograph with title page wrapped in manuscript paper with printer's mark: Néocopie Musicale, Paris (No. 8)
Title page: A Mademoiselle Nadia Boulanger. | LENNOX BERKELEY | SONATA [No 2] | FOR | VIOLIN & PIANO
Page 1: Sonata ["No.2" appears to be a later addition]
32 pages:

p. [i]	Title page
p. [ii]	Blank
pp. 1–12	I. Allegro: risoluto
pp. 13–17	II. Andante
pp. 18–26	III. Rondo: Allegro moderato
pp. [27–30]	Blank

The manuscript is dedicated "A Mademoiselle Nadia Boulanger" by composer on title page
No date or location apparent
Signed by composer on upper right hand corner of p. 1
Present location: British Library: LOAN 101.85c
First edition
© 1934 by J. & W. Chester Ltd (J.W.C.377). Unpriced

SONATINA FOR OBOE AND PIANO (Opus 61)
Holograph in black ink with pencil annotations
The unbound score is written:
I. on one double sheet of 18-stave paper measuring 36.6 × 27.1 cm
II. on both sides of a single sheet of 18-stave paper measuring 36.6 × 27.1 cm
III. on one double sheet of 12-stave paper measuring 31 × 24.2 cm and on both sides of one single sheet of 12-stave paper measuring 31.1 × 23.5 cm

[sellotaped to double sheet]
No manuscript paper printer's mark except on final page: R.C.1 | [encircled galleon] | Printed in England on lower left hand corner
No title page; page 1 [autograph]: SONATINA
12 pages:

p. [1]	Blank
pp. [1–3]	I. Molto moderato
pp. [4–5]	II. Andante
pp. [6–11]	II. Allegro

Dated Sept–Oct 1962 by composer and dedicated "To Janet and John Craxton"
No location apparent
Signed by composer on upper right hand corner of page [1]
Present location: Royal Academy of Music: RAM MS NO. 523 with part
First edition (Score and part)
Lennox Berkeley | Sonatina | for Oboe and Piano | J&W Chester Ltd Eagle Court London EC1M 5QD | [International Distributors]
Score, 16 pages; Part, 4 pages. 297 × 221 mm
White stiff paper wrappers. Lettered in blue and gold. Trimmed edges
Publication: © 1964 by J. &.W. Chester Ltd (J.W.C.1619) @ 12/-
Printed by Caligraving Ltd, Thetford, Norfolk, England

SONATINA FOR PIANO DUET (Opus 39)
Location of complete holograph unknown
Movement III
Holograph in blue ink with pencil corrections and instructions to engraver
The score is written on one double sheet and on both sides of a single sheet of 22-stave paper measuring 35.5 × 26.2 cm
The manuscript paper printer's mark is shown as [encircled galleon] | A. L. No 16 | Printed in England
Spine bound with sellotape
No title page
6 pages:

pp. [1–5]	III. Allegro (alla breve)
p. [6]	[autograph in blue ink] "Last bars of Slow movement" with note in pencil; [not autograph] "This is the new part to end page 13 of proof"

No date, dedication, location or signature is apparent
Present location: British Library: LOAN 101.90B
First edition
LENNOX BERKELEY | SONATINA | FOR | PIANO DUET | PRICE 10s.

NET* | J. & W. CHESTER, Ltd. | 11 Great Marlborough Street, London W.1
20 pages. 305 × 240 mm.
Blue stiff paper wrappers. Lettered in black. Trimmed edges
Publication: © 1954 by J. & W. Chester Ltd (J.W.C.2944) @ 10s

SONATINA FOR TREBLE RECORDER (OR FLUTE) AND PIANO (Opus 13)
Score
Holograph in black and blue ink with extensive autograph additions and corrections in pencil; overlays. Bars crossed out in pencil. Editorial annotations in blue and orange pencil, including rehearsal numbers in blue pencil
The unbound score is written on three double sheets of 28-stave paper measuring 35.8 × 26.8 cm
No manuscript paper printer's mark is apparent
Title page: [Op.13 – added in pencil, not autograph] | SONATINA | for Recorder (or flute) and Piano | Lennox Berkeley
12 pages:

p. [i]	Title page
p. [ii]	3-bar sketch of Sonatina (autograph in pencil)
pp. 1–6	I. Moderato
pp. 6–7	II. Adagio
pp. 7–9	III. Allegro Moderato
p. [10]	Blank

The manuscript is dated "April–May 1939" by the composer after the double bar page 9
No location or dedication is apparent
Signed by the composer on title page and on upper right hand corner of page 1
Present location: British Library: LOAN 101.85e with part

Part
Holograph in black ink. Some sketches in pencil on inside front cover of piano part, bar 10
The unbound score is written on one double sheet of 18-stave paper measuring 35.5 × 25.6 cm
No manuscript paper printer's mark is apparent
4 pages:

pp. [1–2]	I. Moderato
p. [2]	II. Adagio
p. [3]	III. Allegro Moderato
p. [4]	Blank

Signed by the composer on upper right hand corner of page [1] of the flute part

Present location: British Library: LOAN 101.85e with score
First edition
Publication: © 1940 Schott
Other versions
Arrangement for flute and string orchestra

SONATINA FOR TWO PIANOS, FOUR HANDS (Opus 52, no.2)
Location of holograph in private hands
First edition
LENNOX BERKELEY | SONATINA | FOR | TWO PIANOS FOUR HANDS | J. & W. CHESTER, LTD. | 11, Great Marlborough Street, London, W.1
20 pages. 310 × 245 cm
Blue stiff paper wrappers. Lettered in black. Trimmed edges
Publication: © 1959 by J. & W. Chester Ltd (J.W.C.2946) @ 6/-

SONATINE (or SONATINA) FOR VIOLIN AND PIANO (Opus 17)
Location of holograph unknown; details from photocopy
The score is written on 20-stave paper
No manuscript paper printer's mark is apparent
Appears to have been bound with sellotape
Title page: LENNOX BERKELEY | SONATINA | FOR | VIOLIN & PIANO | Op.17
[14 pages]:

p. [i]	Title page
pp. [1]–5	I.
pp. 6–7	II. Adagio
p. 8	III. Allegretto
pp. 8–9	Var:I. Un poco piu Vivo
pp. 9–10	Var:II. Allegro
pp. 10–11	Var:III. Allegro moderato (Tempo Rubato)
pp. 11–12	Var:IV. Tempo di Valse
pp. 12–13	Var:V. Andante
p. 13	Tempo Primo

Dedicated to Gladys Bryans by composer on upper left hand corner of page 1
No date or location apparent
Signed by composer on upper right hand corner of page 1
Present location of holograph: in private hands
First edition
SONATINA | for | Violin and Piano | by | LENNOX BERKELEY | Duration

of performance, 14 minutes | J. & W. CHESTER LTD. | 11 GREAT MARLBOROUGH STREET, LONDON, W.1
17 pages. 305 × 240 mm
Blue paper wrappers. Lettered in black. Trimmed edges
Publication: © 1945 by J. & W. Chester Ltd (J.W.C.391) @ 7/6
Violin part edited by Max Rostal
Also: Printed first edition of score with minor corrections
Present location: British Library: LOAN 101.85f

SONATINA POUR CLARINETTE ET PIANO
Holograph in parts but mostly copyist manuscript in black ink; extensive autograph overlays
The score is written on four double sheets and on both sides of five single sheets of 12-stave paper measuring 31.4 × 23.4 cm
Bound in blue/grey boards (worn) in collection with "Prelude-Intermezzo-Finale" for flute, violin, viola, and piano, and other works
No manuscript paper printer's mark is apparent
Title page of collection: [black ink, not autograph] LENNOX BERKELEY | PRELUDE. INTERMEZZO. FINALE | FOR | FLUTE. VIOLIN. VIOLA. PIANO [autograph addition in black ink] + | SONATINA for Clarinet et [stet] Piano (p. 40) | [sketch in black ink of figure behind open book with musical instruments]
Title page: SONATINE | pour | Clarinette et piano | Lennox Berkeley | Paris 1928
26 pages:

p. 40	Title page
p. 41	Autograph sketches in pencil for Sonatine
pp. 42–45	I. Moderato
p. 52	"II."
pp. 53–57	II. Largo Lento
p. 58	"III."
pp. 59–65	III. Vivace Allegro

The manuscript is dated "Paris 1928" by the composer on title page
No dedication or signature is apparent
Present location: British Library: LOAN 101.83b
No printed first edition

SONGS OF THE HALF-LIGHT (Opus 65)
Two holographs

A: Holograph in blue ink with minimal autograph annotations/corrections in pencil on pages 11 and 20

The score is written on seven double sheets and on both sides of one single sheet of 12-stave paper measuring 30.2 × 23.8 cm

The manuscript paper printer's mark is shown as: [vertical along spine] WH Nr.5.F.16 [only on one page] – none on any other pages

No title page

16 pages:

pp. 1–3   I. Rachel: Allegro Moderato
pp. 4–6   II. Full Moon: Lento. Very quiet and sustained
pp. 7–10   III. All That's Past: Allegretto (Flowing)
pp. 11–12   IV. The Moth: Andante con moto
pp. 13–16   V. The Fleeting: Andante

The manuscript is dated "Dec. 1963–Jan: 1964" after double bar on page 16 and dedicated "To Peter Pears" upper centre page 1

Signed by the composer on upper right hand corner of page 1

Present location: British Library: LOAN 101.93e

B: Holograph in black ink

The score is written on seven double sheets and on both sides of one single sheet of 12-stave paper measuring 30.2 × 23.8 cm

No manuscript paper printer's mark apparent

Title page [autograph]: SONGS OF THE HALF-LIGHT | (FIVE POEMS BY WALTER DE LA MARE). | for high voice and guitar | LENNOX BERKELEY

28 pages:

p. [i]   Title page
p. [ii]   Blank
pp. 1–5   I. Rachel: Allegro moderato
pp. 6–10   II. Full Moon: Lento
pp. 10–15   III. All That's Past: Allegretto
pp. 16–20   IV. The Moth: Lento
pp. 21–26   V. The Fleeting: Andante
pp. [27–28]   Blank

No date, dedication, location or signature is apparent

Present location: British Library: LOAN 101.93e with annotated dyeline and sketches

First edition

Commissioned by Peter Pears | First performed by Peter Pears and Julian Bream | at the Aldeburgh Festival, 1965 | SONGS OF THE HALF-LIGHT | for High Voice and Guitar | by | LENNOX BERKELEY | Op. 65 | Five Poems by Walter de la Mare | 1. Rachel | 2. Full Moon | 3. All that's past | 4. The Moth | 5. The Fleeting | J. & W. CHESTER LTD LONDON [text encircling JWC emblem] | [international distributors]

20 pages. 306 × 238 mm
Dark grey, white and black stiff paper wrappers with drawing of moon shining through trees designed by Doreen Roberts. Lettered in white and black. Trimmed edges
Publication: © 1966 by J. & W. Chester Ltd (J.W.C.4066) @ 12/6
Guitar part edited and fingered by Julian Bream
Printed by Lowe and Brydone (Printers) Ltd, Haverhill

SONNET FOR HIGH VOICE AND PIANO (Opus 102)
Sketches
Present location: British Library: LOAN 101.94g
Sketches
A: Holograph in black ink with autograph annotations in pencil within sketches for Faldon Park
The score is written on one side of one single sheet of 18-stave paper measuring 36.7 × 27 cm
The manuscript paper printer's mark is shown as B&H [incorporated into music globe design]
2 pages:
p. [1]   Clere Venus – bien mieux. [13 bars]
p. [2]   Faldon Park: pencil sketch of end Act I duet for Barbara and Martin
Present location: British Library: LOAN 101.62
B: Holograph sketches within score for Three Pieces for Clarinet
p. [4] autograph sketch in pencil includes first two verses and 2 lines of the third stanza in pencil with one line of music; words not accurately transcribed
Present location: British Library: LOAN 101.85b
First edition
SONNET in collection: LENNOX BERKELEY (1903–1989) | THE COMPLETE FRENCH SONGS | SOLO VOICE & PIANO | CHESTER MUSIC
4 pages (pp. 53–56). 304 × 229 mm
Glossy white stiff paper wrappers with full colour portrait of Berkeley by John Greenidge in Paris. Lettered in black. Trimmed edges
Publication: © 1992 by Chester Music (CH55985) @ £12.95 (0-7119-3289-1)
Original publication: © 1982 by Chester Music; available from Hire Library

SPRING AT THIS HOUR (Opus 37, no.2)
Holograph in blue ink with minimal autograph corrections in pencil
The unbound score is written on three double sheets of 28-stave paper torn in half (= 14-stave paper) measuring approximately 22.5 × 30.5 cm

The manuscript paper printer's mark is shown on bottom left of page as [encircled] J&W CHESTER LTD. | LONDON
Title page [autograph]: 'SPRING AT THIS HOUR' | FOR | UNACCOMPANIED CHOIR | POEM By PAUL DEHN | Music By LENNOX BERKELEY
10 pages:

p. [i]   Title page
p. [ii]   Blank
pp. 1–6   Music
pp. [7–8]   Blank; p. [8] has coffee ring stain

No date, dedication or location is apparent
Signed by the composer on upper right hand corner of p. 1
Present location: British Library: LOAN 101.95f; also sketches in pencil
First edition (Separate vocal score)
No title page: SPRING AT THIS HOUR
8 pages. 253 × 178 mm
White paper. Lettered in black. Trimmed edges
Publication: © 1953 by J. & W. Chester Ltd (J.W.C.7740). Unpriced
Lowe and Brydone (Printers) Ltd, London
(Vocal score of entire collection)
[Within a gold ornament, surmounted by a crown and E II R] | A | GARLAND | FOR | THE QUEEN | Songs for Mixed Voices | Stainer & Bell Limited, 69, Newman Street, London W.1 | Made in England
86 pages: 272 × 193 mm
Turquoise and gold stiff paper wrappers. Lettered in white. Trimmed edges
Publication: © 1953 @ 12/6

STABAT MATER (Opus 28)
Full score
Holograph in blue and black ink with autograph correction, additions and sketches in pencil; extensive overlays. Annotations for production in orange. Page 39 is a page of corrections attached over original page, for Part 7, "Fac me Tecum pie flere" at "In planc tu" ...
The score is written on 15 double sheets and on one side of one single sheet of 24-stave paper measuring 36.8 × 27.1 cm. Single sheet attached as correction page to ½ double sheet, p. 39
The manuscript paper printer's mark is shown as [encircled] CORRECT TO CAPS "J&W Chester Ltd. London No. 24"
Inside, unbound, stiff orange paper wrappers
Title page [autograph]: STABAT MATER | For Six Soloists and Chamber Orchestra | LENNOX BERKELEY | Duration of performance 33 minutes.

[Chester Library stamps including no. 26269]
60 pages:

p. [i]	Title page
p. [ii]	Voices & Orchestra SI,SII,C,T,Bar,B/111(bcl)1/1000/hp/1 perc/str
pp. 1–6	I. Lento [Stabat Mater dolorosa]
pp. 7–13	II. Andante con moto [O quam tristis et afflicta]
pp. 14–18	III. Adagio [Quis est homo]
pp. 19–23	IV. Allegro [Pro peccatis suae gentis]
pp. 24–28	V. Andantino [Eia Mater, fons amoris]
pp. 29–31	VI. Lento [Sancta Mater]
pp. 32–40	VII. Moderato [Fac me Tecum pie flere]
pp. 41–43	VIII. Andante [Virgo virginum]
pp. 43–50	IX. Allegro moderato [Fac me plagis vulnerari]
pp. 50–56	X. Andante [Christe cum sit hinc exire]
pp. [57–58]	Blank

The manuscript is dated "London June–July 1947" after db p. 56 and dedicated "To Benjamin Britten" by the composer on upper left page side of p. 1

Signed by the composer upper right p. 1

Present location: British Library: LOAN 101.74

Other versions

Movement I only

Holograph in black ink with annotations in pencil and overlays. Orchestration expanded on the page as compared to holograph

The unbound score is written on both sides of five single sheets of 24-stave music paper measuring 36.8 × 26.5 cm wrapped inside a double sheet of manuscript paper

Untitled

14 pages:

pp. [i–ii]	Blank
pp. [1–9]	Music: Untitled [I. Stabat etc]
pp. [10–12]	pp. [11–12] have been cut up

No date, dedication, location or signature is apparent

Present location: British Library: LOAN 101.74

Vocal score

Holograph in blue ink and pencil with autograph annotations in pencil; another hand has written in text in V & VI in pencil

The unbound score is written on two double sheets and on both sides of 13 single sheets of approx. 14-stave paper (cut from larger paper, probably in half)

The manuscript paper printer's mark is shown as [encircled] J & W | CHESTER | LTD | LONDON on some sheets

Title page [autograph in pencil]: STABAT MATER. | Lennox Berkeley [signature] | 33 mins. [Chester copyright stamp]

Annotation: Please send to Mr Lennox Berkeley 8 Warwick Ave. W.9. [pencil, unknown hand]

34 pages:

p. [i]	Title page
p. [ii]	Blank except for 2-bar pencil sketch
pp. 1–3	I. Lento
pp. 4–6	II. Andante con moto
pp. 7–9	III. Adagio
pp. 9–11	IV. Allegro
pp. 12–14	V. Andantino
pp. 15–16	VI. Andante maestoso
pp. 17–20	VII. Allegro moderato
pp. 21–22	VIII. Lento
pp. 23–26	IX. Moderato
pp. 26–32	X. Lento

Dedicated "To Benjamin Britten" on upper left hand corner of p. 1

No date or location

Signed by composer on title page and on upper right and corner of p. 1

Present location: British Library: LOAN 101.74

First edition

STABAT MATER | FOR | SIX SOLO VOICES AND CHAMBER ORCHESTRA | Music by | LENNOX BERKELEY | The cover design is a reproduction of | a 13th Century Statue of the Blessed Virgin | in Naumberg Cathedral, Germany | J. & W. CHESTER Ltd. | 11 Great Marlborough Street | London, W.1

79 pages. 336 × 258 mm

Buff stiff paper wrappers with reproduction of a Statue of the Virgin Mary. Lettered in black. Trimmed edges

Publication: © 1950 by J. & W. Chester Ltd (J.W.C.9744) @ 20/-

Printed in England

SUITE FOR FLUTE (PICCOLO), OBOE, VIOLIN, VIOLA, AND 'CELLO (1930)

Holograph in black ink with minimal autograph annotations in pencil; overlays, especially page 14. Bar lines in pencil. Tattered condition. The name "John Dursley" is crossed out or pasted over on score and all parts

The score is written on three double sheets and on both sides of eight single sheets of 18-stave paper measuring 34.9 × 26.9 cm

No manuscript paper printer's mark is apparent; stamped: "N.B. | 36, RUE BALLU | PARIS-9o."

Title page: [autograph overlay in black ink] Lennox Berkeley [underneath overlay: JOHN DURSLEY] | [stamp upper right hand corner] N. B. | 36, RUE BALLU | PARIS-9o | [not autograph in black ink] SUITE | for | Flute, (Piccolo) oboe, violin, viola & 'cello. | I. Introduction & Pastorale | II. Galliard. | III. Passepied. | IV. Aria. | V. Hornpipe | [autograph in pencil] Calvet [Quartet] | 37 R Ruisselet

28 pages:

p. [i]	Title page
p. [ii]	Blank
pp. 1–2	SUITE	Introduction	Lento
pp. 2–6	Pastorale	Allegretto
pp. 7–9	II.	Galliard	Moderato
pp. 10–16	III.	Passepied	Allegro
pp. 17–19	IV.	Aria	Andante
pp. 20–24	V.	Hornpipe	Allegro
pp. 25–26	Blank

No date, dedication or location is apparent

Signed by the composer [overlays covering "John Dursley"] on title page and on upper right hand corner of page 1

Present location: British Library: LOAN 101.84d with five parts

Parts

Four holograph parts in black ink; viola part is copyist manuscript; annotations in pencil

Five parts: each part written on one double sheet of 12-stave paper measuring 29.8 × 23 cm

No manuscript paper printer's mark is apparent

No date, dedication or location is apparent

Signed by "John Dursley" on upper right hand corner of page 1 on all parts; crossed out on flute, violin and cello parts

Present location: British Library: LOAN 101.84d with holograph score

No printed first edition

SUITE FOR HARPSICHORD

Holograph in black ink

The score is written on four double sheets of 12-stave paper measuring 34.4 × 26.5 cm

Spine is stapled

No manuscript paper printer's mark is apparent

Title page [autograph]: TO | VERE PILKINGTON | SUITE | FOR THE | HARPSICHORD | LENNOX BERKELEY

16 pages:

p. [i]	Title page
p. [ii]	Blank
pp. 1–2	I. Lento
pp. 3–5	II. Allegro moderato
pp. 6–7	III. "Sarabande" – Lento
pp. 8–9	IV. "Allegretto" – Tranquillo
pp. 10–12	V. "March" – Introduction: Moderato (quasi cadenza) – Tempo di marcia
p. [13]	Blank
p. [14]	[Piece for Clavichord]

Dated by composer "Paris May–June 1930" after double bar page 12
Dedicated "To Vere Pilkington" upper left hand corner of page 1
Signed by the composer on upper left hand corner of page 1
Present location: British Library ADD MS 63848, leaves 1–8 with copyist manuscript and "Piece for Clavichord"
No printed first edition

SUITE FOR STRING ORCHESTRA (Opus 87)

Holograph in black ink with minimal autograph annotations in pencil; overlays. Bar lines added in pencil
The unbound score is written on six double sheets and on both sides of one single sheet of 18-stave paper measuring 36.8 × 26.8 cm
No manuscript paper printer's mark is apparent
Title page: SUITE FOR STRINGS | LENNOX BERKELEY

26 pages:

p. [i]	Title page
p. [ii]	Blank
pp. 1–6	I. Introduction + Fugue.	Lento
pp. 7–10	II.	AIR	Andantino
pp. 11–20	III.	Scherzo
pp. 21–22	IV. Epilogue	Lento sostenuto
pp. [23–24]	Blank

The manuscript is dated "Nov:1973–Jan:1974" by the composer after double bar page 22
No dedication or location is apparent
Signed by the composer on title page and on upper right hand corner of page 1
Present location: British Library: LOAN 101.34 with drafts and sketches in

pencil; photocopy of holograph with minimal annotations [not autograph] for performance
No printed first edition
Publication: © 1974 by J. & W. Chester Ltd; score and parts housed in hire library

SUITE FROM "A WINTER'S TALE" (Opus 54)
Holograph in black and blue ink with autograph additions in pencil; overlays. Autograph sketches on inside back cover sheets
The score is written on both sides of five single sheets and 13 double sheets of 24-stave paper measuring 36.8 × 27.1 cm and one double sheet of 22-stave paper measuring 35.4 × 26.2 cm
No manuscript paper printer's mark is apparent
Title page: THE WINTER'S TALE. | LENNOX BERKELEY. | FULL SCORE
Title on first page: "A Winter's Tale", the "A" has "The" written over it in pencil
A [The] Winter's Tale
64 pages:

pp. 1–6	A THE [pencil] Winter's Tale	Prologue	Lennox Berkeley	1960	Lento
pp. 7–17	The Banquet: Allegro vivace
pp. 17–20	Andante (Nocturne)
pp. 21–24	Allegretto (Mamillius)
pp. 25–39	Andante (The Storm)
p. 39	Lento
pp. 40–45	Florizel and Perdita: Andante
pp. 46–53	Shepherd's Dance: Allegro moderato
pp. 54–59	The Statue: Andante
pp. [60–62]	[pencil sketches]
pp. [63–64]	Blank

The manuscript is dated Oct–Dec. 1960 after double bar page 59
No dedication or location is apparent
Signed by the composer on title page and on upper right hand corner of page 1
Present location: British Library: LOAN 101.21a
First edition (Miniature score)
Cover: LENNOX BERKELEY | SUITE: | "A WINTER'S TALE" | OPUS 54 | FOR | ORCHESTRA | J. & W. CHESTER, LTD. | LONDON: | 11 GREAT MARLBOROUGH STREET, W.1
64 pages. 190 x 140 mm
Light green stiff paper wrappers. Lettered in black. Trimmed edges
Publication: © 1962 by Chester Music (J.W.C.127) @ 12/6
Printed by Lowe and Brydone (Printers) Ltd, London

SUITE FROM "NELSON" (Opus 42)
Holograph in blue ink with autograph corrections and additions in pencil; extensive overlays. Production annotations in blue and pencil. Performance annotations
The score is written on 32 sheets of 28-stave paper measuring 35.4 × 26.3 cm
No manuscript paper printer's mark is apparent
Bound in dark green cloth boards with flyleaves, spine is sewn and taped. Cover lettered in gold embossed: NELSON SUITE | BERKELEY
Title page: [stamp] 26375.B | NELSON SUITE | 1. The Sailing of the Victory 2. The Cockpit 3. Portsmouth | Lennox Berkeley | [FULL SCORE] | [Chester stamp] | [Copyright stamp]
64 pages:

p. [i]	Title page
p. [ii]	Blank
pp. 1–24	I THE SAILING OF THE VICTORY	Molto moderato
pp. 25–29	II THE COCKPIT	Lento
pp. 30–61	III PORTSMOUTH	Allegro con brio
p. [62]	Blank

No date, dedication or location is apparent
Signed by the composer on title page and on upper right hand corner of page 1
Present location: British Library: LOAN 101.17
No printed first edition
Publication: © 1955 by J. & W. Chester Ltd; score and parts housed in hire library

SWEET WAS THE SONG (Opus 43, no.3)
Location of holograph unknown
First edition
No title page; To Alvilde | SWEET WAS THE SONG | Carol for Choir and Organ
8 pages. 254 × 178 mm
White paper. Lettered in black. Trimmed edges
Publication: © 1957 by J. & W. Chester/Edition Wilhelm Hansen London Ltd (J.W.C.5709) @ 1/6
Printed by Halstan & Co. Ltd, Amersham, Bucks, England

SYMPHONY NO. 1 (Opus 16)
Location of holograph unknown. Description taken from annotated copy
The score is written on 18-stave paper
No manuscript paper printer's mark is apparent
No title page from holograph

111 pages
p. [i]   BBC Symphony Orchestra | Cond. Stanford Robinson
p. [ii]   Blank with annotation: "Duration of performance 33 minutes"
pp. 1–44   I. Allegro moderato
pp. 45–68   II. Allegretto
pp. 69–78   III. Lento
pp. 79–111   IV. Allegro

The manuscript is dated 1940–41after double bar on page 111
No dedication or location is apparent
Signed by the composer on upper right hand corner of page 1
Present location: British Library: LOAN 101.6; also autograph sketches in BL LOAN 101.5 and 101.102a [Autograph in black ink]

First edition (Miniature score)
SYMPHONY | FOR ORCHESTRA | BY | LENNOX BERKELEY | 1. Allegro moderato | 2. Allegretto | 3. Lento | 4. Allegro | J. & W. CHESTER, Ltd., | 11 Great Marlborough Street, London, W.1
100 pages. 190 × 139 mm
Mottled blue/grey paper wrappers. Lettered in black. Trimmed edges
Publication: © 1951 by J. & W. Chester Ltd (J.W.C.95) @ 12/6
Printed in England

SYMPHONY NO. 2 (Opus 51)
Original Version
Holograph in blue ink with autograph annotations in black ink, pencil and blue crayon; notes scratched out; overlays. Performance annotations in pencil, including rewrite of clarinet and bassoon parts on p. 19 with annotation "altered Jan '59 by composer J.W.". Title page ripped top centre and repaired

The score is written on 40 single sheets of 24-stave paper measuring 26.8 (approx.) × 36.5 cm; on one double sheet of 28-stave paper measuring 26 (approx.) × 35.8 cm; and on 33 single sheets of 22-stave paper measuring 26.4 (approx.) × 36.4 cm
No manuscript paper printer's mark is apparent
Bound in green Morocco leather binding with embossed gold lettering
Cover: SECOND SYMPHONY | LENNOX BERKELEY
Title page: [autograph in blue ink] LENNOX BERKELEY | SECOND SYMPHONY | I
150 pages:
p. [i]   Title page
p. [ii]   Blank
pp. 1–39   I | Adagio
                p. 4 Allegro Moderato

	p. 20 A Tempo
pp. [39a–e]	Blank
p. [39f]	Title page: [autograph in blue crayon] L. BERKELEY | Second Symphony | II | Full Score
p. [39g]	Blank
pp. 40–74	II
pp. [74a–c]	Blank
p. [74d]	Title page: [autograph in pencil] L. Berkeley | Second Symphony. | III
p. [74e]	Blank
pp. 75–94	III. | Lento
	p. 78 Un poco con mosso (Tempo II)
	p. 86 Tempo I
	p. 87 Un poco piu vivo (Tempo II)
	p. 92 Tempo I – Tempo II
pp. [94a–b]	Blank
p. [94c]	Title page: [autograph in blue crayon] L. Berkeley | Second Symphony | IV. | Full Score
p. [94d]	Blank
pp. 95–130	IV | Allegro Moderato
	p. 127 Lento
	p. 128 Allegro
pp. [131–132] Blank	

No date, dedication or location noted. Copyright date given as 1958 on bottom left of page 1

Signed by the composer on title page and on top right hand corner of page 1

Present location: University of Birmingham, Main Library, Special Collections, Feeney Collection

Also: Dyeline copy of holograph with autograph annotations and two pages of corrections inside front cover

Present location: Private collection

No printed first edition

Publication: © 1958 by J. & W. Chester Ltd; score and parts from hire library

Revised version (1976)

Holograph [incomplete] in black ink with autograph annotations in pencil; sketches in pencil on cover sheets; overlays

The score is written on 27 double sheets of 24-stave paper measuring 36.8 × 27 cm with five double sheets of dyeline copy of original holograph

No manuscript paper printer's mark is apparent

Title page [autograph]: L. BEKELEY [stet] \| 2nd Symphony \| I̶V̶ [crossed out in pencil] \| Revised Version

128 pages:
p. [i]	Title page
p. [ii]	Blank
pp. 1–36	I. Lento – Allegro
pp. 37–64	II. Allegro vivace
[p.65	Missing]
pp.74–93 [66–85]	III. Lento [annotated dyeline: "Revised 1972"]
pp. 85–121	IV. Allegro
pp. [122–124]	Blank
p. [125]	Sketches in pencil
p. [126]	Blank

The manuscript is dated "April–May 1976 Revised version" (Mvts. 1&2); November 1972 (Mvt. 3)
No dedication or location is apparent
Signed by the composer on title page
Present location: British Library: LOAN 101.19 with two heavily annotated dyelines LOAN 101.20. No printed first edition
Publication: © 1976 by J. & W. Chester Ltd; score and parts housed in hire library

SYMPHONY NO. 3 (Opus 74)
Full score
Location of holograph unknown
Details taken from annotated dyeline of holograph
The score is written on 72 pages of 24-stave paper
The manuscript paper printer's mark is shown as [vertical bottom left] WH Nr.9.F.24
No title page; p. 1: [autograph] to Antony and Lili Hornby | Symphony in One Movement (No.3)
72 pages:
pp. 1–72	Allegro Moderato
p. 14	Un poco meno vivo
p. 18	Tempo I
p. 31	Piu Lento
p. 33	Lento
p. 49	Tempo

The manuscript is dated "December 1967–April 1969" after double bar page 72 and dedicated "To Antony and Lili Hornby" on top of page 1
No location is apparent
Signed by the composer on upper right hand corner of page 1
Dyeline of holograph
Dyeline with extensive autograph annotations in pencil – corrections and performance annotations. Performance annotations in blue pencil

Cover title: Symphony 3 in One Movement
Present location: British Library: LOAN 101.28
Short score
Holograph in pencil with extensive autograph corrections and additions in pencil; overlays. Orchestration indicated and some pages of scoring included. Also some additional related sketches
The unbound score is written on four double sheets and on both sides of six single sheets of 24-stave paper measuring 34 × 27 cm and on both sides of a single sheet of 16-stave paper measuring 33.9 × 27.1 cm
The manuscript paper printer's mark is shown as [vertical bottom left] WH Nr.9.F.24
No title page or any title information apparent
30 pages:
pp. 1–22   Rough page numbering; many extra pages and pages removed
p. 13   Allegro [no tempo in full score holograph at this point, p. 57]
No date, dedication, location or signature is apparent
Present location: British Library: LOAN 101.28 with dyeline of full score holograph
First edition (Miniature score)
LENNOX BERKELEY | Symphony No. 3 in one movement | Duration: 14 minutes | Orchestral parts on hire only | J. & W. CHESTER LTD LONDON [text encircling JWC emblem] | EDITION WILHELM HANSEN, LONDON
88 pages. 190 × 136 mm
White stiff paper wrappers. Lettered in blue and grey. Trimmed edges
Publication: © 1971 by J. & W. Chester Ltd (J.W.C.459). Unpriced
Printed by Halstan & Co. Ltd, Amersham, Bucks

SYMPHONY NO. 4 (Opus 94)
Holograph in black ink with autograph additions and corrections in pencil; extensive overlays. Pencil bar lines. Last four bars of Mvmt III crossed out with annotation "see revised ending"; revised ending not attached to this holograph
The unbound score is written on two alternating types of paper:
1. Written on eight double sheets and on both sides of six single sheets of 28-stave paper measuring 36.9 × 27.1 cm
No manuscript paper printer's mark is apparent
2. Written on 19 double sheets and on both sides of seven single sheets of 24-stave paper measuring 38 × 27.1 cm
The manuscript paper printer's mark is shown as B&H [incorporated into music globe design]
No title page; p. 1: [autograph in black ink] To Burnet Pavitt. | Symphony | (No.4) LB
134 pages:

pp. 1–45	Lento
p. [45a]	Blank
pp. 46–81	II	Andante
	p. 48 Var:I	Allegretto
	p. 53 Var:II	Allegro
	p. 60 Var:III	Andante Lento
	p. 66 Var:IV	Allegro Moderato
	p. 76 Var:V	Adagio
pp. [82a–b]	Blank
p. [82c]	[autograph in black ink]: L. Berkeley	Symphony No 4.	(Third Movement | Full Score)	
p. [82d]	Blank
pp. 83–126	III.
	p. 100 Meno Vivo
	[no p. 101]
	p. 118 Meno Vivo
	p. 120 Tempo I
pp. [127–31]	Blank

The manuscript is dedicated "To Burnet Pavitt" on upper left hand corner of page 1. (Not on dyeline of holograph below)
No dedication or location is apparent
Signed by the composer on title page and on upper right hand corner of page 1
Present location: British Library: LOAN 101.37B; see also LOAN 101.37A for extensive pencil drafts and sketches
Completely revised version
Dyeline with autograph additions including:
Title page not on holograph: [autograph] 4th Symphony | L. Berkeley
[No dedication line on this version]
Autograph addition in blue ink on page 41: Allegro appassionato – new opening bars for violas and cellos
Movement III: [not autograph] Allegro (added to version before dyeline)
Present location: British Library: LOAN 101.38
Also: Extensive pencil drafts and sketches
Present location: British Library: LOAN 101.37A
No printed first edition
Publication: © 1978 by J. & W. Chester/Edition Wilhelm Hansen London Ltd; score and parts housed in hire library

TANT QUE MES YEUX (A Memory) (Opus 14, no.2)
Location of holograph unknown

First edition
TANT QUE MES YEUX | (A Memory) | The words by | LOUISE LABÉ | with | English text by | M. D. CALVOCORESSI | Set to music by | LENNOX BERKELEY | Oxford University Press
4 pages. 310 × 240 mm
Grey paper wrappers. Lettered in black with design of flowers and squares. Trimmed edges
Publication: © 1941 by Oxford University Press. Unpriced
Printed in England

THE TEMPEST: INCIDENTAL MUSIC
Location of holograph unknown
Where the Bee Sucks
For voice and orchestra
Holograph in black ink with minimal autograph annotations in red ink and pencil
The score is written on one side of a single sheet and on two double sheets of 18-stave paper measuring 36.7 × 27.9 cm
Bound with brown tape
Title page [part autograph]: SONG: WHERE THE BEE SUCKS from | INCIDENTAL MUSIC to [autograph] The Tempest | [autograph crossed out] (Where the Bee suck [sic]) | L. Berkelly [sic]
10 pages:

p. [1]	Title page with pencil annotation [not autograph]: "Pencil marks in score were made when performed by Mulland [sp?] Light Orch."; also BBC stamp and "H.1.H" and "T/55"
pp. 1–8	Allegro moderato "Where the bee sucks"
p. [9]	Blank with BBC stamp

Present location: BBC Music Library (BBC MSS 20325) with parts
No printed first edition

THEME AND VARIATIONS FOR GUITAR (Opus 77)
Location of complete holograph unknown
Description taken from dyeline copy of holograph
The score appears to be written on three double sheets of 16-stave
The manuscript paper printer's mark is shown as [vertical on left] WH Nr.5.F.16
Title page: THEME + VARIATIONS. | for | GUITAR | LENNOX BERKELEY
12 pages:

p. [i]	Title page
p. [ii]	Blank

p. 1   Theme: Moderato
p. 2   Var I: Allegro
p. 3   Var II: Allegretto
p. 4   Var III: Andantino Lento
p. 5   Var IV: Andante
p. 6   Var V: Allegro
p. 7   Var VI: Lento
[pp. [8–10]   Blank]

The manuscript is dated "August 1970" by the composer after double bar page 7
No location or dedication is apparent
Signed by the composer on upper right hand corner of page 1
Dyeline of complete holograph
Present location: British Library: LOAN 101.87e with pencil draft and sketches

Fragment

Holograph (incomplete) in pencil with non-autograph additions in blue ink
The score is written on one double sheet of 16-stave paper measuring 34.1 × 27 cm
No manuscript paper printer's mark apparent
No title page
4 pages:

p. 3   Var:II/Allegretto
p. 3   Var:III/Andantino
p. 4   Var: IV Andante cantabile
p. 5   Var: V Allegro
p. 6   Var: VI Lento

No date, location, dedication signature is apparent
Present location: British Library: LOAN 101.87e with sketches

First edition

COLLEZIONE DI MUSICHE PER CHITARRA | DIRETTA DA ANGELO GILARDINO | LENNOX BERKELEY | THEME | AND VARIATIONS | for guitar | Revisione e diteggiatura di | ANGELO GILARDINO | [Berben symbol] | EDIZIONI MUSICALI Berben [script] ANCONA-MILANO
9 pages. 312 × 234 mm
Rust paper wrappers. Lettered in black. Trimmed edges
Publication: © 1972 by Lennox Berkeley/Edizioni Musicali BERBEN – Ancona (Italy) (E. 1643 B.). Unpriced

THEME AND VARIATIONS FOR PIANO DUET (Opus 73)

Holograph in black ink with autograph corrections in pencil; overlays
The score is written on four double sheets and on both sides of a single sheet of 16-stave paper measuring 34 × 27.1 cm

The manuscript paper printer's mark is shown as [vertical along spine] WH Nr.5.F.16
Title page [autograph]: To Gerald Stofsky & Annie Alt | THEME & VARIATIONS | for | Piano DUET | LENNOX BERKELEY | [pencil annotation] Op. 73 (1968)
18 pages

p. [i]	Title page
p. [ii]	Blank
pp. 1–2	Moderato
pp. 2–4	VAR.I.	Allegro
pp. 5	Lento.Var:II.
pp. 5–7	Var:III. Allegro
p. 8	Var:IV. Lento
pp. 9–10	Var:V. Andante
pp. 10–12	Var:VI.	Allegro
pp. 12–[14]	Tempo I [see below for original pp. 13–14]
pp. [15–16]	Blank

The manuscript is dated 1968 and dedicated to Gerald Stofsky and Annie Alt on title page
No location is apparent
Signed by the composer on upper right hand corner of page 1
Original ending
Holograph in black ink with overlays
The score is written on both sides of a single sheet of 16-stave paper measuring 34 × 27.1 cm
The manuscript paper printer's mark is shown as [vertical along spine] WH Nr.5.F.16
2 pages:
pp. 13–14   original copies of final bar with Var VII | Tempo del Principio
Dated October–December 1968
Present location: British Library: LOAN 101.90c with extensive autograph sketches in pencil
No printed first edition
Publication: © 1971 by J. & W. Chester/Edition Wilhelm Hansen London Ltd (Copyist MS available in photocopy)

THEME AND VARIATIONS FOR VIOLIN (Opus 33, no.1)
Location of holograph unknown
First edition
LENNOX BERKELEY | THEME and VARIATIONS | for | Solo Violin | Price 3/- net* | J. & W. Chester Ltd. | 11, Great Marlborough Street, London, W.1
7 pages. 309 × 241 mm

Buff paper wrappers. Lettered in black. Trimmed edges
Publication: © 1951 by J. & W. Chester Ltd (J.W.C.1306) @ 3/-
Printed in England

THERE WAS NEITHER GRASS NOR CORN
Location of holograph unknown
Copyist versions
A: Annotated copyist manuscript with autograph pencil sketch on page 1. Includes annotation in pencil: Benjamin Britten | Lennox Berkeley on page 1
B: Two dyeline copies of second copyist manuscript with any autograph annotations
The manuscript is dated "Nov. 1949 T.M." by copyist and dedicated "For Edward Sackville-West"
Present location: British Library: LOAN 101.95d
No printed first edition

THOU HAST MADE ME (Opus 55, no.1)
Location of holograph unknown
First edition
Written for the St Cecilia's Day Service (1960) | of the Musicians' Benevolent Fund. | THOU HAST MADE ME | For Mixed Choir and Organ | Words by | JOHN DONNE | Music by | LENNOX BERKELEY | CHESTER MUSIC | J. & W. Chester / Edition Wilhelm Hansen London Ltd. | Eagle Court London EC1M 5QD
12 pages. 258 × 177 mm
White paper wrappers. Lettered in black. Trimmed edges
Publication: © 1960 by J. & W. Chester Ltd (J.W.C.8826) @ 2/6
Printed by Halstan & Co. Ltd, Amersham, Bucks

THREE EARLY SONGS
Location of holograph unknown
Copyist manuscript in black ink; text written in by composer. No annotations
The score is written on four double sheets of 12-stave paper measuring 31 × 23.4 cm
The manuscript paper printer's mark is shown as R C 3 on lower left hand corner; clefs printed on paper
Bound together; sewn at spine
Title page [autograph in black ink]: THREE SONGS | Lennox Berkeley
16 pages:
p. [i]   Title page

p. [ii]   Blank
pp. 1–3   I. To John Greenidge | "D'un vanneu de blé aux vents" | (J. du Bellay) No.1 | LENNOX BERKELEY
p. 4   Text of poem written out by composer
p. 5   Title page [autograph in black ink]: Pastourelle
pp. 6–7   Allegretto; Pastourelle [No2] ; Words XIIIth century (anonymous). | From the "Oxford Book of French Verse" (No.2)
p. 8   Text of Pastourelle written out by composer
pp. 9–11   To G.M.B.; No.III Rondeau (Charles d'Orléans)1391–1465 | Joyeaux et animé
p. 12   Text of Rondeau written out by composer
pp. [13–14] Blank

No date or location is apparent
Dedicated by composer to John Greenidge (No.1) and Geraldine Berkeley (No.3)
Signed by composer on title page and on upper right hand corner of page 1
Present location: British Library: LOAN 101.92a

First edition
THREE (EARLY) SONGS in collection: LENNOX BERKELEY (1903–1989) | THE COMPLETE FRENCH SONGS | SOLO VOICE & PIANO | CHESTER MUSIC
11 pages (pp. 5–15). 304 × 229 mm
Glossy stiff paper wrappers with full colour portrait of Berkeley in Paris. Lettered in black. Trimmed edges
Publication: 1992 by Chester Music (CH55985) @ £12.95

Separate publication
D'un Vanneur de Blé aux Vents (The Thresher)
Location of holograph unknown

First edition
D'un Vanneur de blé aux Vents | The words by JOACHIM DU BELLAY | Set to music by LENNOX BERKELEY | OXFORD UNIVERSITY PRESS
4 pages. 310 × 240 mm
Grey paper wrappers. Lettered in black with design of flowers and squares. Trimmed edges
Publication: © 1927 by Oxford University Press. Unpriced
Printed by Henderson & Spalding Ltd

THREE GREEK SONGS (Opus 38)
Holograph in blue ink with autograph corrections and additions in pencil and blue ink; bars crossed out. Copyright and publication information added in blue ink at bottom of first page. Queries in pencil [not autograph] and autograph block

print words in pencil. Paper is fragile; partially torn from being folded in half
The score is written on one double sheet and on both sides of a single sheet of 22-stave paper measuring 37 × 27.4 cm
No manuscript paper printer's mark is apparent
No title page; p. 1 [autograph]: 3 Greek Poems [pencil] Three Greek Poems [blue ink] | I. | Lennox Berkeley
6 pages:
pp. 1–2   I. Andante; Epitaph of Timas (Sappho)
pp. 2–5   II. Allegro; Spring Song (Antipater)
p. 6   III. Lento; To Aster (Plato)
The manuscript is dated "1951" by the composer after the double bar on p. 6 ["1950" crossed out by composer]
No dedication or location is apparent
Signed by the composer on upper right hand corner of p. 1
Present location: British Library: LOAN 101.92i
First edition
LENNOX BERKELEY | THREE GREEK SONGS | for | Medium Voice | Epitaph of Timas (Sappho) | Spring Song (Antipater) | To Aster (Plato) | Price 4/- net* | J. & W. Chester Ltd. | 11 Great Marlborough Street, London, W.1
8 pages. 357 x 247 mm
Beige stiff paper wrappers. Lettered in black. Trimmed edges
Publication: © 1953 by J. & W. Chester Ltd (J.W.C.4053) @ 4/-

THREE IMPROMPTUS FOR PIANO (Opus 7)
Location of holograph unknown
Correction sheet
Holograph in pencil
The unbound score is written on one side of a single sheet of 18-stave paper measuring 36.7 × 27.1 cm
No date or signature is apparent
Present location: British Library: LOAN 101.89a
First edition
CONCERT SERIES | [image of man at piano] | No. 7 | THREE IMPROMPTUS | by | LENNOX BERKELEY | Price 2/- net | WINTHROP ROGERS | EDITION | [Boosey & Hawkes international distribution addresses]
7 pages. 310 × 235 mm
White paper wrappers. Lettered in dark blue. Trimmed edges
Publication: © 1937 by Hawkes & Son (London) Ltd (H. 14663) @ 2/-
Printed in England

THREE LATIN MOTETS FOR FIVE UNACCOMPANIED VOICES (Opus 83, no.1)

Holograph in three distinct sections wrapped inside cover sheets

Covers

Cover sheets are written on one double sheet of 18-stave paper measuring 34.4 × 25.9 cm

The manuscript paper printer's mark is shown as [decorative lyre motif] B.C. No.5 [bottom left]. Made and printed in England by Bosworth & Co., Ltd. [bottom right]

Title page: [autograph in blue ink] 3 Latin Motets. | Original M.S.

4 pages:

p. [1]   Title page
p. [2]   Blank
pp. [3–4]   [not autograph] pencil sketch of 3rd movement of string quartet by Sheila Lennox Robertson (signed)

No date, location, dedication or signature is apparent

Eripe me

Holograph in black ink with minimal autograph annotations in pencil and black ink; overlays

The unbound score is written on two double sheets of 12-stave paper measuring 30.1 × 24.3 cm

No manuscript paper printer's mark is apparent

No title page; p. 1: [autograph in black ink] To Alec Robertson. | This work was commissioned by the North Wales Music Festival with funds provided by the | Welsh Arts Council, and first performed by the St John's College Cambridge Choir under George Guest. | Eripe me

8 pages:

pp. 1–8   Lento

Dated "April 1972" after double bar page 8 and dedicated "To Alec Robertson" by the composer on top of page 1

No location is apparent

Signed by the composer on upper right hand corner of page 1

Veni Sponsa Christi

Holograph in black ink with minimal autograph annotations; overlays. Bar lines added in pencil

The unbound score is written on one double sheet of 12-stave paper measuring 29.4 × 23.3 cm

No manuscript paper printer's mark is apparent

No title page; p. 1: [autograph] II. | Veni sponsa Christi

4 pages:

pp. 1–4   Andantino

No date, dedication or location is apparent

Signed by the composer on upper right hand corner of page 1
Regina coeli
Holograph in black ink with autograph sketches and corrections in pencil; extensive overlays
The score is written on two double sheets and on both sides of one single sheet of 12-stave paper measuring 30.2 × 24.2 cm
Bound with clear tape
No title page; p. 1: [autograph] III | Regina Coeli
10 pages:
pp. 1–10 Allegro
        p. 1 Autograph pencil sketch on top stave of rejected version of bass part, partially rubbed out
        pp. 3–7 Andante
        pp. 7–10 Tempo I
The manuscript is dated "May–June 1972" by the composer after double bar page 10
No dedication, location or signature is apparent
Present location: British Library: LOAN 101.96a with pencil drafts and sketches, clean copy of holograph, letter
Letter
"From Dr. G.H. [George] Guest, organist" dated "1 May 1986"
Dear Lady Berkeley
It was most kind of you to go to such trouble over the text of Lennox's beautiful motet (we greatly enjoy singing them all, and they have been heard in Japan, the USA, Australia, as well as in many European countries). The only thing is that the text he set differs from the photo copied one you sent me – and I enclose a copy of L's text.
Don't worry, though, it was just that we wanted to make sure we were singing the right words.
George Guest
[with list of textual variants]
First edition
Contemporary Church Music Series | LENNOX BERKELEY | Three Latin Motets | for five voices | J. & W. CHESTER/EDITION WILHELM HANSEN LONDON LTD | Eagle Court, London EC1M 5QD
24 pages. 255 × 180 mm
Cream paper wrappers. Lettered in black. Trimmed edges
Publication: © 1974 by J. & W. Chester Ltd (J.W.C.8895). Unpriced
Printed by Halstan & Co. Ltd, Amersham, Bucks
American edition
Lennoc Berkeley | Three Latin Motets | for Five-Part Chorus of Mixed Voices (SSATB) | a cappella

24 pages. 266 × 173 mm
White paper wrappers. Lettered in black. Trimmed edges
Publication: © 1974 by J. & W. Chester Ltd. American edition published by Tetra Music Corporation (ABC11). (same plates)

THREE MAZURKAS (HOMAGE A CHOPIN) FOR PIANO (Opus 32, no.1)
Holograph (incomplete) in black and blue ink with extensive annotations; overlays. Tattered condition; pages 5/6 torn
The unbound score is written on both sides of three single sheets of 18-stave paper measuring 36.4 × 27 cm
The manuscript paper printer's mark is shown as [encircled] J & W | CHESTER | L.TD | LONDON No.18
No title page
6 pages:
pp. 1–3   I. Allegro
pp. 3–5   II. Allegretto
p. 6   III. Allegro
No date, dedication or location is apparent
Signed by the composer on upper right hand corner of page 1
Present location: British Library: LOAN 101.89e
First edition
Publication: © 1951 by J. & W. Chester Ltd (J.W.C.2316)

THREE PIECES FOR CLARINET
Holograph in black ink with autograph annotation in pencil in I. and overlays in III
The score is written on one double sheet of 12-stave paper measuring 35 × 27 cm
No manuscript paper printer's mark is apparent
No title page; p.[1]: [autograph] THREE PIECES | For Clarinet | Lennox Berkeley
4 pages:
p. [1]   I. Moderato [ma in tempo rubato]
p. [2]   II. Lento
p. [3]   III. Allegro
p. [4]   autograph sketch of the song "Sonnet," Opus 102 includes first two stanzas and two lines of the third stanza in pencil; words not accurately transcribed
No date, location or dedication is apparent
Signed by composer on upper right hand corner of p. [1]
Present location: British Library: LOAN 101.85b

First edition
Lennox Berkeley | THREE PIECES | for clarinet | Edited by Thea King | [Photocopy warning] | CHESTER MUSIC | J.&W. Chester/Edition Wilhelm Hansen London Ltd. | Eagle Court London EC1M 5QD
4 pages. 305 × 229 mm
White stiff paper wrappers. Lettered in dark and light blue. Trimmed edges
Publication: © 1983 by J. & W. Chester/Edition Wilhelm Hansen London Ltd (CH55492). Unknown
Edited by Thea King
Printed in England

THREE PIECES FOR ORGAN (Opus 72, no.1)
Aubade
Holograph in blue and black ink with autograph corrections and additions in pencil; overlays. Bars crossed out. Organ registrations [not autograph] added in blue and black ink
The unbound score is written on two double sheets of 24-stave paper measuring 34.1 × 27.1 cm
The manuscript paper printer's mark is shown as [horizontal bottom left] W.H.Nr.9.F.24
Title page: [autograph in blue ink] Aubade | for | Organ | Lennox Berkeley
8 pages:
p. [i]   Title page
p. [i]   Autograph sketch in pencil of mss. 24 crossed out
pp. [1–4]   Aubade | for Organ | Allegro Moderato
p. [5]   Fragmentary pencil sketches
p. [6]   Blank
No date, location or dedication is apparent. Copyright date given as © 1966
Signed by the composer on upper right hand corner of page [1]
Copyist manuscript
Dyeline of copyist manuscript heavily annotated for performance [not autograph] in pencil with corrections, registrations, fingerings. List of corrections on inside front cover
Present location: British Library: LOAN 101.91c with Aria and Toccata; dyelines and draft
Aria and Toccata
Holographs of each separate work inside double sheet of manuscript paper
Cover
Title page of covers: [autograph in pencil] Aria + Toccata for organ. | Lennox Berkeley

Aria
Holograph in blue ink with minimal autograph annotations
The unbound score is written on one double sheet of 16-stave paper measuring 34.2 × 27 cm
The manuscript paper printer's mark is shown as [vertical along spine] WH Nr.5 F.16
No separate title page
4 pages:
pp. 1–3   "Aria" | Slow
p. 4   Blank
No date, dedication or location is apparent. Copyright date shown as © 1968
Signed by the composer on upper right hand corner of page 1

Toccata
Holograph in black ink with minimal autograph corrections in pencil; overlays. Bars crossed out in black ink on page 6
The unbound score is written on three double sheets of 16-stave paper measuring 34.2 × 27 cm
The manuscript paper printer's mark is shown as [vertical along spine] WH Nr.5 F.16
No title page
12 pages
pp. 1–8   Fairly Fast | (Allegro moderato)
p. 3   Meno vivo. Quiet and sustained
p. 5   Tempo Primo
pp. 9–12   Blank
No date, dedication or location is apparent
Signed by the composer on upper right hand corner of page 1
Present location: British Library: LOAN 101.91c with holograph of Aubade; annotated dyelines and incomplete autograph pencil draft

First edition
Lennox Berkeley | Three Pieces | for Organ | Chester Music
17 pages. 298 × 220 mm
White stiff paper wrappers. Letters in blue and grey
Publication: © 1971 by J. & W. Chester Ltd (J.W.C.2352). Unpriced
Printed in England

THREE PIECES FOR PIANO: ETUDE, BERCEUSE and CAPRICCIO (Opus 2)

Holograph in black ink with publication and some autograph annotations in pencil, black and orange ink and green pencil; autograph overlays
The unbound score is written on two double sheets of 14-stave paper measuring 35.2 × 27.2 cm and on both sides of two single sheets of 14-stave paper measuring

35.2 × 26.8 cm, wrapped inside one double sheet of 16-stave paper measuring 32.9 × 26.8 cm

The manuscript paper printer's mark, only on 16-stave paper, is shown as Néocopie Musicale, Paris (No.6)

Title page for all three: A2629 [red ink] 649/651 [green pencil] reg.14.12.36 [pencil] | LENNOX BERKELEY [autograph in black ink] | THREE PIECES FOR PIANO [marked through in pencil] | Separate or Complete [black ink, not autograph] | I | 17671/2/3 | II | CR

16 pages:

p. [i]	Title page
p. [ii]	Blank
pp. 1–3	I. Étude: Allegro moderato
pp. 4–6	II. Berceuse: Allegretto
pp. 7–9	III. Capriccio: Allegro
p. [10]	Short score in pencil in Berkeley's hand: "Choral from L'Histoire du Soldat – Stravinsky"
p. [11]	Errata [autograph]
p. [12]	[autograph] Lennox Berkeley	28 Great Ormond Street	London W.C.1
pp. [13–14]	Blank

The manuscripts of each piece are dedicated as follows:

Étude is dedicated to Miss Harriet Cohen

Berceuse is dedicated to Alan Searle

Capriccio is dedicated to Vere Pilkington

No date or location is apparent

Signed by the composer on upper right hand corner of page 1

Present Location: British Library: ADD MS 54395, leaves 25–34 (one of Galliard MSS)

First edition

LENNOX BERKELEY | THREE PIECES FOR PIANO | ETUDE | BERCEUSE | CAPRICCIO | Each 2/- net | AUGENER Ltd. | 18 GREAT MARLBOROUGH STREET. | & 57 HIGH STREET, MARYLEBONE | LONDON. W.1

4, 4, 3 pages. 311 × 236 mm

Buff paper covers. Lettered in black. Trimmed edges

Publication: © 1937 by Augener Ltd. (17672 R) @ 2/- (each)

Printed in England by Augener Ltd, Acton Lane, London, W.4

THREE SONGS FOR FOUR MALE VOICES (Opus 67, no.1)

Holograph in pencil, crossed out sketches. Final bars of music (p. 12) written on recto of first page of music (p. 1). Copyright and publisher information in blue ink at the bottom of the first page

The score is written on four double sheets of 12-stave paper measuring 30.2 × 23.8 cm

No manuscript paper printer's mark is apparent

Title page [autograph in pencil]: THREE SONGS | for | Men's Voices | L. Berkeley

16 pages:

p. [i]	Title page
p. [ii]	Blank
p. 12	End of III. Kissing Usurie
pp. 1–5	I. Fair Daffodils	Herrick	Andante con moto
pp. 6–8	II. Spring goeth all in White	Bridges	Lento
pp. 9–11	III. Kissing Usurie	Herrick	Allegro
p. [iii]	Unidentified sketch
p. [iv]	Crossed out 6-bar sketch of Fair Daffodils

No date, dedication or location is apparent

Signed by the composer on upper right hand corner of page 1

Other versions

Dyeline of holograph with autograph corrections in pencil in answer to non-autograph queries in blue ink. Also some additions and autograph pencil sketch crossed out on p. 5

Dated 1965 and identified as Opus 67 no.1 by composer in pencil on cover of buff foolscap folder containing holograph and dyeline

Present location: British Library: LOAN 101.95k

First edition

THREE SONGS | for | FOUR MALE VOICES | by | LENNOX BERKELEY | 1. Fair Daffodils (Herrick) | 2. Spring goeth all in white (Bridges) | 3. Kissing Usurie (Herrick) | [Chester logo]

14 pages. 272 × 191 mm

Stiff blue paper wrappers. Lettered in white. Trimmed edges

Publication: © 1966 by J. & W. Chester Ltd (J.W.C.5710) @ 5/-

Printed by Lowe and Brydone (Printers) Ltd, London

TOCCATA FOR PIANO

Holograph in blue ink

The score is written on two double sheets of 10-stave paper measuring 30.8 × 23.4 cm stapled at spine

The manuscript paper printer's mark is shown as A L [gothic script] | Manuscript Music | No. 60. at bottom left hand corner of folded page

No title page; p. 1 [autograph] To J.F. Waterhouse | TOCCATA | Lennox Berkeley 1925

8 pages:
pp. 1–8   Vif – Molto Meno Mosso – Tempo Primo
Dated "Negron Sept–Oct: 1925" by composer after double bar p. 8
Dedicated "To J.F. Waterhouse" by composer on top of p. 1
Signed by composer on upper right hand corner of p. 1
Present location: Private collection but due to go to the British Library as LOAN 101.89j
No printed first edition

TOCCATA FOR VIOLIN AND PIANO (Opus 33, no.3)
Location of holograph unknown
First edition
TOCCATA | for | Violin & Piano | by | LENNOX BERKELEY | J. & W. CHESTER, LTD., | LONDON: 11, GREAT MARLBOROUGH STREET, W.1
7 pages. 304 × 248 mm
Light blue paper wrappers. Lettered in black. Trimmed edges
Publication: © 1951 by J. & W. Chester Ltd (J.W.C.396) @ 3/6
(Later published with Elegy Op.33 No.2)

TOMBEAUX
Location of holograph unknown
Copyist manuscript in purple and black ink with autograph additions such as tempo markings and corrections; one autograph overlay, p. 12
The score is written on four double sheets of 12-stave paper measuring 34.8 × 27 cm and on one side of a single sheet of 15-stave paper measuring 34.6 × 27 cm
The manuscript paper printer's mark is shown as [lyre motif] B.C.No.13 Made and Printed in England
Title page: 8 Minutes | TOMBEAUX | Q̶U̶A̶T̶R̶E̶ CINQ CHANTS SUR DES POEMES | de | Jean Cocteau | [drawing] | LENNOX BERKELEY
Bound in grey stiff paper covers lettered in black, very worn, entitled Cinq Chants with same ink drawing as on title page
16 pages:
p. [i]   Title page; drawing in black ink, on cover and title page, is attributed to John Greenidge
p. [ii]   Autograph annotation in pencil: 19 Rue du Mont Ceris | Paris XVIII
pp. 1–4   1. Le Tombeau de Sappho: Tres Lent
pp. 5–6   2. De Socrate: Moderato
pp. 7–8   3. D'un Fleuve: Con moto
pp. 9–10   4. De Narcisse: Triste et lent

pp. 11–14   5. De Don Juan: Vif
The manuscript is dated "Paris 1926" after double bar page 14
No dedication, location or signature is apparent
Present location: British Library: LOAN 101.92b
First edition
TOMBEAUX in collection: LENNOX BERKELEY (1903–1989) | THE COMPLETE FRENCH SONGS | SOLO VOICE & PIANO | CHESTER MUSIC
15 pages (pp. 20–34). 304 × 229 mm
Glossy stiff paper wrappers with full colour portrait of Berkeley in Paris. Lettered in black. Trimmed edges
Publication: © 1992 by Chester Music (CH55985) @ £12.95
Chamber orchestra version
Location of holograph unknown
No printed first edition

TRIO FOR FLUTE, OBOE AND PIANO
Holograph (incomplete) in black ink with pencil annotations
The score is written on two double sheets of 28-stave paper measuring 36.4 × 27.1 cm
Title page: [autograph in pencil] Lennox Berkeley | Trio Suite | for | Flute Oboe + Piano
8 pages:
p. [i]   Title page
p. [ii]   Blank
pp. [1–3]   I. Prelude: Andante con moto
pp. [4–6]   Blank
No date, location, or dedication is apparent
Signed by the composer on title page and on upper right hand corner of page [1]
Present location: British Library: LOAN 101.85 with copyist manuscript of parts
No printed first edition

TRIO FOR HORN, VIOLIN AND PIANO (Opus 44)
Holograph in blue ink with minimal autograph corrections and additions in pencil; overlays. Extensive publication annotations and corrections in red ink; rehearsal numbers added in blue
The score is written on four double and both sides of 13 single sheets of 22-stave paper measuring 37 × 26.8 cm in tattered condition

The manuscript paper printer's mark is shown as [encircled galleon] | A. L. No 16 | Printed in England
No title page
42 pages:

pp. [1]–12	I. Allegro
pp. 13–18	II. Lento
pp. 19–41	III. Tema & Variations

	p. 19	Tema
	pp. 20–23	Var.I Allegro vivace
	pp. 23–25	Var.II Allegretto
	pp. 25–26	Var.III Lento
	pp. 27–29	Var.IV Vivace
	pp. 29–31	Var.V Allegretto
	pp. 31–33	Var.VI Moderato
	pp. 33–35	Var.VII Adagio
	pp. 35–37	Var.VIII Moderato
	pp. 37–40	Var.IX Allegro vivo
	pp. 40–41	Var.X Moderato
	p. [42]	Blank

The score is dated "Oct. 16th 1953" after double bar p. 41, and dedicated "To Sheila Robertson"
No location is apparent
Signed by the composer on upper right hand corner of page 1
Present location: British Library: LOAN 101.86a; also includes sketches
First edition
Publication: © 1956 by J. & W. Chester Ltd (J.W.C.271)

TRIO FOR VIOLIN, VIOLA AND CELLO (Opus 19)
Holograph draft in black ink with extensive autograph corrections and additions in pencil; overlays, especially last page. Editorial annotations in red ink
The score is written on two double sheets and on both sides of five single sheets of 18-stave paper measuring 36.5 × 26.7 cm
The manuscript paper printer's mark is shown as J&W Chester Ltd., No. 18
Bound in orange paper wrapper with taped spine (tattered condition). Contained in orange file folder
Cover of file folder: [not autograph, black ink] MS | BERKELEY | Trio for Strings (1943) | STRING TRIO (1943) | [not autograph, pencil] Op. 19
Cover of score: [not autograph] Original score | [Chester Library label] | Lennox Berkeley | String Trio | Duration 17 minutes | [Copyright stamp]
No title page

18 pages:
pp. 1–8   I. [autograph annotation in pencil] Moderato
pp. 9–11   II. Adagio
pp. 11–17   III. Allegro
p. [18]   Autograph 5-bar sketch in pencil of III. Allegro
The manuscript is dated "1943" on top of page 1
No location, dedication or signature is apparent
Present location: British Library: LOAN 101.85g
First edition (Miniature score)
LENNOX BERKELEY | TRIO | FOR | VIOLIN, VIOLA AND CELLO | J. & W. CHESTER LTD. | 11 Great Marlborough Street, London, W.1 | MADE IN ENGLAND
24 pages. 191 × 140 mm
Blue stiff paper wrappers. Lettered in black. Trimmed edges
Publication: © 1944 by J. & W. Chester Ltd (J.W.C.259) @ 5/-
Printed in England

TROIS POÈMES DE VILDRAC
Holograph in black ink with durations added in pencil
The score is written on two double sheets of 12-stave paper measuring 32.9 × 26.9 cm
The manuscript paper printer's mark is shown as Néocopie Musicale, Paris (No. 5) on lower left-hand corner of paper
Title page [autograph]: à Mademoiselle Nadia Boulager | en toute admiration et gratitude | 3 POÈMES | DE | VILDRAC | LENNOX BERKELEY
8 pages:
p. [i]   Title page
p. [ii]   Blank
p. [1]   I. Lento tranquillo
p. [2]   II. Andante con moto
p. [3]   III. Andante
pp. [4–6]   Blank
The manuscript is dated "Paris 1929" after the double bar page [3] and dedicated "à Mademoiselle Nadia Boulanger en toute admiration et gratitude" upper centre page [1]
Signed by the composer on upper right hand corner of page [1]
Present location: British Library: LOAN 101.92c; together with copyist manuscript without autograph annotations
First edition
TROIS POÈMES DE VILDRAC in collection: LENNOX BERKELEY (1903–1989)

| THE COMPLETE FRENCH SONGS | SOLO VOICE & PIANO | CHESTER MUSIC
4 pages (pp. 35–38). 304 × 229 mm
Glossy stiff paper wrappers with full colour portrait of Berkeley in Paris. Lettered in black. Trimmed edges
Publication: © 1992 by Chester Music (CH55985) @ £12.95

UBI CARITAS ET AMOR (1969)
Holograph in black ink with autograph corrections in pencil; overlays
The unbound score is written on two double sheets of 12-stave paper measuring 37.8 × 28.4 cm
No manuscript paper printer's mark is apparent
No title page; p. 1: [autograph] Ubi Caritas et Amor | Motet | Lennox Berkeley
8 pages:
pp. [1–6]   Lento
pp. [7–8]   Blank
The manuscript is dated "Jan–Feb: 1969" by the composer after double bar page [6]
No dedication or location is apparent
Signed by the composer on upper right hand corner of page [1]

UBI CARITAS ET AMOR (Opus 96, no.2)
Holograph in black ink with partially erased pencil sketch on the bottom of p. 1; overlays
The score is written on one double sheet and on both sides of a single sheet of 18-stave paper measuring 38 × 29 cm
The manuscript paper printer's mark is shown as B&H inscribed within picture of globe with musical note and appears upside down on holograph
No title page; page 1: [typescript] Commissioned for the celebration of the fifteen hundredth Anniversary | of the birth of Saint Benedict (480–1980) and dedicated to the | Benedictine Order. | [autograph] Ubi Caritas et Amor. | Motet. | Lennox Berkeley
6 pages:
pp. 1–6   Andante – Piu Vivo – Tempo Primo
The manuscript is dated "Feb–March 1980" by composer after double bar p. 6
Dedicated to the Benedictine Order on top of p. 1
No location is apparent
Signed by composer on top right hand corner of p. 1
Present location: British Library: LOAN 101.96g

First edition
CONTEMPORARY CHURCH MUSIC SERIES | LENNOX BERKELEY | UBI CARITAS | ET AMOR | for unaccompanied chorus | SSATB | CHESTER MUSIC
6 pages. 254 × 177 mm
White paper wrappers. Lettered in black. Trimmed edges
Publication: © 1982 by J. & W. Chester Ltd (J.W.C.55419). Unpriced
[Contemporary Church Music Series]
Printed by Caligraving Ltd, Thetford, Norfolk

UNA AND THE LION (Opus 98)
Holograph in black ink with minimal autograph clarifications in pencil; overlays. Partially erased pencil sketch on p. 1. Autograph sketches in black ink and pencil on front cover. One notebook page enclosed with Spenser poems written in ink by composer
The score is written on four double sheets of 18-stave paper measuring 36.8 × 27.2 cm and on one side of a single sheet of 16-stave paper measuring 37 × 28 cm
The manuscript paper printer's mark for 18-stave paper is shown at the bottom left of the page as B&H [incorporated into music globe design]
Contained in brown envelope with cover markings: Rosalind 3995. Una and the Lion Berkeley FS
No title page; p. 1: [autograph] UNA and the LION. | Moderato; (Edmund Spenser); Lennox Berkeley (op:98)
18 pages:

pp. 1–5	Moderato "It fortuned out of the thickest wood"
pp. 5–10	Andante "O how can beauty master the most strong"
pp. 6–10	Sarabande (Andante) [instrumental]
pp. 10–11	Allegro moderato "The lion Lord of every beast"
pp. 11–12	Lento "But he my lion and my noble Lord"
p. 13	Allegro Moderato "Redowning tears did choke"
pp. 13–16	L'Istesso tempo "With pity calmed down fell his angry mood"
pp. 16–17	Andante con moto "Still When She Slept"

The manuscript is dated "Nov 1978–Jan 1979" after the double bar p. 17
No dedication or location is apparent
Signed by the composer on upper right hand corner of page 1
Present location: British Library: LOAN 101.82 with drafts and sketches
No printed first edition
Publication: © 1979 by J. & W. Chester Ltd; score and parts housed in hire library

VARIATION ON AN ELIZABETHAN THEME: SELLINGER'S ROUND
No. 3 of a collaboration entitled Variations on Sellinger's Round (transcribed from Byrd's setting for the virginals) including settings by Michael Tippett, Arthur Oldham, Benjamin Britten, Humphrey Searle, William Walton, all written at Benjamin Britten's invitation. Imogen Holst transcribed Byrd's theme
According to Professor Craggs: "The whole manuscript, consisting of 7 items, is unbound and kept in a folder." The collected work is dated 1953
Holograph in Yale University Library. Details taken from photocopy
The score is written on 28-stave paper
No manuscript paper printer's mark is apparent
No title page; p. [1] [autograph] Variation on Sellinger's Round | Lennox Berkeley
4? pages:
pp. [1–3]   Andante
No date, location or dedication apparent on manuscript
Signed by composer on upper right hand corner of p. [1]
Present location: The James Marshall and Marie-Louise Osborn Collection, Yale University Library, New Haven, Connecticut, USA
Microfilm of score available in the hire library of Boosey & Hawkes (mu9008060)
British Library: Mus.Mic.H.3.(1.) [1990] = "A microfilm of the score in the hire library of B&H London"
No printed first edition

VARIATIONS ON A HYMN TUNE BY ORLANDO GIBBONS (Opus 35)
Location of holograph unknown
Copyist manuscript with autograph annotations
Title: [autograph] VARIATIONS ON A HYMN | BY | ORLANDO GIBBONS
Dedication by composer to Dorothy Cranbrook on top of page 1
Signed by the composer on upper right hand corner of page 1
Piano arrangement
Holograph draft in pencil torn in half
The score is written on four double sheets of torn paper
The manuscript paper printer's mark is shown as "J&W Chester Ltd. London"
Contained in buff folder
Cover: Two copies of Piano Arrangement. Incomplete. For chorus and instruments
The manuscript is dedicated by composer "To Dorothy Cranbrook" on top of p. 1
No date or location is apparent
Signed by the composer on upper right hand corner of page 1
Present location: British Library: LOAN 101.76
First edition (Choral score)
No title page; p. 1: To Dorothy Cranbrook | Variations on a Hymn by Orlando

Gibbons | for tenor solo, chorus, strings and organ | CHORUS PART
15 pages. 254 × 177 mm
No wrappers. Trimmed edges
Publication: © 1981 by J. & W. Chester/Edition Wilhelm Hansen London Ltd (J.W.C.55357). Unpriced
Score and parts located in hire library

VOICES OF THE NIGHT (Opus 86)
Fair copy
Location of holograph unknown
Details taken from annotated dyeline copy (See description of dyeline below)
The score is written on approximately seven double sheets of 24-stave paper
No manuscript paper printer's mark is apparent
Title page: [autograph] VOICES of the NIGHT | LENNOX BERKELEY | [Chester Hire Stamp]
28 pages:

p. [i]	Title page
p. [ii]	[autograph] Written for The Three Choirs Festival 1973.	and commissioned by the Arts Council.	Dedicated to Charlotte Bonham Carter
pp. 1–26	Voices of the Night	Andante

The manuscript is dated "June–July 1973" after double bar page 26 and dedicated to Charlotte Bonham Carter by the composer on page [ii]
No location is apparent
Signed by the composer on the upper right hand corner of page 1
Dyeline of holograph
Dyeline of holograph with one autograph annotation in pencil; publication annotation © 1973 added
Present location: British Library: LOAN 101.33 with pencil draft and sketches
Pencil draft
Holograph (incomplete) in pencil with extensive annotations; bars crossed out. Corresponds with pages 1–17 of holograph above
The unbound score is written on two double sheets and on both sides of one single sheet of 24-stave paper measuring 40.1 × 26.6 cm
No manuscript paper printer's mark is apparent
No title page or any title details
10 pages:

pp. 1–8a, 8–9	Music
p. 8	Un poco piu vivo

No date, dedication, location or signature is apparent

Present location: British Library: LOAN 101.33 with sketches and annotated dyeline copy of complete fair copy holograph
First edition (Miniature score)
LENNOX BERKELEY | VOICES OF THE NIGHT | or Orchestra | CHESTER MUSIC | J. & W. Chester / Edition Wilhelm Hansen London Ltd. | Eagle Court, London EC1M 5QD
28 pages. 191 × 140 mm
White stiff paper covers. Lettered in dark and light blue. Trimmed edges
Publication: © 1978 by J. & W. Chester/Edition Wilhelm Hansen London Ltd (J.W.C.55064). Unpriced
Printed by Panda Press, Haverhill, Suffolk

THE WALL OF TROY
Holograph in black and blue ink with autograph additions, including cues, in black and blue ink and pencil with overlays
The unpublished score is written on seven double sheets of 22-stave paper measuring 36.9 × 27.5 cm
The manuscript paper printer's mark is shown as [embossed and encircled] J.&W. Chester Ltd. | London & Geneva | No.22
No title page; page 1 [autograph]: THE WALL OF TROY | Andante – Lennox Berkeley
28 pages:

pp. 1–2	I.	Andante
pp. 3–6	II.	Allegro
p. 7	III.a	(horn solo)
	III.b	(horn solo)
	IV.a	Allegro
p. 8		Andante
	IV.b	Lento (flute solo) – [cut in BBC parts]
pp. 8–11	V.	Andante
pp. 11–12	VI.	Andante
pp. 12–13	VII.	Allegro moderato
pp. 13–14		Andante
pp. 14–18		Allegro Vivace
pp. 19–20	VIII.	Andante
pp. 21–22	IX.	[No tempo] "What a funny old boy with her"
pp. 22–23	X.	Allegro
p. 23		Andante
pp. 24–26	XI.	Moderato ["XI" crossed out and "X" added]
pp. 27–28	XII.	Allegretto ["XII" crossed out and "XI" added]

No date, dedication or location is apparent
Signed by composer on upper right hand corner of page 1
Present location: British Library: LOAN 101.65
Parts location: BBC Music Library (MS20418)
No printed first edition

WESTMINSTER ABBEY
Holograph in black ink used for performance with annotations in pencil
The score is written on three double sheets of 20-stave paper measuring 36.4 × 27 cm
The manuscript paper printer's mark is shown as [encircled] J & W | CHESTER | LTD. | LONDON | No. 20
WESTMINSTER ABBEY | (Incidental Music).). | Lennox Berkeley
12 pages:

p. [1]   Title page with annotation "1.30 Thurs." in pencil and BBC stamp
p. [2]   Blank
pp. 1–2 I. Moderato
pp. 2–4 II. Allegretto
pp. 4–6 III.
pp. 6–7 IV. segue to:
         p. 7 Fanfare I: Piu vivo
p. 8   Fanfare II
p. 8   Fanfare III
p. [9]   Blank
p. [10] Blank with BBC stamp

No date, location or dedication is apparent
Signed by the composer on upper right hand corner of p. 1
Present location: BBC Music Library (BBC MS 8325); autograph score with parts copied by P.W. Tilbrook
No printed first edition

THE WINDHOVER: TO CHRIST OUR LORD (Opus 72, no.2)
Holograph [incomplete] in pencil with autograph annotations in black ink
The score is written on both sides of two single sheets of 16-stave paper measuring 34.1 × 27.3 cm
The manuscript paper printer's mark is shown as W H Nr.5.F.16 in lower left hand corner
No title page
4 pages:

pp. 1–4   Music

No date, dedication, location or signature is apparent
Present location: British Library: LOAN 101.95(1)
First edition
MUSICAL TIMES | THE WINDHOVER: | To Christ our Lord | Part-song for S A T B (unaccompanied) | Words by Gerard Manley Hopkins | Music by | LENNOX BERKELEY
7 pages. 244 × 165 mm
Printed in *The Musical Times*, November 1968 (No. 1509)
Publication: © 1968 by Novello & Company Ltd. Unpriced

WINDSOR VARIATIONS FOR CHAMBER ORCHESTRA (Opus 75)
Location of complete holograph unknown
Fragment of full score
Holograph (incomplete) in black ink with pencil annotations and one overlay
The score is written on both sides of a single sheet of 16-stave paper measuring 34 × 27 cm
The manuscript paper printer's mark is shown as [vertical bottom left] WH Nr.5.F.16
No title page
2 pages:
p. 11   last five bars of Variation 1
p. 12   first five bars of Variation 2
No date, dedication, location or signature is apparent
Present location: British Library: LOAN 101.29a with pencil sketch
First edition (Miniature score)
Commissioned for the 1969 Windsor Festival with funds from the Arts | Council of Great Britain and first performed by the Menuhin Festival | Orchestra conducted by Yehudi Menuhin | LENNOX BERKELEY | Windsor Variations | ORCHESTRATION: | Flute | 2 oboes | 2 bassoons | 2 horns in F | Strings | Duration: 13 minutes | Orchestral parts on hire only | [Chester/Hansen logo]
56 pages. 190 × 138 mm
White stiff paper wrappers. Lettered in blue and grey. Trimmed edges
Publication: © 1972 by J. & W. Chester Ltd (J.W.C.8892). Unpriced

A WINTER'S TALE (Incidental music)
Holograph in black ink with extensive annotations; overlays. Much of the music cut or pages taped together. Pages of non-autograph inserts. Tattered condition
The unbound score is written on 14 double sheets and on both sides of five single sheets of 22-stave paper measuring 26.4 × 36.4 cm; also various inserts of all sizes
No manuscript paper printer's mark is apparent

Contained in brown paper wrappers
Title page: [autograph in black ink] THE WINTER'S TALE | Incidental Music. | Lennox Berkeley | [Full Score]
122 pages:

p. [i]	Title page
p. [ii]	Blank
pp. 1–84	Score
	Extensive cuts; pages taped together and renumbered
pp. [85–86]	Blank

No date, dedication or location is apparent
Signed by the composer on title page and on upper right hand corner of page 1
Present location: Stratford upon Avon: The Shakespeare Centre, Box 38 with Autolycus Songs, parts and music cue copy of play; note on wrappers: "Piano score with Lennox Berkeley Dec. 1960"

Autolycus Songs
Holograph in black ink
The score is written on five double sheets of 16-stave paper measuring 34.1 × 27.1 cm
The manuscript paper printer's mark is shown as WH Nr.5.F.16
Title page: [autograph in black ink] Autolycus Songs (LB)
20 pages:

p. [i]	Title page
pp. [ii–vi]	Blank
pp. 1–13	Moderato "When daffodils"
p. [14]	Blank

Present location Stratford upon Avon: The Shakespeare Centre: Box 38 with full score, parts and music cue copy of play
No printed first edition
(See *Suite: A Winter's Tale* (Opus 54) published by Chester Music)

YESTERDAY AND TODAY

Holograph in black and blue ink with autograph additions in blue ink. Timings in pencil
The unbound score is written on one double sheet and both sides of one single sheet of 18-stave paper measuring 36.5 × 27 cm
The manuscript paper printer's mark is shown as [encircled] J.&.W. | CHESTER | LTD. | LONDON No. 18
No title page; page 1 [autograph]: Music for 'Yesterday and Today' | Lennox Berkeley
6 pages:

pp. 1–3   I. Reproaches: Lento "I opened the sea before thee"
pp. 4–6   II. Hymn: [vv1–5 of Vexilla Regis: Hymn for Passiontide]$A.S.
           p. 4 Moderato "The banners of the king go forth"
           pp. 5–6 Andante "Blest on whose arms"
           p. 6 "Hail Holy Cross"
No date, dedication or location is apparent
Present location: British Library: LOAN 101.65
No printed first edition
Choral parts in BBC 324. (no vocal score complete) "SATB parts (×4) [double SATB no.1]

YOUTH IN BRITAIN

Holograph [incomplete] in blue ink with autograph additions, corrections and directions in blue pencil. Timings in pencil. Broadcast production annotations including measure numbers in orange pencil

The unbound score is written on seven double sheets of 22-stave paper measuring 36.8 × 27.2 cm

No title page; p. 1 [autograph]: YOUTH IN BRITAIN | Lennox Berkeley

30 pages:

pp. 1–11   I.M1
            p.1   Moderato
            pp.1–6   (Titles) Allegro moderato
            p. 7   Lento "Boy Down Slide – Girl"
            pp. 7–8+   Allegretto "Boy on Swing"
            pp. 9–10   [Missing]
            p. 11   "Barrow Falls"
pp. 11–13   I.M2
            pp. 11–12 Allegro
            pp. 12–13 Andante "Child and rabbit"
pp. 14–18   I.M3   Allegro
pp. 18–19   I.M4   Lento
pp. 20–23   I.M5
            p. 20   Allegro moderato
            pp. 20–23 Allegretto
pp. 23–24   I.M6   Moderato
pp. 24–30   I.M7   Allegro (Tempo di Marcia)
No date, dedication or location is apparent
Signed by the composer on upper right hand corner of page 1
Present location: British Library: LOAN 101.65
No printed first edition

Discography

This section is divided into the following:

1. A list of commercially-produced recordings (78rpms, LPs, CDs and cassettes) of Lennox Berkeley's music, arranged alphabetically by title.
2. Lennox Berkeley as speaker. Details of interviews (arranged by date) which I have been able to trace from various sources, together with the whereabouts if copies are still in existence.

WORKS BY BERKELEY

Andantino for Organ
J. Bate (organ)   Hyperion A 66061

Another Spring (Opus 93 no.1)
F. Loring (bar)/C. Horsley (pno)   Meridian E 77017

Antiphon (Opus 85)
Westminster Cathedral String Orchestra/C. Mawby   Unicorn UNS 260

Automne (Opus 60 no.3)
M. Dickinson (m-sop)/P. Dickinson (pno)   Argo ZRG 788

Autumn's Legacy: No.3 – Lesbos (Opus 58)
M. Morelle (sop)/D. Wright (pno)   Jupiter JEP 0C36 (45rpm)

Concert Study in E flat (Opus 48 no.2)
Colin Horsley (piano)   Lyrita RCS 9

Concertino for flute/treble recorder, violin, cello and harpsichord/piano (Opus 49)
C. Dolmetsch (rec), A. Schrenfeld (vln), E. Schrenfeld (vlc), J. Saxby (hpsi)
                                                                                Orion ORS 73104

The Endymion Ensemble   Epoch CDLX 7100

Concerto for Flute and Orchestra (Opus 36)
J. Galway (fl)/London Philharmonic Orchestra/Berkeley   RCA Red Seal RS 9011
                                                        RSK 9011 (cassette)

Concerto for Guitar and Orchestra (Opus 88)
J. Bream (guitar)/Monteverdi Orchestra/Gardiner   RCA ARL 1 1181
                                                        09026 61605-2
                                                        RCA GK 81181
                                                        GL 81181

Concerto for Piano and Orchestra (Opus 29)
D. Wilde (piano)/New Philharmonic Orchestra/Braithwaite   Lyrita SRCS 94
                                                          HNH 4079

Concerto for 2 Pianos and Orchestra (Opus 30)
G. Beckett and B. McDonald (pianos)/London Philharmonic Orchestra/ Del Mar
                                                        Lyrita SRCS 80
                                                        HNH 4017
                                            Musical Heritage Society 3696

Concerto for Violin and Chamber Orchestra (Opus 59)
Y. Menuhin (violin)/Menuhin Festival Orchestra/Boult   HMV ASD 2759
                                                        HMV EX 290864-3
                                                HMV EX 290864-9 (cassette)
                                    EMI British Composers CDMS 66121-2

Daffodils (from "A Winter's Tale")
J. MacDougall (tenor)/English Serenata   Meridian CDE 84301

Diversions (Opus 63)
Nash Ensemble   Hyperion A 66086

Divertimento (Opus 18)
London Chamber Orchestra/J. Bernard   Decca K 1882-3 (78rpm)
London Philharmonic Orchestra/Berkeley   Lyrita SRCS 74
                                                        Lyrita SRCD 226
Royal Philharmonic Orchestra/Buketoff   RCA SB 6730
                                                        RCA LSC 3005

D'un vanneur de blé aux vents
W. Brown (ten)/M. McNamee (pno) Jupiter JUR 00A5
M. Dickinson (m-sop)/P. Dickinson (pno) Argo ZRG 788

Duo for Cello and Piano (Opus 81 no.1)
J. Lloyd Webber/J. McCabe (piano) Oiseau-Lyre DSLO 18

Duo for Oboe and Cello (1971)
The Endymion Ensemble Epoch CDLX 7100

Elegy for Violin and Piano (Opus 33, no.2a)
The Endymion Ensemble Epoch CDLX 7100

Fantasia for Organ (Opus 92)
J. Bate (organ) Hyperion A 66061
N. Kynaston (organ – first performance 1/12/76) Organ Club JPS G62
A. Mahon (organ) Woodward MW 916

A Festival Anthem (Opus 21 no.2)
Clare College (Cambridge) Choir/Brown Meridian CDE 84216
  Meridian KE 77216 (cassette)

Five Chinese Songs (Opus 78)
M. Dickinson (m-sop)/P. Dickinson (pno) Argo ZRG 788

Five Poems (Auden) (Opus 53)
T. Helmsley (bar)/E. Lush (pno) HMV DLP 1209
  HMV HQM 1069
Philip Langridge (ten)/S. Bedford (pno) Collins Classics 1490-2
Sarah Leonard (sop)/M. Martineau (pno) Somm Recordings SOMMCD213
F. Lott (sop)/G. Johnson (pno) (No.2 only) Chandos CHAN 8722
  ABTD 1362 (cassette)

Five Short Pieces for Piano (Opus 4)
Christopher Headington (piano) Kingdom Records KCLCD 2012
  CKCL 2012 (cassette)
Raphael Terroni (piano) BMS 416CD

Five Songs (de la Mare) (Opus 26) (No.3 only)
S. Woolf (ten)/S. Bedford (pno) Unicorn RHS 316

Five Songs (Housman) (Opus 14 no.3) (Nos 3 and 5 only)
A. Rolfe Johnson (tenor)/G. Johnson (piano)　　　　Hyperion CDA 66471/2

Four Concert Studies (Opus 14 no.1) (Nos 2, 3 and 4 only)
Colin Horsley (piano)　　　　　　　　　　　　　　　　Lyrita RCS 9

Four Poems of St Teresa of Avila (Opus 27)
P. Bowden (con)/Collegium Musicum Londinii/Minchinton　　HMV DLP 1209
　　　　　　　　　　　　　　　　　　　　　　　　　　HMV HQM 1069
K. Ferrier (con)/String Orchestra/Goldsbrough　　BBC Records REGL 368
　　　　　　　　　　　　　　　　　　　BBC Records ZCF 368 (cassette)
B. Greevy (con)/New Irish Chamber Orchestra/Prieur
　　　　　　　　　　　　　　　　　　　　　New Irish Recordings NIRC 013
S. Walker (con)/London Mozart Players/Sanders　　　　　ACA 519

The Hill of the Graces (Opus 91 no.2)
BBC Northern Singers/S. Wilkinson　　　　　　　　　Abbey LPB 798

How Love came in
P. Pears (ten)/B. Britten (pno)　　　　　　　　　　Decca LW 5241
　　　　　　　　　　　　　　　　　　　　　　　　London 5324
　　　　　　　　　　　　　　　　　　　　　　　London LL 1532
　　　　　　　　　　　　　　　　　　　　　　　Eclipse ECS 545

I Sing of a Maiden
King's College Choir/Willcocks　　　　　　　　　　HMV ALP 2290
　　　　　　　　　　　　　　　　　　　　　　　　HMV ASD 2290
　　　　　　　　　　　　　　　　　　　　　　　　HMV ESD 7050
Leicester Cathedral Choir/White　　　　　　　　　Wealden WS 171
Norwich Cathedral Choir/Runnett　　　　　　　　Cathedral CRL 756
　　　　　　　　　　　　　　　　　　　　　　　Philips 848001 VKY
　　　　　　　　　　　　　　　　　　　　　　　Philips 4FM 10003
St Chad's Metropolitan Cathedral Choir/Harper　　Abbey LPB 768

Improvisation on a theme of Falla (Opus 55 no.2)
Christopher Headington (piano)　　　　Kingdom Records KCLCD 2012
　　　　　　　　　　　　　　　　　　　　　　　CKCL 2012 (cassette)

In Wintertime (Opus 103)
Elysian Singers/Greenall　　　　　　　　　　　Continuum CCD 1043

Introduction and Allegro for double bass and piano (Opus 80)
The Endymion Ensemble　　　　　　　　　　　　Epoch CDLX 7100

Introduction and Allegro for violin (Opus 24)
M. Davis (vln)　　　　　　　　　　　　　　　　Orion ORS 78293

Judica Me (Opus 96 no.1)
Clare College (Cambridge) Choir/Brown　　　　　Meridian CDE 84216
　　　　　　　　　　　　　　　　　　　Meridian KE 77216 (cassette)
Worcester Cathedral Choir/A. Partington (org)/Hunt　　Alpha ACA 533

Justorum animae (Opus 60 no.2)
Canterbury Cathedral Choir/Wicks　　　　　　　Grosvenor GRS 1030

Lay your sleeping head (Opus 14 no.2)
P. Langridge (ten)/S. Bedford (pno)　　　　　　Collins Classics 1490-2

Look up, sweet Babe (Opus 43 no.2)
Canterbury Cathedral Choir/P. Moore (org)/Wicks　　Grosvenor GRS 1030
Choir of St Albans Abbey/A. Parnell (org)/Darlington　　Priory PR 124
　　　　　　　　　　　　　　　　　　　　　　Priory PRCD 003

The Lord is my Shepherd (Opus 91 no.1)
Chichester Cathedral Choir/I. Fox (org)/J. Birch　　　Abbey LPB 770
Chichester Cathedral Choir/J Thomas (org)/A. Thurlow
(Chichester Commissions)　　　　　　　　　　　Priory PRCD 570
Clare College (Cambridge) Choir/Brown　　　　　Meridian CDE 84216
　　　　　　　　　　　　　　　　　　　Meridian KE 77216 (cassette)
King's College (Cambridge) Choir/C. Hughes (org)/S. Cleobury
　　　　　　　　　　　　　EMI British Composers CDC7 54418-2
St Paul's Cathedral Choir/A. Lucas (org)/J. Scott　　Hyperion CDA 66758
Winchester Cathedral Choir/J. Lancelot (org)/M. Neary　　ASV CDQS 6025
　　　　　　　　　　　　　　　　　　　ASD ZCQS 6025 (cassette)

Lord, when the sense of thy sweet grace (Opus 21 no.1)
Chapel Choir of Dean Close School/I. Little (org)/P. Cairns
(Recorded in Tewkesbury Abbey)　　　　　Michael Woodward MW 944
Choir of St Albans Abbey/A. Parnell (org)/Darlington　　Priory PR 124
　　　　　　　　　　　　　　　　　　　　　　Priory PRCD 003

Magnificat (Opus 71)
Combined choirs of St Paul's Cathedral, Westminster Abbey and Westminster Cathedral/London Symphony Orchestra/L. Berkeley (First performance 8 July 1968)   Intaglio INCD 7281

Magnificat and Nunc Dimittis (Opus 99)
Chichester Cathedral Choir/J. Thomas (org)/A. Thurlow
(Chichester Commissions)   Priory PRCD 570
Clare College (Cambridge) Choir/Brown   Meridian CDE 84216
                                                                          Meridian KE 77216 (cassette)

Mass for Five Voices (Opus 64)
Clare College (Cambridge) Choir/Brown   Meridian CDE 84216
                                                                          Meridian KE 77216 (cassette)
Michael Brewer Singers/Brewer   Priory PRCD 292
Norwich Cathedral Choir/M. Archer (org)/Nicholas   Vista VPS 1096

Mazurka (Opus 101, no.2)
Christopher Headington (piano)   Kingdom Records KCLCD 2012
                                                                                 CKCL 2012 (cassette)

Missa Brevis (Opus 57)
Bristol Cathedral Choir/C. Brayne   Priory PRCD 385
Choir of St Albans Abbey Choir/A. Parnell (org)/Darlington   Priory PR 124
                                                                                  Priory PRCD 003
Clare College (Cambridge) Choir/Brown   Meridian CDE 84216
                                                                          Meridian KE 77216 (cassette)
St Chad's Metropolitan Cathedral Choir/J. Pryer (org)/Harper   Abbey LPB 768
St Mary's Collegiate Church Choir (Warwick)/C. Matthews (org)/S. Lole
                                                                                   Abbey CDCA 592
                                                                          Abbey CACA 592 (cassette)

Mont Juic (Opus 9)
English Chamber Orchestra/S. Bedford   Collins Classics 1123-2
                                                                                    1123-4 (cassette)
                                                                           Collins Classics 1031-2
                                                                                    1031-4 (cassette)
London Philharmonic Orchestra/Berkeley   Lyrita SRCS 50
                                                                       Musical Heritage Society 1919

Night covers up the rigid land (Opus 14 no.2)
Philip Langridge (ten)/S. Bedford (pno)   Collins Classics 1490-2

Nocturne for Harp (Opus 67 no.2)
David Watkins (harp)   RCA LRL 1 5087
Danielle Perrett (harp)   ASV CDDCA 1036

Ode du premier jour de mai (Opus 14 no.2)
W. Brown (ten)/M. McNamee (pno)   Jupiter JUR 00A5

Palm Court Waltz (Opus 81 no.2)
I. Brown and K. Stott (pianos)   Hyperion A 66086
R. Terroni and N. Beedle (pianos)   BMS 416CD

Partita (Opus 66)
Frensham Heights School Orchestra/Rice   Waverley LLP 1039
London Philharmonic Orchestra/Berkeley   Lyrita SRCS 74
                                                                     Lyrita SRCD 226

Paysage
Christopher Headington (piano)   Kingdom Records KCLCD 2012
                                                              CKCL 2012 (cassette)

Petite Suite for oboe and cello (1927)
The Endymion Ensemble   Epoch CDLX 7100

Polka, Nocturne and Capriccio (Opus 5) (No.1 only)
C. Headington (piano)   Kingdom Records KCLCD 2012
                                                              CKCL 2012 (cassette)
C. Smith (piano)/P. Sellick (piano) (2 pianos 3 hands)   HMV CLP 3641
                                                                     HMV CSD 3641

Prelude and Capriccio (Opus 95)
Raphael Terroni (piano)   Pearl SHE 576

Prelude and Fugue for Clavichord (Opus 55 no.3)
M. Thomas (clav)   Record Society RSX 16

Quartet for Oboe and String Trio (Opus 70)
Nash Ensemble   Hyperion A 66086
The Endymion Ensemble   Epoch CDLX 7100

Quintet (Opus 90)
Ensemble with Colin Horsley (piano)   Meridian E 77017

Ronsard Sonnets (Set 1) (Opus 40)
W. Whitesides (ten)/Louisville Orchestra/Whitney
                                   Louisville Orchestra LOU 662
                                                       LOU S662

Ronsard Sonnets (Set 2) (Opus 62)
P. Pears (ten)/London Sinfonietta/Berkeley   Decca Head 3

Salve Regina (Opus 48 no.1)
Clare College (Cambridge) Choir/Brown   Meridian CDE 84216
                                   Meridian KE 77216 (cassette)
London Oratory Junior Choir/P. Russill (org)/Hoban   Abbey MVP 782

Scherzo for Piano (Opus 32 no.2)
Colin Horsley (piano)   Lyrita RSC 9
                                                      Meridian E 77017

Serenade for Strings (Opus 12)
Academy of St Martin-in-the-Fields/Sillito   Collins Classics CD 1234-2
                                Collins Classics 1234-4 (cassette)

English Sinfonia/J. Farrer   Carlton Classics MCD60
English Symphony Orchestra/W. Boughton   Nimbus NI 5295
                                                       Nimbus NI 5450/3

Little Orchestra of London/Jones   Pye GSGC 14042
London Philharmonic Orchestra/Berkeley   Lyrita SRCS 74
                                                       Lyrita SRCD 226

Stuttgart Chamber Orchestra/Munchinger   Decca LXT 5153
                                                   Decca Eclipse ECS 688
                                                            London LL 1395

Sextet (Opus 47)
Music Group of London inc. Jack Brymer (cl) and Alan Civil (hn) Argo ZRG 749
Nash Ensemble   Hyperion A 66086
The Endymion Ensemble   Epoch CDLX 7100

Sinfonia Concertante (Opus 84) (4th movement)
Roger Winfield (oboe)/London Philharmonic Orchestra/Berkeley Lyrita SRCS 74
                                                                    Lyrita SRCD 226

Sinfonietta (Opus 34)
English Chamber Orchestra/Del Mar   Lyrita SRCS 111
                                                       Lyrita SRCD 111

Six Preludes for Piano (Opus 23)
John Clegg (piano)   Alpha DB 148C
                                                    Paradisum PDS-CD2
Anthony Goldstone (piano)   Gamut GAMCD 526
Christopher Headington (piano)   Kingdom Records KCLCD 2012
                                                    CKCL 2012 (cassette)
Colin Horsley (piano)   HMV C 3940 (78rpm)
                                                        HMV HQM 1069
                                                           Lyrita RSC 9
                                                       Meridian E 77017
Raphael Terroni (piano)   BMS 416CD

Sonata for Flute and Piano (Opus 97)
J. Galway (fl)/P. Moll (pno)   RCA Red Seal RS 9011

Sonata for Flute and Piano: Poulenc/orch. Berkeley (Opus 93 no.2)
J. Galway (flute)/Royal Philharmonic Orchestra/Dutoit   RL 25109
J. Stinton (flute)/Scottish Chamber Orchestra/Bedford   Collins Classics 70052

Sonata for Piano (Opus 20)
Christopher Headington (piano)   Kingdom Records KCLCD 2012
                                                    CKCL 2012 (cassette)
Colin Horsley (piano)   Lyrita RCS 9
Raphael Terroni (piano)   Pearl SHE 576
                                                            BMS 416CD

Sonata for Violin and Piano (Opus 1)
M. Pounder (vln)/R. Terroni (pno)   Pearl SHE 576

Sonatina for Guitar (Opus 52 no.1)
R. Aussel (guitar)   Mandala MAN 4802
Julian Bream (guitar)   RCA Victor LM 2448
                                                             LSC 2448
                                                          RCA RB 15650
                                       RCA Victor Gold Seal 09026 61595-2
                                                          RCA RB 16239
                                                           RCA SB 6891

C. Heurtefeux (guitar) — Mandala MAN 4806
C. Ogden (guitar) — Nimbus NI 5390
R. Provost (guitar) — Ars Nova AN 1003
J. Savijoki (guitar) — Ondine ODE 779-2

Sonatina for Oboe and Piano (Opus 61)
C. Pluygers (ob)/M. Stanley (pno) — Redbridge RBR 1002

Sonatina for Piano Duet (Opus 39)
I. Brown and K. Stott (pianos) — Hyperion A 66086
R. Terroni and N. Beedle (pianos) — BMS 416CD

Sonatina for Recorder (or Flute) and Piano (Opus 13)
Piers Adams (rec)/J. Rhodes (pno) — Tremula TREM 103-2
James Galway (fl)/Anthony Goldstone (pno) — RCA LRL 1 5127
K. Smith (fl)/P. Rhodes (pno) — ASV CDDCA 768
ZCDCA 768 (cassette)
K. Spratt (fl)/E. Mucha (pno) — KLT 001

Sonatina for Violin and Piano (Opus 17)
Hugh Bean (vln)/David Parkhouse (pno) — Argo ZRG 749
M. Davis (vln)/P. Platt (pno) — Orion ORS 78292

Songs of the Half Light (Opus 65)
N. Mackie (ten)/B. Jeffrey (guitar) (Nos 2 and 5) — Beltona MBE 111
Beltona SBE111
I. Partridge (ten)/J. Savijoki (guitar) — Ondine ODE 779-2

Spring at this Hour – A Garland for the Queen (Opus 37 no.2)
Bristol Bach Choir/Jenkins — Priory PRCD 352
Cambridge University Chamber Choir/Brown — Gamut GAMCD 529
Cambridge University Madrigal Society and Golden Age Singers/Boris Ord
Columbia 33CX 1063
Exultate Singers/O'Brien — RCA GL 25062

String Trio (Opus 19)
J. Georgiadis (vln)/B. Hawkins (va)/D. Cummings (vc) — Pearl SHE 547
D. Greed (vln)/H. Breakspear (va)/A. Wickham (vc)
Max Sound MSCB 16/17 (Dolby B) (cassette)
Max Sound MSCB 16/17 (Dolby C) (cassette)
J. Pougnet (vln)/F. Riddle (va)/A. Pini (vc) — Nixa WLP 20017

	Westminster WL5316
	Westminster XWN 18515
Thamyse String Trio	Altarus Recordings AIR-2-9005
Troester Trio	Polydor 68333-4 (78rpm)

Sweet was the Song: arr. for men's voices (Opus 43 no.3)
The Clerkes of Oxenford/Wulstan   Abbey 603

Symphony No.1 (Opus 16)
London Philharmonic Orchestra/Del Mar   Lyrita SRCS 80
                                                                                    HNH 4017
                                                         Musical Heritage Society 3696

Symphony No.2 (Opus 51)
London Philharmonic Orchestra/N. Braithwaite   Lyrita SRCS 94
                                                                                    HNH 4079

Symphony No.3 (Opus 74)
London Philharmonic Orchestra/Berkeley   Lyrita SRCS 57
                                                                                Lyrita SRCD 226
                                                         Musical Heritage Society 1672

Tant que mes Yeux
M. Dickinson (m-sop)/P. Dickinson (pno)   Argo ZRG 788

Theme and Variations for Guitar (Opus 77)
Julian Bream (guitar)   RCA SB 6876
                                                                                RCA ARS 1 0049
B. Davezac (guitar)   Erato STU 70926
J. Savijoki (guitar)   Ondine ODE 779-2
J. Wolf (guitar)   Partridge PART 1115-2

Theme and Variations for Piano Duet (Opus 73)
R. Terroni and N. Beedle (pianos)   BMS 416CD

Theme and Variations for Violin (Opus 33 no.1)
Frederick Grinke (violin)   Decca LXT 2978
                                                                                London LL 1055

Thou hast made me (Opus 55 no.1)
Canterbury Cathedral Choir/P. Moore (org)/Wicks   Grosvenor GRS 1030

DISCOGRAPHY · 307

Clare College (Cambridge) Choir/Brown | Meridian CDE 84216
| Meridian KE 77216 (cassette)
Guildford Cathedral Choir/P. Wright (org)/A. Millington
| Abbey ALPHA XPS 103
Magdalen College (Oxford) Choir/Harper | Alpha CDCA 915
| CACA 915 (cassette)

Three Greek Songs (Opus 38)
T. Hemsley (bar)/E. Lush (pno) | HMV DLP 1209
| HMV HQM 1069
M. Morelle (sop)/D. Wright (pno) | Jupiter JEP 0C36 (45rpm)

Three Impromptus for Piano (Opus 7 no.1)
Colin Horsley (piano) | Lyrita RCS 9

Three Latin Motets (Opus 83 no.1)
Clare College (Cambridge) Choir/Brown | Meridian CDE 84216
| Meridian KE 77216 (cassette)

Three Mazurkas (Opus 32 no.1)
Christopher Headington (piano) | Kingdom Records KCLCD 2012
| CKCL 2012 (cassette)

Three Pieces for Organ (Opus 72 no.1)
Malcolm Archer (organ) | Vista VPS 1096
Jennifer Bate (organ) (No.1 only) | Hyperion A 66061
S. Hollas (organ) | Wealden WS 149

Three Pieces for Piano (Opus 2)
Christopher Headington (piano) | Kingdom Records KCLCD 2012
| CKCL 2012 (cassette)

Three Songs for Male Voices (Opus 67 no.1)
Gentlemen of St John's College Choir, Cambridge | Etcetera KTC 1192

Toccata for Violin and Piano (Opus 33, no.3)
The Endymion Ensemble | Epoch CDLX 7100

Trio for violin, horn and piano (Opus 44)
H. Moulle (vln)/S. Hermanssen (hn)/H. Gobel (pno) | Thorofon MTM 257
M. Parikian (vln)/D. Brain (hn)/C. Horsley (pno) | HMV CLP 1029

Schiller Trio
HMV HQM 1007
Capitol G 7175
Seraphim 60073
Phoenix BGS 1007

Variation on an Elizabethan theme (Sellinger's Round)
Aldeburgh Festival Orchestra/Britten (first performance 20/6/53)
Decca LXT 2798
London LL 808
Guildhall String Ensemble/Robert Salter RCA Red Seal RD 87846
RCA Red Seal RK 87846 (cassette)

BERKELEY AS SPEAKER

3 April 1969	Berkeley talks about Sir Adrian Boult C.H. on his 80th birthday (BBC R3) 1333 W National Sound Archive
2 August 1971	Berkeley's speech at Sir Arthur Bliss's 80th birthday concert at the Royal Albert Hall T 35120 BBC Sound Archives
29 August 1971	Talks about his approach to composition (BBC R3) M 4137 R National Sound Archive
3 October 1971	Berkeley talks about Alan Rawsthorne in a tribute M 4224 R National Sound Archive T 61139 BBC Sound Archives
25 November 1971	Berkeley discusses musical criticism T 44031 BBC Sound Archives
7 January 1972	Berkeley talks about his years of study in Paris with Nadia Boulanger (BIRS Lecture) T 581 W National Sound Archive
3 March 1972	A discussion about Walton in the 1920s

	with Angus Morrison at a BIRS Lecture P 833 W National Sound Archive
7 August 1972	Berkeley discusses the role of the music critic (BBC R3) M 4543 R National Sound Archive
12 February 1973	Introduces a programme of his songs with Peter Dickinson T 60220 BBC Sound Archives
9 March 1973	Berkeley talks to Colin Mawby about his music T 60223 BBC Sound Archives
22 March 1973	Christopher Headington talks about and assesses the influences that have shaped Berkeley's style (BBC R3) 2235 R National Sound Archive
24 April 1974	An interview on the crisis period and young composers LP 35407 BBC Sound Archives
15 May 1973	Interviewed about his life and work, with mention of Nadia Boulanger LP 35406 BBC Sound Archive
16 May 1973	Berkeley talks about his Quartet for Oboe and String Trio (Op.70) (BBC R3) T 575 Y National Sound Archive
30 September 1973	A discussion about Nadia Boulanger's contribution to music by some former pupils including Lennox Berkeley (BBC R3) T 709 W National Sound Archive
3 March 1975	Berkeley talks about his meetings with Maurice Ravel in Paris (BBC R3) P 1063 W National Sound Archive

17 July 1977	Provides some reminiscences for a programme on the soprano Sophie Wyss T 53021 BBC Sound Archives
1979	Berkeley talks about the 1936 ISCM Festival and Benjamin Britten TR 144495 BBC Transcription Service
31 August 1992	"Lennox Berkeley" Peter Dickinson talking about the composer's life H 596 National Sound Archive
No date apparent	Three Modern British Composers: Britten, Tippett and Berkeley LP 133616 BBC Transcription Service
No date apparent	Berkeley talks about the composers who have influenced him LP 153031 BBC Transcription Service

Select bibliography

This bibliography presents writings relating to Lennox Berkeley and his music from the earliest years to the present day. It is divided into the following sections:

I   **Writings by Lennox Berkeley**
Arranged in chronological order.
Many of the entries are annotated.

II   **General writings about Berkeley and his music**
Arranged in alphabetical order by author's name.
Some of the entries are annotated to clarify contents.

III   **References to specific works**
These are collected under the relevant heading of Berkeley's works if they are specifically concerned with those works. All entries are listed in alphabetical order by author's name within the headings. Again some of the entries are annotated.

I: WRITINGS BY BERKELEY

"A Paris Letter"
Monthly Musical Record, 59 (June 1929), p. 174
(Remarks about a concert of Honegger's works including "Rugby", which Berkeley described as "…a masterpiece" and "Pacific 231". Also mentioned is Roussel's "Le Festin de l'Araignée" and first performances of Poulenc's "Concerto Champêtre", conducted by Pierre Monteaux, and Walton's "Façade".)

"Music in Paris"
Monthly Musical Record, 59 (August 1929), p. 242
(Comments on performances of Mozart and Aaron Copland.)

"Music in Paris"
Monthly Musical Record, 59 (December 1929), p. 370

(Views on concerts conducted by Pierre Monteaux and Henry Wood which included Vaughan Williams' "London Symphony". Also mentioned are two invitation concerts of modern chamber music, given in October 1929, which included Martinu's String Quartet and Arthur Bliss's Oboe Quartet.)

"Music in Paris"
Monthly Musical Record, 60 (May 1930), p. 143
(Details of concerts which included Stravinsky's "Capriccio", Poulenc's "Aubade" and Conrad Beck's "Concerto for Orchestra" conducted by Walter Straram.)

"Music in Paris"
Monthly Musical Record, 60 (August 1930), p. 242
(Mention of Manuel de Falla, Honegger's new cello concerto and Pavlova's short season of ballet.)

"Nadia Boulanger as Teacher"
Monthly Musical Record, 61 (January 1931), p. 4
(Considers her attitude towards music and mentions her methods in general.)

"Music in Paris"
Monthly Musical Record, 61 (March 1931), p. 82
(A discussion about the Paris orchestras and orchestral concerts. There is particular mention of Alfredo Casella.)

"Music in Paris"
Monthly Musical Record, 61 (May 1931), p. 146
(Views on the first performance in Paris of Stravinsky's "Symphony of Psalms" and the piano recitals of Walter Gieseking.)

"Music in Paris"
Monthly Musical Record, 61 (July 1931), p. 210
(Mention of a recital by Roland Hayes, Segovia's concert at the Opera, Milhaud's violin concerto and Honegger's "Chris du monde".)

"Music in Paris"
Monthly Musical Record, 61 (December 1931), p. 360
(Views on concert going in Paris, music teachers and the public's attitude towards music.)

"English music in Paris"
Monthly Musical Record, 62 (February 1932), p. 37

(A letter to the editor of the *Monthly Musical Record*)

"Music in Paris"
Monthly Musical Record, 62 (March–April 1932), p. 63
(A description of the first performance of Stravinsky's violin concerto at the Salle Pleyel.)

"Music in Paris"
Monthly Musical Record, 62 (June 1932), p. 112
(Mention of Alfred Cortot's concert in celebration of the Haydn bicentenary.)

"Music in Paris"
Monthly Musical Record, 62 (September 1932), p. 159
(Views on the Ballet Russes de Monte Carlo.)

"Music in Paris"
Monthly Musical Record, 62 (December 1932), p. 365
(A review of a concert given by the Paris Symphonic Orchestra under Pierre Monteaux which included a symphony by a "... young French composer, Jean Francaix".)

"Music in Paris"
Monthly Musical Record, 63 (March–April 1933), p. 63
(Mention of performances of Kurt Weill's "Mahagonny" and "Der Jasager", Manuel de Falla's Concerto for Harpsichord, Ravel's new Piano Concerto for the left hand, first performed in Paris by Wittgenstein in January 1933, and some orchestral works by Charles Koechlin.)

"Music in Paris"
Monthly Musical Record, 63 (June 1933), p. 112
(Impressions of the Straram Orchestra ("... the best in Paris at the moment ...") and M. Straram who "... has done more for young and unknown composers than any other conductor here ..." Also mentioned is the Italian composer, Alfredo Casella and his compositions including his Partita for piano and orchestra, and Greek conductor Dimitri Mitropoulos.)

"Music in Paris"
Monthly Musical Record, 63 (December 1933), p. 231
(Views on Respighi's "Pines of Rome" which is described as "... second-rate and vulgar ...", and Honegger's "Troisième Movement Symphonique".)

"Music in Paris"
Monthly Musical Record, 64 (June 1934), pp. 110–11
(A description of Madame Ida Rubinstein's performance at the Opera. Particular mention is made of Stravinsky's "Persephone" and Honegger's "Semiramis".)

"Britten and his String Quartet"
The Listener, 27 May 1943, p. 641
(A survey of the String Quartet which "... is full of unusual qualities, but the really surprising thing is its beauty".)

"Maurice Ravel" in Norman Demuth *Ravel* (Master Musician Series)
London, Dent, 1947 (First edition), p. 177
(Quotations from a letter, dated 9 May 1946, written by Berkeley to the author.)

"Open Forum: Variations on a Theme – Tonal or Atonal?" in Rollo Myers (ed)
Music Today No.1 (Journal of the ISCM), London, Dobson, 1949, p. 145
(Replies from eminent composers who were invited to express their views on this controversial question. Schoenberg, Milhaud, Poulenc, Jolivet, Migot, Searle, Murrill, Mellors and Demuth are among the composers who replied. Berkeley writes that he "... never [has] been able to derive much satisfaction from atonal music".)

"The composer looks at the opera"
Philharmonic Post, 5 (March/April 1950), pp. 12–13
("Particular difficulties confront the English opera composer. Three distinguished musicians, each of whom is at present working on an opera [Berkeley, George Lloyd and Michael Tippett], put forward their ideas for the solution of these problems.")

"Britten's Spring Symphony"
Music and Letters, 31 (July 1950), pp. 216–19

"Poulenc's Piano Concerto"
Programme note for the first performance in England (Royal Albert Hall), BBC Symphony Orchestra Concerts, 8 November 1950, pp. 11–12

"Britten's Spring Symphony"
Philharmonic Post, 5 (April/May 1951), pp. 8–9

"The Light Music" in D. Mitchell and H. Keller (eds) *Benjamin Britten: a commentary on his works from a group of specialists*
London, Rockcliffe, 1952, pp. 287–94

Review of Alec Robertson's "More than Music" (Collins)
The Tablet, 9 December 1961, p. 1178

"The Sound of Words"
The Times, 28 June 1962, p. 15
(An account of the composer's reading habits including fiction, English and French, books about religion and music, "... some of which have helped me in my work ...".)

"Britten's characters" *About the House*, 1 no.5 (1963), p. 14
(An examination of the characters in Britten's operas.)

"Francis Poulenc: obituary tribute"
Musical Times, 104 (March 1963), p. 205

"Concert Going in 1963"
The Sunday Times, 30 December 1962, p. 28

"Boulanger the dedicated"
Piano Teacher, 8, no.2 (1965), pp. 6–7
(A tribute to his teacher Nadia Boulanger.)

"Nocturnes, Berceuse, Barcarolle" in A. Walker (ed.) *Frederic Chopin: Profiles of the Man and Musician*
London, Barrie and Rockcliff, 1966, pp. 170–86
(A discussion of these piano works, with music examples.)

"Truth in Music"
Times Literary Supplement, 3 March 1966, p. 158
(A discussion about contemporary composers "... [who] have made much use of religious subjects, either by setting sacred texts to music or by using words or subject matter that are religious or have religious implications.")

"Lili Boulanger"
The Listener, 21 November 1968, p. 692
(A introduction to the composer and her music, prompted by a concert conducted by her sister, Nadia Boulanger, and broadcast by the BBC.)

"Last week's broadcast music"
The Listener, 13 February 1969, p. 218
(Mention of Monteverdi, Peter Maxwell Davies and the pianist Alfred Brendel.)

The Listener, 23 October 1969, p. 579
(A discussion about Ronald Stevenson, Humphrey Searle and Maurice Ravel.)

"Charles Burney's Tour"
The Listener, 5 March 1970, p. 321
(Details of Burney's tour of France and Italy in 1770 to collect material for his *General History of Music* published a few years later.)

"Lennox Berkeley writes about Alan Rawsthorne"
The Listener, 30 December 1971, p. 913
(An appreciation of the composer.)

"Alan Rawsthorne"
Composer, no.42 (Winter 1971–72), pp. 5–7

"A composer speaks – 2"
Composer, no.43 (Spring 1972), pp. 17–19
(A description of his compositional methods with mention of Boulanger and Britten.)

"Walton – yesterday"
Performing Right, no.57 (May 1972), pp. 18–19
(A tribute to Sir William Walton on his 70th birthday.)

[Tribute to Alec Robertson] in *Dear Alec – a tribute for his 80th birthday from his friends known and unknown*
Worcester, Stanbrook Abbey Press, 1972, p. [11]
(A limited edition with 60 specially numbered copies and 135 copies printed in various papers and bindings. Alec Robertson and Lennox Berkeley were colleagues in the Music Division of the BBC.)

"Views from Mont Juic"
Tempo, no.106 (September 1973), pp. 6–7
(Memories about the 1936 ISCM Festival and his first meeting with Britten.)

Comments on the 1975 season of Henry Wood Promenade Concerts:
    Prom no.1   *Radio Times*, 19–25 July, p. 46
    Prom no.2   *Radio Times*, 26 July–1 August, p. 19
    Prom no.3   "   "   "   "   p. 25
    Prom no.4   "   "   "   "   p. 29
    Prom no.5   "   "   "   "   p. 32

Prom no.6	*Radio Times*, 26 July–1 August, p. 36	
Prom no.7	" " " "	p. 40
Prom no.8	" " " "	p. 46
Prom no.9	*Radio Times*, 2–8 August, p. 18	
Prom no.10	" " "	p. 25
Prom no.11	" " "	p. 28
Prom no.12	" " "	p. 32
Prom no.13	" " "	p. 38
Prom no.14	" " "	p. 44
Prom no.15	" " "	p. 51
Prom no.16	*Radio Times*, 9–15 August, p. 17	
Prom nos.17–18	" " "	p. 25
Prom no.19	" " "	p. 33
Prom no.20	" " "	p. 36
Prom no.21	" " "	p. 40
Prom no.22	" " "	p. 46
Prom no.23	*Radio Times*, 16–22 August, p. 18	
Prom no.24	" " "	p. 25
Prom no.25	" " "	p. 28
Prom no.26	" " "	p. 32
Prom no.27	" " "	p. 36
Prom no.28	" " "	p. 40
Prom no.29	" " "	p. 47
Prom no.30	*Radio Times*, 23–29 August, p. 19	
Prom no.31	" " "	p. 31
Prom no.32	" " "	p. 34
Prom no.33	" " "	p. 38
Prom no.34	" " "	p. 42
Prom no.35	" " "	p. 46
Prom no.36	*Radio Times*, 30 August–5 September, p. 21	
Prom nos.37–38	" " " "	p. 30
Prom no.39	" " " "	p. 34
Prom no.40	" " " "	p. 39
Prom no.41	" " " "	p. 44
Prom no.42	" " " "	p. 50
Prom no.43	*Radio Times*, 6–12 September, p. 25	
Prom no.44	" " "	p. 33
Prom no.45	" " "	p. 36
Prom no.46	" " "	p. 42
Prom no.47	" " "	p. 49
Prom no.48	" " "	p. 57

Prom no.49   *Radio Times*, 6–12 September, p. 63
Prom no.50   *Radio Times*, 13–19 September, p. 23
Prom nos.51–52   "   "   "   p. 34
Prom no.53   "   "   "   p. 44
Prom no.54   "   "   "   p. 50
Prom no.55   "   "   "   p. 55
Prom no.56   "   "   "   p. 61
Prom no.57   *Radio Times*, 20–26 September, p. 27

"A composer looks back" in B. Still (ed.) *250 years of the Three-Choirs Festival* [Gloucester], Three-Choirs Festival Association, 1977, p. 45
(Recollections of past Festivals when the composer's works were performed.)

"Foreword" in Pierre Bernac *Francis Poulenc: the man and his songs*
London, Gollancz, 1977, pp. 11–12

"Maurice Ravel"
Adam International Review, no.404–6 (1978), pp. 13–17
(An appreciation of the French composer.)

"Benjamin Britten" in Alan Blythe *Remembering Britten*
London, Hutchinson, 1981, pp. 43–6
(Recollections of Benjamin Britten.)

[Comments] in R. Ricketts (editor and producer) *Bid the World Goodnight*
London, Search Press, 1981, pp. 19–21
(Reflections on old age and death.)

"Introduction" in Christopher Headington *Britten*
London, Methuen/Eyre Methuen, 1981

["Janet Craxton"] in the Thanksgiving Concert Programme Book in memory of Janet Craxton London, Wigmore Hall, 24 April 1982, [p. 7]

"Igor Stravinsky – a centenary tribute"
Musical Times, 123 (June 1982), p. 395

"Michael Tippett – a tribute" in Geraint Lewis (ed.) *Michael Tippett – a Celebration*
Tunbridge Wells, Baton Press, 1985, p. 21

"Tribute to Nadia Boulanger" in Bruno Monsaingeon (trans. Robyn Marsack)

Mademoiselle: conversations with Nadia Boulanger
Manchester, Carcanet Press, 1985 (originally published in France, 1981), p. 120

II: GENERAL WRITINGS ON BERKELEY AND HIS WORKS

ANON. "Berkeley conducts Berkeley: CD Review", *Musical Times*, 134 (July 1993), p. 412
ANON. "The Career of Lennox Berkeley", *The Times*, 19 October 1956, p. 3
ANON. "Choral music: record review", *Tempo*, no.183 (December 1992), pp. 59+
ANON. "Composers of Today", *The Chesterian*, 25 (April 1951), p. 105
ANON. "Composers of Today", *Music Parade*, 2 no.4, opp. page 1
ANON. "Lennox Berkeley", *The Chesterian*, 29 (October 1954), p. 59 (Also includes a photograph of the composer)
ANON. "Lennox Berkeley", *London Music*, 14 (February 1959), p. 22
ANON. "Lennox Berkeley: obituary", *American Organist*, 24 (April 1990), p. 71
ANON. "Lennox Berkeley: obituary", *Catholic Herald*, 5 January 1990, p. 3
ANON. "Lennox Berkeley: obituary", *Central Opera*, 29 (1989–90), pp. 73–4
ANON. "Lennox Berkeley: obituary", *Classical Music*, 20 January 1990, p. 9
ANON. "Lennox Berkeley: obituary", *Dolmetsch Bulletin*, 57 (February 1990), p. 13
ANON. "Lennox Berkeley: obituary", *Gramophone*, 67 (February 1990), p. 1444
ANON. "Lennox Berkeley: obituary", *Hymn*, 44 no.4 (1993), p. 30
ANON. "Lennox Berkeley: obituary", *Notes*, 46 no. 4 (1990), p. 929
ANON. "Lennox Berkeley: obituary", *Opera*, 41 (February 1990), p. 186
ANON. "Lennox Berkeley: obituary", *Opera News*, 55 (August 1990), p. 51
ANON. "Lennox Berkeley: obituary", *Variety*, 338 (24 January 1990), pp. 192–93
ANON. "Lennox Berkeley honoured", *Musical Opinion*, 96 (June 1973), p. 456
ANON. "Living British composers", *Hinrichsen's Musical Yearbook*, 6 (1949–50), p. 121
ANON. "M.T.A. composer of the Year", *Music Teacher*, 33 (December 1954), p. 607
ANON. [Memorial Requiem Mass for Lennox Berkeley], *The Daily Telegraph*, 21 March 1990, p. 23
ANON. "Miscellanea", *Musical Opinion*, 77 (March 1954), p. 335
ANON. "Mr. Lennox Berkeley on the composer's need to hear his own works", *The Times*, 2 April 1959, p. 14
ANON. "Musical Memory", *The Sunday Times*, 15 May 1983, p. 35
ANON. "New and Old", *Dolmetsch Bulletin*, no.28 (September 1977), p. 1
ANON. "The new appointment", *Performing Right*, no.64 (November 1975), pp. 12–13

ANON. "New Year Honours", *London Music*, 12 (February 1957), p. 9

ANON. "Newcomers: Lennox Berkeley", *The Chesterian*, 15 (April 1934), pp. 114–15 (An introduction to the composer on joining the firm of J. & W. Chester.)

ANON. "P.R.S. elects new President", *Music Teacher*, 54 (November 1975), p. 13

ANON. "Recordings : piano works", *Musical Opinion*, 112 (October 1989), p. 357

ANON. "Sir Lennox and the Festival go well together …", *Gloucestershire Echo*, 8 July 1977, p. 10

ANON. "Sir Lennox Berkeley – composer of restrained and courteous virtues" [obituary], *The Times*, 27 December 1989, p. 14

ANON. "Sir Lennox Berkeley" [obituary], *The Daily Telegraph*, 27 December 1989, p. 19

APRAHAMIAN, F. "The golden notes of Spring", *The Sunday Times*, 6 March 1983, p. 39 (Mention of a concert which provided an "… early 80th birthday homage to Sir Lennox Berkeley …")

BAKER, G. "What are they like at home?", *Music Teacher*, 33 (September 1954), pp. 434, 438

BANFIELD, S. "The cultivated ear", *Musical Times*, 132 (January 1991), p. 709

BANFIELD, S. [Lennox Berkeley] in "Sensibility and English Song: Critical Studies of the Early Twentieth Century", 2 volumes, Cambridge, Cambridge University Press, 1985, pp. 389–92

BOOSEY, L. and BERKELEY, L. "Tributes to Sir Arthur Bliss", *Performing Right*, no.64 (November 1975), pp. 15–16

BRITTEN, B. *My brother Benjamin*, Bourne End (Bucks), Kensal Press, 1986, pp. 91, 94, 106, 124, 141

BROOK, D. "Lennox Berkeley" in *Composers Gallery*, London, Rockliff, 1946, pp. 20–22

BRYAN, G. "The younger English composers: Part V – Lennox Berkeley", *Monthly Musical Record*, 59 (June 1929), pp. 161–62 (A brief survey of his life and music to date.)

CARPENTER, H. [Lennox Berkeley] in *Benjamin Britten: a biography*, London, Faber & Faber, 1992, pp. 80, 83–84, 97, 104, 110–12, 179, 315, 352, 442

CECIL, M. "The composition of Number 8", *Harper and Queen*, April 1990, pp. 198–201 (An investigation of Berkeley's tastes and lifestyle at 8, Warwick Avenue in Little Venice, London.)

CHISSELL, J. "Success at 70", *The Sunday Times*, 6 May 1973, p. 37

COHEN, H. *A Bundle of Time: the memoirs of Harriet Cohen*, London, Faber & Faber, 1969, pp. 89 and 247 (Mention of a visit to a Promenade concert, and letter about Berkeley's three piano pieces.)

COLE, H. "Elizabeth Hall: Berkeley's 80th", *The Guardian*, 16 May 1983, p. 11
COLE, H. "Music with a French accent" [obituary], *The Guardian*, 27 December 1989, p. 23
COLE, H. "Thirteen composers leap to their feet to acknowledge the applause", *The Guardian*, 5 July 1983, p. 11 (An account of the 80th birthday concert at Cheltenham when musical tributes from former pupils of Berkeley were played.)
COLLINS, S. "In competition", *Strad*, 89 (October 1978), pp. 539+
COOPER, M. "Lennox Berkeley", *Canon*, 13 (January 1960), pp. 135–36
COOPER, M. "Lennox Berkeley", *The Listener*, 9 May 1963, p. 805 (A survey of Berkeley's life and compositions, prompted by broadcasts of the "Sonatina for two pianos" and "Autumn's Legacy".)
CRICHTON, R. "Berkeley", *The Financial Times*, 15 May 1978, p. 13 (A 75th birthday tribute)
CRICHTON, R. "Between Britten and France", *Times Literary Supplement*, 22 December 1989, p. 1409 (A review of Peter Dickinson's book on the composer.)
CRICHTON, R. "Lennox Berkeley 1903–1989" [obituary], *Opera*, 41 (March 1990), pp. 293–94
CRICHTON, R. "Lennox Berkeley – an obituary", *Financial Times*, 28 December 1989, p. 9
DEAN, W. "Heroic Stature", *The Listener*, 20 October 1983, p. 32 (A consideration of Berkeley's operas, prompted by broadcasts of *Nelson*, *Castaway* and *A Dinner Engagement*.)
DEAN, W. "Lennox Berkeley's Orchestral Music", *The Listener*, 7 April 1955, p. 637 (A discussion about Berkeley's development, prompted by a broadcast of *Symphony No.1*.)
DEAN, W. "Review of Peter Dickinson's *The Music of Lennox Berkeley*", *Music and Letters*, 71 (August 1990), pp. 439–42
DICKINSON, P. "Aldeburgh – I", *Musical Times*, 131 (September 1990), pp. 499–500 (Details of a tribute to Berkeley at the 1990 Aldeburgh Festival.)
DICKINSON, P. "An unobtrusive man: Sir Lennox Berkeley's wide-ranging achievement", *The Listener*, 14 June 1990, pp. 44–45 (A survey of Berkeley's life and work.)
DICKINSON, P. "Berkeley at 75", *Radio Times*, 119 (May 1978), pp. 409–11 (The text of an interview marking the composer's 75th birthday.)
DICKINSON, P. "Berkeley on the keyboard", *Music and Musicians*, 11 (April 1963), pp. 10–11, 58 (Includes a portrait and musical examples.)
DICKINSON, P. "Berkeley's music today", *Musical Times*, 109 (November 1968), pp. 1013–14 (Includes a portrait of the composer.)
DICKINSON, P. [Interview with Lennox Berkeley] in *Twenty British Composers, prepared for the Feeney Trust*, London, Chester Music, 1975, pp. 23–29
DICKINSON, P. "Lennox Berkeley", in S. Sadie (ed.) *The New Grove Dictionary*

of Music and Musicians: 6th edition (Volume 2), London, Macmillan, 1980, pp. 560-63

DICKINSON, P. "Lennox Berkeley", *Music and Musicians*, 13 (August 1965), pp. 20-23, 54 (+ portrait), reprinted in "Senior British Composers 2: Lennox Berkeley" in *Composer*, no.36 (Summer 1970), pp. 3-9, 11

DICKINSON, P. "Lennox Berkeley", *Radio 3 Magazine*, 2 (6) June 1983, pp. 4-6 (A celebration of the composer's 80th birthday.)

DICKINSON, P. *Lennox Berkeley: 75th birthday year*, London, Chester Music, 1978 (Includes an introductory essay, photographs, a list of works and a discography.)

DICKINSON, P. *Lennox Berkeley: the 80th year*, London, Chester Music, 1983 (Includes an essay, list of works, discography and photographs.)

DICKINSON, P. *Lennox Berkeley: the 85th year*, London, Chester Music, 1988 (Includes a survey of his life and music, a full list of works, a select bibliography, a list of recordings and photographs.)

DICKINSON, P. "The Music of Lennox Berkeley", *Musical Times*, 104 (May 1963), pp. 327-30 (Written in celebration of Berkeley's 60th birthday.)

DICKINSON, P. *The Music of Lennox Berkeley*, London, Thames Publishing, 1988 (A detailed survey of Berkeley's life and music with many musical examples and illustrations.)

DICKINSON, P. "Sir Lennox Berkeley" [obituary], *The Independent*, 27 December 1989, p. 18

DICKINSON, P. "Sir Lennox Berkeley" (Repertoire Guide No.12), *Classical Music*, 23 March 1991, pp. 12-13

DICKINSON, P. "Sir Lennox Berkeley as teacher – a master of musical integrity" [obituary], *The Guardian*, 28 December 1989, p. 31

DICKINSON, P. "Sir Lennox Berkeley in British Music", Programme of the 39th Cheltenham International Festival of Music, July 1983, p. 7

DREWRY, V. "Lennox Berkeley – some recent compositions", *The Chesterian*, 26 (October 1951), pp. 1-4

E.R.A. "Alice Esty ... Soprano", *Musical America*, April 1989, p. 39

EAST, J.M. "Works that will make Sir Lennox remembered for all time", *Westminster Record*, January 1990, p. 3

EAST, L. "Berkeley at 70", *Music and Musicians*, 21 (May 1973), pp. 22-23 (Includes a photograph of the composer as conductor.)

ERICSON, R. "English music shows many facets", *The New York Times*, 26 August 1984, pp. 22, 24

FLOTHUIS, M. *Modern British Composers*, Stockholm/London, The Continental Book Company/Sidgwick & Jackson, 1949, pp. 31-35

FORD, C. "Berkeley Square", *The Guardian*, 3 August 1973, p. 10 (+ portrait)

FRANK, A. "A composer with style and grace", *Radio Times*, 25 June 1954, p. 7

FRANK, A. "Contemporary Portraits", *Music Teacher*, 29 (September 1950), pp. 395, 404, reprinted in *Modern British Composers*, London, Dobson, 1953, pp. 64–68

GILARDINO, A. "Contemporary guitar music in Great Britain", *Fronimo*, 1 (October 1973), pp. 8–14 [in Italian]

GREENFIELD, E. "Here and there: James Galway", *Gramophone*, 60 (May 1983), p. 1025

HANSEN, R.H. "Lennox Berkeley: His Influence and His Songs", *The NATS Journal*, 46 (March/April 1990), pp. 4–11, 50

HANSEN, R.H. "The Songs of Lennox Berkeley", Dissertation for DMA, 1987. North Texas State University

HEADINGTON, C. "Berkeley's 70th birthday", *WH-News*, no.9 (1974), pp. 1–2 (originally appeared in *Audio*)

HEADINGTON, C. "The instrumental music of Lennox Berkeley", *The Chesterian*, 32 (Winter 1958), pp. 82–85

HENDERSON, R. "Sir Lennox Berkeley: a tribute", *The Daily Telegraph*, 16 May 1983, p. 13

HOWES, F.S. [Lennox Berkeley] in *The English Musical Renaissance*, London, Secker and Warburg, 1966, pp. 274–77

HUGHES, A. "At 73, Sir Lennox Berkeley visits the United States", *The New York Times*, 1 February 1976, p. 37

HUGHES, E. and DAY, T. "Discographies of British composers – 1: Sir Lennox Berkeley", *Recorded Sound*, no.77 (January 1980), pp. 63–79 (+ portrait)

HULL, R. "The music of Lennox Berkeley", *The Listener*, 16 March 1944, p. 309 (Prompted by a performance of *Symphony No.1*, with musical examples.)

HULL, R. "The music of Lennox Berkeley", *The Chesterian*, 23 (January 1948), pp. 61–64

HULL, R. "The style of Lennox Berkeley", *The Chesterian*, 24 (April 1950), pp. 84–87

HUNT, K. "Lennox Berkeley: an obituary", *Keyboard Magazine*, 16 (June 1990), p. 21

JOHNSON, S. "Review of Peter Dickinson's *The Music of Lennox Berkeley*", *Notes*, 50 (December 1993), pp. 599–600

KENNEDY, M. *Britten* (Master Musician Series), London, Dent, 1993 (Revised ed., pb.), pp. 20, 21, 25, 51, 52, 60, 110, 133, 312

LE FLEMING, C. "The shorter works of Lennox Berkeley: an appreciation", *The Chesterian*, 27 (April 1953), pp. 98–104, reprinted in *Making Music*, no.22 (Summer 1953), pp. 9–11

LEVI, E. "Music by Lennox Berkeley – I: Chamber Music", *WH-News*, no.1 (1983), pp. 2–6

LEVI, P. "Just how much is a composer worth?", *The Sunday Times*, 6 March 1977,

p. 35 (A discussion about various British composers and their income from composing.)

LOCKSPEISER, E. "The music of Lennox Berkeley", *The Listener*, 10 July 1947, p. 76 (Comments on Berkeley's music and influences.)

LOCKSPEISER, E. *The Music of Lennox Berkeley*, London, J & W Chester, c. 1950 (Introduction to a booklet describing the music of Berkeley.)

MacCRINDLE, S. "Sir Lennox Berkeley: an 80th birthday tribute", Sleeve note for Hyperion A66086, published in association with the Performing Right Society, 1983

MASON, C. "The progress of Lennox Berkeley", *The Listener*, 27 September 1956, p. 485 (Mention of influences on the composer and his operas, prompted by the first performance of *Ruth*.)

MAYCOCK, R. "A breath of French air", *The Independent*, 27 May 1988, p. 14 (Views on a concert celebrating Berkeley's 85th birthday.)

MEARES, S. "In Recent Times – a Personal Choice" [Sir Lennox Berkeley] in *British Opera in Retrospect* (ed. Meares), London, British Music Society, 1986, pp. 124–25

MELLERS, W.H. "Lennox Berkeley" in E.Blom (ed.) *Grove's Dictionary of Music and Musicians: 5th edition* (Volume 1), London, Macmillan, 1954, pp. 645–46

MELLERS, W.H. "The Music of Lennox Berkeley", *The Listener*, 24 June 1954, p. 1113 (A discussion putting Berkeley's music in context, prompted by the appearance of *A Dinner Engagement*.)

MITCHELL, D. and EVANS, J. (comps.) *Benjamin Britten: Pictures from a Life 1913–1976*, London, Faber & Faber, 1978 (pb.1980)
(Photograph 83: ISCM Festival, Barcelona 1936;
Photographs 85–86: Crantock, July–August 1936 – "The Composers at Work";
Photograph 110: The Old Mill, Snape;
Photograph 130: Boyd Neel;
Photograph 131: Details of the printed programme when *Serenade for String Orchestra* (Op.12) was first performed in January 1940.)

MITCHELL, D. and REED, P. *Letters from a Life: selected letters and diaries of Benjamin Britten, volume 1 1923–1939*, London, Faber & Faber, 1991, pp. 40, 46, 168, 318, 421, 424, 425, 438, 457, 477, 481, 491, 520, 528, 537–40, 552, 569, 574–75, 590, 586, 592–93, 597, 605, 606–07, 611, 616

MITCHELL, D. and REED, P. *Letters from a Life: selected letters and diaries of Benjamin Britten*, volume 2 1939–1945, London, Faber & Faber, 1991, pp. 633–34, 660, 668, 690, 705, 707–08, 717–18, 720, 723, 730–31, 732, 738, 739, 742, 751, 752, 781, 784, 804, 816, 848, 851, 859, 923, 924, 1080, 1096, 1106, 1111, 1125–26, 1134, 1139, 1153, 1165, 1178, 1230, 1232, 1240, 1241

MUNDY, S. "Lennox Berkeley at 75", *Classical Music Weekly*, 27 May 1978, p. 14

NAGLEY, J. "Orchestral", *Musical Times*, 119 (July 1978), p. 611

NICHOLS, R. "Sir Lennox Berkeley" [obituary], *The Independent*, 27 December 1989, p. 18

NOBLE, J. "Youth's turn", *The Sunday Telegraph*, 16 January 1972, p. 19

NORRIS, G. "Philharmonia/Priestman", *The Times*, 5 July 1983, p. 16 (Comments on the opening concert of the 1983 Cheltenham Music Festival when A *Bouquet for Lennox* was first performed, "... Happy Birthday to You ... [being] more overtly stated in the variation by William Mathias.")

NORTHCOTT, B. "Music: Restoring the Magic", *The Sunday Telegraph*, 10 July 1983, p. 15

NORTHCOTT, B. "Since Grimes: a concise survey of the British musical stage", *Music News*, 4 no.2 (1974), pp. 9–10

OAKES, M. "Respectful retrospection", *The Independent*, 29 June 1990, p. 14

OLIVER, M. "British Composers – Lennox Berkeley: a profile", *Gramophone*, 51 (July 1973), p. 178

"PETERBOROUGH" "Upper most in thought", *The Daily Telegraph*, 8 June 1983, p. 20

"PETERBOROUGH" "Varied bouquet", *The Daily Telegraph*, 31 March 1983, p. 18 (Details of "Bouquet for Lennox" written by 15 of the composer's former pupils to celebrate his 80th birthday.)

PETRE, J. "Unchained Melody", *The Catholic Herald*, 13 May 1983, p. 5

PORTER, A. "Berkeley", *The Financial Times*, 4 August 1973, p. 9

REDDING, J. "A descriptive list of the musical manuscripts of Sir Lennox Berkeley" (Part dissertation for Master of Science in Library Science, July 1988, University of North Carolina at Chapel Hill.)

REDDING, J. "Lennox Berkeley": introduction to a booklet describing Berkeley's works, published by Chester Music, 1993 (Also includes a list of works, a select bibliography and discography.)

REDDING, J. "President Emeritus – In memoriam Sir Lennox Berkeley", Cheltenham Music Festival Programme, 1990, p. 6

REDLICH, H.F. "Lennox Berkeley", *Music Survey*, 31 (June 1951), pp. 245–49 (with music examples)

REES, C.B. "Impressions: Lennox Berkeley", *London Music*, 7 (July 1952), pp. 20–22

REES, C.B. "Lennox Berkeley is 60", *Musical Events*, 18 (May 1963), pp. 6–7

ROUTH, F. [Lennox Berkeley] in *Contemporary British Music*, London, Macdonald, 1972, pp. 191, 281, 312, 344–46, 357, 382, 384, 389, 390, 392, 403, 405

RUSHTON, J. "Lennox Berkeley at 80 – some reflections on his church music", *W.H. News*, no.1 (1983), pp. 33–34

SCHAFFER, M. "Lennox Berkeley", in *British Composers in Interview*, London, Faber and Faber, 1963, pp. 83–91

SHAWE-TAYLOR, D. "Berkeley – homage to a craftsman", *The Sunday Times*, 21 May 1978, p. 39

SHAWE-TAYLOR, D. "Berkeley's achievement", *The Sunday Times*, 16 January 1972, p. 30

SHAWE-TAYLOR, D. "Lennox Berkeley – the master's touch", *The Sunday Times*, 14 May 1978, p. 38 (A review of Lyrita SRCS 94. Also contains Barry Fantoni's drawing of the composer.)

SHAWE-TAYLOR, D. "Lennox Berkeley: success at 70", *The Sunday Times*, 6 May 1973, p. 37

SHAWE-TAYLOR, D. "A man at peace with melody" [obituary], *The Sunday Times*, 31 December 1989, p. B5

SHAWE-TAYLOR, D. "The master of melody", *The Sunday Times*, 15 May 1983, p. 43 (+ portrait)

SIMMONS, D. "London Music", *Musical Opinion*, 96 (September 1973), pp. 601–03

STEPTOE, R. "Lennox Berkeley", *Composer*, no.90 (Spring 1987), pp. 12–14

STEPTOE, R. "Lennox Berkeley" [Contemporary composers series], *Music Teacher*, 65 (July 1986), pp. 21–24

STEVENS, A. "Lennox Berkeley: an obituary", *Crescendo International*, 27 (February 1990), p. 9

SUDLOW, P. "Lennox Berkeley at 75", *Music and Musicians*, 26 (May 1978), p. 27

TAVENER, J. "Lennox Berkeley at 70", *The Listener*, 10 May 1973, p. 625

TAYLOR, T.N. "British One Act Operas 1960–1970: a critical survey." Chapter 8 – Berkeley and Walton (PhD thesis, 1981. University College, Cardiff)

THOMAS, E. "Sir Lennox Berkeley", *The Independent*, 30 December 1989, p. 22

TREND, M. "The good book he deserves", *The Spectator*, 13 January 1990, p. 26 (A review of *The Music of Lennox Berkeley* by Peter Dickinson.)

VARIOUS "Birthday tributes to Sir Lennox Berkeley by some of his former pupils", *WH-News*, no.1 (1983), pp. 6–10

VOGEL, A. "Lennox Berkeley", *The Chesterian*, 33 (Spring 1959), pp. 121–23

WARMAN, C. "Salute to Sir Lennox", *The Times*, 11 May 1983, p. 12 (An 80th birthday tribute.)

WEBSTER, E. "Birthday Tribute to Sir Lennox", *The Gloucestershire Echo*, 4 July 1983, p. 5

WEBBER, J.L. "The cello music of Sir Lennox Berkeley", *Strad*, 87 (September 1976), pp. 361, 363

WHITE, M. "The persuasive voice of Lennox Berkeley", *The Independent on Sunday*, 8 April 1990, p. 28

WILLIAMSON, M. "Genius out of tune with the voice of Britain", *The Independent*, 4 April 1990, p. 19 (Review of "The Music of Lennox Berkeley" by Peter Dickinson.)

WILLIAMSON, M. "Sir Lennox Berkeley (1903–1989)", *Musical Times*, 131 (April 1990), pp. 197–99
WOOD, A. "Lennox Berkeley, 70, hits the high point of his career", *Oxford Mail*, 3 August 1973, p. 12 (Recollections about the composer by his godmother, Miss Sybil Jackson.)
WORDSWORTH, D. "Sir Lennox Berkeley: a personal tribute", *British Music Society Journal*, 12 (1990), pp. 3–6

III: REFERENCES TO SPECIFIC WORKS

ANDANTINO FOR CELLO AND PIANO (1955)

ANON. "Review of New Music", *Musical Opinion*, 79 (April 1956), p. 413
PIRIE, P.J. "Review of New Music", *Music and Letters*, 37 (July 1956), p. 310

ANDANTINO FOR CELLO AND PIANO (MUSIC FOR A PRINCE)

ANON. "PRS Luncheon", *Performing Right*, no.54 (1970), pp. 11–12 (Details of the annual PRS luncheon when the bound manuscript of *Music for a Prince* was presented to the Prince of Wales by Sir Arthur Bliss.)

ANOTHER SPRING (Op. 93, no.1)

BERKELEY, L. Sleeve note for Meridian E 77017

ANTIPHON (Op. 85)

ANON. "Cheltenham", *Music and Musicians*, 22 (September 1973), pp. 78+
ANON. "Fine Arts Orchestra at the Queen Elizabeth Hall", *Musical Events*, 28 (October 1973), p. 23
ANON. "First Performances", *World Music*, 16 no.1 (1974), p. 68
BERKELEY, L. Programme note for the first performance (7/7/73)
LOPPERT, M. "Festivals – Cheltenham", *Musical Times*, 114 (September 1973), pp. 927, 929
MAYCOCK, R. "Nearly New", *Music and Musicians*, 22 (December 1973), pp. 71–72

NICOLE, J. Sleeve note for Unicorn UNS 260
SADIE, S. "A Serious Business", *The Times*, 9 July 1973, p. 8
WARRACK, J. [Antiphon], *Gramophone*, 57 (March 1980), p. 1385
WEBSTER, E.M. "Cheltenham Festival: God and Mammon", *Musical Opinion*, 96 (September 1973), pp. 599–600

ASK ME NO MORE (Op. 37, no.1)
KEYS, I. "Reviews of Music", *Music and Letters*, 34 (July 1953), pp. 269–70

AUTOMNE (Op. 60, no.3)
MANN, W.S. "Contemporary Songs", *Gramophone*, 53 (August 1975), p. 355

AUTUMN'S LEGACY (Op. 58)
BERKELEY, L. Programme note for the first performance (6/7/62)
COOPER, M. "Great Britain: a welter of music", *Musical America*, 82 (September 1962), p. 95
SHAWE-TAYLOR, D. "Young Blood at Cheltenham", *The Sunday Times*, 8 July 1972, p. 33 ("Berkeley had three great assets as a song-writer ... natural feeling for the voice, for the piano, and for poetry. ...")
WEBSTER, E.M. "Cheltenham: feast of contemporary music?", *Musical Opinion*, 85 (September 1962), p. 723

BATTER MY HEART (Op. 60, no.1)
PAYNE, A. "Birthday for Berkeley", *Music and Musicians*, 12 (January 1964), p. 37

CASTAWAY (Op. 68)
ANON. "The English Opera Group", *Musical Opinion*, 90 (August 1967), pp. 617–18
ANON. "London Opera Diary", *Opera*, 18 (September 1967), pp. 772–74
ANON. "Twentieth Aldeburgh Festival", *About the House*, 2 no.7 (1967), pp. 43+
CHAPMAN, E. "New one-act operas by Berkeley and Walton", *Musical Events*, 22 (August 1967), pp. 33–34
COOPER, M. [Castaway], *The Daily Telegraph*, 5 June 1967, p. 15
DEAN, W. "English Opera Group", *Musical Times*, 108 (September 1967), pp. 821–82
DEHN, P. "New Operas for Aldeburgh – The Bear and Castaway", *About the House*, 2 no.6 (1967), pp. 35–37

Synopsis for the first performance (3/6/67)
FINCH, H. "Lennox Berkeley double bill", *The Times*, 17 June 1983, p. 6 (Comments on an 80th birthday production of *Castaway* at Trinity College of Music, London.)
FOREMAN, L. "Castaway" in *The Viking Opera Guide* (ed. A. Holden), London, Viking, 1993, pp. 89–90 (also available on CD-ROM)
GOODWIN, N. "Vaudeville from the Vienna boys", *Music and Musicians*, 15 (August 1967), p. 21
GREENFIELD, E. "Britten and the Aldeburgh miracle", *HiFi/Musical America*, 17 (September 1967), p. MA25
GREENFIELD, E. [Castaway], *The Guardian*, 5 June 1967, p. 5
MANN, W.S. [Castaway], *The Times*, 5 June 1967, p. 6
PORTER, A. "Aldeburgh", *Musical Times*, 108 (July 1967), p. 632
REID, C. [Castaway], *The Spectator*, 9 June 1967, pp. 607–08
ROSENTHAL, H. "The 1967 Aldeburgh Festival", *Opera*, 18 (Autumn 1967), pp. 24–25
SADIE, S. [Castaway], *The Times*, 13 July 1967, p. 8
SENIOR, E. "Three-way link", *Music and Musicians*, 15 (July 1967), p. 43
SHAWE-TAYLOR, D. [Castaway], *The Sunday Times*, 11 June 1967, p. 50
URQUHART, T. "Bath, Aldeburgh", *Opera News*, 32 (23 September 1967), p. 27
WARRACK, J. [Castaway], *The Sunday Telegraph*, 11 June 1967, p. 11

CHRIST IS THE WORLD'S REDEEMER (Gartan)

SACKVILLE-WEST, E. "Reports from Abroad", *Musical Times*, 104 (July 1963), pp. 496–97 (Reprinted from *The Sunday Times*)

COLONIUS' PRAISE (Op. 31)

ANON. "Colonius' Praise – first performance", *Music Survey*, 2 (Autumn 1949), pp. 127–28
ANON. "Promenade Concert – new choral work by Lennox Berkeley", *The Times*, 14 September 1949, p. 8
McNAUGHT, W. Programme note for the first performance (13/9/49)

CONCERTINO FOR CHAMBER ORCHESTRA

ANON. "Harrogate Musical Festival", *The Times*, 23 September 1927, p. 8

EVANS, E. "Contemporary Music Centre", *Musical Times*, 68, May 1927, p. 453

CONCERTO FOR CELLO AND ORCHESTRA

ANON. "News Section – composers", *Tempo*, no.145 (June 1983), p. 53
DALE, S.S. "Contemporary Cello Concerti, 49: Baeck, Busser and Berkeley", *Strad*, 87 (February 1977), pp. 821, 823, 825, 827, 829, 831
DICKINSON, P. Programme note for first London performance (23/10/83)
DREYER, M. "New Music", *Musical Times*, 124 (December 1983), p. 759
LOVELAND, K. "Cheltenham", *Musical Times*, 124 (September 1983), p. 564

CONCERTO FOR FLUTE AND ORCHESTRA (Op. 36)

ANON. "Promenade Concert – Two Contemporary Concertos", *The Times*, 30 July 1953, p. 10
MacCRINDLE, S. Sleeve note for RCA Red Seal RS 9011
MITCHELL, D. "In my opinion – The Promenade Concerts", *Musical Opinion*, 76 (September 1953), pp. 703–04
PIRIE, P.J. "Reviews of new music", *Music and Letters*, 38 (July 1957), p. 302
RAYMENT, M. "Promenade Concerts", *Musical Times*, 94 (September 1953), p. 422

CONCERTO FOR GUITAR AND ORCHESTRA (Op. 88)

CRICHTON, R. "City of London Festival", *Musical Times*, 115 (September 1974), pp. 769–70
EAST, L. "City Festival", *Music and Musicians*, 23 (September 1974), p. 56
GRIER, C. Sleeve note for RCA Red Seal ARLI-1181
MacDONALD, M. "Berkeley – Guitar Concerto", *Gramophone*, 53 (November 1975), p. 807

CONCERTO FOR PIANO AND DOUBLE STRING ORCHESTRA (Op. 46)

ANON. "Poetical Piano Concerto – Lennox Berkeley's new work", *The Times*, 12 February 1959, p. 5
CHAPMAN, E. "Musical survey", *London Music*, 14 (April 1959), pp. 35–36
GODDARD, S. "London Letter", *The Chesterian*, 33 (Spring 1959), pp. 130–34
HULL, R. Programme note for the first performance (11/2/59)

OTTAWAY, H. "Radio Notes", *Musical Opinion*, 82 (April 1959), p. 465
RUTLAND, H. "Music in London", *Musical Times*, 100 (April 1959), p. 211

CONCERTO FOR PIANO AND ORCHESTRA (Op. 29)

ANON. "Promenade Concert – Lennox Berkeley's Piano Concerto", *The Times*, 1 September 1948, p. 7
BERKELEY, L. Programme note for the first performance (31/8/48)
BERKELEY, L. Sleeve note for Lyrita SRCS 94
JACOBSON, B. "British Music", *Stereo Review*, 43 (September 1979), p. 108
MacDONALD, M. [Berkeley], *Gramophone*, 55 (April 1978), p. 1713

CONCERTO FOR TWO PIANOS AND ORCHESTRA (Op. 30)

ANON. "Concerto for two pianos and orchestra", *Music Review*, 15 (May 1954), pp. 153–54
ANON. "New Concerto given its first performance", *Strad*, 59 (January 1949), p. 196
ANON. "A New Concerto: Henry Wood Society's Programme", *The Times*, 14 December 1948, p. 6
ANON. "Philharmonic Concert: Mr Goossens and Modern Music", *The Times*, 11 February 1954, p. 3
ANON. "Reviews of new music", *Musical Opinion*, 75 (October 1951), p. 31
ANON. "Reviews of new music", *Musical Opinion*, 76 (March 1953), pp. 351–53
DICKINSON, P. Sleeve note for Lyrita SRCS 80
FOSS, H. Programme note for Promenade concert performance (1/9/49)
HOWES, F. "Berkeley's Concertos", *Musical Times*, 90 (January 1949), p. 27
HUSSEY, D. "Broadcast Music", *The Listener*, 23 December 1948, pp. 983–84
KEYS, I. "Reviews of music", *Music and Letters*, 33 (January 1952), p. 93
MASON, C. "New Music", *The Chesterian*, 26 (October 1951), pp. 25–27
ROBERTS, M.W. "An Introduction to the Literature for Two Pianos and Orchestra, 1915–1950" (Dissertation for DMA, 1981. Southern Baptist Theological Seminary)
ROSE, B. "Reviews of music", *Music and Letters*, 34 (July 1953), p. 271

CONCERTO FOR VIOLIN AND ORCHESTRA (Op. 59)

ANON. "Berkeley's new concerto – performance at Bath Festival", *The Times*, 3 June 1961, p. 4

ANON. "Concerto for Violin and Chamber Orchestra", *Music and Musicians*, 10 (July 1962), p. 52

ANON. "The Soloist as Conductor: Berkeley's Violin Concerto", *The Times*, 18 May 1962, p. 15 (A review of the first London performance at the Royal Festival Hall)

CHISLETT, W.A. "Lennox Berkeley: an appreciation, and introduction to the Violin Concerto" (Bath Festival Programme Book (1961), pp. 11–12)

DALE, S.S. "Contemporary Violin Concerti", *Strad*, 90 (December 1979), pp. 614–15

NIEMAN, A. "Berkeley Concerto", *Music and Musicians*, 10 (July 1962), pp. 43–44

RUBBRA, E. "Reviews of music", *Music and Letters*, 43 (1962), p. 392

SHAWE-TAYLOR, D. "The Many-sided Menuhin", *The Sunday Times*, 4 June 1961, p. 40 (Also contains impressions of the Bath Festival)

STADLEN, P. "New work by Berkeley", *The Daily Telegraph*, 2 June 1961, p. 16

COUNTING THE BEATS (Op. 60, no.4)

DICKINSON, P. & BERKELEY, L. "Counting the Beats – Music and Poetry", *Composer*, no.12 (1963), pp. 3–4

CRUX FIDELIS (Op. 43, no.1)

ANON. "Purcell Singers", *The Times*, 8 March 1953, p. 4

MITCHELL, D. "London Music – some first performances", *Musical Times*, 96 (May 1955), p. 268

DIALOGUE FOR CELLO AND ORCHESTRA (Op. 79)

BERKELEY, L. Programme note for the first performance (30/7/71)

DALE, S.S. "Contemporary Cello Concerti: Baeck, Busser and Berkeley", *Strad*, 87 (February 1977), pp. 829+

EAST, L. "Modern British", *Music and Musicians*, 20 (July 1972), p. 67

WATSON, S. "New Music", *Musical Times*, 113 (April 1972), pp. 381–82

A DINNER ENGAGEMENT (Op. 45)

ANDERSON, W.R. "Radio Music", *Musical Times*, 95 (August 1954), p. 426

ANON. "Aldeburgh Festival – A Dinner Engagement", *The Times*, 18 June 1954, p. 2
ANON. "A Dinner Engagement", *London Music*, 9 (August 1954), pp. 13–14
ANON. "A Dinner Engagement", *Musical Opinion*, 79 (November 1955), p. 95
ANON. "The English Opera Group", *London Music*, 9 (December 1954), p. 45
ANON. "The English Opera Group", *Musical Opinion*, 78 (November 1954), p. 73
ANON. "London Opera Centre", *Opera*, 18 (June 1967), p. 525
ANON. "News", *The Chesterian*, 30 (October 1955), p. 51
ANON. "Sadler's Wells – A Dinner Engagement", *The Times*, 8 October 1954, p. 10 ("The opera is certainly an engagement to be kept.")
DEHN, P. "A Dinner Engagement", *Opera*, 5 (June 1954), pp. 335–38
DEHN, P. Synopsis of the opera for the first performance and later printed in the vocal score
FINCH, H. "Lennox Berkeley double bill", *The Times*, 17 June 1983, p. 6 (Comments on an 80th birthday production of *A Dinner Engagement* at Trinity College of Music, London)
FOREMAN, L. "A Dinner Engagement" in *The Viking Opera Guide* (ed. A. Holden), London, Viking, 1993, pp. 89–90 (also available on CD-ROM)
GODDARD, S. "London Letter", *The Chesterian*, 29 (October 1954), pp. 48–50
HUSSEY, D. "A Dinner Engagement", *The Listener*, 8 July 1954, pp. 76–77
KELLER, H. "The half-year's new music", *Music Review*, 16 (February 1955), pp. 54–55
MASON, C. "New Music", *The Chesterian*, 30 (October 1955), pp. 57–58
MITCHELL, D. "Aldeburgh", *Opera*, 5 (August 1954), pp. 478–80
MITCHELL, D. "The Aldeburgh Festival", *Musical Opinion*, 77 (August 1954), pp. 645–46
RUTLAND, H. "The English Opera Group", *Musical Opinion*, 78 (November 1954), p. 73
SHAW-TAYLOR, D. "The Arts and Entertainment: Aldeburgh", *The New Statesman*, 26 June 1954, p. 829
SMITH, C. "London premieres include two new operas by Lennox Berkeley", *Musical America*, 74 (15 December 1954), p. 3
WAGNER, W. "Sydney", *Canon*, 9 (September 1955), p. 66

DITHYRAMB AND HYMN

ANON. "A Choral Concert: Mlle. Nadia Boulanger", *The Times*, 25 November 1936, p. 12
ANON. "Nadia Boulanger's Concert", *The Sunday Times*, 29 November 1936, p. 7

McNAUGHT, W. "Boulanger, Fauré and Schütz", *Musical Times*, 77 (December 1936), p. 1127

DIVERSIONS (Op. 63)

BERKELEY, L. Programme note for the first performance (13/7/64)
MacDONALD, M. "Lennox Berkeley: an 80th birthday tribute", *Gramophone*, 61 (December 1983), p. 797
RUSHTON, J. Sleeve note for Hyperion A66086
WEBSTER, E.M. "Cheltenham: growing child of our time", *Musical Opinion*, 87 (September 1964), p. 709

DIVERTIMENTO IN B FLAT (Op. 18)

ANGLES, R. Sleeve note for RCA Victor RB 6730
DICKINSON, P. Sleeve note for Lyrita SRCS 74
FOSS, H. Programme note for Promenade concert performance (25/8/47)
HARVEY, T. [Berkeley], *Gramophone*, 45 (January 1968), p. 373
HUSSEY, D. "Music: Two New Works by Berkeley and Britten [Serenade]", *The Spectator*, 22 October 1943, p. 383 ("... the Divertimento makes no pretensions to do more than entertain its audience, and its importance lies less in what it is than in its further manifestation of the composer's complete self-realisation and mastery of style")
MacDONALD, M. "Berkeley", *Gramophone*, 53 (September 1975), pp. 451–52
SACKVILLE WEST, E. [Berkeley's Divertimento], *The New Statesman*, 23 October 1943, p. 268
SIMMONS, D. "London Music", *Musical Opinion*, 91 (May 1968), p. 424

DOMINI EST TERRA (Op. 10)

ANON. "Modern Music: Festival at Queen's Hall", *The Times*, 18 June 1938, p. 12
BLOM, E. "Contemporary Music Society", *The Birmingham Post*, 20 June 1938, p. 14 (This article had appeared in later editions of *The Birmingham Post* on Saturday 18 June 1938)
EVANS, E. "ISCM Festival", *The Chesterian*, 19 (July–August 1938), pp. 171–74
FOX-STRANGWAYS, A.H. "Three Choirs Festival", *The Observer*, 11 September 1938, p. 12

H., G.A. "Three Choirs Festival: Musical Contrasts", *The Manchester Guardian*, 9 September 1938, p. 15

WESTRUP, J.A. "Debussy at Worcester", *The Daily Telegraph*, 9 September 1938, p. 10

DUO FOR CELLO AND PIANO (Op. 81, no.1)

BERKELEY, L. Programme note for the first performance (11/1/72)

BERKELEY, L. Sleeve note for Decca DSLO 18

EAST, L. "Young artists", *Music and Musicians*, 20 (April 1972), p. 74

ELEGY (Op. 33, no.2a) and TOCCATA (Op. 33, no.3) FOR VIOLIN AND PIANO

KEYS, I. "Reviews of music", *Music and Letters*, 33 (April 1952), pp. 180–81

FANTASIA FOR ORGAN (Op. 92)

APRAHAMIAN, F. Programme note for the first performance (1 December 1976)

BREMSER, M. "Festival Hall", *Musical Times*, 118 (February 1977), p. 155

FESTIVAL ANTHEM (Op. 21, no.2)

HUSSEY, W. "Patron of Art", London, Weidenfeld & Nicholson, 1985, pp. 94–96 (Includes details of letters exchanged)

LA FÊTE ETRANGE

BEAUMONT, C. "La Fête Etrange" in C. Beaumont, *Supplement to the Complete Book of Ballets*, London, Beaumont, 1942, pp. 143–46

BREMSER, M. (ed.) International Dictionary of Ballet (Volume 1), Chicago & London, St. James Press, 1993, pp. 485++ (Useful detail about the history of the ballet)

FIVE CHINESE SONGS (Op. 78)

CRICHTON, R. "Lennox Berkeley", *Musical Times*, 112 (May 1971), p. 465

MANN, W.S. "Contemporary Songs", *Gramophone*, 53 (August 1975), p. 355
RUSHTON, J. Programme notes [1971]

FIVE DE LA MARE SONGS (Op. 26)

ANON. "Five Songs", *Music Review*, 10 (May 1949), pp. 149–50
H., A. "New Music: Chester", *Musical Times*, 90 (May 1949), pp. 159–60
KEYS, I. "Reviews of music", *Music and Letters*, 30 (January 1949), p. 89
MELLERS, W. "New music reviewed", *The Chesterian*, 23 (January 1949), pp. 76–78

FIVE HERRICK POEMS (Op. 89)

ANON. "First performances", *World Music*, 16 (1974), p. 60

FIVE PIECES FOR VIOLIN AND ORCHESTRA (Op. 56)

ANON. "Editorial notes", *Strad*, 73 (September 1962), p. 157
ANON. "New Berkeley work at the Proms", *Musical Events*, 17 (August 1962), p. 8
ANON. "Promenade Concerts", *Musical Opinion*, 85 (September 1962), p. 712
BERKELEY, L. Programme note for the first performance (31/7/62)
CARDUS, N. "London Proms", *The Manchester Guardian*, 2 August 1962, p. 7 ("The solo writing is another example of Mr Berkeley's ability to write a fluent, flexible, sometimes gyrating sequence of figuration; and the orchestral texture is judiciously contrasted... The fourth movement, a flowing, beautifully inflected melody, is the most appealing of the five.")
CHAPMAN, E. "The Proms", *Musical Events*, 17 (September 1962), p. 27
COOPER, M. "Veiled Unity of new Violin work", *The Daily Telegraph*, 1 August 1962, p. 12
CRICHTON, R. "Promenade Concerts", *Musical Times*, 103 (September 1962), p. 618
LOCKSPEISER, E. "Music", *The Listener*, 9 August 1962, pp. 224–25
SHAWE-TAYLOR, D. "Lennox Berkeley conducts his Five Pieces", *The Sunday Times*, 5 August 1962, p. 20 (Includes a photograph of the composer conducting the BBC Symphony Orchestra)
SIMMONS, D. "Berkeley and Shostakovitch", *Music and Musicians*, 11 (September 1962), p. 38

FIVE POEMS BY W.H. AUDEN (Op. 53)

RUTLAND, H. "Music in London – Macnaghten Concert", *Musical Times*, 100 (December 1959), p. 672

FOUR POEMS OF ST TERESA OF AVILA (Op. 27)

ANON. "Four Poems of St Teresa", *Making Music*, no.12 (Spring 1950), p. 23
BERKELEY, L. Sleeve note for BBC Records REGL 368
KEYS, I. "Reviews of music", *Music and Letters*, 31 (January 1950), p. 91
WARBURTON, A.O. "Set works for O-level GCE", *Music Teacher*, 47 (February 1968), pp. 10+
WARRACK, J. [Four Poems of St Teresa of Avila], *Gramophone*, 60 (November 1982), p. 608

FOUR RONSARD SONNETS – SET 1 (Op. 40)

BARRELL, B. [Ronsard Sonnets Set 1 – revised version], *Composer*, no.64 (Summer 1978), p. 32
BERKELEY, L. Programme note for the first performance of the revised version (14/6/78)
KELLER, H. "The half-year's new music", *Music Review*, 14 (August 1953), p. 212

FOUR RONSARD SONNETS – SET 2 (Op. 62)

BERKELEY, L. Programme note for the first performance (9/8/63)
CHAPMAN, E. "At the Proms", *Musical Events*, 18 (September 1963), p. 23
MURRAY, D. "Contemporary vocal works", *Gramophone*, 51 (May 1974), p. 2063
PAYNE, A. "Berkeley Sonnets", *Music and Musicians*, 12 (September 1963), p. 12
PORTER, A. "Proms", *Musical Times*, 104 (October 1963), pp. 719–20
SHAWE-TAYLOR, D. "Lennox Berkeley Sonnets", *The Sunday Times*, 11 August 1963, p. 28 (A review and comments on the first performance)

THE HILL OF THE GRACES (Op. 91, no.2)

GRIFFITHS, P. "New music", *Musical Times*, 116 (December 1975), p. 1081
OLIVER, M. [The Hill of the Graces], *Gramophone*, 57 (July 1979), p. 238

PROTHEROE, G. Sleeve note for ABBEY LPB 798 (1979)

HOW LOVE CAME IN

ROBERTSON, A. "Early Songs", *Gramophone*, 48 (June 1970), p. 85

I SING OF A MAIDEN

HARPER, J. Sleeve note for Abbey LPB 768
WEBB, S. "Christmas Music from King's", *Gramophone*, 55 (December 1977), p. 1156

IMPROVISATIONS ON A THEME OF MANUAL DE FALLA (Op. 55, no.2)

C., G-F. [Macnaghten Concerts], *Musical Opinion*, 84 (April 1961), p. 407

IN MEMORIAM IGOR STRAVINSKY

DENISOV, E., etc. "In memoriam – Igor Fedorovich Stravinsky: canons and epitaphs", *Tempo*, no.97 (1971), between pp. 24–25

IN WINTERTIME (Op. 103)

STEANE, J.B. "Christmas", *Gramophone*, 69 (December 1991), p. 141

INTRODUCTION AND ALLEGRO FOR DOUBLE BASS AND PIANO (Op. 80)

ANON. "Recent publications", *ISB*, 2 no.2 (1976), p. 148
KEMP, I. "Reviews of music", *Music and Letters*, 30 (July 1949), p. 285

INTRODUCTION AND ALLEGRO FOR VIOLIN (Op. 24)

ANON. "Introduction and Allegro for solo violin", *Strad*, 60 (May 1949), p. 28

ANON. "Introduction and Allegro for solo violin", *Music Review*, 10 (November 1949), p. 315
BONAVIA, F. "New Music – Violin", *Musical Times*, 91 (March 1950), pp. 100–01
MELLERS, W. "New in review", *The Chesterian*, 24 (July 1949), pp. 24–25

INTRODUCTION AND DANCE

ANON. "London Chamber Orchestra", *The Times*, 27 April 1926, p. 14
MILLAN, D. Programme note for the first performance (26/4/26)

JONAH (Op. 3)

A., H.A. "New works at Leeds Festival", *The Yorkshire Post*, 8 October 1937, p. 5
ANON. "Berlioz Oratorio at Leeds", *The Daily Telegraph*, 8 October 1937, p. 14
ANON. "Contemporary Music – Broadcasting House", *The Morning Post*, 22 June 1936, p. 5
ANON. "Jonah: a new oratorio technique", *The Yorkshire Post*, 8 October 1937, p. 5
ANON. "Leeds Music Festival: Bach's St Matthew Passion", *The Times*, 9 October 1937, p. 10
ANON. "Leeds Music Festival: The Childhood of Christ", *The Times*, 8 October 1937, p. 12
BRADBURY, E. [Jonah] in Arthur Jacobs (ed.) *Choral Music*, Harmondsworth, Penguin Books, 1962, pp. 347–48
CALVOCORESSI, M.D. "Oratorio – modern idiom", *Radio Times*, 12 June 1936, p. 12
CAPELL, R. "Jonah, the Whale and Mr Berkeley", *The Daily Telegraph*, 20 June 1936, p. 8 (Impressions of the work after a BBC broadcast)
CARDUS, N. "Mr Berkeley's Jonah", *The Manchester Guardian*, 8 October 1937, p. 14
FOREMAN, L. "Jonah – Lennox Berkeley", *BMS Newsletter*, no.46 (June 1990), pp. 158–59
FRANK, A. "Jonah", *The Listener*, 10 June 1936, p. 1134
GREENFIELD, E. [Revival of Jonah], *The Guardian*, 3 April 1990, p. 38
GRIER, C. "Hot Line to Haydn", [London] *Evening Standard*, 2 April 1990, p. 37
HOWES, F.S. "Jonah": programme note for the Leeds Festival performance (7/10/37), (With musical examples)
RENNERT, J. "Jonah – Opus 3 (1933–35)", programme note for 1990 performance (31/3/90)
RUDLAND, M. "Berkeley's Jonah", *Musical Times*, 131 (June 1990), p. 341

THOMPSON, H. "The Leeds Festival", *Musical Times*, 78 (November 1937), pp. 993–94

THE JUDGEMENT OF PARIS (Op. 10, no.2)

ANON. "Sadler's Wells Theatre", *The Times*, 11 May 1938, p. 14
ANON. "The Sitter Out", *The Dancing Times*, no.333 (June 1938), pp. 263–67 (Comments appear on p. 266, together with photographs of the production)
HORSNELL, H. "Sadler's Wells: Gala Performance", *The Observer*, 15 May 1938, p. 15
VAUGHAN, D. "Frederick Ashton and his ballets", London, A & C Black, 1977, pp. 164–65 (+ photograph of production)

JUDICA ME (Op. 96, no.1)

BERKELEY, L. Programme note for the first performance (2/9/78)
LOVELAND, K. "Three Choirs", *Musical Times*, 119 (November 1978), p. 980

JUSTORUM ANIMAE (Op. 60, no.2)

WEBB, S. "Choral Music", *Gramophone*, 52 (November 1974), p. 946

LOOK UP, SWEET BABE (Op. 43, no.2)

RUSHTON, J. Sleeve note for Priory PR 124
WEBB, S. "Choral Music", *Gramophone*, 52 (November 1974), p. 946

THE LORD IS MY SHEPHERD (Op. 91, no.1)

HUSSEY, W. "Patron of Art", London, Weidenfeld & Nicholson, pp. 94–96
ROBERTSON, N. Sleeve note for Abbey LPB 770
STEANE, J.B. "English Anthems", *Gramophone*, 71 (June 1993), pp. 94, 97

LORD WHEN THE SENSE OF THY SWEET GRACE (Op. 21, no.1)

RUSHTON, J. Sleeve note for Priory PR 124

MAGNIFICAT (Op. 71)

BERKELEY, L. "A description of his setting of the Magnificat", *The Listener*, 4 July 1968, p. 25
CRANKSHAW, G. "Lucid Octet", *Music and Musicians*, 18 (October 1969), p. 58
CRICHTON, R. "Music in London – the Proms", *Musical Times*, 110 (October 1969), pp. 1051, 1053
McVEAGH, D. "City of London", *Musical Times*, 109 (September 1968), pp. 832–33
MAWBY, C. "Berkeley's Magnificat", *Church Music*, 2 no.28 (1968), p. 26
SIMMONS, D. "London music", *Musical Opinion*, 92 (September 1969), p. 621
WALSH, S. "Four choirs", *Music and Musicians*, 17 (September 1968), p. 45

MASS FOR FIVE VOICES (Op. 64)

BERRY, M. "English and French Works", *Gramophone*, 68 (July 1990), p. 271
NICHOLAS, M. Sleeve note for Vista VPS 1096
REYNOLDS, G. "Twentieth Century Music from Norwich Cathedral", *Gramophone*, 59 (December 1981), pp. 924, 929
YOUNG, P.M. "Choral performances", *American Choral Review*, 9 no.2 (1967), p. 36

MAZURKA (Op. 101, no.2)

ANON. "Berkeley Birthday Present", *Music and Musicians*, November 1983, p. 2

MISSA BREVIS (Op. 57)

HARPER, J. Sleeve note for Abbey LPB 768

MONT JUIC (Op. 9)

ANON. "Record Review", *Tempo*, no. 178 (September 1991), p. 48+
BERKELEY, L. Prefatory note for the published score
CRANKSHAW, G. Sleeve note for Lyrita SRCS 50
HARVEY, T. "British Music", *Gramophone*, 49 (June 1971), pp. 42, 45
KENNEDY, M. "Britten/Berkeley", *Gramophone*, 68 (December 1990), p. 1201

NELSON (Op. 41)

ANON. "Berkeley's Nelson", *The Times*, 16 February 1953, p. 10 (Details of the concert performance of Nelson)

ANON. "Music Man's Diary – Plans for Nelson", *Music and Musicians*, 3 (September 1954), pp. 18–19

ANON. "Nelson: the composer and librettist", *Canon*, 8 (February 1955), p. 297

ANON. "Nelson: first performance", *London Music*, 9 (September 1954), p. 36

ANON. "Nelson: a new British opera", *Musical Opinion*, 78 (October 1954), p. 11

ANON. "Nelson on the stage", *Music and Musicians*, 2 (March 1954), pp. 16–17

ANON. "News", *The Chesterian*, 27 (April 1953), p. 104

ANON. "Sadler's Wells Opera: Nelson", *The Times*, 23 September 1954, p. 10

BARKER, F.G. "At last the admiral sings", *Music and Musicians*, 3 (October 1954), p. 17

BARKER, F.G. "Current London opera", *Opera News*, 19 (1 November 1954), pp. 22–23

BERKELEY, L. "Composers' forum", *London Music*, 9 (November 1954), pp. 23–24

BERKELEY, L. Programme note for the first performance (22 September 1954)

BLOM, E. "Music: Nelson", *The Observer*, 26 September 1954, p. 11

COOPER, M. "Nelson: an impressive drama", *The Daily Telegraph*, 23 September 1954, p. 8

DEAN, W. "Lennox Berkeley and Nelson", *The Listener*, 16 September 1954, p. 461 (An article prompted by the first performance of Nelson which was broadcast by the BBC)

DEAN, W. "Opera Diary – Sadler's Wells", *Opera*, 5 (November 1954), pp. 690–94 (Includes photographs of the production)

DEAN, W. "Opera: Nelson (Sadler's Wells)", *The Spectator*, 1 October 1954, p. 389

DEAN, W. "Sadler's Wells", *Opera*, 5 (November 1954), pp. 690–94

FINCH, H. [Nelson], *The Times*, 9 April 1988, p. 20

FOREMAN, L. "Nelson" in *The Viking Opera Guide* (ed. A. Holden) London, Viking, 1993, pp. 89–90 (also available on CD-ROM)

GODDARD, S. "London letter", *The Chesterian*, 27 (April 1953), pp. 117–19

HOPE-WALLACE, P. "Lennox Berkeley's First Opera", *The Manchester Guardian*, 24 September 1954, p. 7

JONES, E. "When love and duty conflict", *Radio Times*, 17 September 1954, p. 5

KELLER, H. "The half-year's new music", *Music Review*, 16 (February 1955), pp. 54–55

KLEIN, J.W. "A plea for Berkeley's Nelson", *Musical Opinion*, 92 (March 1969), pp. 295, 297, 299

KLEIN, J.W. "Some reflections on Berkeley's Nelson", *The Chesterian*, 29 (January 1955), pp. 73–80

MITCHELL, D. "London music", *Musical Times*, 95 (November 1954), pp. 612–15

MITCHELL, D. "Wigmore Hall", *Opera*, 4 (April 1953), pp. 245–46

MONTAGU, G. "Nelson at Sadler's Wells", *London Music*, 9 (November 1954), pp. 24–25

NEWMAN, E. "Nelson: some hints to librettists", *Score*, no.10 (December 1954), pp. 71–72 (Reprinted from *The Sunday Times*, 3 October 1954)

NEWMAN, E. "The Vienna Makeshifts", *The Sunday Times*, 26 September 1954, p. 11

NOTCUTT, A. "Four new British operas", *Musical Courier*, 151 (June 1955), p. 18

NOTCUTT, A. "London", *Musical Courier*, 150 (1 November 1954), pp. 32–33

PORTER, A. and DEAN, W. "Opera Diary", *Opera*, 5 (November 1954), pp. 690–94

PRYCE-JONES, A. "Nelson: libretto", London, J & W Chester, 1954

PRYCE-JONES, A. "Some notes on the text of *Nelson*", *Opera*, 5 (October 1954), pp. 595–98

REDLICH, H.F. "New British operas", *The Chesterian*, 29 (April 1955), pp. 110–17

SENIOR, E. "Nelson", *Music and Musicians*, 2 (March 1954), pp. 24–25

SENIOR, E. "Nelson: Music at Home and Abroad", *Music and Musicians*, 3 (May 1955), p. 24

SHAWE-TAYLOR, D. "The Arts and Entertainment: Nelson", *The New Statesman*, 2 October 1954, pp. 387–88

SMITH, C. "London premieres include two new operas by Lennox Berkeley", *Musical America*, 74 (December 1954), p. 3

THAMES, E. "Sir Lennox Berkeley", *The Independent*, 30 December 1989, p. 22

WATERHOUSE, J.F. "World of Music: Composer and Librettist", *The Birmingham Post*, 27 September 1954, p. 4

WHITE, M.J. "Berkeley's happy Kismet", *The Independent*, 9 April 1988, p. 11 (A concert performance of *Nelson* by the Chelsea Opera Group, conducted by Grant Llewellyn, which is described as a "… brilliantly alive, sophisticated score")

NELSON: SUITE FOR ORCHESTRA (Op. 42)

BERKELEY, L. "Nelson: suite – Programme Note", Cheltenham Festival Programme, 20 July 1955

COOPER, M. "Cheltenham Festival", *Musical Times*, 96 (September 1955), p. 489

GODDARD, S. "London letter", *The Chesterian*, 30 (October 1955), pp. 52–54

RAYNOR, H. "Berkeley's Nelson suite", *Musical Times*, 97 (November 1956), p. 601

NIGHT COVERS UP

CARPENTER, H. "W H Auden: a biography", London, G. Allen & Unwin, 1981, p. 188

NOCTURNE FOR HARP (Op. 67, no.2)

M., G. "The London Concert and Recital World – Symphonic Emphyllos", *Musical Opinion*, 90 (December 1966), p. 127

OVERTURE FOR CHAMBER ORCHESTRA (Op. 8)

C., D.M. Programme note for the first British performance (1/10/35)

PALM COURT WALTZ (Op. 81, no.2)

BERKELEY, L. Sleeve note for Hyperion A66086
MacDONALD, M. "Lennox Berkeley: an 80th birthday tribute", *Gramophone*, 61 (December 1983), p. 797

PARTITA (Op. 66)

DICKINSON, P. Sleeve note for Lyrita SRCS 74
FLUCK, A. "Festival of Youth", *Composer*, no.25 (Autumn 1967), p. 16
GREENFIELD, E. "Best foot forward and otherwise", *Hi-Fi/Musical America*, 15 (August 1965), p. 135
HENDERSON, R. "Farnham", *Musical Times*, 106 (July 1965), p. 529
HURD, M. "Farnham 1965", *Music in Education*, 29 (1965), p. 174
MacDONALD, M. "Berkeley", *Gramophone*, 53 (September 1975), pp. 451–52

PRELUDE AND CAPRICCIO FOR PIANO (Op. 95)

BISHOP, J. Sleeve note for Pearl SHE 576

BOYD, M. "South Wales" *Musical Times*, 119 (May 1978), pp. 438–40

QUARTET FOR OBOE AND STRINGS (Op. 70)

BERKELEY, L. Sleeve note for Hyperion A66086
MacDONALD, M. "Lennox Berkeley: an 80th birthday tribute", *Gramophone*, 61 (December 1983), p. 797

QUARTET FOR STRINGS NO.3 (Op. 76)

BERKELEY, L. Programme note for the first London performance (23/3/71)
CRICHTON, R. "Lennox Berkeley", *Musical Times*, 112 (May 1971), p. 465
RUBBRA, E. "Last week's broadcast music", *The Listener*, 9 September 1971, p. 345

QUINTET FOR WIND AND PIANO (Op. 90)

ANON. "Chamber Music Society: Berkeley premiere", *Hi-Fi/Musical America*, 26 (May 1976), p. MA31
ANON. "Premieres", *Music Education Journal*, 62 (March 1976), p. 104
ANON. "Premieres", *Music Journal*, 34 (March 1976), p. 28
BERKELEY, L. Sleeve note for Meridian E 77017

RUTH (Op. 50)

ANON. "English Opera Group", *London Music*, 11 (March 1956), p. 41
ANON. "English Opera Group", *Musical Opinion*, 80 (November 1956), p. 73
BERKELEY, L. "Composers' forum", *London Music*, 11 (October 1956), pp. 20–21
CROZIER, E. [Symposis for the first performance, 2 October 1956]
GODDARD, S. "London letter", *The Chesterian*, 31 (Winter 1957), pp. 93–96
HAMBURGER, P. "Ruth – an introduction", *Opera*, 7 (October 1956), pp. 590–94
KELLER, H. "The new in review", *Music Review*, 17 (November 1956), pp. 335–36
LITTLEFIELD, I. "A decade for the Group", *Opera News*, 21 (11 March 1957), p. 26
LOVELAND, K. "Cheltenham", *Musical Times*, 124 (September 1983), p. 564
LOVELAND, K. "Cheltenham: Birthday offering", *Opera*, 34 (November 1983), pp. 1205–07

MITCHELL, D. "Some first performances: Ruth", *Musical Times*, 97 (November 1956), pp. 596–97
NOBLE, J. "Third Programme", *Opera*, 9 (February 1958), p. 133
OTTAWAY, H. "Radio notes", *Musical Times*, 97 (December 1956), p. 645
PORTER, A. "Scala Theatre (EOG)", *Opera*, 7 (November 1956), pp. 699–70 (Includes photographs of the first production)
WEBSTER, E. "Berkeley's opera Ruth is a joy", *Gloucestershire Echo*, 8 July 1983, p. 2

SALVE REGINA (Op. 48, no.1)

BERRY, M. "Sacred Choral Works", *Gramophone*, 57 (November 1979), p. 900

SCHERZO FOR PIANO (Op. 32, no.2)

ANON. "Scherzo for piano", *Music Review*, 11 (November 1950), p. 333
BERKELEY, L. Sleeve note for Meridian E 77017
KEYS, I. "Scherzo", *Music and Letters*, 32 (January 1951), p. 91
ROBERTSON, A. "New Music – Piano", *Musical Times*, 91 (July 1950), p. 275

SERENADE FOR STRING ORCHESTRA (Op. 12)

ANON. "Common Ground", *About the House*, 6 no.12 (1984), pp. 56–57 (Details about the ballet "Common Ground" which is danced to the Serenade for Strings)
ANON. "Serenade for Strings", *Music Review*, 16 (May 1955), pp. 161, 163
DICKINSON, P. Sleeve note for Lyrita SRCS 74
DOUGILL, D. "Terms of endearment", *The Sunday Times*, 15 April 1984, p. 35 (A description of the ballet "Common Ground" which uses the score of the Serenade for Strings)
MacDONALD, M. "Berkeley", *Gramophone*, 53 (September 1975), pp. 451–52
MILNER, A. Sleeve note for Decca Eclipse ECS 688

THE SEVEN AGES OF MAN, ETC.

ANON. "Mercury Theatre – amiable puppets", *The Times*, 23 June 1938, p. 14
D., W.A. "Puppets at the Mercury", *The Daily Telegraph*, 23 June 1938, p. 12

H., H. "Mercury – Puppet Show 1938", *The Observer*, 26 June 1938, p. 13

SEXTET (Op. 47)

ANON. "First performances at Cheltenham", *Tempo*, no.37 (Autumn 1955), p. 2
BERKELEY, L. Programme note for the first performance, Cheltenham Festival Programme Book 11 July 1955
BERKELEY, L. Sleeve note for Argo ZRG 749
HARRISON, M. [Lennox Berkeley], *Gramophone*, 52 (October 1974), p. 714
MacDONALD, M. "Lennox Berkeley: an 80th birthday tribute", *Gramophone*, 61 (December 1983), p. 797
MITCHELL, D. "Some first performances", *Musical Times*, 97 (February 1956), p. 90
RUSHTON, J. Sleeve note for Hyperion A66086

SIGNS IN THE DARK (Op. 69)

BRADBURY, E. Programme note for the first performance (27/78/68)
McVEAGH, D. "The Proms – British Music", *Musical Times*, 109 (October 1968), pp. 934–35
PIRIE, P.J. "Music Reviews – Cantatas", *Musical Times*, 109 (December 1968), pp. 1146–47
PIRIE, P.J. "Radio", *Musical Times*, 108 (December 1967), p. 1136

SINFONIA CONCERTANTE (Op. 84)

ANON. "Promenade Concerts 1973", *Music Review*, 35 no.1 (1974), p. 97
ANON. "Survey – new works at the Proms", *Musical Events*, 28 (October 1973), pp. 26–28
BENNETT, R.R. "First performance: Lennox Berkeley's Sinfonia Concertante", *Tempo*, no.106 (September 1973), p. 60
BERKELEY, L. Programme note for the first performance (3 August 1973)
BOWEN, M. "Contemporary Proms", *Music and Musicians*, 22 (October 1973), pp. 64+
DICKINSON, P. Sleeve note for Lyrita SRCS 74
MacDONALD. M. "Berkeley", *Gramophone*, 53 (September 1975), pp. 451–52
PAYNE, A. "Promenade Concert: Enchanting Sinfonia by Berkeley at 70", *The Daily Telegraph*, 4 August 1973, p. 9

PORTER, A. "Proms", *Musical Times*, 114 (October 1973), pp. 1028–29

SINFONIETTA (Op. 34)

ANON. "Reviews of new music – Sinfonietta", *Musical Opinion*, 75 (January 1952), p. 219
ANON. "Sinfonietta", *London Music*, 6 (January 1951), pp. 39–40+
GODDARD, S. "London letter", *The Chesterian*, 25 (January 1951), pp. 76–78
KENNEDY, M. Sleeve note for Lyrita SRCS 111
KEYS, I. "Reviews of music – Sinfonietta", *Music and Letters*, 33 (July 1952), pp. 271–72
OLIVER, M. "British Music", *Gramophone*, 59 (May 1982), p. 1498

SIX PRELUDES FOR PIANO (Op. 23)

BERKELEY, L. Sleeve note for Meridian E 77017
ROBERTSON, A. "New music – Six Preludes", *Musical Times*, 90 (August 1949), pp. 282–83
ROSE, B. "Reviews of music – Six Preludes for Piano", *Music and Letters*, 38 (July 1957), pp. 300–01
TODD, D. "Berkeley: Six Preludes", *Music Teacher*, 57 (April 1978), pp. 14–15
WHITTALL, A. "The British Connection", *Gramophone*, 69 (March 1992), p. 88

SONATA FOR FLUTE AND PIANO (Op. 97)

ANON. "News section: Composers", *Tempo*, no.127 (December 1978), p. 53
BROKAW, R. "New flute music contest", *Instrument*, 35 (October 1980), p. 62
McALLISTER, R. and DEAN, W. "Edinburgh", *Musical Times*, 119 (November 1978), p. 981
MacCRINDLE, S. Sleeve note for RCA Red Seal RS 9011

SONATA FOR FLUTE AND PIANO: F. POULENC (orch. Berkeley, Op. 93, no. 2)

JACOBS, Arthur "Festival Hall: James Galway", *The Financial Times*, 25 March 1977, p. 3

LAYTON, R. "Twentieth Century Flute Concertos", *Gramophone*, 69 (August 1991), p. 59

SONATA FOR PIANO (Op. 20)

HULL, R. "New music reviewed", *The Chesterian*, 22 (September 1947), pp. 51–52
SUTTON, W. "Contemporary British piano sonatas", *Music Teacher*, 44 (December 1965), p. 488

SONATA FOR VIOLA AND PIANO (Op. 22)

ANON. "Sonata in D minor for viola and piano", *Music Review*, 12 (November 1950), pp. 326–27
ANON. "Sonata for viola and piano", *Strad*, 60 (August 1949), p. 124
KEYS, I. "Sonata in D minor for viola and piano", *Music and Letters*, 31 (January 1950), p. 91
ROBERTSON, A. "New music", *Musical Times*, 90 (August 1949), pp. 282–83

SONATINA FOR GUITAR (Op. 52, no.1)

ANON. "News", *The Chesterian*, 32 (Summer 1957), p. 19
KOLODIN, I. Sleeve note for RCA Victor LM 2448

SONATINA FOR OBOE AND PIANO (Op. 61)

ANON. "Redcliffe Festival Concert", *Musical Opinion*, 86 (January 1963), p. 199

SONATINA FOR PIANO DUET (Op. 39)

ANON. "Reviews of new music", *Musical Opinion*, 77 (July 1954), p. 593
MacDONALD, M. "Lennox Berkeley: an 80th birthday tribute", *Gramophone*, 61 (December 1983), p. 797
MASON, C. "New music", *The Chesterian*, 29 (October 1954), pp. 54–56
MITCHELL, D. "Some first performances", *Musical Times*, 96 (March 1955), p. 151
ROWLEY, A. "New music – Piano", *Musical Times*, 95 (December 1954), p. 660

RUSHTON, J. Sleeve note for Hyperion A66086

SONATINA FOR TREBLE RECORDER (OR FLUTE) AND PIANO
(Op. 13) – arranged for flute and string orchestra by R. Newton

LOVELAND, K. "Cheltenham Festival", *Musical Times*, 131 (October 1990), pp. 557–58

SONATINA FOR VIOLIN AND PIANO (Op. 17)

HARRISON, M. [Lennox Berkeley], *Gramophone*, 52 (October 1974), p. 714
PAYNE, A. "Songs without words", *Music and Musicians*, 11 (May 1963), p. 20

SONGS OF THE HALF-LIGHT (Op. 65)

GOODWIN, N. "Suffolk constellation", *Music and Musicians*, 13 (August 1965), p. 17

SPRING AT THIS HOUR (Op. 37, no.2)

ANON. [A Garland for the Queen], *The Times*, 26 January 1953, p. 2
ANON. [A Garland for the Queen], *The Times*, 13 April 1953, p. 10
BARTLETT, C. Sleeve note for Gamut GAMCD 529
BLOM, E. "A Garland for the Queen", *The Observer*, 7 June 1953, p. 11
DODD, N. Sleeve note for Priory PRCD 352
FISKE, R. "A Garland for the Queen", *Gramophone*, 55 (June 1977), p. 90
GODDARD, S. "London letter", *The Chesterian*, 28 (July 1953), pp. 26–29
KELLER, H. "The half-year's new music", *Music Review*, 14 (August 1953), p. 212
MASON, C. [A Garland for the Queen], *Musical Times*, 94 (July 1953), p. 327
STEANE, J.B. "A Garland for the Queen", *Gramophone*, 69 (April 1992), p. 150

STABAT MATER (Op. 28)

ANON. "News", *The Chesterian*, 23 (April 1949), p. 98
HOLST, I. "Lennox Berkeley's Stabat Mater", *Making Music*, no.24 (Spring 1954), pp. 8–9. Reprinted in *The Chesterian*, 28 (April 1954), pp. 115–18

KEYS, I. "Reviews of music", *Music and Letters*, 31 (April 1950), pp. 172–74
MASON, C. "New music – some recent scores", *Musical Times*, 91 (July 1950), pp. 274–75
NOBLE, J. "Music in London", *Musical Times*, 106 (April 1965), p. 279

SUITE FOR ORCHESTRA

ANON. "Promenade Concert: British Music", *The Times*, 13 September 1929, p. 10
C., D.M. Programme note for the first British performance (12 September 1929)

SYMPHONY NO.1 (Op. 16)

DICKINSON, P. Sleeve note for Lyrita SRCS 80
HULL, R. Programme note for the first performance (8 July 1943)
KEYS, I. "Reviews of music", *Music and Letters*, 33 (April 1952), pp. 183–84

SYMPHONY NO.2 (Op. 51)

BERKELEY, L. Programme note for the first performance (24 February 1959)
BERKELEY, L. Sleeve note for Lyrita SRCS 94
COOPER, M. "Lennox Berkeley and his new symphony", *The Listener*, 19 February 1959, p. 351 (A survey of choral and orchestral music, together with background and a brief analysis of Symphony No.2)
GODDARD, S. "London letter", *The Chesterian*, 33 (Spring 1959), pp. 130–31
GOODWIN, N. "Berkeley's 2nd Symphony at Birmingham", *Musical Times*, 100 (April 1959), p. 215
JACOBSON, B. "British music", *Stereo Review*, 43 (September 1979), p. 108
MacDONALD, M. [Berkeley], *Gramophone*, 55 (April 1978), p. 1713
OTTAWAY, H. "Radio notes", *Musical Opinion*, 82 (April 1959), p. 465

SYMPHONY NO.3 (Op. 74)

ANON. "Cheltenham", *Musical Opinion*, 92 (September 1969), p. 631
ANON. "Festivals", *Musical Opinion*, 116 (October 1993), p. 325
ANON. "First performances", *World Music*, 11 no.4 (1969), p. 78
ANON. "Promenade Concerts, 1973", *Music Review*, 35 no.1 (1974), p. 97

BERKELEY, M. "Lennox Berkeley's 3rd Symphony", *The Listener*, 3 July 1969, p. 25
BERKELEY, M. Programme note for the first performance (9 July 1969)
BOWEN, M. "Contemporary Proms", *Music and Musicians*, 22 (October 1973), pp. 64+
COOPER, M. "Cheltenham Festival: Powerful tension of Berkeley's symphony", *The Daily Telegraph*, 7 July 1973, p. 9
CRICHTON, R. "Music in London", *Musical Times*, 113 (February 1972), p. 165
CRICHTON, R. "Music in London", *Musical Times*, 114 (May 1973), p. 511
DOMMETT, K. "Festival revitalised", *Music and Musicians*, 18 (September 1969), p. 30
HARVEY, T. "Contemporary English orchestral music", *Gramophone*, 50 (October 1972), p. 711
HENDERSON, R. "Festivals – Cheltenham", *Musical Times*, 110 (September 1969), p. 957
LAURENCE, R. "Orchestral", *Music and Musicians*, 21 (June 1973), pp. 74+

SYMPHONY NO.4 (Op. 94)

BERKELEY, L. Programme note for the 1978 Cheltenham Festival
BRACEFIELD, H. "Proms modern and British", *Music and Musicians*, 27 (December 1978), p. 44

THEME AND VARIATIONS FOR GUITAR (Op. 77)

HARRISON, M. "Contemporary British guitar works", *Gramophone*, 51 (October 1973), pp. 690, 695
OLIVER, M. "English Guitar Music", *Gramophone*, 59 (January 1982), p. 1037

THOU HAST MADE ME (Op. 55, no.1)

STEANE, J.B. "The English Anthem", *Gramophone*, 69 (November 1991), p. 151
WEBB, S. "Choral Music", *Gramophone*, 52 (November 1974), p. 946

THREE GREEK SONGS (Op. 38)

KELLER, H. "The half-year's new music", *Music Review*, 14 (August 1953), p. 212

THREE LATIN MOTETS (Op. 83, no.1)

ANON. "Recitals", *Church Music*, 3 no.18 (1972), p. 25
MESSENGER, T. "North Wales", *Musical Times*, 114 (July 1973), p. 728
RICHARDS, D. "St Asaph", *Music and Musicians*, 21 (January 1973), p. 67

THREE MAZURKAS (Op. 32, no.1)

ANON. "Reviews of new music", *Musical Opinion*, 74 (June 1951), p. 475
ANON. "Three mazurkas", *Music Review*, 12 (August 1951), p. 244

THREE PIECES FOR ORGAN (Op. 72, no.1)

NICHOLAS, M. Sleeve note for Vista VPS 1096
WEBSTER, E. "Cheltenham", *Musical Opinion*, 92 (September 1969), p. 629

THE THRESHER

LEWIS, C. DAY "C. Day Lewis: An English Literary Life", London, Weidenfeld & Nicholson, 1980, p. 42

TRIO FOR HORN, VIOLIN AND PIANO (Op. 44)

ANON. "Lennox Berkeley's New Work: a Horn Trio", *The Times*, 30 March 1954, p. 3
BERKELEY, L. Sleeve note for HMV HQM 1007
BROWN, D.J. "Recordings", *Tempo*, no.153 (June 1985), pp. 34–37
MITCHELL, D. "Some first performances", *Musical Times*, 95 (May 1954), pp. 266–67
PIRIE, P.J. "Reviews of music", *Music and Letters*, 38 (July 1957), p. 302

TRIO FOR VIOLIN, VIOLA AND CELLO (Op. 19)

HARRISON, M. [String Trio], *Gramophone*, 56 (October 1978), p. 702
MACDONALD. M. [String Trio], *Gramophone*, 65 (July 1987), pp. 191–92
OLIVER, M. "British Chamber Music", *Gramophone*, 65 (August 1987), p. 322

TWO (AUDEN) SONGS

LEWIS, C. DAY "The Buried Day", London, Chatto and Windus, 1960, p. 186
LEWIS, Sean DAY "C.Day Lewis: An English Literary Life", London, Weidenfeld & Nicholson, 1980, p. 42

UNA AND THE LION (Op. 98)

ANON. "Berkeley returns to Wigmore Hall recital", *Dolmetsch Bulletin*, no.32 (September 1979), p. 8
ANON. "Carl Dolmetsch at the Wigmore Hall", *Recorder and Music*, 6 no.6 (1979), pp. 183–84

VARIATION ON AN ELIZABETHAN THEME (SELLENGER'S ROUND)

"DIAPASON" [Aldeburgh Festival], *East Anglian Daily Times*, 22 June 1953, p. 7
MITCHELL, D. [Aldeburgh Festival], *Musical Times*, 94 (July 1953), p. 376
ROBERTSON, A. "Aldeburgh Festival: Variations on Sellinger's Round", *Gramophone*, 31 (October 1953), p. 1554

VARIATIONS ON A HYMN-TUNE BY ORLANDO GIBBONS (Op. 35)

BERKELEY, L. Programme note for the first performance (21 June 1952)

VOICES OF THE NIGHT (Op. 86)

BERKELEY, L. Programme note for the first performance (22 August 1973)
WEBSTER, E. "Three Choirs", *Music and Musicians*, 22 (October 1973), pp. 84–85
WEBSTER, E. "Three Choirs", *Musical Opinion*, 97 (October 1973), pp. 3–4

WINDSOR VARIATIONS (Op. 75)

BOWEN, M. "Flesch finalists", *Music and Musicians*, 19 (September 1970), pp. 60–61
CRICHTON, R. "Festivals: Windsor", *Musical Times*, 110 (November 1969), p. 1161

A WINTER'S TALE: SUITE FOR ORCHESTRA (Op. 54)

ANON. "Suite – A Winter's Tale", *Music and Musicians*, 12 (November 1963), p. 59

DICKINSON, P. "Berkeley: Suite – A Winter's Tale", *Musical Times*, 104 (July 1963), p. 301

Appendix 1: Classified index of main works

Arrangements and transcriptions of music by other composers
Fauré, Gabriel – Berkeley orchestrated the following for the ballet La Fête Étrange (1947):
  Barcarolle No.5 (Op.66)
  Impromptu No.2 (Op.31)
  "Mandoline" (words by Verlaine)
  Nocturne No.6 (Op.63)
  Nocturne No.7 (Op.74)
  Prelude No.5 (Op.103)
  Prelude No.8 (Op.103)
  "Soir" (words by Albert Samain)
Poulenc, Francis – Sonata for flute and piano (orchestrated by Berkeley)
Sarawak National Anthem
Tolhurst, George – Air and recitative from *Ruth* (orchestrated by Berkeley)

Ballets
Ballet (no title)
The Judgement of Paris (Op.10, no.2)

Chamber music
Allegro for two recorders
Andantino for cello and piano (1955)
Andantino for cello and piano (Music for a Prince)
Canon for string trio
Concertino for recorder, violin, cello and harpsichord (Op.49)
Diversions for eight instruments (Op.63)
Duo for cello and piano (Op.81, no.1)
Duo for oboe and cello
Elegy for violin and piano (Op.33, no.2a)
Four pieces for flute, oboe and piano
In Memoriam Igor Stravinsky: canon for string quartet
Introduction and Allegro for double bass and piano (Op.80)
Introduction and Allegro for violin (Op.24)
Minuet for two recorders
Nocturne for harp (Op.67, no.2)
Petite Suite
Piece pour flute, clarinette et basson

Prelude–Intermezzo–Finale for flute, violin, viola and piano
Quartet for oboe and string trio (Op.70)
Quartet for strings no.1 (Op.6) Quartet for strings no.2 (Op.15)
Quartet for strings no.3 (Op.76)
Quintet for oboe, clarinet, horn, bassoon and piano (Op.90)
Serenade for flute, oboe, violin, viola and cello
Sextet for clarinet, horn and string quartet (Op.47)
Sonata for flute and piano (Op.97)
Sonata for viola and piano (Op.22)
Sonata for violin and piano, No.1
Sonata for violin and piano, No.2 (Op.1)
Sonatina for guitar (Op.52, no.1)
Sonatina for oboe and piano (Op.61)
Sonatina for treble recorder (or flute) and piano (Op.13)
Sonatina for violin
Sonatina for violin and piano (Op.17)
Sonatine pour clarinette et piano
Suite for flute, oboe, violin, viola and cello
Suite for oboe and cello
Theme and Variations for guitar (Op.77)
Theme and Variations for violin (Op.33, no.1)
Three pieces for clarinet
Toccata for violin and piano in E minor (Op.33, no.3)
Trio for flute, oboe and piano
Trio for horn, violin and piano (Op.44)
Trio for violin, viola and cello (Op.19)
Two Pieces for String Quartet

Choral works
Colonus' Praise (Op.31)
Deux poèmes de Pindare
Domini est Terra (Op.10)
The Hill of the Graces (Op.91, no.2)
Jonah (Op.3)
Judica me (Op.96, no.1)
Magnificat (Op.71)
Ode (Partition)
Stabat Mater (Op.28)
Una and the Lion (Op.98)
Variations on a hymn by Orlando Gibbons (Op.35)

Church music
Adeste fideles
Batter my heart, three person'd God (Op.60, no.1)
Boar's Hill: hymn tune (Hear'st thou, my soul)
Crux fidelis (Op.43, no.1)
Gartan: hymn tune (Christ is the World's Redeemer)
Hail Holy Queen

Hear'st thou, my soul
I sing of a Maiden
In Wintertime (Op.103)
Justorum animae (Op.60, no.2)
Look up sweet babe (Op.43, no.2)
The Lord is my Shepherd (Op.91, no.1)
Lord, when the sense of thy sweet grace (Op.21, no.1)
Magnificat and Nunc Dimittis (Op.99)
Mass for five voices (Op.64)
Melfort: hymn tune (Hail Gladdening Light)
Missa Brevis (Op.57)
Salve Regina (Op.48, no.1)
Sion's Daughters, Sons of Jerusalem (Op.21, no.2)
Sweet was the song (Op.43, no.3)
Thou hast made me (Op.55, no.1)
Ubi caritas et amor (1969)
Ubi caritas et amor (Op.96, no.2)
Wiveton: hymn tune (Lord, by whose breath)

Fanfares
Fanfare for the Royal Academy of Music Banquet

Film music
The First Gentleman
Hotel Reservé
Out of chaos
(The) Sword of the Spirit
Youth in Britain

Keyboard
Andantino for organ
Bagatelle for two pianos (Op.101, no.1)
Concert Study in Eb (Op.48, no.2)
Fantasia for organ (Op.92)
Five short pieces for piano (Op.4)
Four concert studies (Op.14, no.1)
Four piano studies (Op.82)
Four pieces for organ
Impromptu for organ
Improvisation on a theme by Manuel de Falla (Op.55, no.2)
March for piano
Mazurka for piano (1939)
Mazurka for piano (Op.101b)
Mr Pilkington's Toye
Palm Court Waltz (Op.81, no.2a)
Paysage [de France]
Piece for Vere (piano or harpsichord)
Polka, Nocturne and Capriccio (Op.5)

Prelude and Capriccio for piano (Op.95)
Prelude and Fugue for clavichord (Op.55, no.3)
Scherzo for piano (Op.32, no.2)
Six preludes for piano (Op.23)
Sonata for piano in A (Op.20)
Sonatina for piano
Sonatina for piano duet in Eb (Op.39)
Sonatina for two pianos (Op.52, no.2)
Suite for harpsichord
Theme and Variations for piano duet (Op.73)
Three Impromptus for piano (Op.7, no.1)
Three Mazurkas (Homage à Frederic Chopin) (Op.32, no.1)
Three Pieces for Organ (Op.72, no.1)
Three pieces for piano
Three short pieces for piano
Toccata for piano
Two dances for piano duet

Operas
Castaway (Op.68)
(A) Dinner Engagement (Op.45)
Faldon Park (Op.100)
Nelson (Op.41)
Ruth (Op.50)

Orchestral (including Suites)
Antiphon (Op.85)
Concertino for Chamber Orchestra
Concerto for cello and orchestra
Concerto for flute and orchestra (Op.36)
Concerto for guitar and orchestra (Op.88)
Concerto for piano and double string orchestra (Op.46)
Concerto for piano and orchestra (Op.29)
Concerto for two pianos and orchestra (Op.30)
Concerto for violin and chamber orchestra (Op.59)
Dialogue for cello and orchestra (Op.79)
Diana and Actaeon Waltz (Palm Court Waltz)
Divertimento in Bb (Op.18)
Elegy for String Orchestra (Op.33, no.2b)
Esterel: suite for orchestra
Five Pieces for Violin and Orchestra (Op.56)
Four pieces for small orchestra
Interlude (Nelson) (Op.41)
Introduction and Allegro for two pianos and orchestra (Op.11)
Introduction and Dance
Mont Juic (Op.9)
Nocturne (Op.25)
Overture (Op.8)

Overture for chamber orchestra
Overture for Light Orchestra
Partita (Op.66)
Serenade for string orchestra (Op.12)
Sinfonia Concertante for oboe and orchestra (Op.84) – 4th movement
Sinfonietta
Sinfonietta (Op.34)
Suite for orchestra (1927)
Suite for orchestra (1953)
Suite for strings (Op.87)
Suite: Nelson (Op.42)
Suite: A Winter's Tale (Op.54)
Symphony for string orchestra
Symphony no.1 (Op.16)
Symphony no.2 (Op.51)
Symphony no.3 (Op.74)
Symphony no.4 (Op.94)
Variation on an Elizabethan theme (Sellinger's Round)
Voices of the Night (Op.86)
Windsor Variations (Op.75)

Part songs, etc.
Ask me no more (Op.37, no.1)
A Grace
Hymn for Shakespeare's Birthday (Op.83, no.2)
Legacie
The Midnight Murk
(La) Poulette Grise
Signs in the Dark (Op.69)
Spring at this hour (Op.37, no.2)
There was neither grass nor corn
Three Latin Motets (Op.83, no.1)
Three songs for four male voices (Op.67, no.1)
The Windhover (Op.72, no.2)

Radio incidental music
A Glutton for Life
Iphigenia in Taurus
Look back to Lyttletoun
(The) Seraphina
(The) Wall of Troy
Westminster Abbey
Yesterday and Today

Songs and song-cycles
Another Spring (Op.93, no.1)
Automne (Op.60, no.3)
Autumn's Legacy (Op.58)

(The) Beacon Barn (Op.14, no.2)
(La) belle dame sans merci
Bells of Cordoba (Op.14, no.2)
Counting the beats (Op.60, no.4)
(Les) Dimanches
D'un Vanneur de blé aux vents (The Thresher)
(The) Ecstatic
Eleven-fifty (Op.14, no.2)
Five Chinese Songs (Op.78)
Five Herrick Poems (Op.89)
Five Housman Songs (Op.14, no.3)
Five Poems by W.H. Auden (Op.53)
Five songs (Walter de la Mare) (Op.26)
Four poems of St Teresa of Avila (Op.27)
Four Ronsard Sonnets (Set 1) (Op.40)
Four Ronsard Sonnets (Set 2) (Op.62)
Four score years and ten
How love came in
i carry your heart
Lay your Sleeping Head, My Love (Op.14, no.2)
The Low Lands of Holland
Lullaby
Night covers up the rigid land (Op.14, no.2)
Ode du premier Jour de Mai (Op.14, no.2)
Releasing a migrant yen
So sweet love seemed
Sonnet de Ronsard
Songs of the Half-Light (Op.65)
Sonnet for high voice and piano (Op.102)
Tant que mes yeux (Op.14, no.2)
Three Early Songs
Three Greek Songs (Op.38)
Three poems by Mary Webb
Tombeaux
Trois poèmes de Vildrac
Two (Auden) Songs

Theatre incidental music
Incidental music for puppet play and farce (1938)
Jigsaw: music for Oranges and Lemons (a review)
The Tempest
A Winter's Tale

Appendix 2: Lost or missing manuscripts

Automne (Op.60, no.3)

Ballet (no title): 1932
(La) belle dame sans merci
Boar's Hill: hymn tune

Capriccio (Op.5)
Concertino for Chamber Orchestra
Concertino for recorder, violin, cello and harpsichord (Op.49)
Crux fidelis (Op.43, no.1)

(Les) Dimanches
Divertimento in Bb (Op.18)
Domini est Terra (Op.10)
D'un Vanneur de blé aux vents

Elegy for violin and piano (Op.33, no.2a)
Esterel: suite for orchestra

Fantasia for organ (Op.92)
La Fête Etrange: ballet
The First Gentleman: music for the film
Five Chinese songs (Op.78)
Five short pieces for piano (Op.4)
Four concert studies (Op.14, no.1)
Four pieces for flute, oboe and piano
Four pieces for small orchestra
Four pieces for organ

Gartan: hymn tune

Hotel Reservé: music for the film
How love came in

In memoriam Igor Stravinsky: canon for string quartet
Introduction and Allegro for double-bass and piano (Op.80)
Introduction and Allegro for violin (Op.24)
Introduction and Dance
Iphigenia in Taurus: incidental music

The Judgement of Paris

(The) Low Lands of Holland

Mazurka for piano (Op.101, no.2)
Melfort: hymn tune
Minuet for two recorders

Overture for chamber orchestra (1947)

Petite Suite for oboe and cello
Polka (Op.5) – orchestral version

Quartet for strings no.1 (Op.6)
Quartet for strings no.2 (Op.15)

Sarawak National Anthem: arrangement
The Seraphina
Seven Ages of Man
Sinfonietta (1929)
Sonata for piano (Op.20)
Sonata for viola and piano (Op.22)
Sonatina for guitar (Op.52, no.1)
Sonatina for piano
Sonatina for violin
Sonatina for violin and piano (Op.17)
Sonette de Ronsard
(The) Station Master (1938)
Suite for oboe and cello
Suite for Orchestra (1927)
Suite for Orchestra (1953)
Sweet was the song (Op.43, no.3)
(The) Sword of the Spirit: music for the film
Symphony for string orchestra
Symphony no.3 (Op.74)

Tant que mes yeux (Op.14, no.2)
The Tempest: incidental music
Theme and variations for guitar (Op.77)
Theme and variations for violin (Op.33, no.1)
There was neither grass nor corn
Thou hast made me (Op.55, no.1)
Three Early Songs
Three improvisations for piano (Op.7)
Three poems by Mary Webb
Three short pieces for piano
Toccata for violin and piano in E minor (Op.33, no.3)
Tombeaux
Two (Auden) Songs
Two dances for piano duet
Two Pieces for String Quartet

Variations on a hymn-tune by Orlando Gibbons (Op.35)
Voices of the Night (Op.86)

Windsor Variations (Op.75)

Appendix 3: Personalia

Ashton, Frederick (1904–1988), English choreographer, dancer and producer, founder-choreographer of the Royal Ballet, of which he was Principal Choreographer, 1933–1970, and Director, 1963–70. Knighted in 1962. Wrote *The Judgement of Paris* in 1938 with music by Berkeley.

Auden, Wystan Hugh (1907–1973), English-born poet (later American citizen) who had a profound influence on Britten and his friends. Both Berkeley and Britten composed songs using Auden's poems.

Bartlett, Ethel (1896–1978), English pianist who settled in America with her husband, Rae Robertson, with whom she played music for two pianos. They featured much English music by Bliss, Britten and Walton, in their programmes and Berkeley dedicated his *Three Pieces for Two Pianos* (Op.5) to them.

Bernac, Pierre (1899–1979), French baritone, recitalist and teacher. Associated with French composer Francis Poulenc with whom he gave many song recitals. Both gave the first performance of Berkeley's *Five (de la Mare) Songs* in 1946/47.

Bernard, Anthony (1891–1963), English conductor, pianist and composer who found the London Chamber Orchestra in 1921. Featured many of Berkeley's early works at its concerts and recorded the Divertimento in Bb (Op.18) on two 78s for Decca (K1882–3). The *Sinfonietta* (Op.34) is dedicated to him.

Binyon, Helen and Margaret, twin daughters of the poet Laurence Binyon. Both Berkeley and Britten wrote music for the Binyon Puppets presentations in 1938.

Birch, John (1929–   ), English organist and choirmaster. Organist at Chichester Cathedral from 1958 to 1980. Directed the first performances of *The Lord is My Shepherd* (Op.91, no.1) at the cathedral's 900th celebrations in 1975, and the *Magnificat and Nunc Dimittis* (Op.99) which is dedicated to him.

Bliss, Arthur (1891–1975), English composer and conductor. Master of the Queen's Music from 1953 to 1975. Worked with Berkeley as Director of Music at the BBC during World War II. Questioned the refusal of the BBC to broadcast *String Quartet No.2* (Op.15) in 1942, and commissioned the *Divertimento* (Op.18) for Section C of the BBC Symphony Orchestra the following year. Berkeley contributed his *Canon for String trio* to Bliss's 80th birthday celebrations in 1971.

Boosey, Leslie (1887–1979), English music publisher. Became Chairman of Boosey & Hawkes Ltd in 1930, and on retirement in 1963 became the firm's President. Also Chairman of the Performing Right Society in 1929. Berkeley wrote *Four Score Years and Ten* to words by Vivian Ellis in celebration of Boosey's 90th birthday in 1977.

Boulanger, Nadia (1887–1979), French composer, conductor and teacher of composition who led the revival of Monteverdi, and championed Stravinsky. She had studied with Paul Vidal, Louis Vierne, Alexandre Guilmant (organ), Charles Marie Widor and Gabriel Fauré (composition). She succeeded Paul Dukas in 1921 as professor of composition at the Ecole Normale, a post she kept until 1939. Her pupils included Aaron Copland, Roy Harris, Virgil Thomson, Elliott Carter and Walter Piston from the USA, and Berkeley (between 1927 and 1932), Igor Markevitch, Thea Musgrave, Henryk Szeryng and Hugo Cole from Europe. Ravel introduced Berkeley to her. She conducted the first performance of *Dithyramb* and *Hymn* in London on 24 November 1936, and received the dedication of the *Trois Poèmes de Vildrac, Domini est Terra* (Op.10), *Sonata No.2 for Violin and Piano* (Op.1) and *Divertimento in Bb* (Op.18).

Brain, Dennis (1921–1957), English horn player who studied at the Royal Academy of Music. Killed in a car crash. Played the horn in the first performance of Berkeley's *Trio* (Op.44) in March 1954.

Bream, Julian (1933–), English guitarist and lutenist. Commissioned the *Sonatina for Guitar* (Op.52 no.1) and the *Guitar Concerto* (Op.88), both of which are dedicated to him. He gave the first performance of *Songs of the Half-Light* (Op.65) with Peter Pears.

Britten, Benjamin (1913–1976), English composer, pianist and conductor whose friendship with Berkeley began in 1936 when they were both in Barcelona for the ISCM Festival. Collaborated with Berkeley in the orchestral suite *Mont Juic* (Op.9), each contributing two movements. Also dedicated his Piano Concerto (1938) to Berkeley who in turn dedicated his *Introduction and Allegro for two pianos and orchestra* (Op.11) to Britten.

Bryan, Gordon (1895–1958), English pianist, teacher and composer who studied with Percy Grainger. From 1924 he was a frequent broadcaster, and in 1927–29 he organized a series of chamber concerts at the Aeolian Hall in London. These series included two appearances of Maurice Ravel (in October 1928 and January 1929) who took part in works of his own as pianist and conductor. Wrote a very early article on Berkeley (June 1929), and played with the Aeolian Players at a recital in Oxford which included Berkeley's *Prelude, Intermezzo (Blues) and Finale* (1927).

Burra, Peter (1909–1937), English writer on art, music and literature. Twin brother of Nella Burra and a close friend of Peter Pears. Died in a plane crash in April 1937. Berkeley and Britten first met Burra at the 1936 ISCM Festival at Barcelona, and later jointly inscribed their orchestral suite, *Mont Juic*, to his memory.

Cohen, Harriet (1895–1967), English pianist and noted interpreter of Bach. Berkeley wrote his *Etude* (Op.2) specially for her.

Craxton, Janet (1929–1981), English oboe player. Daughter of Harold Craxton. Studied and later professor of oboe at the Royal Academy of Music. Gave the first performance of *Sinfonia Concertante* (Op.84) which is dedicated to her.

Cuenod, Hugues (1902–), Swiss tenor. *Sonnet* (Op.102) was written for and is dedicated to him with "love and admiration".

Curzon, Clifford (1907–1982), English pianist who studied with Boulanger in Paris and Schnabel in Berlin. He gave the first performance of Berkeley's *Sonata in A for piano* (Op.20) in July 1946.

Dehn, Paul (1912–1976), English poet, film critic, film script writer, song writer and opera librettist who wrote *A Dinner Engagement* (Op.45) and *Castaway* (Op.68) which is dedicated to him. Also wrote the libretto for Walton's *The Bear* (1967), and an acrostic sonnet in celebration of Sir Lennox and Lady Freda's Silver Wedding (December 1971).

Dickinson, Meriel (1940–), English mezzo-soprano who studied at the Royal Manchester College of Music and the Vienna Academy. Gave the first performance of the *Chinese Songs* (Op.78), with her brother Peter (see below) in 1974.

Dickinson, Peter (1934–), English composer, pianist and writer. Professor of music at Keele University and Goldsmiths College, London. Wrote *The Music of Lennox Berkeley* to mark Berkeley's 85th birthday in 1988. Has also made arrangements of Berkeley's music. The *Five Chinese Songs* (Op.78) are dedicated to Professor Dickinson and his sister Meriel.

Dolmetsch, Carl (1911–1997), English recorder player. Studied with his father, Arnold, and at 15 was a virtuoso. Berkeley wrote his *Sonatina for recorder (flute) and piano* (Op.13), the *Concertino for recorder (or flute), violin, cello and harpsichord (or piano)* (Op. 49) and *Una and the Lion* (Op.98) for him.

Ferrier, Kathleen (1912–1953), English contralto who worked with Britten and Pears. Berkeley wrote his *Four Poems for St Teresa of Avila* (Op.27) for her.

Forbes, Watson (1909–1997), Scottish viola player who studied with Albert Sammons. Professor of chamber music at the RAM from 1956, and viola from 1958. The *Sonata for viola and piano* (Op.22) is dedicated to him and he took part in the first performance of the *Trio* (Op.19) in August 1944.

Francis, John (1908–1992), English flute player who commissioned Berkeley's *Flute Concerto* (Op.36) and played his *Trio for flute, oboe and Piano* with the Sylvan Trio.

Galway, James (1939–), Irish flute player who studied with John Francis at the Royal College of Music, and at the Paris Conservatoire. Commissioned Berkeley to orchestrate the Poulenc flute sonata (Op.93 no.2) and also commissioned the *Sonata for Flute* (Op.97) in 1978 which he played at the Edinburgh Festival.

Grinke, Frederick (1911–1987), British violinist of Canadian birth. Member of the Kutcher Quartet and leader of the Boyd Neel Orchestra (1937–46). Commissioned and gave the first performances of *Theme and Variations* (Op.33 no.1), *Elegy* (Op.33 no.2a) *and Toccata*

(Op.33 no.3) and *Five Pieces for Violin and Orchestra* (Op.56). Also received the part dedication of Berkeley's *Trio for violin, viola and cello* (Op.19).

Holst, Imogen (1907–1984), English conductor, composer, editor and writer. Daughter of Gustav Holst who became music assistant to Benjamin Britten and Director of the Aldeburgh Festival (1952–64). Berkeley dedicated *Crux Fidelis* (Op.43 no.1) to her and she directed its first performance.

Horsley, Colin (1920–   ), New Zealand pianist who studied at the Royal College of Music. Commissioned the *Trio for horn, viola and piano* (Op.44). Gave the first performance of Berkeley's *Concerto for Piano and Orchestra* (Op.29) in 1948, the *Scherzo for Piano* (Op.32 no.2) and the *Concerto for Piano and Double String Orchestra* (Op.46). Also gave the first British performance of *Three Mazurkas* (Op.32 no.1).

Hussey, Walter (1909–1985), English cleric who was vicar of St Matthew's Northampton (1937–55) and Dean of Chichester Cathedral (1955–77). Encouraged church patronage of the arts and was responsible for commissioning Henry Moore ("Madonna and Child"), Graham Sutherland ("Crucifixion"), Marc Chagall, John Piper and Ceri Richards, and music from Britten ("Rejoice in the Lamb" in 1943), Tippett, Walton, Rubbra and Bernstein ("Chichester Psalms"). It was Britten who suggested to Hussey that Berkeley be asked to write the 1945 commission for St Matthew's and *Sion's Daughters, Sons of Jerusalem (A Festival Anthem)* (Op.21 no.2) was the result. Hussey also commissioned *The Lord is My Shepherd* (Op.91 no.2) for the 900th celebrations at Chichester Cathedral in 1975.

Lewis, C. Day (1904–1972), Irish poet, critic and writer. Whilst at Oxford University (Wadham College), he gave the first performance of some of Berkeley's early songs at the Oxford University Musical Club and Union. Wrote the text for *Hymn for Shakespeare's Birthday* (Op.83 no.2).

MacCrindle, Sheila (1931–1993), Promotions Manager at Chester Music from October 1972 to May 1991. Responsible for the catalogues of many twentieth-century composers including Lennox Berkeley who dedicated *Judica Me* (Op.96 no.1) to her in 1978.

Manduell, John (1928–   ), South African-born English administrator and composer. Studied at the RAM where he was a pupil of Berkeley. Director of the Cheltenham Festival 1969–1994. *Antiphon* (Op.85) is dedicated to him, and he was responsible for organizing the birthday tribute "A Bouquet for Lennox" at Cheltenham in 1983 to which he contributed.

Mawby, Colin (1936–   ), English composer, organist and choirmaster. Director of Music at Westminster Cathedral, and later for Irish Radio. Directed the first performance of the *Mass for five voices* (Op.64) in Westminster Cathedral and the *Suite* (Op.87) in 1974.

Menuhin, Yehudi (1916–1999), American-born violinist and conductor who studied with Busch and Enescu. Played and directed the first performance of Berkeley's *Concerto for Violin and Chamber Orchestra* (Op.59) at the Bath Festival in 1961. Also directed the first performances of Berkeley's *Windsor Variations* (Op.75) in Windsor and London.

APPENDIX 3: PERSONALIA · 369

Neel, Boyd (1905–1981), English-born conductor. Qualified as naval officer and doctor of medicine. Founded the Boyd Neel Orchestra in 1933. Gave the first public performance of Britten's "Variations on a Theme of Frank Bridge" (1937) and Berkeley's *Serenade for String Orchestra* in 1940.

Nettleship, Ursula (1886–1968), English singer, choir trainer and director. She met Berkeley in 1936 when he and Britten stayed at her sister's, Ethel Nettleship's, house. Berkeley dedicated *The Beacon Barn* (Op.14 no.2) to her in 1938.

Pears, Peter (1910–1986), English tenor whose musical partnership with Britten began in 1937. Created several important roles in Britten's operas and Boaz in Berkeley's *Ruth* (Op.50). Commissioned Berkeley for the *Ronsard Sonnets (Set 1)* (Op.40) and *Five Herrick Poems* (Op.89). Gave the first performance of the second set of *Ronsard Sonnets* (Op.62) and *Songs of the Half-Light* (Op.65) with Julian Bream.

Pilkington, Charles Vere (1905–1983), Friend of Berkeley's at Oxford. Educated at Ludgrove and Eton College. Went up to Christ Church, Oxford in Hilary term 1924, originally to study history. Received a BA in English in 1927, and took his MA in 1968. Had an interest in music as he requested permission to conduct the orchestra in the Headington pageant on 9 and 10 June 1927, and Berkeley wrote several pieces for him including the *March* for harpsichord or piano (1924), *Mr Pilkington's Toye* for harpsichord or piano (1925), *For Vere* for harpsichord or piano (1927) and *Suite for Harpsichord* (1930).

Poulenc, Francis (1899–1963), French composer and pianist. Close friend of Berkeley from his student days in Paris. Berkeley wrote *Automne* (Op.60 no.3) in his memory and dedicated the *Four Ronsard Sonnets (Set 2)* (Op.62) to him.

Rafaelli, José (19 –19). Shared a flat in Paris with Berkeley and was later killed fighting in the French resistance. Berkeley dedicated his *Five Short Pieces* (Op.4) to him.

Raybould, Clarence (1886–1972), English conductor, pianist and composer. Joined the BBC in 1936. Assistant conductor of the BBC Symphony Orchestra 1939–45. Conducted the first performance of Berkeley's *Divertimento in Bb* (Op.18) in 1943.

Robertson, Alec (1892–1982), English scholar, author and broadcaster. Ordained in 1934 and held an appointment at Westminster Cathedral until 1938 when he resumed his professional career. Returned to the priesthood in 1969. Chief producer of music talks on the BBC Third and Home programmes from 1943. The *Three Latin Motets* (Op.83 no.1) are dedicated to him.

Robertson, Rae (1893–1956), Scottish pianist who formed a piano duo with his wife Ethel Bartlett (q.v.)

Sellick, Phyllis (1911–), English pianist who played with her husband Cyril Smith (1907–1974). Berkeley wrote his *Concerto for Two Pianos and Orchestra* (Op.30) for them.

Smeterlin, Jan (1892–1967), Polish-born pianist who settled in England. Gave the first performance of Berkeley's *Three Short Pieces* in 1929 at the start of his career.

Straram, Walter (1876–1933), French conductor who founded his own concert society in Paris in 1925, giving first performances of works by Honegger, Roussel and Milhaud, etc. Conducted the first performance in Paris of Berkeley's *Suite* for orchestra in February 1928.

Tausky, Vilem (1910–), Czech-born conductor and composer who settled in England. As guest conductor of the Sadler's Wells Opera, he conducted the premiere of *Nelson* (Op.41) and many of the subsequent performances. Berkeley dedicated his *Overture [in B flat]* to Tausky and his wife Peggy.

Wyss, Sophie (1897–1983), Swiss soprano who settled in England in 1925. Gave the first performances of Britten's "Our Hunting Fathers", "On this Island" and "Les Illuminations". She also gave the first performance of Berkeley's *Tombeaux* in the orchestral form on the BBC in March 1929. Berkeley dedicated *Tant que Mes Yeux* (Op.14 no.2) and *The Low Lands of Holland* to her.

General index

This index contains personal and other names which appear in the chronology and other sections on works and performances, manuscripts and first editions, recordings and the bibliography.

A Cappella Singers, 62
Academy of St. Martin-in-the-Fields, 114, 303
Adams, Piers, 305
Adeney, Richard, 54
Aeolian Players, 53
Aichinger, Gregor, 125
Alain-Fournier,
    Le Grand Meaulnes, 76
Alberni String Quartet, 109
Aldeburgh Festival,
    1952, 83
    1953, 25, 26, 85
    1954, 27, 86
    1965, 32, 102, 256
    1966, 32, 106
    1967, 33
Aldeburgh Festival Choir, 83
Aldeburgh Festival Orchestra, 83, 85, 308
Alexandra, HRH Princess, 31
Allen, Patrick, 96
Allister, Jean, 104
Alt, Annie, 107, 272
Ambler, Eric, 71
Ambrosian Singers, 93
American Academy and Institute of Arts and Letters, 44
Anne, HRH Princess, 38
Annelle, R., 180
Anthony, Trevor, 88
Antipater, 83, 275
Apollinaire, Guillaume, 100, 130
Archer, Malcolm, 301, 307
Argyle, Pearl, 63
Arnell, Richard, 100
Arts Council of Great Britain, 26, 44, 85, 108, 111, 114, 115, 117, 119, 120, 122, 290, 293
Ashby, Arnold, 91
Ashcroft, Peggy, 96
Ashton, Frederick, 63
Askwith, Betty, 121, 186
Atkins, James, 104
Auden, W.H., 51–2, 63, 169, 194, 213
    The Shield of Achilles, 94
    Songs and other musical pieces, 94
Aumont, Jean-Pierre, 79
Aussel, R., 304
Avila, St Teresa of, 77, 172–4

Bach, J.S., 42
Bach Choir, 41, 42
Baker, Janet, 118, 127, 128
Baker-Smith, Malcolm, 68
Ballet, William, 92
Ballet Russe de Monte Carlo, 57, 313
Barbirolli, Evelyn, 45
Barbirolli, John, 89
Barker, Charles, 73
Barker, George, 92
Bartlett, Ethel, 60, 225
Bartok, Bela, 21
Bate, Jennifer, 73, 126, 163, 296, 298, 307
Bates, Verity Ann, 104
Bath Festival,
    1961, 30, 98, 331, 332
Bath Festival Chamber Orchestra, 98
Bath Festival Society, 98
Bathori, Jane, 52
Bax, Arnold,
    A Garland for the Queen –contribution, 85

Bax, Clifford, 85
Baxter, Timothy, 113
BBC Choral Society, 25, 80
BBC Chorus, 59, 105
BBC Concert Orchestra, 95
BBC Light Music Festival,
    1959, 95
BBC Northern Orchestra, 23, 68, 71, 99,
    105, 107, 114, 245
BBC Northern Singers, 99, 105, 106, 299
BBC Orchestra, 25, 59, 62, 63, 70
BBC Radio Theatre, 69
BBC Scottish Military Band, 68
BBC Singers, 69, 72, 89, 117
BBC Symphony Orchestra, 22, 26, 58, 69,
    75, 80, 84, 85, 89, 93, 94, 96, 98, 101,
    115, 265, 314, 336
Bean, Hugh, 305
Becker, Maria, 87
Beckett, G., 297
Beamish, Sally,
    *Variation on a theme by Lennox
    Berkeley (Bouquet for Lennox)*, 46–7
Beck, Conrad,
    Concerto for Orchestra, 312
Beddoes, Thomas L., 98
Bedford, David,
    *Variation on a theme by Lennox
    Berkeley (Bouquet for Lennox)*, 47
Bedford, Steuart, 84, 298, 300, 301, 302,
    304
Beecham, Thomas, 79
Beedle, N., 302, 305, 306
Behrend, Mrs J.L., 64
Bellas, Joachim du, 50, 274
Benedictine Order, 120, 287
Benjamin, George,
    Homage to Haydn – contribution,
    121, 206
Bennett, Richard Rodney, 38
    Homage to Haydn – contribution,
    121, 206
    *Variation on a theme by Lennox
    Berkeley (Bouquet for Lennox)*, 47
    Victory, 35
Berkeley, Aline Carla (née Harris)
    (mother), 12, 13, 17
Berkeley, Claude (cousin), 19, 66
Berkeley, Elizabeth Freda (née Bernstein)
    (wife), 13, 24, 27, 28, 32, 35, 36, 37, 47,
    91, 105, 237, 277
Berkeley, George Lennox Rawdon
    (paternal grandfather), 11

Berkeley, Geraldine M. (sister), 12, 48, 51,
    274
Berkeley, (Captain) Hastings George
    FitzHardinge (father), 11, 12, 13, 15, 17
Berkeley, Julian Lennox (son), 25, 34, 97,
    106, 117
Berkeley, Lennox Randal Francis, 12
    as conductor: 23, 29, 34, 39, 54, 58,
    59, 69, 73, 76, 78, 83, 87, 92, 93,
    94, 98, 99, 100, 101, 105, 111, 114,
    115, 297, 301, 302, 303, 306
    as performer: 23, 50, 52, 64, 67, 69,
    72, 77
    as speaker: 308–10
    as writer: 311–19, 320, 327, 328, 331,
    332, 334, 335, 336, 337, 340, 341,
    342, 343, 344, 345, 346, 347, 348,
    351, 352, 353, 354
Berkeley, Michael FitzHardinge (son), 24,
    34, 97, 106, 108, 201
    arranger of the *Stabat Mater* (Lennox
    Berkeley), 42, 78
    *Variation on a theme by Lennox
    Berkeley (Bouquet for Lennox)*, 47
Berkeley, Nicholas Eadnoth (son), 28,
    117, 182
Bernac, Pierre, 36, 75, 170
Bernard, Anthony, 52, 53, 55, 56, 76, 77,
    82, 83, 246
Bernard, James, 36, 297
Berners, (Lord) Gerald, 17
Berrow, Jim, 45
Besch, Anthony, 104
Betjaman, John, 36, 47
Binge, Ronald,
    Music for a Prince – contribution, 108
Binyon, Helen, 64
Binyon, Margaret, 64
Birch, John, 117, 120, 300
Blackburn, Harold, 88
Blades, Christopher, 79
Blans, Patricia, 104
Bliss, Arthur, 22, 35, 36, 39, 40, 111, 135,
    308, 320, 327
    A Garland for the Queen – contribution,
    85
    Music for a Prince – contribution, 108
    Oboe Quartet, 312
    The Olympians, 37
Bliss, (Lady) Trudy, 135
Blunden, Edmund, 85
Bonham Carter, Charlotte, 114, 290
Boosey, Leslie, 118

Boughton, W., 303
Boulanger, Lili, 34, 315
Boulanger, Nadia, 18, 19, 31, 38, 44, 55, 57, 62, 70, 156, 251, 286, 308, 309, 312, 315, 316, 318–19, 333, 334
Boulez, Pierre, 35
Boult, Adrian, 22, 75, 106, 115, 297, 308
Bouquet for Lennox (2 July 1983), 46–7
Bowden, Pamela, 299
Bowen, Kenneth, 113
Bowring, Jennifer, 121
Boyd Neel Orchestra, 65
Boyle, Edward, 38
Boyle, Rory,
    Variation on a theme by Lennox
        Berkeley (*Bouquet for Lennox*), 47
Bradshaw, Susan, 38, 160, 161
Brae, June, 76
Brahms, Carl, 92
Brahms, J.,
    Trio (Op. 40), 86
Brain, Dennis, 86, 307
Braithwaite, Nicholas, 78, 297, 306
Brayne, Christopher, 301
Breakspear, H., 305
Bream, Julian, 39, 92, 102, 116, 143, 256, 257, 297, 304, 306
Brendel, Alfred, 315
Brewer, Michael, 301
Bridges, Robert, 95, 282
Bristol Bach Choir, 305
Bristol Cathedral Choir, 301
Britannia Band of Derry, 100
British Broadcasting Corporation (see also BBC), 16, 17, 19, 21, 22, 23, 24, 25, 26, 28, 29, 31, 32, 33, 34, 37, 42, 46, 47, 52, 68, 70, 72, 74, 75, 80, 85, 87, 88, 89, 90, 92, 93, 95, 101, 104, 106, 114, 117, 121, 180, 205, 238, 245, 270, 291, 292, 295, 315
British Institute of Recorded Sound, 36, 308, 309
British Music Society, 15, 44, 53
Britten, Benjamin, 17, 18, 19, 20, 21, 26, 28, 29, 30, 41, 42, 43, 58, 62, 63, 64, 78, 125, 157, 187, 194, 200, 206, 213, 259, 260, 273, 299, 308, 310, 315, 316, 318, 320, 321, 323, 324
    Billy Budd, 30
    Chorale, 72
    Death in Venice, 38
    Mont Juic, 18, 19, 208-209
    Peter Grimes, 23
    Serenade, 334
    Shepherd's Carol, 72
    Spring Symphony, 314
    String Quartet No.1, 22, 314
    Variation on an Elizabethan Theme, 85, 289
    War Requiem, 31
Britten-Pears Library, 62, 153, 157, 168, 175, 179, 200, 206, 208
Britton, Donald, 76
Brookes, Oliver, 102
Brown, Christopher,
    Variation on a theme by Lennox
        Berkeley (*Bouquet for Lennox*), 47
Brown, Iona, 302, 305
Brown, Timothy, 298, 300, 301, 303, 305, 307
Brown, Wilfred, 298, 302
Browne, Laidman, 68, 76
Bruce, Margaret, 112, 121, 171
Bryan, Gordon, 53, 230, 231
Bryans, Gladys, 56, 69, 251, 254
Brymer, Jack, 303
Buckle, Richard, 111, 218
Buketoff, Igor, 297
Burke, Anthony, 76
Burke, Nigel, 79
Burney, Charles, 35, 316
Burra, Peter, 18, 62
Burrow, Brian, 78
Burrowes, Norma, 113
Büsser, Paul, H., 332
Byles, Edward, 122
Byrd, William, 289

Cable, Margaret, 63
Cahill, Teresa, 78
Cairns, P., 300
Calder, Beryl, 93
Calvocoressi, M.D., 50, 66, 270
Cambridge Hymnal (1967), 104–5, 184, 198
Cambridge University Chamber Choir, 305
Cambridge University Madrigal Society, 85, 305
Cameron, Basil, 53, 79, 89
Cameron, Francis, 97, 207
Cantelo, April, 86, 91
Canterbury Cathedral Choir, 96, 300, 306
Carew, Thomas, 84, 129
Carter, Peter, 110
Casella, Alfredo, 312
    Partita for Piano and Orchestra, 313

Catholic Film Society, 68
Cavalcanti, Alberto, 78
Chagrin, Francis, 218
Chamber Music Society of Lincoln Center (New York), 116
Chapel Choir of Dean Close School, 300
Chaplin, Anthony (Lord), 109, 112, 171, 233
Chappell, William, 63, 79, 87
Chapple, Brian,
　Variation on a theme by Lennox Berkeley (Bouquet for Lennox), 46
Chard, Geoffrey, 104
Charles, Prince of Wales, 35, 108
Chatellier, Marc, 66
Chávez, Carlos, 81
Chelsea Opera Group, 89, 343
Cheltenham Music Festival, 41
　1955, 27, 90
　1962, 31, 99, 131
　1964, 32, 101
　1968, 34, 100, 106
　1969, 34, 107
　1973, 38, 114
　1981, 110
　1983, 46–7, 325
Chester, J.& W., 17, 38, 46, 185
Chichester Cathedral Choir, 117, 120, 300, 301
Chichester 902 Festivities (1977), 118, 128
Chopin, Frederic, 81, 315
City Arts Trust, 106
City of Birmingham Symphony Orchestra, 29, 94, 115
City of London Festival,
　1968, 33, 106
Civil, Alan, 303
Clare College (Cambridge) Choir, 298, 300, 301, 303, 307
Claridge, Norman, 87
Clark, Kenneth, 71
Clark, Patricia, 104
Clarke, Ashley, 29, 95
Clarkson, Stanley, 88
Clegg, John, 304
Cleobury, Stephen, 120, 121, 122, 186, 300
Clerkes of Oxenford, 306
Cleverdon, Douglas, 92
Cocteau, Jean, 52, 283
Cohen, Harriet, 58, 281, 320
Coleridge, Hartley, 99

Collegium Musicum Londinii, 85, 99, 299
Columba, St, 99, 100
Comfort, Lance, 71
Composers' Guild of Great Britain, 38, 40, 47, 111
Constable, John, 100
Cook, Brian Raynor, 89
Cooke, Arnold,
　Symphony No. 4, 39
Cooper, Elizabeth, 79
Cooper, Gerard, 77
Copland, Aaron, 311
　Variations for Piano, 19
Cornford, Frances, 72
Corp, Ronald, 56
Cortot, Alfred, 313
Couper, Barbara, 93
Cowsill, David, 101
Craggs, Stewart R., 289
Craigie, Jill, 71
Cranbrook, Dorothy (Countess), 83, 289
Crashaw, Richard, 71, 90, 104, 199
Craxton, Essie, 82, 158
Craxton, Janet, 101, 105, 114, 232, 245, 252, 318
Craxton, John, 101, 252
Crichton, Ronald, 76
Crosby & Co. Ltd., 103, 220
Croser, Peter, 100
Cross, Joan, 59
Crozier, Eric, 74, 91, 234
Cuenod, Hughes, 84, 121
Cummings, D., 305
cummings, e.e., 109
Curzon, Clifford, 19, 22, 72, 73, 171, 226, 250
Cusack, Cyril, 92

Daniel, Nicholas, 45
Danielou (Cardinal), 35
Darlington, Stephen, 300, 301
Dartington String Quartet, 109
Dashwood, Helen (Lady), 121, 132
Davenport, Clement, 65, 241
Davenport, John, 65, 241
Davezac, B., 306
Davies, Andrew, 116
Davies, Meredith, 104
Davies, Peter Maxwell, 315
Davies, W.H., 99
Davis, M., 300, 305
Day Lewis, Cecil, 36, 37, 50, 52, 70, 113, 157, 183

Dean, Winton, 36, 41, 122, 159, 161
Debussy, Claude, 14, 16, 42
    Pelléas and Mélisande, 14
Dehn, Paul, 26, 36, 85, 86, 103, 136, 138, 152, 153, 258
Deller, Alfred, 92
Delphos Ensemble, 101
Delroy, Albert, 92
Demuth, Norman, 314
Denison, John, 26
Desert Island Discs, 42
Devine, George, 89
Dickinson, Meriel, 52, 63, 78, 95, 110, 164, 296, 298, 306
Dickinson, Patric, 75, 100, 149
Dickinson, Peter, 52, 53, 56, 57, 63, 95, 110, 164, 227, 296, 298, 306, 309, 310
Dolmetsch, Carl, 66, 91, 120, 296
Dolmetsch, Jeanne, 120
Dolmetsch, Marguerite, 120
Donne, John, 70, 96, 99, 133, 134, 272
Dotrice, Roy, 96
Douglas, Basil, 86, 152, 153
Downes, Frank, 102
Downes, Ralph, 83
Draper, Charles, 88
Drewry, Val, 74, 247
Drummond, Cecile, 12
Duff, Leslie, 78
Duran, Elena, 66
Durrell, Lawrence, 98
Dursley, John, 260, 261
Dusseau, Jeanne, 52
Dutoit, Charles, 117, 304
Dykes Bower, John, 97

Eaves, Sylvia, 55
Edinburgh International Festival, 1978, 43, 119
Edith Sitwell Memorial Concert (1966), 106
Edmund de Polignac, Princess, 62, 150
Eisenberg, Maurice, 65
Elizabeth II, Queen, 33, 37, 42, 85
Elizabeth, Queen (Queen Mother), 35
Elliott, Victoria, 88
Ellis, Osian, 115, 155
Ellis, Vivian, 40, 118
    Music for a Prince – contribution, 108
Elysian Singers, 299
Endymion Ensemble, 297, 298, 300, 302, 303, 307
English, Gerald, 100

English Chamber Orchestra, 110, 116, 301, 304
English National Opera, 44, 122
English Opera Group, 78, 83, 91, 104, 153
English Opera Group Association, 26, 88
English Opera Group Chamber Orchestra, 87, 93, 104
English Serenata, 297
English Sinfonia, 303
English Symphony Orchestra, 303
Espla, Oscar, 81
Esty, Alice, 94, 169, 322
Evans, Geraint, 45
Evans, Nancy, 78, 88, 94
Exultate Singers, 113, 305

Falla, Manuel de, 312
    Concerto for Harpsichord, 313
    El Amor Brujo, 97
Farnham, Festival, 1965, 103, 220
Farrer, J., 303
Fauré, Gabriel, 334
    Barcarolle No.6, 76
    Impromptu No.2, 76
    "Mandoline", 76
    Nocturne No.6, 76
    Nocturne No.7, 76
    Prelude No.5, 76
    Prelude No.8, 76
    "Soir", 76
Fedorovitch, Sophie, 76
Feeney Trust, 29, 94
Fenby, Eric, 113
Ferber, Albert, 74
Ferrier, Kathleen, 24, 77, 174, 299
Festival of the City of London, 1974, 116
Festival of Nine Lessons and Carols (1983), 121, 186
Festival of Poetry (1963), 100, 149
Fine Arts Orchestra, 114
Finzi, Gerald,
    A Garland for the Queen – contribution, 85
Forbes, Watson, 71, 73
Ford, John, 86
Foundation Prince Pierre de Monaco, 31
Fox, Ian, 117, 120, 300
Françaix, Jean, 18, 19, 313
Francis, Hannah, 105, 213
Francis, John, 84, 141
Francis, Sarah, 54, 60

Franck, César, 154
Frank, Alan, 40
Franklin, Gretchen, 93
Franklin, Norman, 94
Fraser, Peter, 67, 167, 168
French Broadcasting Company, 81
Frensham Heights School Orchestra, 103, 302
Fry, Christopher, 85
Fuchsova, Liza, 87
Fulton, Arnold, 63

Galway, James, 41, 43, 117, 119, 297, 304, 305, 323
Gardiner, J.E., 297
Gardner, John, 83, 113
   Music for a Prince – contribution, 108
Garrod, H.W., 14
Gau, Geraldine von (maternal grandmother), 11
Gendron, Maurice, 110
Georgiadis, John, 305
Gever, Bep, 66
Gibson, Douglas, 21, 30, 31, 97
Gielgud, Val, 75, 87
Gieseking, Walter, 312
Gilardino, Angelo, 109, 271
Gill, Colin, 21, 68, 184, 185
Ginsburg, Norman, 78
Gitlis, Ivry, 75, 187
Gittings, Robert, 68
Glock, William, 31, 64
Glossop, Peter, 88
Gobel, H., 307
Goehr, Walter, 74
Goethe, Johann W. von, 87
Golden Age Singers, 85, 305
Goldsborough, Arnold, 77, 299
Goldsborough String Orchestra, 77, 299
Goldstone, Anthony, 304, 305
Goossens, Eugene, 97
Goren, Eli, 90
Goring, Marius, 87
Graves, Robert, 100, 149
Greed, D., 305
Greenall, Matthew, 299
Greene, Max, 71
Greenidge, John, 50, 77, 173, 257, 274
Greevy, Bernadette, 299
Gregg, Hubert, 68
Griffith, Hugh, 74, 79
Grinke, Frederick, 71, 82, 98, 306
Groves, Charles, 45, 119

Gucht, Jan van der, 59
Guest, George, 113, 276, 277
Guildford Cathedral Choir, 307
Guildhall School of Music and Drama, 45
Guildhall String Ensemble, 308

Hale, Una, 91
Hall, John, 140
Hallé Orchestra, 45, 65, 89
Hamburger, Paul, 87
Hanbury, Victor, 71
Handford, Maurice, 87
Hanson, Howard, 81
Hardy, Trevor, 72, 199
Harewood, George (Lord), 44, 122, 161
Harper, John, 299, 301, 307
Harrhy, Eiddwen, 89
Harris, James Charles (maternal grandfather), 11
Harris, Robert, 74
Harris, William H., 13
Harrogate Festival,
   1927, 15, 53
Hart, Perry, 105
Harverson, Alan, 113
Harvey, Trevor, 69
Harwood, Elizabeth, 120
Hassall, Christopher, 85
Hawkes, Ralph, 18, 19
Hawkins, Brian, 105, 110, 305
Haworth, Elgar, 89
Haydn, Josef, 45, 46, 121, 205, 313
Hayes, Roland, 312
Head, Michael, 113
Headington, Christopher, 78, 298, 299, 301, 302, 304, 307, 309
   Variation on a theme by Lennox Berkeley (Bouquet for Lennox), 47
Heath, Kenneth, 105
Heawood, John, 79
Heenan, John (Cardinal), 32, 38, 102
Helpman, Robert, 63
Hemsley, Thomas, 88, 91, 298, 307
Henderson, Roy, 59
Henry Wood Concert Society, 80
Henry Wood Symphony Orchestra, 54
Herbert, George, 73
Hermanssen, S., 307
Herrick, Robert, 58, 103, 282
Heurtefeux, C., 305
Heyworth, Peter, 39
Hickox, Richard, 65
Hill, Derek, 100

Hill, Martyn, 60
Hinkins, C., 206
Hoban, John, 303
Hobbs, Carleton, 70
Hoddinott, Alun, 42, 44, 118
Hollas, S., 307
Holm, Ian, 96
Holst, Imogen, 89, 125, 150
 Variation on an Elizabethan Theme, 85, 289
Homage to Haydn (1982), 121
Honneger, Arthur,
 Chris du monde, 312
 Concerto for Cello and Orchestra, 312
 Pacific 231, 311
 Rugby, 311
 Semiramio, 314
 Troisième Movement Symphonique, 313
Hooke, Emelie, 86
Hopkins, Antony, 113
Hopkins, Gerard M., 99, 106, 292
Hopkins, Joan, 79
Hornby, Anthony, 107, 267
Hornby, Lili, 107, 267
Horovitz, Joseph, 113
 Music for a Prince – contribution, 108
Horsley, Colin, 24, 25, 79, 81, 86, 90, 93, 144, 296, 299, 303, 304, 307
Housman, A.E., 67, 167
Howard, Andrée, 76
Howells, Herbert,
 A Garland for the Queen – contribution, 85
Hughes, C., 300
Hughes, Patricia, 76
Huhne, Ella, 66
Hume, Basil (Cardinal), 48
Hunt, Donald, 119, 300
Hussey, Walter, 73, 116, 117, 118, 127, 163, 199

Ibert, Jacques, 81
Igloi, Thomas, 110
Ireland, John, 97
 A Garland for the Queen – contribution, 85
Ireland, Patrick, 90
Institute of Contemporary Art, 105
ISCM Festival,
 1936, 17, 58, 310, 316
 1938, 19, 63
 1949, 25, 79

Jackson, Jennifer, 66
Jackson, Richard, 78
Jackson, Sybil, 20, 66
Jeffrey, B., 305
Jeffrey, Peter, 96
Jeffreys Consort of Voices, 108
Jenkins, Glyn, 305
John Paul II, Pope, 46
Johnson, Anthony Rolfe, 299
Johnson, Graham, 298, 299
Johnson, Robert Sherlaw,
 Homage to Haydn – contribution, 121, 206
Johnston, David, 89
Jolivet, André, 314
Jones, Parry, 59
Jones, Sybil, 87
Joubert, John, 113

Keats, John, 50
Keble, John, 95
Kells, Iris, 83
Kennard, Cecile, 64
Kennard, Frank, 64
Kenny, Courtney, 55
Keys, Robert, 88, 212
King, Thea, 54, 65, 279
King's College (Cambridge) Choir, 121, 122, 186, 299
King's Lynn Music Festival, 1971, 36, 110
Kirkup, James, 85
Knott, Zoë, 218
Koechlin, Charles, 313
Kossoff, David, 76
Kotewell, R., 110, 163, 164
Kutcher, Samuel, 52
Kynaston, Nicholas, 41, 117, 298

Labé, Louise, 66, 121, 270
L'Academie Royale des Sciences, des Lettres et des Beaux-Arts de Belgique, 46
Lack, Simon, 93
Lakin, Roderick, 218
Lamb, Charles, 70, 74
Lambert, Constant, 19, 63, 76, 79
Lancelot, James, 300
Landen, Dinsdale, 96
Langridge, Philip, 298, 300, 302
Lassimonne, Denise, 73
Latin Mass Society, 39
Lawson, Catherine, 87, 88

Lee, Clifford, 111
Lee, Laurie, 105
Leeds Festival Chorus, 59
Leeds Music Festival,
    1937, 18, 59
Lees-Milnes, Alvilde, 90, 92, 242, 264
Lefeaux, Charles, 92
Legge, Anthony, 50, 53, 57, 60, 61, 63
Leicester Cathedral Choir, 299
Leighton, Margaret, 76
Leonard, Sarah, 298
Leppard, Raymond, 107, 110, 114, 245
Lewis, Anthony, 113
Lewis, Gwent, 88
Lewis, Joseph, 62
Lewis, Richard, 99, 131
Linden Singers, 111
Linsey, Michael, 87
Lister, Laurier, 79
Little, Ian, 300
Little Orchestra of London, 303
Livesey, Jack, 79
Llewellyn, Grant, 189, 343
Lloyd, Cecil, 88
Lloyd, George, 314
Lloyd Webber, Julian, 298
Lole, Simon, 301
Lom, Herbert, 71
London Bach Group, 99
London Chamber Orchestra, 52, 53, 55,
    56, 76, 77, 83, 297
London Contemporary Music Centre, 53,
    54, 65, 66
London Mozart Players, 299
London Oboe Quartet, 105
London Oratory Junior Choir, 303
London Philharmonic Orchestra, 59, 69,
    297, 301, 302, 303, 306
London Select Choir, 63
London Sinfonietta, 303
London Symphony Orchestra, 62, 64, 65,
    71, 77, 79, 80, 301
Lorca, Federico Garcia, 64, 135
L'Orchestre National de L'Office de
    Radiodiffusion Télévision Française,
    107
Loring, F., 296
Lott, Felicity, 298
Loughran, James, 65
Louisville Orchestra, 303
Lovell, Raymond, 71
Lubbock, John, 82
Lucas, Adrian, 300

Lucas, Audrey, 74
Lumsden, Norman, 78
Lush, Ernest, 82, 298, 307
Lutoslawski, Witold, 37

McCabe, John, 121, 205, 298
    Homage to Haydn – contribution,
    121, 206
MacCrindle, Sheila, 119, 248
McDonald, B., 297
MacDonald, Kenneth, 104
Macdonald, Malcolm, 113
MacDougall, J., 297
McElligott, J.B., 70
MacGregor, Duncan, 99
Macintosh, Jack, 93
McKechnie, James, 68, 93
Mackerras, Charles, 91
Mackie, N., 305
McKie, William, 90
McLeod, John,
    Variation on a theme by Lennox
    Berkeley (Bouquet for Lennox), 47
McMahon, Ivor, 90
McNamee, M., 298, 302
MacNeice, Louis, 68, 74, 85
Maconchy, Elizabeth, 41, 218
Maddox, Diana, 92
Magdalen College (Oxford) Choir, 307
Mahon, A., 298
Maia, Carolyn, 104
Malcolm, George, 30, 84
Malipero, Gian F., 81, 97
Mandikian, Arda, 88
Manduell, John, 41, 114, 129
    Variation on a theme by Lennox
    Berkeley (Bouquet for Lennox), 46
Mar, Norman del, 93, 297, 304, 306
Mare, Walter de la, 23, 75, 85, 102, 118,
    127, 128, 170, 256
Marion-Crawford, Howard, 74
Marriner, Neville, 114
Martineau, Malcolm, 298
Martinon, Jean, 107
Martinů, Bohuslav, 81
    String Quartet, 312
Mason, James, 71
Massey, Roy, 106
Mathias, William, 28, 325
    Variation on a theme by Lennox
    Berkeley (Bouquet for Lennox), 47
Mathieson, Muir, 71
Matters, Arnold, 88

Matthews, Colin, 301
Maupassant, Guy de, 74, 180
Maw, Nicholas, 28, 100, 149
  *Variation on a theme by Lennox
    Berkeley (Bouquet for Lennox)*, 47
Mawby, Colin, 37, 102, 113, 115, 296, 309
Mayer, Robert, 44
Mayger, Graham, 60
Mellors, Wilfred, 314
Melos Ensemble, 90, 116
Menuhin, Yehudi, 35, 98, 108, 148, 293, 297
Menuhin Festival Orchestra, 108, 293, 297
Merchant Taylors' Company, 111, 181
Michael Brewer Singers, 301
Migot, Georges, 314
Milhaud, Darius, 314
  Concerto for Violin and Orchestra, 312
Miller-Jones, Keith, 121
Millington, Andrew, 307
Minchinton, John, 85, 99, 299
Mitchell, Julian, 71
Mitropoulos, Dimitri, 313
Mitterand, François, 47
Moll, Phillip, 119, 304
Montagu, Diana, 78
Monteaux, Pierre, 311, 312, 313
Monteverdi, Claudio, 315
Monteverdi Orchestra, 297
Moore, Henry, 71
Moore, Phillip, 300, 306
Morelle, M., 296, 307
Morley, Matthew, 60
Morris, Victor, 122
Morrison, Angus, 309
Mortimer, Raymond, 72, 221, 222
Moulle, H., 307
Mozart, W.A., 42, 311
Mucha, E., 305
Munchinger, Karl, 303
Murray, Mitch,
  Music for a Prince – contribution, 108
Murrill, Herbert, 21, 314
Music Group of London, 303
Musicians' Benevolent Fund, 96, 272
Musicians' Company, 40

Nash, Paul, 71, 217
Nash Ensemble, 297, 302, 303
National Music Council, 45
National Symphony Chamber Orchestra, 74

Neary, Martin, 300
Neel, Boyd, 65
Nettleship, Ursula, 18, 64
Neville, Paul, 112
New English Music Society, 56
New Irish Chamber Orchestra, 299
New London Children's Choir, 56
New London Orchestra, 56
New Philharmonic Orchestra, 297
Newton, Eric, 71
Newton, Rodney, 66
Nicholas, Michael, 301
Nichols, Roger, 11
Nielson, Flora, 87
North Wales Music Festival,
    1972, 113, 276
Norton, Lady, 105
Norton Foundation, 105
Norwich Cathedral Choir, 299, 301

O'Brien, Garrett, 113, 305
Ogden, C., 305
Oldham, Arthur,
  Variation on an Elizabethan Theme, 85, 289
O'Malley, Patrick, 64, 134, 159
Ord, Boris, 85, 305
Organ Club, 117
Oriana Madrigal Society Choir, 62
Orleans, Charles d', 51, 274
Orr, Robin, 113
Oxford and Cambridge Musical Club, 43, 116
Oxford University Musical Club and
    Union, 13, 14, 15, 45, 50, 51, 52

Page, Kenneth, 102
Panufnik, Andrzej, 81, 94
Parikian, Manoug, 86, 148, 307
Park Lane Group, 110, 112, 157
Park Lane Music Group Players, 78
Parker, Cecil, 79
Parkhouse, David, 305
Parnell, Andrew, 300, 301
Parsons, Geoffrey, 99, 131
Parsons, William, 59
Partington, Andrew, 300
Partridge, Ian, 67, 84, 305
Partridge, Jennifer, 67
Pascal, Roy, 87
Passarat, Jean, 67, 215
Patterson, Paul, 113
Pavitt, Burnett, 111, 119, 219, 268, 269

Pavlova, Anna, 312
Pears, Peter, 42, 48, 58, 70, 78, 83, 84, 88, 89, 91, 101, 102, 115, 121, 165, 168, 174, 175, 178, 179, 208, 214, 256, 299, 303
Peasgood, Osborne H., 97
Performing Right Society, 18, 21, 27, 29, 35, 40, 46, 47, 108
Perrett, Danielle, 302
Peyer, Gervase de, 90
Philip, Duke of Edinburgh, 42
Phillips, James, 71
Pignari, Helena, 81
Pilkington, Vere, 14, 15, 50, 51, 53, 56, 58, 203, 204, 209, 224, 262, 281
Pindar, 62
Pini, Anthony, 305
Plato, 83, 275
Platt, P., 305
Plomley, Roy, 42
Pluygers, C., 305
Poetry Book Society, 100, 149
Pollak, Anna, 88, 91
Ponsonby, David, 66
Poole, John, 117
Porter, Eric, 96
Potter, Peter, 91
Pougnet, Jean, 91, 305
Poulenc, Francis, 28, 31, 36, 46, 75, 97, 100, 101, 130, 170, 314, 315, 318, 348
    Aubade, 312
    Concerto Champêtre, 311
    Concerto for Piano and Orchestra, 314
    Sonata for Flute and Piano, 41, 117, 249
Pounder, M., 304
Poyard, 62
Pratley, Geoffrey, 118, 128
Pré, Jacqueline de, 30
Preston, Simon, 32, 106
Priestman, Brian, 96
Price, Olwen, 88
Pritchett, John, 79
Pro Arte String Quartet, 61
Probyn, John, 88
Provost, R., 305
Pryce-Jones, Alan, 87, 210, 212
Pryer, C., 301
Purcell, Henry, 125
Purcell Singers, 89

Quartermaine, Leon, 70, 76
Queen Marie-José Composition Prize, 33

Quilley, Denis, 92

Rabaud, Henri, 76
Race, Steve,
    Music for a Prince – contribution, 108
Rafaelli, José, 17, 61
Raglan, James, 74
Rankin, Molly, 74
Ravel, Maurice, 15, 18, 42, 309, 314, 316, 318
    Piano Concerto for the Left Hand, 313
Rawsthorne, Alan, 36, 308, 316
    A Garland for the Queen – contribution, 85
Raybould, Clarence, 59, 69, 70, 265
Reed, Henry, 85
Rees, Jonathan, 66
Reigate, John (Lord), 111, 181
Rennert, Jonathan, 60
Respighi, Ottorino,
    Pines of Rome, 313
Rex, Sheila, 88
Rhodes, J., 303
Rhodes, P., 305
Rice, Edward, 103
Rice, Peter, 104
Richards, Bernard, 90
Richards, Ceri, 91
Richardson, Ian, 96
Richardson, Stanley, 64, 135
Riddle, Frederick, 305
Rigg, Diana, 96
Rignold, Hugo, 77
Riley, Ereach, 88
Ritchie, Margaret, 78, 100
Rivers, Malcolm, 104
Riverside Church (New York), 99
Rizza, George, 112
Robb, Betty, 79
Roberts, Doreen, 131, 257
Robertson, Alec, 113, 276, 315, 316
Robertson, Rae, 60, 225
Robertson, Sheila, 86, 276, 285
Roland-Manuel, 33
Rome Radio Orchestra, 79
Ronsard, Pierre de, 50, 84, 101
Roseman, Leonard, 71
Rostal, Max, 23, 69, 255
Roussel, Albert,
    Le Festin de l'Araignée, 311
Royal Academy of Music, 23, 25, 28, 34, 112, 113, 124, 161, 252
Royal College of Music, 46

Royal Marines Band, 112
Royal Northern College of Music, 39, 40, 44
Royal Over-Seas League Music
    Competition (1961), 30
Royal Philharmonic Orchestra, 79, 117,
    119, 297, 304
Royal Philharmonic Society, 93
Royal Shakespeare Company, 96
Royal Society of Musicians, 46
Rubbra, Edmund, 22
    A Garland for the Queen – contribution,
    85
    Homage to Haydn – contribution, 121,
    206
Rubinstein, Artur, 35
Rubinstein, Ida, 314
Runnett, Brian, 299
Russill, P., 303
Rutherford, Jonathan,
    *Variation on a theme by Lennox
    Berkeley (Bouquet for Lennox)*, 47
Rye, Sylvia, 79

Sacher, Paul, 44
Sackville-West, Edward, 72, 99, 273
Sadler's Wells Ballet Orchestra, 76
Sadler's Wells Opera Company, 89
Sadler's Wells Royal Ballet, 66
Sadler's Wells Theatre Ballet, 76
Sagittarius, 69, 206
St. Albans Abbey Choir, 300, 301
St. Cecilia's Day Service (1960), 96
St. Chad's Metropolitan Cathedral Choir,
    299, 301
St. John's College (Cambridge) Choir,
    113, 276, 307
St. Mary's Collegiate Church Choir
    (Warwick), 301
St. Matthew's Church (Northampton)
    Choir, 73, 163
St. Michael's Singers, 60
St. Paul's Cathedral Choir, 96, 300, 301
Salisbury Cathedral Choir, 120
Salter, Robert, 308
Samain, Albert, 76
Sanders, Eric, 105
Sanders, John, 299
Sanders, Neil, 90
Sanderson, Joan, 93
Sappho, 83, 275
Saram, Rohan de, 54
Sargent, Malcolm, 80, 84, 85
Savijoki, Jukka, 305, 306

Saxby, Joseph, 91, 120, 296
Saxton, Michael, 102
Schiller Trio, 308
Schmitt, Florent, 81
Schoenberg, Arnold, 314
Schrenfeld, A., 296
Schrenfeld, E., 296
Schubertians, The, 103
Schütz, Heinrich, 334
Schwarz, Rudolf, 93, 96
Scotland, Tony, 11
Scott, John, 300
Scott, Margaretta, 79
Scottish Chamber Orchestra, 304
Scottish Ensemble, 66
Searle, Alan, 58
Searle, Humphrey, 100, 113, 149, 281,
    314, 316
    Variation on an Elizabethan Theme, 85,
    289
Segovia, Andreas, 312
Sellick, Phyllis, 24, 80, 302
Seyler, Athene, 79
Shakespeare, William, 183
    The Tempest, 23, 74
    A Winter's Tale, 96, 293–4
Shakespeare Memorial Theatre Wind
    Band, 96
Sharp, Frederick, 78, 86, 212
Shelley, Norman, 74, 92
Shen-Yo, 109, 163
Shilling, Eric, 113
Sillito, Kenneth, 303
Sinden, Donald, 74
Sinfonia of London, 92
Slater, Montague, 64
Slatford, Rodney, 111, 186
Smeterlin, Jan, 53
Smith, Cyril, 24, 80, 302
Smith, K., 305
Smith, N.L., 110, 163, 164
Snow, Peter, 87, 153
Société Musicale Independante (Paris),
    55, 57
Society of St Gregory, 91, 238
Söderbaum, Ulla, 79
Southam, Wallace, 99, 131
Southern Cathedrals Festival,
    1980, 120
Speight, Robert, 68, 69
Spencer, Stanley, 71, 217
Spenser, Edmund, 182
    The Faerie Queen, 117, 119, 288

Spratt, K., 305
Squire, Ronald, 79
Ssu-k'ung Shu, 110, 164
Stanley, M., 305
Stevenson, Ronald, 316
Stewart, Gordon, 60
Stewart Craig, Philippa, 69
Stinton, J., 304
Stofsky, Gerald, 107, 272
Stoker, Richard, 113
    Variation on a theme by Lennox
    Berkeley (Bouquet for Lennox), 47
Stolow, Meyer, 102
Stott, Katherine, 302, 305
Straneo, Nini, 95
Straram, Walter, 54, 312, 313
Straram Orchestra, 54, 313
Stratton String Quartet, 67
Stravinsky, Igor, 110, 281, 318
    Capriccio, 312
    Concerto for Violin and Orchestra, 313
    Jeu de Cartes, 18
    Persephone, 314
    Symphony of Psalms, 312
Strode, Rosamund, 62
Stroud Festival,
    1967, 105
Sturrock, Kathleen, 112, 156
Stuttgart Chamber Orchestra, 303
Sutherland, Graham, 71
Sylvan Trio, 60
Symons, Arthur, 77

Tansman, Alexandre, 81
Taplin, Frank, 116
Tausky, Peggy, 95
Tausky, Vilem, 87, 89, 95
Tavener, John,
    Variation on a theme by Lennox
    Berkeley (Bouquet for Lennox), 47
Teachers' Association, 26
Teed, Roy, 78, 113
    Variation on a theme by Lennox
    Berkeley (Bouquet for Lennox), 46
Tennyson, Lord Alfred, 99
Terroni, Raphael, 298, 302, 304, 305, 306
Thamyse String Trio, 306
Thomas, Ambroise,
    Mignon, 12
Thomas, J., 300, 301
Thomas, M., 302

Thomas, Marjorie, 113
Thomas, Robert, 88
Thorne (Father), 13
Three Choirs Festival,
    Worcester (1938), 19, 63, 334, 335
    Hereford (1970), 106
    Hereford (1973), 38, 114, 290
    Worcester (1978), 43, 119
Thurlow, Alan, 300, 301
Tilbrook, P.W., 155, 292
Tippett, Michael, 310, 314, 318
    A Garland for the Queen – contribution, 85
    The Ice Break, 42
    Variation on an Elizabethan Theme, 85, 289
    The Weeping Babe, 72
Todi, Jacopone da, 77
Tolhurst, George,
    Ruth, 113, 124
Tomlinson, Ernest,
    Music for a Prince – contribution, 108
Tranmer, Eileen, 64
Trimble, Joan, 95
Trimble, Valerie, 95
Trinity College of Music, 329, 333
Troester Trio, 306
Tunnell, Charles, 110
Tunnell, John, 110

UNESCO, 81
University of California (Santa Barbara), 103
University of Keele, 41

Varcoe, Stephen, 78
Vaughan, Henry, 73
Vaughan Williams, Ralph,
    A Garland for the Queen – contribution, 85
    London Symphony, 312
Verdi, G., 42
Verlaine, Paul, 76
Vic-Wells Ballet, 63
Vic-Wells Orchestra, 63
Vildrac, Charles, 55, 286
Villa-Lobos, Heitor, 81

Waley, Arthur, 109, 163
Walker, James, 58, 60, 102
Walker, Sarah, 299
Walther, Johann, 125
Walton, Susana, 35

Walton, William, 35, 47, 308, 316
  Façade, 311
  Music for a Prince – contribution, 108
  Troilus and Cressida, 27
  Variation on an Elizabethan Theme, 85, 289
Wannamaker, Sam, 113
Ward, David, 88
Warrack, Guy, 76
  Music for a Prince – contribution, 108
Wastall, Peter, 125
Waterhouse, J.F., 51, 282, 283
Waterhouse, William, 54
Waterman, Dennis, 96
Watkins, David, 105, 214, 302
Watson, Jane, 121
Watts, Isaac, 83
Weagley, Richard, 99
Webb, Mary, 64
Weill, Kurt,
  Das Jasager, 313
  Mahogonny, 313
Welbeck Orchestra, 87
Wells, Alexander, 56
Welsh, Moray, 65
Welsh Arts Council, 113, 118, 276
Welsh Philharmonia Orchestra, 111
Westbury, Marjorie, 74, 92
Westminster Abbey Choir, 90, 96–7, 301
Westminster Cathedral Choir, 97, 102, 113, 120, 301
Westminster Cathedral String Orchestra, 115, 296
Westrup, Jack, 40
Whewell, Michael, 102
Whitesides, W., 303
Whitney, Robert, 303
Wickens, Nigel, 100
Wickham, A., 305
Wicks, Alan, 300, 306
Wilde, D., 297
Wilkinson, Stephen, 106, 299

Willcocks, David, 41, 299
Willey, Brian,
  Music for a Prince – contribution, 108
Williams, Grace,
  Music for a Prince – contribution, 108
Wilson, Elizabeth, 112
Wilson-Johnson, David, 60
Winchester Cathedral Choir, 120, 300
Windsor Festival,
  1969, 108, 293
Winfield, Roger, 303
Wireless Singers, 70
Wittgenstein, Paul, 313
Wolf, J., 306
Wolff, Francis de, 76
Wolfit, Donald, 87
Wood, Christopher, 66
Wood, Helena, 87
Wood, Henry J., 64, 312
Wood, Peter, 96
Wood, Ursula, 85
Woodgate, Leslie, 72, 80, 139
Woodward, Roger, 118
Woolf, S., 298
Worcester Cathedral Choir, 300
Worshipful Company of Musicians, 23, 39
Wright, D., 296, 307
Wright, Peter, 307
Wu-Ti, 109, 163
Wulstan, David, 306
Wynne, David,
  Music for a Prince – contribution, 108
Wyss, Sophie, 52, 67, 77, 310

Yale University, 289
Yang Knang, 110, 163
Yeats, W.B., 70, 80, 139, 140, 200
Young, Alexander, 87
Young, Andrew, 105

Zytowski, Carl, 103